ABOUT THE PUBLISHER

The New York Institute of Finance

... more than just books.

NYIF offers practical, applied education and training in a wide range of financial topics:

* *Classroom training:* evenings, mornings, noon-hour
* *Seminars:* one- and two-day professional and introductory programs
* *Customized training:* need-specific, on your site or ours, in New York City, throughout the United States, anywhere in the world
* *Independent study:* self-paced learning—basic, intermediate, advanced
* *Exam preparation:* NASD licensing (including Series 7), CFA prep, state life and health insurance licensing

Subjects of books and training programs include the following:
* *Account Executive Training*
* *Brokerage Operations*
* *Futures Trading*
* *International Corporate Finance*
* *Options as a Strategic Investment*
* *Securities Transfer*
* *Technical Analysis*
* And much more.

When Wall Street professionals think **training**, they think **NYIF**.

Please write or call for our catalog:
New York Institute of Finance

Marketing Division
70 Pine Street
New York, NY 10270–0003
212/344–2900

Simon & Schuster, Inc.   A Gulf + Western Company
"Where Wall Street Goes to School" ™

SECURITIES TRANSFER:

Principles and Procedures

REVISED FOURTH EDITION

Martin Torosian

NEW YORK INSTITUTE OF FINANCE

Library of Congress Cataloging in Publication Data

```
Torosian, Martin.
    Securities transfer : principles and procedures / Martin Torosian.
   -- 4th ed., rev.
        p.    cm.
    Includes index.
    ISBN 0-13-799081-2
    1. Stock transfer--United States--States.  2. Securities--United
  States.  3. Executors and administrators--United States.  I. Title.
  KF1454.Z95T6 1988
  346.73'092--dc19
  [347.30692]                                                    88-10158
                                                                     CIP
```

This publication is designed to provide accurate and authoritative information in regard to the subject matter covered. It is sold with the understanding that the publisher is not engaged in rendering legal, accounting, or other professional service. If legal advice or other expert assistance is required, the services of a competent professional person should be sought.

—*From a Declaration of Principles jointly adopted by a Committee of the American Bar Association and a Committee of Publishers and Associations.*

Other books by Martin Torosian

Legal Transfer Guide
Modern Stock Market Handbook
The Securities Handbook
The Margin Book
Dynamics of the Options Market
Series 7 Made Ridiculously Simple
Bonds and the Money Market Simplified
What Every Banker Should Know About Broker-Dealers

© 1968, 1971, 1979, 1983, 1988 by Martin Torosian

All rights reserved. No part of this book may be reproduced in any form or by any means without permission in writing from the publisher.

Printed in the United States America

10 9 8 7 6 5 4

NEW YORK INSTITUTE OF FINANCE
70 Pine Street
New York, New York 10270

Contents

Preface, xi

CHAPTER **1**

The Certificate, 1

> *Stock Certificates,* 1
> > The Form of the Certificate, 1
> > The Design and Workmanship, 5
>
> *Bonds,* 6
> > The Form, Design, and Workmanship of the Certificate, 6
> > The Coupons, 9
>
> *Transfer of Bonds and Other Instruments,* 10
> > Registered Bonds, 10
> > Bearer Bonds, 10
>
> *The Impact of the Tax Equity and Fiscal Responsibility Act of 1982,* 10

CHAPTER **2**

The Assignment, 15

> *Legal Aspects of Assignment,* 15
> *Rules for Assignment,* 15
> > Endorsements, 15
> > Forms of Endorsement, 17
>
> *Forms of Assignment,* 20
> > Signature Guarantee, 22

CHAPTER 3
Registration of Certificates, 27

Methods and Practices in Certificate Registration, 27
Abbreviations, 29
Certificate Inscriptions, 30

CHAPTER 4
Custodian to a Minor, 33

Legal Aspects, 33
    Transfer Requirements, 34
    Model Law and Uniform Gifts to Minors Act, 34
    Definition of Minor, 35
    Registration of Securities, 35
    Application of Uniform Gifts to Minors Act, 35
Custodian-Minor Relationships, 35
    Number of Custodians for a Minor, 35
    Eligibility of a Custodian, 37
    Duties and Powers of a Custodian, 37
    Delivery of Registered Securities in the Custodian's Account, 37
    Change of Residence from One State to Another, 37
    Minor Reaching Majority, 40
    Resignation of a Custodian, 40
    Death of a Minor, 40
    Death of a Custodian, 41
Transfer of Securities from a Decedent to a Custodian, 41
Uniform Gifts to Minors Act, 41
Uniform Transfers to Minors Act, 49

CHAPTER 5
Types of Legal Entities, 61

Sole Proprietorships, 61
    Death of a Sole Proprietor, 61
Partnerships, 61
    Sale of Stock in the Name of a Partnership, 62
    Transfer of Stock from the Partnership to the Name of a Partner, 62
    Change in Name of the Partnership, 62
    Death of a Partner, 62

Investment Clubs, 62
    Legal Aspects, 62
    Investment Clubs as Partnerships, 64
    Investment Clubs Organized in Other Ways, 64
    Transfer of Stock into the Name of a Member, 64
    Disbandment of the Club, 65
Exoneration Statutes, 65
Corporations, 67
    Sale of Stock in a Corporate Name, 67
    Transfer of Stock from a Corporate Name into
        the Name of an Officer, 67
    Change of Corporate Name, 69
    Dissolution of a Corporation, 69
Unincorporated Associations, 69
    Unincorporated Association with Governing Body, 69
Churches and Religious Orders, 70
    Stock Registered in the Name of the Church's
        Board of Trustees, 70
    Stock Registered in the Name of a Church, 70

CHAPTER 6
Fiduciary Transfers, 71

Power of Attorney, 71
    Initiation of the Account, 71
    Sale of Stocks, 72
    Transfer of Stocks, 72
    Revocation, 72
    Discretionary Power of Attorney, 72
Bankruptcy and Receivership, 72
    Sale of Stock in the Name of a Bankrupt, 73
    Transfer from the Name of a Bankrupt into the
        Name of a Receiver, 73
    Transfer from the Name of a Bankrupt into the
        Name of a Third Party, 73
Trusts, 73
    Types of Trusts, 73
Living Trusts, 74
    Transfer into the Name of a Trust, 74
    Transfer from the Name of a Trust, 75
    Resignation of a Trustee, 75
    Death of a Trustee, 75

Delegation of Authority, 76
Revocation of the Trust, 76
Testamentary Trusts, 76
Transfer into the Name of a Trust, 76
Transfer from the Name of a Trust, 76
Resignation of a Trustee, 76
Death of a Trustee, 77
Delegation of Authority, 77
Guardianship, 77
Transfer into the Name of a Guardian, 77
Transfer from the Name of a Guardian, 77
Termination of the Guardianship, 77
Death of the Guardian, 78
Death of the Ward, 78
Stocks Issued in the Name of a Minor, 78
Committee and Conservatorship, 78
Transfer into the Name of a Committee or Conservator, 79
Transfer from the Name of a Committee or Conservator, 79
Transfer into the Individual Name of the Ward, 79
Delegation of Authority, 79

CHAPTER 7

Joint Ownership, 81

Joint Tenancy with Right of Survivorship, 81
Types of Joint Ownership in Fifty States and District of Columbia, 82
Death of a Tenant, 84
Death of Both Tenants, 84
Tenancy in Common, 85
Death of a Tenant in Common, 85
Death of Both Tenants in Common, 85
Registration without Tenancy Clause, 86
Tenants by Entirety, 86
Life Tenancy, 86
Transfer into the Name of a Life Tenant, 86
Transfer from the Name of a Life Tenant, 86
Death of a Life Tenant, 86
Community Property, 87

CHAPTER 8
Estates, 89

   Decedents with Last Will and Testament, 89
   How the Will Is Probated, 90
   Executor of Estate, 91
      Transfer into the Name of an Executor, 92
      Transfer from the Name of an Executor, 92
      Death of an Executor, 92
      Delegation of Authority, 92
      Decedents with No Will, 92
   Administrator of Estate, 93
      Transfer into the Name of an Administrator, 93
      Transfer from the Name of an Administrator, 93
      Delegation of Authority, 93
   Decedent, 93
      Transfer into the Name of a Decedent, 94
      Transfer from the Name of a Decedent, 94
      Transfer to Beneficiary, 94
      Distribution and Sale under a Court Order, 94
      Settlement of Small Estates without Administration, 94
      Stock Dividends, 95
      Death of a Beneficiary, 95
      More than One Executor or Administrator, 95
      Delegation of Authority, 96
   Estate and Gift Tax Provisions Under Economic Recovery Act of 1981, 96
      Increase in Unified Credit, 96
      Reduction in Maximum Tax Rate, 97
      Marital Deduction, 97
      Joint Tenancy, 97
      Increase in Annual Gift Tax Exclusion, 97
      Highlights of the Tax Reform Act of 1986, 97

CHAPTER 9
Foreign Securities Transfer, 99

   Canada, 99
      Inter Vivos Trust, 99
      Testamentary Trust, 99
      Executor or Administrator of Estate, 99
      Decedent, 100

Requirements for Transfer, 100
    Alberta, 100
    British Columbia, 100
    Manitoba, 102
    New Brunswick, 102
    Newfoundland, 102
    Nova Scotia, 102
    Ontario, 103
    Prince Edward Island, 103
    Quebec, 103
    Saskatchewan, 104
    Yukon Territory, 104
England, 104

CHAPTER 10
Stock Transfer Taxation, 105
Plan of Operation, 105
New York State Transfer Tax Rates, 106
Maximum Tax, 106
Taxable Transactions, 106
Nontaxable Transactions, 108
Exempt Transactions, 108

CHAPTER 11
Inheritance Tax Waivers, 111
Special Affidavits, 112
Federal Transfer Certificate, 112
Inheritance Tax Offices, 112
Birth and Death Certificates, 112

CHAPTER 12
Rules of Delivery, 123
Types of Deliveries, 123
    Cash Contracts, 123
    Regular Way Contracts, 123
    Seller's Option, 124
Acceptable Denominations for Delivery, 124
    For Stocks, 124
    For Bonds, 124

Contents

CHAPTER 13
Beneficial Ownership, 127
- Purpose of Street Name Registration, 128
- Disclosure of Beneficial Ownership, 129
  - SEC Regulation 13D, 130

CHAPTER 14
SEC Rule 144, 131

CHAPTER 15
Stock Transfer Turnaround, 143
- Operation of the Rules 240.17Ad-1 through 17 Ad-7, 143
  - SEC Turnaround Rules, 143
- Rule 496 of the New York Stock Exchange, 146
- Transfer Agent Drop Facility in New York, 147

CHAPTER 16
Stock Transfer Services, 149
- National Transfer Service (NTS), 149
- Procedure for Record Date Transfers in New York through the NTS, 151
- Agent-Originated Envelope, 152
- Broker-Originated Window Ticket (BOWT), 152
- FAST and Transfer Agent Custodian (TAC), 152
- Appendix: SEC Rules for Registration of Transfer Agents, 153

CHAPTER 17
Missing, Lost, or Stolen Securities, 155
- Operation of Rule 17f-1, 155
  - Reporting Institutions, 155
  - Reporting Requirements, 156
  - Method of Reporting, 157
  - Requirement for Inquiry, 157
  - Method of Inquiry, 157
  - Recordkeeping, 158
  - Exceptions to the Rule, 158
  - Replacement of Lost Certificates, 158
  - Procedure to Replace Lost Instruments, 159

APPENDIX A
Glossary, 161

APPENDIX B
Certifications in Securities Transfer, 171

APPENDIX C
SEC Rules of Transfer Agents Turnaround, 175

APPENDIX D
SEC Lost and Stolen Securities Program, 185

APPENDIX E
Uniform Commercial Code, 189

APPENDIX F
Participant Operating Procedures at Depository Trust Company Pertaining to Securities Processing and Transfer, 205

APPENDIX G
New York Stock Exchange: Rules Pertaining to Securities Transfer and Processing, 273

APPENDIX H
National Association of Securities Dealers: Rules Pertaining to Securities Transfer and Processing, 293

APPENDIX I
Uniform Disposition of Unclaimed Property, 317

Index, 319

Preface

Legislative and administrative changes in securities transfer requirements necessitate revision of the Fourth Edition of *Securities Transfer*.

The revised edition is generally based on new procedures and practices in the securities transfer industry following the Tax Reform Act of 1986 and the Uniform Transfers to Minors Act adopted by most states.

We continue to include the procedures of the Depository Trust Company, which has played a dominant role in securities processing and transfer during the last decade. Since the three depository organizations, custodians of over $3000 billion worth of securities, directly and indirectly impact bank, brokerage office, and transfer agent operation, inclusion of their procedures greatly aids securities personnel, as they have the entire text at their fingertips.

With all changes and additions, the book now provides a more comprehensive guide to securities transfers and registrations—a complete, authoritative, and up-to-date reference guide for transfer agents, registrars, corporate secretaries, trustees, bank trust operation and brokerage office personnel.

Through all editions of this book since 1968, the goal has remained the same—to inform readers of the fundamental requirements of securities transfers.

Martin Torosian

CHAPTER 1

The Certificate

STOCK CERTIFICATES

Issuance of corporate securities is governed by the statutes of the state of incorporation of the firm issuing the securities as well as by other rules and regulations. One of the powers of a corporation's board of directors is to issue the original stock in accord with the corporation's charter.

A stock certificate evidences the holder's ownership—his or her proportionate share and control, if any, in the business. It also indicates any contractual rights of the holder, such as the right to vote, to attend meetings, and to receive dividends in proportion to his or her shares. Issuance of a certificate of stock to a shareowner is a prerequisite of ownership, and the owner is entitled to receive the document.

The Form of the Certificate

Statutory laws and stock exchange requirements are primary considerations in deciding the form of a certificate (see Figure 1-1 on pages 3–4). In general, stock certificates come in registered form. They contain standard conditions and stipulations with respect to capital authorization or the transferability of the shares. A typical certificate of stock contains the following characteristics:

The Face of the Certificate

1. *The name of the corporation.*
2. *The state of incorporation.*
3. *Par value and capital authorization.* The certificate should indicate par value of the shares and capital authorized by the board of directors. If no par value, this should be indicated.

4. *The class of stock* (common, preferred, and the like).
5. *The number of shares.* The number of shares on a typical stock certificate is usually inscribed in three places. It is spelled out in the body of the certificate, written as a figure in the upper right-hand corner, and punched on the right-hand margin. This punch-out section should contain sufficient panels to provide for issue of certificates in denominations of up to 100,000 shares. To identify different denominations, certificates usually come in three variations:

    a. *round lots—one hundred share pieces*—usually preprinted, engraved, indicating the amount of shares;
    b. *odd lots*—generally bearing the statement, "For less than one hundred shares"; and
    c. *over one hundred shares*—usually inscribed, "Over one hundred shares."

    To maintain proper bookkeeping, transfer agents ordinarily avoid issuing fractional shares.
6. *The number of the certificate.* Numbering is hardly consistent. The general practice is to use different sequences for each group of certificates: one sequence of numbers with a distinguishable prefix for odd lots, another for round lots, and still another for over one hundred shares pieces. Certificate numbers might also indicate the location of a particular transfer agent in those cases where there are two or more agents for the same stock. Generally, the class of stock is also identified by a prefix in the certificate number, such as C1234 or P2678.
7. *The name of the stockholder.*
8. *A statement that the shares are fully paid and nonassessable.*
9. *A statement that the shares are transferable* on the books of the corporation.
10. *The seal of the corporation.* An impression of the corporate seal is affixed on the certificate when the bylaws or the statutes of the state require it.
11. *The signatures of the corporate officers.* A certificate is not valid until it is signed by the officers representing the corporation. Generally, facsimile signatures are used. This authority to validate the certificate is usually derived from the bylaws of the corporation or from a statutory requirement of the state of incorporation. The usual requirement is two officers acting in the respective corporate capacity. The signature of one officer holding two offices signed in both capacities is not valid—for example, "John Doe, Vice President and Secretary."
12. *The name of the transfer agent* and *the signature of its officer* on the right-hand side of the certificate. Instead of signing individual certificates, a transfer agent may employ a facsimile signature.

Figure 1-1. A Stock Certificate (Front)

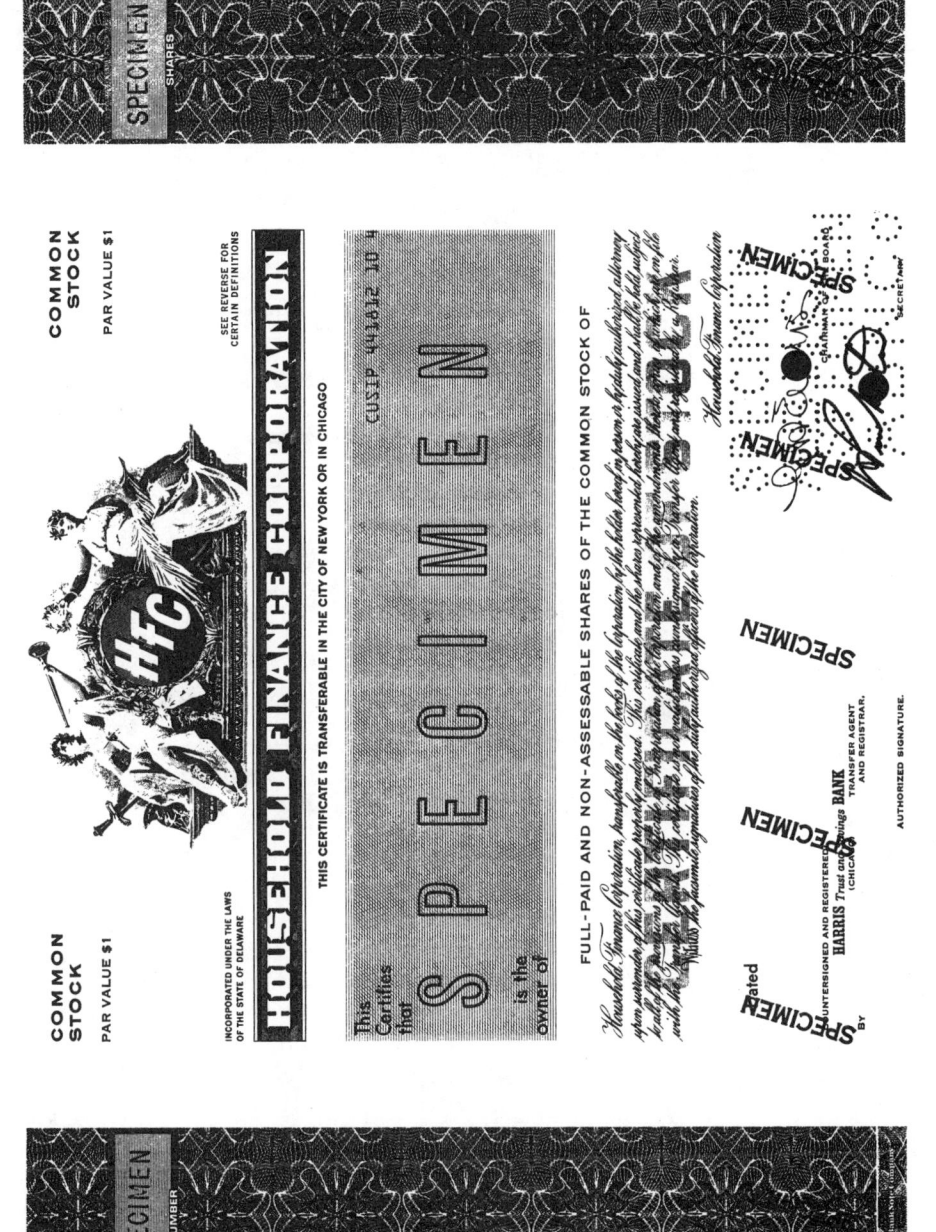

Figure 1-1 (cont.).   A Stock Certificate (Back)

The following abbreviations, when used in the inscription on the face of this certificate, shall be construed as though they were written out in full according to applicable laws or regulations:

TEN COM	—as tenants in common	UNIF GIFT MIN ACT — ....Custodian............	
TEN ENT	—as tenants by the entireties		(Cust) (Minor)
JT TEN	—as joint tenants with right of survivorship and not as tenants in common	under Uniform Gifts to Minors Act..................	
		(State)	

Additional abbreviations may also be used though not in the above list.

HOUSEHOLD FINANCE CORPORATION

HOUSEHOLD FINANCE CORPORATION will furnish without charge to each stockholder who so requests a statement of the powers, designations, preferences and relative, participating, optional or other special rights of each class of stock or series thereof which HOUSEHOLD FINANCE CORPORATION is authorized to issue and the qualifications, limitations or restrictions of such preferences and/or rights. Any such request is to be addressed to the Secretary of HOUSEHOLD FINANCE CORPORATION, Prudential Plaza, Chicago, Illinois 60601.

For Value received,_____ hereby sell, assign and transfer unto

PLEASE INSERT SOCIAL SECURITY OR OTHER IDENTIFYING NUMBER OF ASSIGNEE

_____

PLEASE PRINT OR TYPEWRITE NAME AND ADDRESS INCLUDING POSTAL ZIP CODE OF ASSIGNEE.

_____

_____ *Shares of the capital stock represented by the within Certificate, and do hereby irrevocably constitute and appoint _____*

_____ *Attorney to transfer the said stock on the books of the within-named Corporation with full power of substitution in the premises.*

Dated, _____

NOTICE: THE SIGNATURE TO THIS ASSIGNMENT MUST CORRESPOND WITH THE NAME AS WRITTEN UPON THE FACE OF THE CERTIFICATE, IN EVERY PARTICULAR, WITHOUT ALTERATION OR ENLARGEMENT OR ANY CHANGE WHATEVER.

Securities Transfer 5

13. *The name of the registrar and the signature of its officer.* The name of the registrar usually appears on the left-hand side of the certificate.
14. *The date of the certificate.* The date on the face of the certificate indicates the date of issuance in the books of the corporation.
15. *CUSIP.* The identifying number of the security issue.

The Reverse Side of the Certificate

1. *The form of assignment:*

   > For value received, _____ hereby sell, assign and transfer unto _____, _____ shares of the capital stock represented by the within certificate, and do hereby irrevocably constitute and appoint _____ Attorney to transfer the said stock on the books of the within named Company with full power of substitution in the premises.
   > Dated _____ X _____

   Adjacent to this assignment form, the following legend usually appears:

   > The signature to this assignment must correspond with the name as written upon the face of the certificate, in every particular, without alteration or enlargement, or any change whatever.

2. *Stockholder's identifying number.* Generally appearing on the first line of the assignment, this is either a Social Security number or the identifying number of the assignee.
3. *Definitions of abbreviated forms.* Explanatory legends of acceptable abbreviations to be used in stockholder descriptions usually appear on the reverse side of the certificate. (The statement, "See reverse for certain definitions," generally appears on the face of the certificate next to the inscription.)
4. At least 2 1/2 inches from the bottom of the reverse side of the certificate a *blank space* is provided to protect the punch-out panels on the face of the certificate. The printing, "This space must not be covered in any way" appears in this space.
5. The signature of a witness to an assignment and the date next to the assignment are not necessary. If they appear on the reverse side of a certificate, they may be ignored.

The Design and Workmanship

The securities exchanges require specific techniques in the design, printing, and engraving of a certificate. It is considered essential that the certificates of publicly held corporations contain safeguards against fraudulent duplication. Standards and functions established by securities exchanges are given to the corporations and bank note companies manufacturing these certificates.

BONDS

The Form, Design, and Workmanship of the Certificate

As in the case of stock certificates, stock exchange requirements and state statutes dictate the form of a bond (see Figure 1-2 on pages 7–8) to safeguard against the duplication of the security. The technical requirements for printing, engraving, and design are generally the same as for stock certificates. The paper used by the bank note company is a heavy grade of bond paper. The vignette on the face of the bond is usually unique for that issue and is required by the exchange to deter counterfeiting.

The size of a bond certificate, unlike a stock certificate, varies by the type of issue: the size of a preferred stock certificate is the same as a common stock; but the size and the shape of a coupon bond is quite different from that of a registered bond.

The bank note company, in printing the bonds, uses two engraved steel or nickel plates. One plate, inked in one color, is used to print the border and the face of the bond. The second plate is used to print the vignette, the name, and the contract provisions of the bond in another color.

The border used on the bond is unique for that issue and cannot be used for any other company. The exchange requires that the preparation be done in a permanent, secure place on the premises of the bank note company.

A typical bond certificate has the following characteristics:

The Face of a Bond

1. *The vignette.*
2. *The name of the issuer.*
3. *The denomination.*
4. *The serial number.*
5. *The title* of the bond.
6. *The contract provisions* containing the terms of principal and interest payments, provisions for redemption or conversion, and so on.
7. *The date* of the issue.
8. *The facsimile signatures* of two officers of the corporation.
9. *Certification by the trustees.* Bonds are authenticated by an actual signature of an officer of the trustee. A facsimile signature may not be used.
10. *CUSIP.* The identifying number of the bond.

Figure 1-2. A Bond (Front)

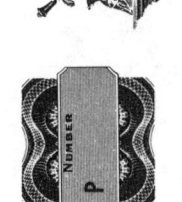

HOUSEHOLD FINANCE CORPORATION

8.45% SENIOR SUBORDINATED DEBENTURE, SERIES 1M, DUE JANUARY 15, 1997

Household Finance Corporation, a Delaware corporation (hereinafter called the "Company," which term includes any successor corporation under the Indenture hereinafter referred to), for value received, hereby promises to pay

.... or registered assigns, the principal sum of ....

8.45%
DUE 1997

SPECIMEN

DOLLARS

8.45%
DUE 1997

CUSIP 441812 BD 5
SEE REVERSE FOR CERTAIN DEFINITIONS

on January 15, 1997, and to pay interest thereon from January 15, 1977, or from the most recent Interest Payment Date to which interest has been paid or duly provided for, semi-annually (beginning July 15, 1977) on January 15 and July 15 of each year, at the rate of 8.45% per annum, until the principal hereof is paid or made available for payment. The interest so payable, and punctually paid or duly provided for, on any Interest Payment Date will, as provided in the Indenture, be paid to the Holder of this Debenture (or one or more Predecessor Debentures) of record at the close of business on the Regular Record Date for such interest, which shall be the last day (whether or not a Business Day) of the calendar month next preceding such Interest Payment Date. Any such interest not so punctually paid or duly provided for shall forthwith cease to be payable to the Holder on such Regular Record Date, and may be paid to the Holder of this Debenture (or one or more Predecessor Debentures) of record at the close of business on a Special Record Date fixed by the Trustee for the payment of such defaulted interest, notice whereof shall be given to Holders not less than 10 days prior to such Special Record Date, or may be paid at any time in any other lawful manner not inconsistent with the requirements of any securities exchange on which the Debentures may be listed, and upon such notice as may be required by such exchange, all as more fully provided in the Indenture. Payment of the principal of this Debenture and, unless otherwise paid as hereinafter provided, the interest thereon will be made at the office or agency of the Company in the City of Pittsburgh, Pennsylvania or, at the option of the Holder, at the office or agency of the Company in the Borough of Manhattan, City and State of New York, in such coin or currency of the United States of America as at the time of payment is legal tender for payment of public and private debts; provided, however, that payment of interest may be made at the option of the Company by check or draft mailed to the person entitled thereto at his address appearing in the Debenture Register. Additional provisions of this Debenture are set forth on the reverse hereof.

Unless the certificate of authentication hereon has been executed by or on behalf of the Trustee by manual signature, this Debenture shall not be entitled to any benefit under the Indenture, or be valid or obligatory for any purpose.

In Witness Whereof, the Company has caused this instrument to be duly executed under its corporate seal.

Household Finance Corporation

Dated:

By ....
Chairman of the Board

Attest: ....
Secretary

TRUSTEE'S CERTIFICATE OF AUTHENTICATION
This is one of the Debentures of the series designated herein referred to in the within-mentioned Indenture.

MELLON BANK, N.A.,
as Trustee

By ....
Authorized Officer

Figure 1-2 (cont.).   A Bond (Back)

HOUSEHOLD FINANCE CORPORATION
8.45% SENIOR SUBORDINATED DEBENTURE, SERIES 1M, DUE JANUARY 15, 1997

This Debenture is one of a duly authorized issue of Senior Subordinated Debentures of the Company (herein called the "Debentures"), issuable in series, unlimited in aggregate principal amount except as may be otherwise provided in respect of the Debentures of a particular series, issued and to be issued under and pursuant to an Indenture dated January 15, 1977 (herein called the "Indenture"), duly executed and delivered by the Company to MELLON BANK, N.A., Trustee, and is one of a series designated as 8.45% Senior Subordinated Debentures, Series 1M, due January 15, 1997 (herein called the "Series 1M Debentures"), unlimited in aggregate principal amount. Reference is hereby made to the Indenture and all indentures supplemental thereto for a description of the rights, limitations of rights, obligations, duties and immunities thereunder of the Trustee, the Company and the Holders.

The Series 1M Debentures may not be redeemed before January 15, 1987, except as stated below. On and after that date and prior to maturity the Company may, at its option, redeem the Series 1M Debentures, either as a whole or from time to time in part, upon not less than 30 nor more than 60 days notice as provided in the Indenture, at their principal amount plus the following redemption premiums (expressed in percentages of principal amount) if redeemed during the twelve-months period beginning January 15 in any of the following years:

Year	Redemption Premium	Year	Redemption Premium	Year	Redemption Premium
1987....	2.00	1989....	1.20	1991....	.40
1988....	1.60	1990....	.80		

and thereafter at their principal amount without premium; together in each case with interest accrued to the date fixed for redemption. Under certain circumstances of declining instalment notes receivable described in the Indenture, the Series 1M Debentures may be redeemed in the manner provided above on and after January 15, 1982 and prior to January 15, 1992, at their principal amount plus the following redemption premiums (expressed in percentages of principal amount) if redeemed during the twelve-months period beginning January 15 in any of the following years:

Year	Redemption Premium	Year	Redemption Premium	Year	Redemption Premium
1982....	2.00	1984....	1.60	1986....	1.20
1983....	1.80	1985....	1.40		

and thereafter, prior to January 15, 1992, at their principal amount plus one-half of the applicable redemption premium referred to in the first of the preceding tables; or, under certain other such circumstances, at their principal amount without premium; together in each case with interest accrued to the date fixed for redemption; all upon the conditions set forth and as more fully provided in the Indenture.

If an Event of Default shall occur, the principal of all the Debentures may be declared due and payable in the manner and with the effect provided in the Indenture.

The Indenture permits, with certain exceptions as therein provided, the amendment thereof and the modification of the rights and obligations of the Company and the rights of the Holders under the Indenture at any time by the Company with the consent of the Holders of at least 66⅔% in aggregate principal amount of the Debentures at the time Outstanding which are affected by such amendment or modification. The Indenture also contains provisions permitting the Holders of 66⅔% in aggregate principal amount of the Debentures at the time Outstanding to waive on behalf of the Holders of all the Debentures compliance by the Company with certain provisions of the Indenture and certain past defaults under the Indenture and their consequences. Any such consent or waiver by the Holder of this Debenture shall be binding upon such Holder and upon all future Holders of this Debenture and of any Series 1M Debenture issued upon the transfer hereof or in exchange herefor or in lieu hereof whether or not notation of such consent or waiver is made upon this Debenture.

The indebtedness evidenced by the Debentures is, to the extent and in the manner provided in the Indenture, subordinate and subject in right of payment to the prior payment in full of the principal of (and premium, if any) and interest on all Senior Indebtedness as defined in the Indenture, and this Debenture is issued subject to such provisions and each Holder, by accepting the same, agrees to and shall be bound by such provisions, and authorizes the Trustee in his behalf to take such action as may be necessary or appropriate to effectuate the subordination as provided in the Indenture and appoints the Trustee his attorney-in-fact for such purpose.

As provided in the Indenture and subject to certain limitations therein set forth, this Debenture is transferable on the Debenture Register, upon surrender of this Debenture for transfer at the office or agency of the Company in the City of Pittsburgh, Pennsylvania, or, at the option of the Holder, at the office or agency of the Company in the Borough of Manhattan, City and State of New York, duly endorsed by, or accompanied by a written instrument of transfer in form satisfactory to the Company and the Debenture Registrar duly executed by, the Holder hereof or his attorney duly authorized in writing, and thereupon one or more new Series 1M Debentures, of authorized denominations and for a like aggregate principal amount, will be issued to the designated transferee or transferees.

The Series 1M Debentures are issuable only as registered Debentures without coupons in denominations of $1,000 or any integral multiple thereof authorized by the Company. As provided in the Indenture and subject to certain limitations therein set forth, Debentures are exchangeable for a like aggregate principal amount of Debentures of the same series and of different authorized denominations, as requested by the Holder surrendering the same.

No service charge will be made for any such transfer or exchange, but the Company may require payment of a sum sufficient to cover any tax or other governmental charge payable in connection therewith.

The Company, the Trustee and any agent of the Company or the Trustee may treat the person in whose name this Debenture is registered as the owner hereof for the purpose of receiving payment as herein provided and for all other purposes whether or not this Debenture be overdue, and neither the Company, the Trustee nor any such agent shall be affected by notice to the contrary.

All terms used in this Debenture which are defined in the Indenture have the meanings assigned to them in the Indenture.

ABBREVIATIONS

The following abbreviations, when used in the inscription on the face of this instrument, shall be construed as though they were written out in full according to applicable laws or regulations:

TEN COM — as tenants in common
TEN ENT — as tenants by the entireties
JT TEN — as joint tenants with right of survivorship and not as tenants in common

UNIF GIFT MIN ACT —................Custodian................
          (Cust)   (Minor)
under Uniform Gifts to Minors
Act ....
    (State)

Additional abbreviations may also be used though not in the above list.

FOR VALUE RECEIVED the undersigned hereby sell(s), assign(s) and transfer(s) unto

PLEASE INSERT SOCIAL SECURITY OR OTHER
IDENTIFYING NUMBER OF ASSIGNEE

_____

Please print or typewrite name and address including postal zip code of assignee

_____

the within Debenture and all rights thereunder, hereby irrevocably constituting and appointing

_____ attorney

to transfer said Debenture on the books of the Company, with full power of substitution in the premises.

Dated : _____

NOTICE: The signature to this assignment must correspond with the name as written upon the face of the instrument in every particular, without alteration or enlargement or any change whatever.

The Reverse Side of a Bond

1. *The name* of the issuer.
2. *The title* of the bond.
3. *The denomination.*
4. *The interest dates.*
5. *The serial number* of the bond.
6. *The place for payment* of the principal and interest.
7. The lower portion of the bond may contain a space to register *the name of the principal.*
8. A registered bond, generally the same size as a standard stock certificate, also contains the assignment form:

> For value received, _____ hereby sell, assign and transfer unto _____ the within bond of _____ for _____ ($_____) No. _____ herewith standing in _____ name on the books of said _____ and do hereby irrevocably constitute and appoint _____ attorney to transfer the said bonds on the books of the within named _____ with full power of substitution in the premises.
> Dated _____ X _____ In the presence of _____

9. The *bondholder's taxpayer identifying number* for a registered bond.

The Coupons

Each coupon (see Figure 1-3 on pages 11–12) contains:

1. the same vignette used on the bond,
2. the name of the issuer,
3. some provisions of the contract,
4. the serial number, and
5. the payment date.

The technical requirements listed above are for long-term bonds, having a term of five years or more. The requirements for short-term bonds, maturing in five years or less, are generally the same with the exception that a vignette is not required and engraving requirements to manufacture the notes are different.

Registered and coupon bonds of the same corporation listed on the New York Stock Exchange must be fully interchangeable.

The usual denomination of a bond is the unit of trading, $1,000 or multiples of $1,000. The bank note company also prepares bonds in denominations of $500.

TRANSFER OF BONDS AND OTHER INSTRUMENTS

The requirements for the transfer of registered bonds, warrants, certificates of deposit, and voting trust certificates are similar to those of stock. With certain minor exceptions, the rules, statutes, and regulations governing the transfer of common and preferred stocks also govern the transfer of other corporate instruments.

Registered Bonds

The assignment form of a bond is called a "bond power," and the registrar is the trustee. The preparation for transfer of a registered bond is similar to that of stock. Corporate bonds are not subject to transfer tax.

The transfer of bonds registered in the name of a fiduciary is governed by the same principles of the Simplification Statutes Act and the Uniform Commercial Code.

Bearer Bonds

There are no transfer requirements for bearer bonds because they are negotiable instruments. However, the broker should obtain the legal documents evidencing the death of the owner of a bearer bond and an inheritance tax waiver from the decedent's state of domicile, if required by statute. These documents are for the broker's records only and need not be submitted to the trustee of the bond.

THE IMPACT OF THE TAX EQUITY AND FISCAL RESPONSIBILITY ACT OF 1982

The Tax Equity and Fiscal Responsibility Act of 1982 passed by Congress in August of 1982 provides a series of provisions designed to increase taxpayer compliance. The major change to securities operation and processing is the elimination of most bearer bonds in order to ensure reporting of interest.

Following are the relevant provisions:

1. The Act prohibits the United States from issuing bearer obligations.
2. The Act provides sanctions for the issuance of bearer bond instruments by corporations, municipalities, organizations, and other entities.
3. The sanctions include the following:
    a. If the municipality or the corporation issues a bearer bond, it will not be allowed to deduct the interest paid on the debt.
    b. In computing earnings and profits, the issuing entity will be precluded from deducting the interest on the obligation.
    c. Tax exemption for interest income otherwise available will be denied.
    d. A loss deduction and capital gain treatment will be denied in certain cases.

Figure 1-3. A Coupon (Front)

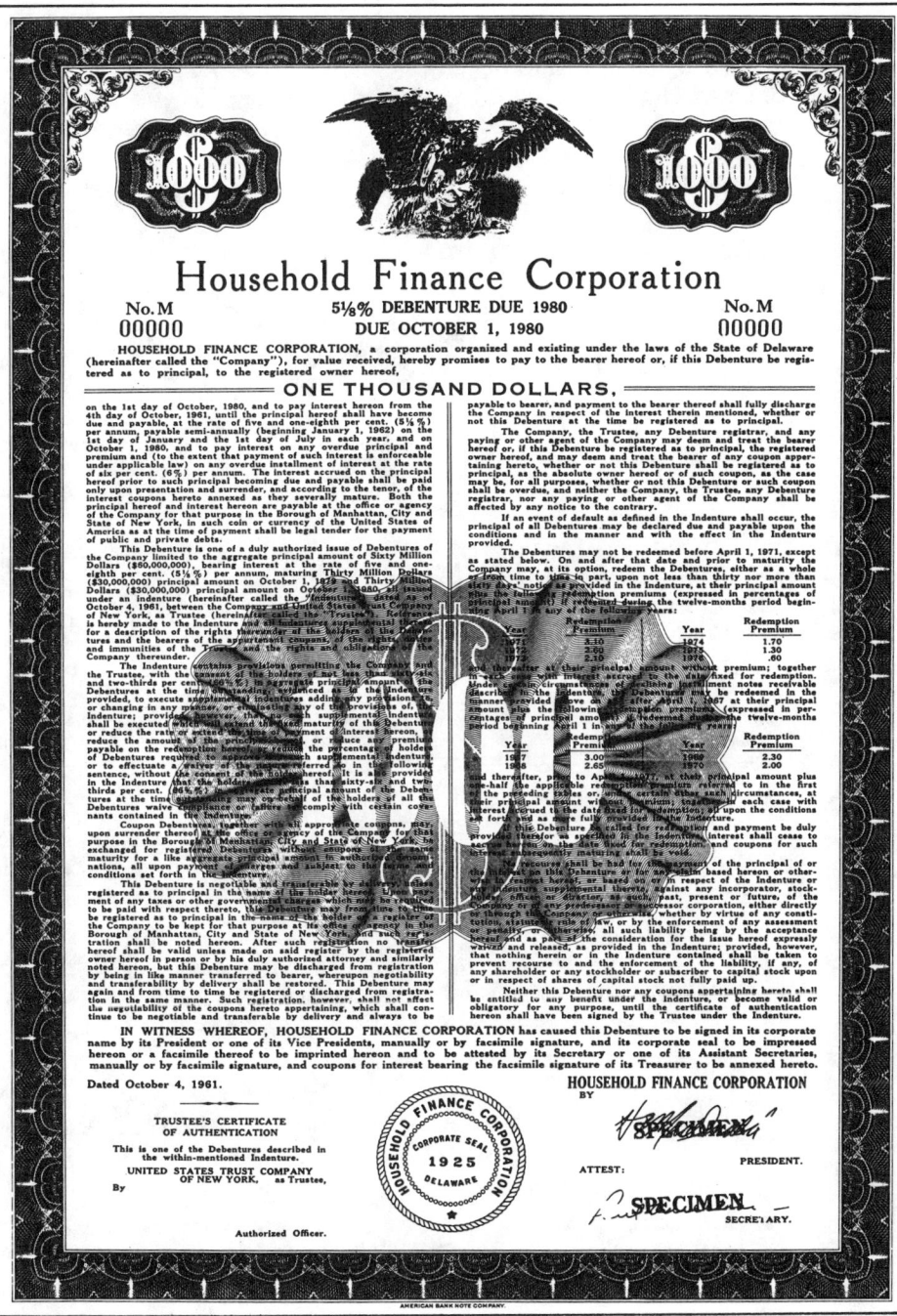

Figure 1-3. (cont.). A Coupon (Back)

Securities Transfer 13

   e. An excise tax will be imposed on the issuance of bearer bonds equal to 1 percent of the principal amount multiplied by the number of years in the term of the bond.

Exceptions are provided for bonds:

   1. issued by individuals,
   2. with a maturity of one year or less,
   3. not offered to the public, or
   4. issued and held by foreign persons.

These provisions apply to bonds issued after July 1, 1983. However, bonds issued pursuant to conversion or exercise of an instrument issued before August 10, 1982 are not subject to these rules.

CHAPTER 2

The Assignment

LEGAL ASPECTS OF ASSIGNMENT

Cancellation and issuance of securities involve many complicated questions of law. The transfer of title from one person to another is accomplished by the delivery of the instrument with a proper assignment.

A stock certificate or a registered bond is accompanied by a proper assignment executed on the reverse side of the certificate or on a stock/bond power (see Figure 2-1 on page 16). The transfer agent, acting on behalf of the corporation, follows a pattern within the scope of law and makes certain that all requirements for a securities transfer are met.

RULES FOR ASSIGNMENT

Endorsements

An endorsement may be "in blank" or "special." When assigned *in blank* the endorsement does not include the name of the transferee. A *special* endorsement specifies the name of the transferee in the assignment space.

The endorsement must be made by an *appropriate person*. The Code defines *appropriate person* as follows:

a. the person specified by the security or by special endorsement to be entitled to the security; or
b. when the person is described as a fiduciary but is no longer serving in the described capacity; or
c. when the security or endorsement so specifies more than one person as fiduciary and one or more are no longer serving in the described capacity—the remaining fiduciary or fiduciaries (whether or not a successor has been appointed or qualified); or

Figure 2-1. Stock/Bond Power

```
FOR VALUE RECEIVED _____ HEREBY SELL ASSIGN AND TRANSFER  [    |    ]
UNTO _____

           ( (_____) SHARES OF THE _____ STOCK OF THE _____
IF STOCK  {
           ( STANDING IN _____ NAME ON THE BOOKS OF SAID _____ REPRESENTED BY CERT. NO. _____

           ( $_____ OF THE _____ PRINCIPAL AMOUNT OF THE _____ COMPANY
IF BONDS  {
           ( REPRESENTED BY BOND NO.(s) _____

HEREWITH AND DO HEREBY IRREVOCABLY CONSTITUTE AND APPOINT
_____
ATTORNEY TO TRANSFER THE SAID STOCK OR BONDS, AS THE CASE MAY BE, ON THE BOOKS OF SAID COMPANY WITH FULL
POWER OF SUBSTITUTION IN THE PREMISES.

                                        X _____
                                        X _____
                                            SIGNATURE(S) GUARANTEED

DATED _____

                              BY _____
                                    AUTHORIZED SIGNATURE
                                 (AUTHORIZING RESOLUTIONS FILED
                                  WITH NEW YORK STOCK EXCHANGE)
```

Securities Transfer

d. when the person so specified is an individual and is without capacity to act by virtue of death, incompetence, infancy, or otherwise—the executor, administrator, guardian, or like fiduciary; or
e. where the security or endorsement specified more than one person as tenants by the entirety or with right of survivorship and by reason of death all cannot sign—the survivor or survivors; or
f. a person having power to sign under applicable law or controlling instrument; or
g. to the extent that any of the foregoing persons may act through an agent—an authorized agent.

The Code further states, "An issuer who registers the transfer of a security upon the unauthorized endorsement is subject to liability for improper registration." The issuer has the duty to issue a similar security to the owner and if necessary, to purchase available securities in the open market for delivery to the owner. The issuer's recourse in this case is against the forger or the signature guarantor. A bona fide purchaser holding a new certificate in his or her name is protected.

To prevent wrongful transfers and adverse claims, the issuer may require the following assurances in processing a securities transfer:

1. A guarantee of the signature of the endorsing person.
2. Where the endorsement is by an agent, appropriate assurance of the authority to sign.
3. Where the endorsement is by a fiduciary, appropriate evidence of appointment.
4. Where there is more than one fiduciary, reasonable assurance that all who are required to sign have done so.

Forms of Endorsement

1. The stockholder should sign his or her name exactly as it appears on the face of the certificate. The abbreviation or enlargement of the signature may restrict the validity of the endorsement. (See Figure 2-2 on page 18 for types of assignments.) A certificate in the name of a corporation must be endorsed by an officer who is authorized to effect the transfer of securities on behalf of the corporation.

2. A certificate registered in the corporate name of a brokerage firm may be transferred if the assignment is executed by an authorized person of the organization or the endorsement is done mechanically by the use of a facsimile signature. In both cases, the assignment must contain the notation "Authorizing resolutions filed with New York Stock Exchange."

3. A certificate registered in the name of a brokerage firm that is organized as a partnership must be endorsed by a partner or an authorized person of the

Figure 2-2. Reverse Side of a Stock Certificate

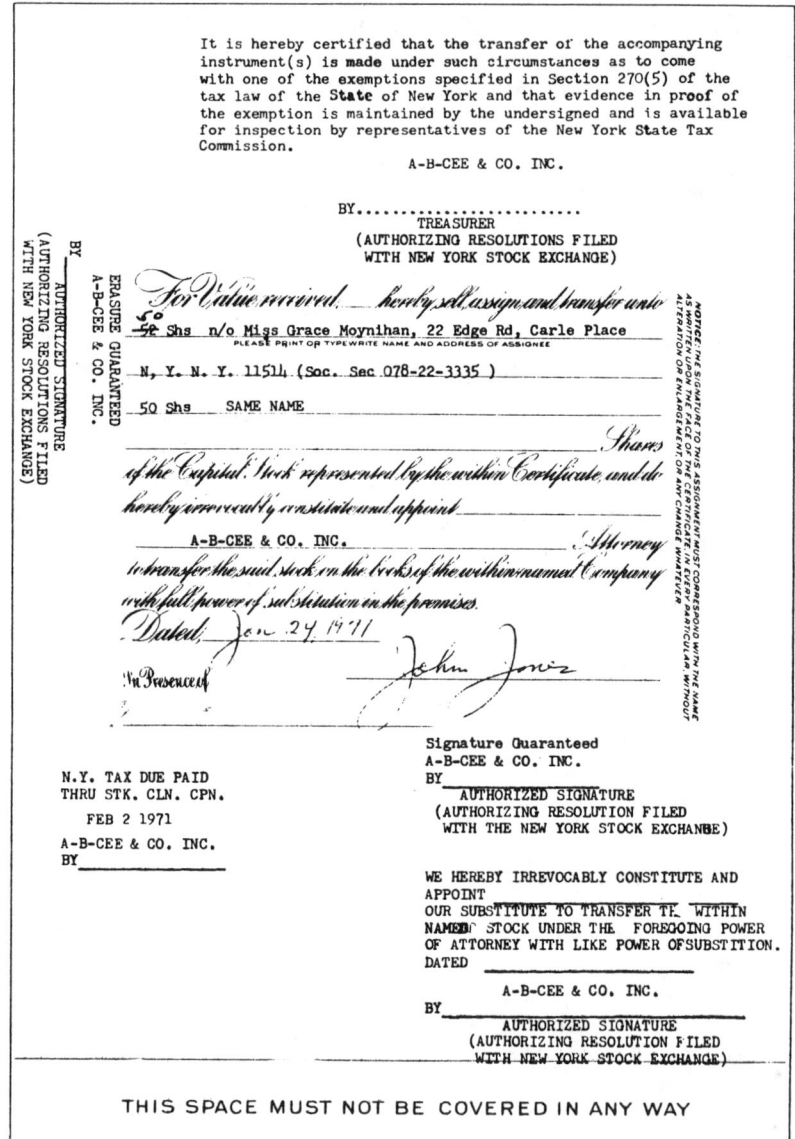

firm. The endorsement must have the name of the firm rather than the name of the person signing—"Abeecee & Co." and not "John Doe, partner, Abeecee & Co." Partnership brokerage firms may also use facsimile signatures providing that the signature is approved by the New York Stock Exchange.

4. If the brokerage firm has changed its name and operates under a new name, the certificate registered under the old name must have the statement "Execution guaranteed" in the assignment.

5. A certificate registered in the name of two or more persons is transferable only if it is endorsed by all the registered owners.

6. A certificate registered in the name of a married woman and endorsed by her is transferable except where applicable law limits the right of a married woman to transfer securities. In such cases the assignment must be executed jointly by husband and wife. No inquiry is made by transfer agents as to the marital status on transfers made by women.

7. A certificate registered in the name of a fiduciary must be endorsed by the fiduciary.

8. The endorsement must be placed on the proper line of the reverse side of the certificate or the stock/bond power (Figure 2-1). An endorsement in the assignment space of the certificate is not recognized. To make such an endorsement acceptable, a certification is submitted to the effect that the signature constitutes the valid endorsement of the registered owner and is affixed for the purpose of assigning the shares.

9. In the case of two tenants, the certificate is transferable if one has endorsed the certificate and if the other has a stock/bond power attached to the certificate.

10. If the signature of the stockholder differs from the name appearing on the certificate, the broker must guarantee the signature to be that of the person named on the face of the certificate.

11. An endorsement may be written in pencil, although the practice is discouraged.

12. An endorsement pasted on the back of the certificate or on a stock power is not recognized.

13. The stockholder's signature is not required when the transfer is to split up the certificate into other denominations in the same name.

14. Endorsements by "X" marks are acceptable if they are witnessed by two persons who furnish their addresses and sign the following statement:

We hereby certify that the assignment has been read to the assignor in our presence; that he made his mark in our presence; that he signified his intention thereby to transfer the shares of stock represented by certificate _____ (number of certificate) _____ of _____ (name of corporation) _____ .

15. An endorsement by a person who has since deceased is not valid. The certificate must be endorsed by a duly appointed representative of the estate.

16. An endorsement by a person who is empowered to act as attorney by the stockholder is acceptable with the statement "attorney-in-fact" next to the signature.

17. When there are two assignments for the same shares, one of which is on the reverse side of the certificate and the other on a stock power, the transfer is acceptable only after one assignment is released by the assignee.

18. No endorsement is necessary when a temporary certificate is presented in exchange for a permanent one, provided there is no transfer of title.

19. A certificate registered in the maiden name of a stockholder may be transferred to the married name if the assignment is executed as "Mary Doe, formerly Mary Smith."

FORMS OF ASSIGNMENT

1. *Power of Attorney.* The practice of appointing an attorney to transfer shares on the books of a corporation is an old one. The attorney designated on the certificate acts on behalf of the stockholder and not the corporation. The practice no longer has legal significance. It is merely used to make the certificate non-negotiable.

When the name of an individual or an organization has been inserted in the attorney space on the reverse side of the certificate or on a stock/bond power, a power of substitution must be executed in blank by such person. The release of the power of attorney makes the certificate a negotiable instrument.

> We hereby irrevocably constitute and appoint _____ our substitute to transfer the within named stock under the foregoing power of attorney with like power of substitution.
> Dated _____ By _____

2. *Alterations or Corrections.* Any alterations, erasures or corrections on the assignment must be guaranteed in this manner: "Erasure guaranteed."

3. *Transferee in Error.* A certificate on which the name of the transferee has been filled in by error is transferable only if the name is erased with the proper erasure guarantee signed by an authorized person. Some transfer agents require a letter of indemnity (see Figure 2-3 on facing page) executed by an authorized person before effecting the transfer. There is no need of an erasure guarantee if the certificate is accompanied by a stock power endorsed by the transferee.

4. *Attorney Designated in Error.* If a person or an organization is designated as attorney in error, the transfer agents generally accept an erasure guarantee certification to effect the transfer.

5. *Blank Assignment.* A stock power may be assigned in blank without the necessity of inserting the certificate number of the security.

Figure 2-3. Letter of Indemnity

LETTER OF INDEMNITY

ERRONEOUS TRANSFERS

Gentlemen:

    At our request, you transferred on _____,19__ certificates for _____ shares of _____ and issued certificates in transfer thereof represented by the following certificate numbers:

in the name of _____ who was erroneously designated by us as the transferee of said shares and who at no time had any interest in or to said shares.

    If you will cancel the certificate(s) so issued in transfer, which certificate(s) are enclosed herewith, and if you will issue new certificate(s) representing the same amount of shares to:

the person rightfully entitled thereto, we agree, for ourselves, our successors, assigns, heirs, executors and administrators, to all times indemnify and save harmless the _____ and you, as Transfer Agent from and against any and all claims, liabilities, damages, actions, charges and expenses sustained or incurred by reason of your action.

                                                                     Very truly yours,

                                                                     A.B. Cee & Co., Inc

                                                                     BY_____

                                                                     Authorized Signature

6. *Witness.* Even though the form of a stock certificate continues to have the word "witness" in the assignment space, the endorsement need not be witnessed to make the instrument transferable. The requirement of a signature guarantee has eliminated this practice.

7. *Date.* The date on an assignment is meaningless.

8. *British Stocks.* A British deed is required to transfer stocks of corporations organized in Great Britain (see Figure 2-4 on pages 23–24). The following are some of the requirements for the proper execution of the deeds:

   a. The deed must be signed by both the transferor and the transferee.
   b. Both signatures must be properly witnessed by a notary public.
   c. A signature with initials is not acceptable.
   d. Full names, including the full middle name, must be used. Middle initials do not suffice.
   e. A certificate that is split up into denominations in the same name does not require the British deed.

Signature Guarantee

The genuineness of the endorsement is extremely important for the transfer of stock. Transfer of title on a forged endorsement makes the transfer agent liable for any damages. The transfer agent must receive assurances from the presentor of the stock before a transfer is effected on the books of the corporation. A century or so ago, the practice was for the assignor to appear before a transfer clerk, disclose his identity, and request the transfer of his shares. This was the only sure way of verifying the endorsement. In today's securities markets, this procedure is certainly not practical. It is now the custom of the transfer agent to request a guarantee of the signature from a responsible institution to protect itself and the issuer against any liability. The guarantors are generally members of the securities exchanges who have filed their authorized signatures with every transfer agent throughout the exchange facility. The transfer agent has the responsibility of checking the guarantor's signature in the file before processing the transfer.

Attestation by a notary public in lieu of a signature guarantee is not acceptable since this procedure does not fulfill all the requirements for transfer.

In addition to the members of the securities exchanges, local banks and trust companies may be authorized to guarantee the signatures of shareowners. The guarantees of these banks are accepted only if their signatures are on file with each transfer agent. Guarantees by savings banks are usually not accepted since their activities in securities transactions are limited in nature. Savings banks in the State of New York are exceptions to this rule. Recent legislation in that state has broadened their powers. The form of guarantee is "Signature guaranteed." No other form is acceptable for transfer. Forms such as "Signature compared," "Endorsement guaranteed," "Signature correct," are not recognized even though the Uniform Commercial Code discusses the form

Figure 2-4. Stock Transfer Form (Side One)—British Deed

STOCK TRANSFER FORM

(Above this line for Registrars only)

Consideration Money £ ....

Certificate lodged with the Registrar

(For completion by the Registrar/Stock Exchange)

Full name of Undertaking.

Full description of Security.

Number or amount of Shares, Stock or other security and, in figures column only, number and denomination of units, if any.

Words

Figures

(units of)

Name(s) of registered holder(s) should be given in full; the address should be given where there is only one holder.

If the transfer is not made by the registered holder(s) insert also the name(s) and capacity (e.g., Executor(s)) of the person(s) making the transfer.

In the name(s) of

I/We hereby transfer the above security out of the name(s) aforesaid to the person(s) named below *or to the several persons named in Parts 2 of Brokers Transfer Forms relating to the above security:*

Delete words in italics except for stock exchange transactions.

Signature(s) of transferor(s)

1. ....

2. ....

3. ....

4. ....

Bodies corporate should execute under their common seal.

Stamp of Selling Broker(s) or, for transactions which are not stock exchange transactions, of Agent(s), if any, acting for the Transferor(s)

Date ....

Full name(s) and full postal address(es) (including County or, if applicable Postal District number) of the person(s) to whom the security is transferred.

Please state title, if any, or whether Mr., Mrs. or Miss.

Please complete in typewriting or in Block Capitals.

I/we request that such entries be made in the register as are necessary to give effect to this transfer.

Stamp of Buying Broker(s) (if any)

Stamp or name and address of person lodging this form (if other than the Buying Broker(s))

No. 740 10-63
Julius Blumberg, Inc.
80 Exchange Place
New York 4, N. Y.

Figure 2-4 (cont.). Stock Transfer Form (Side Two)—British Deed

The security represented by the transfer overleaf has been sold as follows :—

.... Shares/Stock		.... Shares/Stock
.... Shares/Stock		.... Shares/Stock
.... Shares/Stock		.... Shares/Stock
.... Shares/Stock		.... Shares/Stock
.... Shares/Stock		.... Shares/Stock
.... Shares/Stock		.... Shares/Stock
.... Shares/Stock		.... Shares/Stock
.... Shares/Stock		.... Shares/Stock
.... Shares/Stock		.... Shares/Stock
.... Shares/Stock		.... Shares/Stock

Balance (if any) due to Selling Broker(s) ....

Amount of Certificate(s) ....

Brokers Transfer Forms for above amounts certified

Stamp of certifying Stock Exchange   *Stamp of Selling Broker(s)*

FORM OF CERTIFICATE REQUIRED WHERE TRANSFER IS NOT LIABLE TO
AD VALOREM **STAMP DUTY**

Instruments of transfer are liable to a fixed duty of 10s. when the transaction falls within one of the following categories:—
(a) Transfer vesting the property in new trustees on the appointment of a new trustee of a pre-existing trust, or on the retirement of a trustee.
*(b) Transfer by way of security for a loan or re-transfer to the original transferor on repayment of a loan.
(c) Transfer to a beneficiary under a will of a specific legacy of stock, etc. (NOTE—Transfers by executors in discharge or partial discharge of a pecuniary legacy are chargeable with *ad valorem* duty on the amount of the legacy so discharged unless the will confers on the executors power so to discharge the pecuniary legacy without the consent of the legatee.)
(d) Transfer of stock, etc., forming part of an intestate's estate to the person entitled to it, not being a transfer in satisfaction or part satisfaction of (i) a sum of £1,000, £5,000 or £20,000 to which the surviving spouse is entitled under the intestacy where the total value of the residuary estate exceeds that amount, or (ii) the sum due to the surviving spouse in respect of the value of a life interest which he or she has elected to have redeemed in accordance with Section 2 of the Intestates Estate Act, 1952.
(e) Transfer to a residuary legatee of stock, etc., forming part of the residue divisible under a will.
(f) Transfer to a beneficiary under a settlement, on distribution of the trust funds, of stock, etc., forming the share or part of the share of those funds to which the beneficiary is entitled in accordance with the terms of the settlement.
(NOTE—Categories (e) and (f) do not include a transfer to a beneficiary under a will or settlement who takes not only by reason of being entitled under the will or settlement but also
(i) following a purchase by him of some other interest in the trust property, e.g., a life interest or the interest of some other beneficiary; in such a case *ad valorem* transfer on sale duty is payable; or
(ii) where there is an element of gift *inter vivos* in the transaction in consequence of which a beneficiary under a will or settlement takes a share greater in value than his share under the will or settlement; in such a case *ad valorem* voluntary disposition duty is payable.)
(g) Transfer on and in consideration of marriage of stocks, etc., to either party to the marriage or to trustees to be held on the terms of a duly stamped settlement made in consideration of the marriage. (NOTE—A transfer made to the husband or wife after the date of the marriage is not within this category unless it is made pursuant to an ante-nuptial contract.)
(h) Transfer by the liquidator of a company of stocks, etc., forming part of the assets of the company to the persons who were shareholders, in satisfaction of their rights on a winding-up.
*(j) Transfer, not on sale and not arising under any contract of sale and where no beneficial interest in the property passes: (i) to a person who is a mere nominee of, and is nominated only by, the transferor; (ii) from a mere nominee who has at all times held the property on behalf of the transferee; (iii) from one nominee to another nominee of the same beneficial owner where the first nominee has at all times held the property on behalf of that beneficial owner. (NOTE—This category does not include a transfer made in any of the following circumstances: (i) by a holder of stock, etc., following the grant of an option to purchase the stock, to the person entitled to the option or his nominee; (ii) to a nominee in contemplation of a contract for the sale of the stock, etc., then about to be entered into; (iii) from the nominee of a vendor, who has instructed the nominee orally or by some unstamped writing to hold stock, etc., in trust for a purchaser, to such purchaser.)

(1) "I" or "We."   (1) .... hereby certify that the transaction in respect of which this transfer is made is one which falls
(2) Insert "(a),"   (2)
"(b)" or   within the category .... above.
appropriate
category.   (3) ....

(3) Here set out
concisely the
facts explaining
the transaction in
cases falling within
(b) and (j) or in
any case which
does not clearly
fall within any
of the categories
(a) to (j).
Adjudication may
be required.   Date .... 19 ....   *Signature ....
                Description ....

Transferors   *Transferees*

N.B.—A transfer by way of a gift *inter vivos* is chargeable with *ad valorem* stamp duty and must be adjudicated.
* NOTE—The above certificate should be signed in the case of (b) or (j) either by all the transferors and transferees, or a member of a Stock Exchange or a Solicitor acting for one or other of the parties, or an accredited representative of a Bank; where the bank or its official nominee is a party to the transfer, the certificate may be to the effect that "the transfer is excepted from Section 74 of the Finance (1909-10) Act, 1910." In other cases the certificate should be signed by a Solicitor or other person (e.g., a Bank acting as trustee or executor) having a full knowledge of the facts.

Securities Transfer

"Endorsement guaranteed." The form does not include a date, nor is it used in combination with other guarantees.

Signature guarantee under the Uniform Commercial Code is as follows:

1. Any person guaranteeing a signature of an endorser of a security warrants that at the time of signing,

   a. the signature was genuine; and
   b. the signer was an appropriate person to endorse; and
   c. the signer had legal capacity to sign.

But the guarantor does not otherwise warrant the rightfulness of the particular transfer.

2. Any person may guarantee an endorsement of a security, and by so doing warrants not only the signature but also the rightfulness of the particular transfer in all respects. But no issuer may require a guarantee of endorsement as a condition to registration of transfer.

Guidelines for Signature Guarantee

1. Except with respect to registered securities of the United States Government, the signature to an assignment of a certificate must be guaranteed by a member or member organization of a securities exchange that has provided a signature guarantee program for its members.

2. Signatures may also be guaranteed by a commercial bank or trust company organized under the laws of the United States or the State of New York with its principal office in the vicinity of the New York Stock Exchange. "Vicinity of the exchange" means the part of the City of New York south of Chambers Street.

3. Signatures may be guaranteed by a national bank and trust company or by a member of the Federal Reserve System whose signature is on file with and acceptable to the transfer agent.

4. Certificates registered in the name of member brokerage firms do not require signature guarantees for transfer.

5. A signature guaranteed by an out-of-town member brokerage firm not having an office in the vicinity of the New York Stock Exchange must be reguaranteed by a New York member firm. Instead of reguarantee, the New York member firm may inscribe "Delivered by [name of the New York firm]."

6. Transfer agents may accept signature guarantees by savings banks organized in the State of New York.

7. The place of the signature guarantee in the assignment must be within the proximity of the signature of the shareholder.

8. A signature may be guaranteed by an officer of the issuing corporation if he or she is empowered to do so.

9. A signature guarantee by a brokerage firm that has since failed or merged with another firm is acceptable only if reguaranteed by the succeeding organization.

Medallion Signature Guarantee

Manual signature guarantees can now be replaced by an insurance backed, mechanically affixed medallion image. Arrangements have been made between the Stock Transfer Association and the American Bankers Association under which medallion signature guarantees of participating members will be accepted. This is a seal bearing the words "Signature Guaranteed," the name of the guarantor, the wording "ABA-STA Signature Guarantee Plan," and identification numbers. The impression is three-colored.

The program, when fully implemented, will bring an end to the costly procedure of maintaining and updating signature cards. It will also relieve the transfer agent of the impractical requirement of verifying the individual guarantor's signature, thus facilitating the processing of transfers.

The participating member is issued a tamper-proof machine and an exclusively numbered medallion plate. When presented with the stock, the transfer agent affixes the medallion impression on each certificate. This procedure will replace the manual signature guarantee. The program has a surety bond coverage planned to be $3 million per instrument with $12–25 million aggregate coverage.

One of the requirements of the plan is an indemnity agreement executed by the subscriber in favor of issuers and their transfer agents indemnifying them against any loss incurred in relying upon the medallion guarantee.

CHAPTER 3

Registration of Certificates

Ownership of a share is expressed by the registration of the stock certificate. A bona fide purchaser is entitled to a certificate of stock registered in his or her name. Ownership is identified in a proper and distinctive manner within the scope of regulations and statutes. Employing only essential words or phrases, the registration on the face of the certificate must have no ambiguities of ownership. Words giving unnecessary amplification to the registration or limitations to its meaning should be avoided. Such phrases might justify the transfer agent's request for supporting documents. Properly inscribed certificates eliminate unnecessary paperwork, inconvenience, and delay on subsequent transfers.

METHODS AND PRACTICES IN CERTIFICATE REGISTRATION

Registration of certificates starts with initiation of the customer's account at the brokerage house. This provides a basis for preparation of registration instructions containing the name and the address of the transferee. The form in which the certificates are recorded on the books of the corporation is based, therefore, on these instructions. Statutes minimize the transfer agent's inquiry as to the nature and propriety of the transferee. The responsibility rests on the person requesting the transfer. Erroneous representations cause irregularities in the ownership of the shares. Following are some prescribed methods and procedures in certificate registration:

1. The full given name of the transferee is used, without initials.

2. For female stockholders, the practice is to indicate Miss, Mrs., or Ms.

3. The transfer agents use acceptable and generally recognized abbreviations to describe ownership. These abbreviations have the same effect as though the words were written out in full.

4. Words such as "of," "the," "for," "an," "as," and "made by" are omitted except for corporate stockholder's descriptions.

5. With the exception of the apostrophe and hyphen, all other punctuation is omitted.

6. Titles or abbreviations of titles are omitted in the stockholder's descriptions to dismiss doubt as to the ownership of the shares in a representative capacity.

7. References describing the shareholder's ownership such as "Account No. 1," "Reserve Account," "Special Account," and so on, are not included in the inscription on certificates.

8. Suffixes such as "Senior" or "Junior" are abbreviated on the face of the certificate.

9. Alternative ownership, such as "John Doe or Mary Doe," to describe joint registration is not allowed.

10. The description of a fiduciary transferee always contains reference to the instrument under which the securities are to be held. In all fiduciary registrations the instruction indicates:

   a. If the fiduciary is an individual, it should be the full given name of the individual; if the fiduciary is a corporation, the corporate title. If there are two fiduciaries, one an individual and the other a corporation, the corporate title should appear first. It is not necessary to disclose the names of the trustees on the certificate if the stockholder is a pension or a profit sharing trust established by a corporation.
   b. The capacity of the fiduciary—administrator, executor, and so on.
   c. The instrument governing the fiduciary relationship, that is, "under the will of," "under agreement of."
   d. The date of the instrument—"under agreement dated October 3, 1978."
   e. If applicable, as in the case of living trusts, the name of the maker.
   f. If applicable, as in the case of living trusts, the name of the beneficiary.

11. Abbreviations used to describe ownership are the same for singular, plural, male, or female.

12. Legally recognized entities should be described by their full titles whether they are partnerships or corporations: "A. B. Cee & Co. Inc." or "A. B. Cee & Co., a partnership."

13. Ownership of securities by institutions is described by using the full legal title of the account. The fact that the securities are controlled by treasurers and cashiers should not lead the transfer agent to include their names as part of the title: "John Brown, Treasurer, A. B. Cee College." This inscription is misleading and creates a doubt as to whether John Brown or the institution owns the security. The same is true for corporate accounts. The registration should not include the name of the officer of the corporation as part of the title: "John Brown, President, A. B. Cee Corp."

Securities Transfer

14. The instruction should include the stockholder's permanent address:
    a. street and apartment number,
    b. name of street, avenue, drive, road, and so on,
    c. city and state,
    d. zip code, and
    e. taxpayer identifying number.

15. Registrations describing joint ownership must have appropriate tenancy clause—JTTEN, TEN COM, and so on.

16. Transfers to an individual name of a minor or to a fictitious name are not permissible.

ABBREVIATIONS

Brevity in security registrations is important from an economic and practical standpoint. It is good practice to utilize acceptable and easily recognized abbreviations in stockholder description. Table 3-1 below contains a list of standard abbreviations in stockholder descriptions.

Table 3-1

Account	AC	De Bonis Non	DBN
Adminstrator	ADM	Department	DEPT
American	AMER	District	DIST
Ancillary	ANC	Division	DIV
And	&	Drive	DR
And others	ET AL	Estate	EST
Apartment	APT	East	E
Article	ART	Et Cetera	ETC
Assistant	ASST	Executor, Executrix	EX
Association	ASSN	Federal	FED
Attention	ATT	Foreign	FGN
Avenue	AVE	Foundation	FDN
Bank	BK	General	GEN
Beneficiary	FBO	Guardian	GDN
Boulevard	BLVD	Highway	HWY
Brothers	BROS	Hospital	HOSP
Building	BLDG	Including, Inclusive	INCL
Care of	C-O	Incorporated	INC
Chapter	CH	Independent Executor	IND EX
Clause	CL	Insurance	INS
Company	CO	Joint Tenants with Rights	
Commercial	COML	of Survivorship	JT TEN
Committee	COMM	Life Tenant	LIFE TEN
Conservator	CONS	Limited	LTD
Corporation	CORP	Manufacturing	MFG
Court	CT	National	NATL
Cum Testamento Annexo	CTA	North	N
Custodian	CUST	Page	P

Paragraph	PAR	Station	STA
Parkway	PKWY	Street	ST
Place	PL	Temporary	TEMP
Post Office	PO	Tenants in Common	TEN COM
President	PRES	Tenants by Entirety	TEN ENT
Public Law	PL	Trustee, Trustees	TR
Railroad	RR	Trust Department	TR DEPT
Railway	RY	Trust Officer	TR OFF
Receiver	REC	Treasurer	TREAS
Residuary Trust	RES TRUST	Under Agreement	UA
		Under Court Order	UCO
Revised	REV	Under Uniform Gifts to Minors Act	UNIF GIFT MIN ACT
Rural Delivery	RD		
Savings	SVGS	Under Will	UW
Section	SEC	United States	US
Secretary	SECY	University	UNIV
Society	SOC	Vice President	VP
South	S	West	W
Special	SPL		

CERTIFICATE INSCRIPTIONS

Table 3-2 below lists alphabetically legally recognized inscriptions on certificates. This is used as a format in initiating brokerage accounts or requesting security registrations:

Table 3-2

Administrator	John Brown ADM EST Mary Brown
Administrator with will annexed	John Brown ADM CTA EST Mary Brown
Administrator (successor) with will annexed	John Brown ADM DBN CTA EST Mary Brown
Administrator—special	John Brown SPL ADM EST Mary Brown
Administrator—temporary	John Brown TEMP ADM EST Mary Brown
Agency relationship	John Brown AGENT UA OCT 2, 64
Association (unincorporated)	XYZ Association
Bank	A.B. CEE Bk
Bank (as fiduciary with an individual)	A.B. Cee Bk C & John Brown TR UW Mary Brown
Church	Roman Catholic Church
Church (in certain cases according to state laws)	Roman Catholic Diocese of Chicago
College	Dartmouth College

Securities Transfer

Committee	John Brown COMM Mary Brown incompetent
Community property	John Brown & Mary Brown Community Property
Conservator	John Brown CONS Mary Brown
Corporation	XYZ Corporation
Corporation (as fiduciary with an individual)	XYZ Corp. & John Brown TR UW Mary Brown
Curator (in certain cases)	John Brown Curator Mary Brown
Custodian	(Use correct statutes of states)
Executor	John Brown EX EST Mary Brown
Foundation (as corporation or association)	XYZ Foundation
Guardian	John Brown GDN Mary Brown a minor
Incompetent	John Brown COMM Mary Brown an incompetent
Independent executor	John Brown IND EX EST Mary Brown
Individual	John Brown
Intervivos trust (living trust)	John Brown TR UA Oct. 2, 64 MB Mary Brown FBO William Brown
Intervivos trust with beneficiaries	John Brown TR UA Oct. 2, 62 MB Mary Brown FBO William Brown ET AL
Investment club	XYZ Investment Club
Joint tenants	John Brown & Mary Brown JT TEN
Life tenants	John Brown LIFE TEN UW Mary Brown
Nominee	Brown & Co.
Partnership	XYZ & Co., (a partnership)
Pension trust	John Brown & Mary Brown TR XYZ Corp. Pension Fund UA Feb. 6, 51
Pledgee	Brown Trust Co. Pledgee UA John Brown Oct. 2, 64
Receiver	John Brown Receiver XYZ Corp.
Sole proprietorship	John Brown Co.
Tenants in common	John Brown & Mary Brown TEN COM
Tenants by entirety	John Brown & Mary Brown TEN ENT
Testamentary guardian	John Brown Testamentary GDN Mary Brown UW William Brown
Testamentary trust	John Brown TR UW Mary Brown
Testamentary trust with beneficiary	John Brown TR UW Mary Brown FBO William Brown
Trustee in bankruptcy	John Brown TR in bankruptcy Mary Brown
Usufructuary	John Brown USUFRUCT Mary Brown naked owner

CHAPTER 4

Custodian to a Minor

LEGAL ASPECTS

Giving gifts of securities to minors is regulated by law throughout the United States. While the laws vary from state to state, there is a degree of uniformity created by the enactment of the Uniform Gifts to Minors Act and the Uniform Transfer to Minors Act. The Acts provide a relatively simple procedure for donating securities or money to minors and enable a third party to deal with a minor on the same basis as an adult. Prior to this legislation it was difficult for a broker, bank, or transfer agent to deal with minors as individuals, because the minor had the power to repudiate the contract.

These statutes provide a convenient method for transacting a donation of securities to a minor, making these gifts possible without appointing a guardian or establishing a living trust for the benefit of the minor. While making a gift is a simple matter, it is important that securities personnel understand the requirements and the applicability of these statutes and advise their customers accordingly. The Uniform Gifts to Minors Act clearly states that the minor is the beneficial owner of the security at all times, and the custodian is merely the supervisor of the account. Under these laws a gift is complete and irrevocable. The donor gives up all rights to the property. The gift made under these provisions cannot be returned to the donor. To make the transaction complete, however, the securities must be registered in the name of the custodian for the benefit of the minor.

One of the reasons for making a donation of money and securities to minors is to reduce taxes. Once the donation is consummated, properties owned by minors are not taxable to the parents or donors. The donor reduces his or her income tax liability. The minor may be in a low or zero tax bracket, so he or she may not have any tax liability either.

Caution must be exercised, however, to avoid future complications. If the donor wants to shift his or her income tax liability to the minor, the gift must be irrevocable and away from the donor's control. The donor cannot receive income from the gift once the gift is made, nor can the donor make the gift to the minor to contribute to the child's legal support or needs.

If securities are involved, they must be registered with proper inscription describing the method in which the gift was made: guardian, trustee, custodian, and so on. A minor, who is presumably under 18 years old, cannot own securities with the parent or donor in joint tenancy. If the gift is being made under the Uniform Gifts to Minors Act, the donor must realize that the minor is the beneficial owner of the security at all times.

Other methods of making gifts to minors are:

1. *Short-term revocable trusts.* These are generally known as Clifford trusts; the donor gives assets or money for a minimum of ten years. At the termination of the trust, the gift reverts to the donor. Here again, care must be exercised in the structure of the trust. In the absence of specific provision, any capital gains on the gift are generally taxable to the donor. To establish a Clifford trust, one must place stocks, bonds, savings certificates—generally, income-producing assets—into a trust and name the beneficiary. The instrument appoints a trustee to manage the assets. The trust income is taxable to the beneficiary if the trust instrument provides annual distribution of income to the beneficiary. If there are no provisions to that effect, the income will be taxable to the trust. A transfer of property to this type of trust results in a gift for gift tax considerations. The grantor may have to pay gift tax on the present value of the income that the trust will generate. The principal itself, however, is not taxable. If the trust income is distributed annually to the beneficiary, the gift tax exclusion of $10,000 per beneficiary is applied ($20,000 for a joint gift). At the termination of the trust, the trust property becomes part of the grantor's estate. If the trust assets are sold, the grantor will have to pay capital-gains tax, not the beneficiary.
2. *Income trust.* This is a living trust in which income generated from the trust is payable to the minor.
3. *Crummey trust.* This is similar to an income trust, but here the minor has the right to withdraw money.

Transfer Requirements

In custodian registrations, the transfer agent's responsibilities are limited. They are not bound to examine the transaction of the gift, the eligibility of the custodian, or the disability of the minor. Their authority is to see that the statute is properly designated and the account correctly identified.

Model Law and Uniform Gifts to Minors Act

Lesiglation bearing on this procedure began in 1955. Recommended by the National Conference of Commissioners on Uniform State Laws, the Model Law was enacted by fourteen states and the District of Columbia. A year later, a uniform statute called Uniform Gifts to Minors Act was recommended and subsequently enacted by several states. This statute broadened the old Model

Law by allowing gifts of money, as well as of securities, and enlarged the selection of custodians.

Beginning in 1966, the National Conference of Commissioners recommended a revised version of the Uniform Gifts to Minors Act further broadening the scope of the original act and answering a whole series of questions.

At present, most states provide a standard procedure in this area. Before making a gift of money or securities, consult the statutes of the state of residence of the minor, donor, and custodian for local provisions of the law, legal interpretations, and possible tax consequences.

Definition of Minor

Under common law a person reaches majority at age 21. Under 21 he or she is considered a minor. Most states, however, have enacted legislation prescribing the actual age of majority, removing most of the disabilities of a minor. In many states, a person under 21 is no longer considered a minor. At the age of 18, 19, or 20 he or she can make contracts, secure educational loans, enter into marriage agreements, and so on.

Table 4-1 (on page 36) is a list of states specifying the age of majority under the Act.

Registration of Securities

If a gift is a security in registered form, the law requires that the security be registered with the proper designation of the custodian, the minor, the title of the Act, and the name of the state. Table 4-2 (on pages 38–39) contains the applicable phrase for each jurisdiction.

Application of Uniform Gifts to Minors Act

The laws can be applied only within the United States, the Virgin Islands, and the Canal Zone. The donor, the custodian, or the minor should have a permanent address in the United States.

CUSTODIAN-MINOR RELATIONSHIPS

Number of Custodians for a Minor

Section 2 of the Act states that "Any gift made in a manner prescribed in Subsection (a) may be made to only one minor and only one person may be the custodian." Separate custodian accounts must be maintained for each minor.

Table 4-1. Age of Majority for Purposes of Gifts

State	
Alabama	19 (18 for a married person)
Alaska	19 (16 if married)
Arizona	18
Arkansas	18 (16 for women through a judicial process)
California	18
Canal Zone	21
Colorado	18
Connecticut	18
Delaware	18
District of Columbia	18
Florida	18
Georgia	18
Hawaii	18
Idaho	18 (if married regardless of age)
Illinois	18
Indiana	18
Iowa	18 (if married regardless of age)
Kansas	18
Kentucky	18
Louisiana	18
Maine	18 (if married regardless of age)
Maryland	18
Massachusetts	18
Michigan	18
Minnesota	18
Mississippi	21 (18 for a married person)
Missouri	18
Montana	18
Nebraska	19
Nevada	18
New Hampshire	18
New Jersey	18
New Mexico	18
New York	18
North Carolina	18
North Dakota	18
Ohio	18
Oklahoma	18
Oregon	18 (if married regardless of age)
Pennsylvania	18
Rhode Island	18
South Carolina	18
South Dakota	18
Tennessee	18
Texas	18
Utah	18
Vermont	18
Virgin Islands	21
Virginia	18
Washington	18
West Virginia	18
Wisconsin	18
Wyoming	19

Eligibility of a Custodian

Following are eligible custodians:

1. A donor of a registered security.
2. Any adult person except in the following jurisdictions: Alaska, Arizona, Florida, Georgia, Kansas, Kentucky, Louisiana, Michigan, Mississippi, Montana, Nebraska, New Hampshire, New Jersey, New Mexico, New York, Oregon, Vermont, and Wisconsin.
3. Any adult member of the minor's family.
4. A guardian of the minor.
5. A trust company except in Georgia and Oregon.

Duties and Powers of a Custodian

Section 4 of the Revised Uniform Gifts to Minors Act states:

> The custodian shall collect, hold, manage, invest and reinvest the custodial property.
>
> The custodian shall invest and reinvest the custodial property as would a prudent man of discretion and intelligence who is seeking a reasonable income and the preservation of his capital.
>
> The custodian may sell, exchange, convert, surrender, or otherwise dispose of custodial property in the manner ... and upon the terms he deems advisable.
>
> The custodian shall keep records of all the transactions with respect to the custodial property and make them available for inspection ... by the parent or the minor if he has attained the age of fourteen years.

Delivery of Registered Securities in the Custodian's Account

The shares must be registered in the proper custodian clause before a delivery of the security is made to the custodian. Securities cannot be shipped to the custodian in "street name"; nor can stock be held in "street name" for the custodian account. The statutes do not allow custodians to purchase securities on margin, nor can they use the property of the minor as collateral for a loan.

Change of Residence from One State to Another

The brokerage firm should establish a new account, giving the proper statutory wording of the new state, and future transactions should take place in that account. There is no provision in the Uniform Act for transferring securities from the old custodian clause to the proper phrase of the new state. Therefore, most transfer agents refuse to effect such transfers. The registration of

Table 4-2

Alabama	John Doe, as Cust for Mary Doe, under the Alabama UGMA
Alaska	John Doe, as Cust for Mary Doe, under the Alaska UGMA
Arizona	John Doe, as Cust for Mary Doe, under the Arizona UGMA
Arkansas	John Doe, as Cust for Mary Doe, under the Arkansas UGMA
California	John Doe, as Cust for Mary Doe, under the California UGMA
Canal Zone	John Doe, as Cust for Mary Doe, under the Canal Zone UGMA
Colorado	John Doe, as Cust for Mary Doe, under the Colorado UGMA
Connecticut	John Doe, as Cust for Mary Doe, under the Connecticut UGMA
Delaware	John Doe, as Cust for Mary Doe, under the Delaware UGMA
District of Columbia	John Doe, as Cust for Mary Doe, under the District of Columbia UGMA
Florida	John Doe, as Cust for Mary Doe, under the Florida Gifts to Minors Act
Georgia	John Doe, as Cust for Mary Doe, a minor under the laws of Georgia
Hawaii	John Doe, as Cust for Mary Doe, under the Hawaii UGMA
Idaho	John Doe, as Cust for Mary Doe, under the Idaho UGMA
Illinois	John Doe, as Cust for Mary Doe, under the Illinois UGMA
Indiana	John Doe, as Cust for Mary Doe, under the Indiana UGMA
Iowa	John Doe, as Cust for Mary Doe, under the Iowa UGMA
Kansas	John Doe, as Cust for Mary Doe, under the Kansas UGMA
Kentucky	John Doe, as Cust for Mary Doe, under the Kentucky UGMA
Louisiana	John Doe, as Cust for Mary Doe, a minor, under the Louisiana Gifts to Minors Act
Maine	John Doe, as Cust for Mary Doe, under the Maine UGMA
Maryland	John Doe, as Cust for Mary Doe, under the Maryland UGMA
Massachusetts	John Doe, as Cust for Mary Doe, under the Massachusetts UGMA
Michigan	John Doe, as Cust for Mary Doe, under the Michigan UGMA
Minnesota	John Doe, as Cust for Mary Doe, under the Minnesota UGMA
Mississippi	John Doe, as Cust for Mary Doe, under the Mississippi UGMA

Securities Transfer

Missouri	John Doe, as Cust for Mary Doe, under the Missouri UGMA
Montana	John Doe, as Cust for Mary Doe, under the Montana UGMA
Nebraska	John Doe, as Cust for Mary Doe, under the Nebraska UGMA
Nevada	John Doe, as Cust for Mary Doe, under the Nevada UGMA
New Hampshire	John Doe, as Cust for Mary Doe, under the New Hampshire UGMA
New Jersey	John Doe, as Cust for Mary Doe, under the New Jersey UGMA
New Mexico	John Doe, as Cust for Mary Doe, under the New Mexico UGMA
New York	John Doe, as Cust for Mary Doe, under the New York UGMA
North Carolina	John Doe, as Cust for Mary Doe, under the North Carolina UGMA
North Dakota	John Doe, as Cust for Mary Doe, under the North Dakota UGMA
Ohio	John Doe, as Cust for Mary Doe, under the Ohio UGMA
Oklahoma	John Doe, as Cust for Mary Doe, under the Oklahoma UGMA
Oregon	John Doe, as Cust under the laws of Oregon, for Mary Doe, a minor
Pennsylvania	John Doe, as Cust for Mary Doe, under the Pennsylvania UGMA
Rhode Island	John Doe, as Cust for Mary Doe, under the Rhode Island UGMA
South Carolina	John Doe, as Cust for Mary Doe, under the South Carolina UGMA
South Dakota	John Doe, as Cust for Mary Doe, under the South Dakota UGMA
Tennessee	John Doe, as Cust for Mary Doe, under the Tennessee UGMA
Texas	John Doe, as Cust for Mary Doe, under the Texas UGMA
Utah	John Doe, as Cust for Mary Doe, under the Utah UGMA
Vermont	John Doe, as Cust for Mary Doe, under the Vermont UGMA
Virgin Islands	John Doe, as Cust for Mary Doe, under the Virgin Islands UGMA
Virginia	John Doe, as Cust for Mary Doe, under the Virginia UGMA
Washington	John Doe, as Cust for Mary Doe, under the Washington UGMA
West Virginia	John Doe, as Cust for Mary Doe, under the West Virginia Gifts to Minors Act
Wisconsin	John Doe, as Cust for Mary Doe, under the Wisconsin UGMA
Wyoming	John Doe, as Cust for Mary Doe, under the Wyoming UGMA

securities should not be changed until the minor reaches majority, at which time the securities should be transferred to the minor as an individual.

A certificate bearing the old custodian description can be deposited in the new account at the time of sale, but the proceeds must be paid bearing the custodian wording of the old state.

Minor Reaching Majority

When the minor reaches majority, the custodian should transfer the shares to the minor's name. The following documents are necessary:

1. an assignment or stock power by the custodian, and
2. a certified copy of the minor's birth certificate.

Resignation of a Custodian

A custodian may resign before a minor has attained majority. In certain states, the custodian should petition the court for the resignation and the appointment of a successor custodian. Required documents are:

1. an assignment or stock power by the custodian, and
2. a court-certified copy of the certificate of appointment of the successor custodian, dated within sixty days of the presentation of the stock to the transfer agent.

In other states, a donor custodian may resign and designate his or her own successor. Required documents are:

1. an assignment by the former custodian, and
2. an instrument of resignation signed by the custodian and witnessed by a notary public.

In all other jurisdictions, the usual requirements are:

1. an assignment by the former custodian,
2. a duly notarized letter of resignation, and
3. a properly notarized letter of designation of a successor custodian.

Death of a Minor

When a minor dies before reaching majority the shares will be part of his estate. The certificates registered in the custodian clause should be endorsed by the custodian for liquidation or delivery, thus terminating the custodianship. Required documents are:

1. an assignment by the custodian, and
2. a certified copy of the minor's death certificate.

Death of a Custodian

In most states, a successor custodian is appointed by the court. The court may appoint a guardian or an adult member of the minor's family to succeed the deceased custodian. Required documents are:

1. an assignment by the successor custodian.
2. a certified copy of the death certificate of the deceased custodian, and
3. a court-certified copy of the certificate of appointment of the successor custodian, dated within sixty days of the submission of the stock to the transfer agent.

Under the Revised Uniform Act, if the minor is 14 years or over, he or she may designate a successor custodian. Required documents are:

1. an assignment by the successor custodian,
2. a certified copy of the death certificate of the deceased custodian,
3. a certified copy of the minor's birth certificate evidencing his or her age of 14 years or over, and
4. a duly notarized letter of designation of a successor custodian signed by the minor.

TRANSFER OF SECURITIES FROM A DECEDENT TO A CUSTODIAN

Securities registered in the name of a deceased stockholder cannot be transferred to a custodian of a minor, since gifts are made during the lifetime of the donor.

UNIFORM GIFTS TO MINORS ACT

The following is the complete text of the Uniform Gifts to Minors Act adopted by most states. The provisions of the Act vary from state to state. For instance, the Act defines an adult person as one who has attained the age of twenty-one years. This age requirement is different in each state. Check the provisions of the Act in the applicable state.

The Act covers gifts to minors of securities, life insurance policies, annuity contracts, and money.

Section 1. Definitions. In this act, unless the context otherwise requires:

(a) An "adult" is a person who has attained the age of twenty-one years.

(b) A "bank" is a (bank trust company, national banking association, savings bank, industrial bank . . .).

(c) A "broker" is a person lawfully engaged in the business of effecting transactions in securities for the account of others. The term includes a bank which effects such transactions. The term also includes a person lawfully engaged in buying and selling securities for his own account, through a broker or otherwise, as a part of a regular business.

(d) "Court" means the [name of the court].

(e) The "custodial property" includes:

(1) all securities, life insurance policies, annuity contracts and money under the supervision of the same custodian for the same minor as a consequence of a gift or gifts made to the minor in a manner prescribed in this act;

(2) the income from the custodial property; and

(3) the proceeds, immediate and remote, from the sale, exchange, conversion, investment, reinvestment, surrender or other disposition of such securities, money, life insurance policies, annuity contracts and income.

(f) A "custodian" is a person so designated in a manner prescribed in this act; the term includes a successor custodian.

(g) A "financial institution" is a bank, a federal savings and loan association, a savings institution chartered and supervised as a savings and loan or similar institution under federal law or the law of a state (or a federal credit union or a credit union chartered and supervised under the laws of a state . . .); a "domestic financial institution" is one chartered and supervised under the laws of this state or a bank chartered and supervised under federal law and having its principal office in this state; an "insured financial institution" is one, deposits (including a savings, share, certificate or deposit account) in which are, in whole or in part, insured by the Federal Deposit Insurance Corporation(,) (or) by the Federal Savings and Loan Insurance Corporation (, or by a fund approved by the state).

(h) A "guardian" of a minor means the general guardian, guardian, tutor or curator of his property or estate appointed or qualified by a court of this state or another state.

(i) An "issuer" is a person who places or authorizes the placing of his name on a security (other than as a transfer agent) to evidence that it represents a share, participation or other interest in his property or in an enterprise or to evidence his duty or undertaking to perform an obligation evidenced by the security, or who becomes responsible for or in place of any such person.

(j) A "legal representative" of a person is his executor or the administrator, general guardian, guardian, committee, conservator, tutor or curator of his property or estate.

(k) A "life insurance policy or annuity contract" means a life insurance policy or annuity contract, issued by an insurance company (authorized to do business in this state) on the life of a minor to whom a gift of the policy or contract is made in the manner prescribed in this act or on the life of a member of the minor's family.

(l) A "member" of a "minor's family" means any of the minor's parents, grandparents, brothers, sisters, uncles and aunts, whether of the whole blood or the half blood, or by or through legal adoption.

(m) A "minor" is a person who has not attained the age of twenty-one years.

(n) A "security" includes any note, stock, treasury stock, bond, debenture, evidence of indebtedness, (certificate of interest or participation in an oil, gas or mining title or lease in payments out of production under such a title or lease), collateral trust certificate, transferable share, voting trust certificate or, in general, any interest or instrument commonly known as a security, or any certificate of interest or participation in, any temporary or interim certificate, receipt or certificate of deposit for, or any warrant or right to subscribe to or purchase, any of the foregoing. The term does not include a security of which the donor is the issuer. A security is in "registered form" when it specifies a person entitled to it or to the rights it evidences and its transfer may be registered upon books maintained for that purpose by or on behalf of the issuer.

The inclusion or omission of the bracketed words relating to oil, gas and mineral interests is optional; if the bracketed words are included and there is doubt whether such interests are "securities" in legal or common parlance, change "An Act, etc. . . ." at the beginning of the Act to encompass such interests.

The second sentence precludes a gift of or investment in an obligation of the donor.

The definition of a security "in registered form" is derived from Uniform Commercial Code Section 8–102(1)(c).

(o) A "transfer agent" is a person who acts as authenticating trustee, transfer agent, registrar or other agent for an issuer in the registration of transfers of its securities or in the issue of new securities or in the cancellation of surrendered securities.

(p) A "trust company" is a bank, corporation (or other legal entity) authorized to exercise trust powers (in the state).

Section 2. Manner of Making Gift. (a) An adult may, during his lifetime, make a gift of a security, a life insurance policy or annuity contract or money to a person who is a minor on the date of the gift:

(1) if the subject of the gift is a security in registered form, by registering it in the name of the donor, another adult person (an adult member of the minor's family, a guardian of the minor) or a trust company, followed, in substance, by the words: "as custodian for [name of minor] under the [name of enacting state] Uniform Gifts to Minors Act";

(2) if the subject of the gift is a security not in registered form, by delivering it to an adult other than the donor (an adult member, other than the donor, of the minor's family, a guardian of the minor) or a trust company, accompanied by a statement of gift in the following form, in substance, signed by the donor and the person designated as custodian:

GIFT UNDER THE [NAME OF ENACTING STATE] UNIFORM GIFTS TO MINORS ACT

I, _____ hereby deliver to _____ as custodian
   [name of donor]   [name of custodian]

for _____ under the [name of enacting state] Uniform Gifts
     [name of minor]

to Minors Act, the following security(ies): [insert an appropriate description of the security or securities delivered sufficient to identify it or them]

_____
          [signature of donor]

_____ hereby acknowledges receipt of the above
   [name of custodian]

described security(ies) as custodian for the above minor under the [name of enacting state] Uniform Gifts to Minors Act.

Date: _____ _____
                                     [signature of custodian]

(3) If the subject of the gift is money, by paying or delivering it to a broker or a (domestic) financial institution for credit to an account in the name of the donor, another adult (an adult member of the minor's family, a guardian of the minor) or a trust company, followed, in substance, by the words:

as custodian for _____ under the [name of enacting state]
                    [name of minor]

Uniform Gift to Minors Act.

(4) if the subject of the gift is money, by paying or delivering it to a broker or a (domestic) financial institution for credit to an account in the name of the donor, another adult (an adult member of the minor's family, a guardian of the minor) or a trust company, followed, in substance, by the words:

as custodian for _____ under the [name of enacting state]
                      [name of minor]

Uniform Gifts to Minors Act.

(b) Any gift made in a manner prescribed in Subsection (a) may be made to only one minor and only one person may be the custodian.

(c) A donor who makes a gift to a minor in a manner prescribed in Subsection (a) shall promptly do all things within his power to put the subject of the gift in the possession and control of the custodian, but neither the donor's failure to comply with this Subsection, nor his designation of an ineligible person as custodian, nor renunciation by the person designated as custodian affects the consummation of the gift.

Section 3. Effect of Gift. (a) A gift made in a manner prescribed in this act is irrevocable and conveys to the minor indefeasibly vested legal title to the security, life insurance policy, annuity contract or money given, but no guardian of the minor has any right, power, duty or authority with respect to the custodial property except as provided in this act.

(b) By making a gift in a manner prescribed in this act, the donor incorporates in his gift all the provisions of this act and grants to the custodian and to any issuer, transfer agent, bank, financial institution, life insurance company, broker or third person dealing with a person designated as custodian, the respective powers, rights and immunities provided in this act.

Section 4. Duties and Powers of Custodian. (a) The custodian shall collect, hold, manage, invest and reinvest the custodial property.

(b) The custodian shall pay over to the minor for expenditure by him, or expend for the minor's benefit, so much of or all the custodial property as the custodian deems advisable for the support, maintenance, education and benefit of the minor in the manner, at the time or times, and to the extent that the custodian in his discretion deems suitable and proper, with or without court order, with or without regard to the duty of himself or of any other person to support the minor or his ability to do so, and with or without regard to any other income or property of the minor which may be applicable or available for any such purpose.

(c) The court, on the petition of a parent or guardian of the minor or of the minor, if he has attained the age of fourteen years, may order the custodian to pay over to the minor for expenditure by him or to expend so much of or all the custodial property as is necessary for the minor's support, maintenance or education.

(d) To the extent that the custodial property is not so expended, the custodian shall deliver or pay it over to the minor on his attaining the age of twenty-one years or, if the minor dies before attaining the age of twenty-one years, he shall thereupon deliver or pay it over to the estate of the minor.

(e) The custodian, notwithstanding statutes restricting investments by fiduciaries, shall invest and reinvest the custodial property as would a prudent man of discretion and intelligence who is seeking a reasonable income and the preservation of his capital, except that he may, in his discretion and without liability to the minor or his estate, retain a security given to the minor in a manner prescribed in this act or hold money so given in an account in the financial institution to which it was paid or delivered by the donor.

(f) The custodian may sell, exchange, convert, surrender or otherwise dispose of custodial property in the manner, at the time or times, for the price or prices and upon the terms he deems advisable. He may vote in person or by general or limited proxy a security which is custodial property. He may consent, directly or through a committee or other agent, to the reorganization, consolidation, merger, dissolution or liquidation of an issuer, a security which is custodial property, and to the sale, lease, pledge or mortgage of any property by or to such an issuer, and to any other action by such an issuer. He may execute and deliver any and all instruments in writing which he deems advisable to carry out any of his powers as custodian.

(g) The custodian shall register each security which is custodial property and in registered form in the name of the custodian, followed, in substance, by the words:

as custodian for _____ under the [name of enacting
[name of minor]

state] Uniform Gifts to Minors Act.

The custodian shall hold all money which is custodial property in an account with a broker or in an insured (domestic) financial institution in the name of the custodian, followed, in substance, by the words:

as custodian for _____ under the [name of enacting
[name of minor]

state] Uniform Gifts to Minors Act.

The custodian shall keep all other custodial property separate and distinct from his own property in a manner to identify it clearly as custodial property.

(h) The custodian shall keep records of all transactions with respect to the custodial property and make them available for inspection at reasonable intervals by a parent or legal representative of the minor or by the minor, if he has attained the age of fourteen years.

(i) A custodian has (and holds as powers in trust), with respect to the custodial property, in addition to the rights and powers provided in this act, all the rights and powers which a guardian has with respect to property not held as custodial property.

(j) If the subject of the gift is a life insurance policy or annuity contract, the custodian:

(1) has, in his capacity as custodian, all the incidents of ownership in the policy or contract to the extent as if he were the owner, except that the designated beneficiary of any policy or contract on the life of a person other than the minor shall be the custodian as custodian for the minor for whom he is acting; and

(2) may pay premiums on the policy or contract out of the custodial property.

Section 5. Custodian's Expenses, Compensation, Bond and Liabilities. (a) A custodian is entitled to reimbursement from the custodial property for his reasonable expenses incurred in the performance of his duties.

(b) A custodian may act without compensation for his services.

(c) Unless he is a donor, a custodian may receive from the custodial property reasonable compensation for his services determined [by one of the following standards in the order stated:

Securities Transfer 47

(1) a direction by the donor when the gift is made;

(2) a statute of this state applicable to custodians;

(3) the statute of this state applicable to guardians;

(4) an order of the court.]

(d) Except as otherwise provided in this act, a custodian shall not be required to give a bond for the performance of his duties.

(e) A custodian not compensated for his services is not liable for losses to the custodial property unless they result from his bad faith, intentional wrongdoing or gross negligence or from his failure to maintain the standard of prudence in investing the custodial property provided in this act.

Section 6. Exemption of Third Persons from Liability. No issuer, transfer agent, bank, life insurance company, broker or other person or financial institution acting on the instructions of or otherwise dealing with any person purporting to act as a donor or in the capacity of a custodian is responsible for determining whether the person designated as custodian by the purported donor or by the custodian or purporting to act as custodian has been duly designated or whether any purchase, sale or transfer to or by or any other act of any person purporting to act in the capacity of custodian is in accordance with or authorized by this act, or is obliged to inquire into the validity or propriety under this act of any instrument or instructions executed or given by a person purporting to act as a donor or in the capacity of a custodian, or is bound to see to the application by any person purporting to act in the capacity of a custodian of any money or other property paid or delivered to him. No issuer, transfer agent, bank, life insurance company, broker or other person or financial institution acting on any instrument of designation of a successor custodian, executed as provided in Subsection (a) of Section 7 of this act by a minor to whom a gift has been made in a manner prescribed in this act and who has attained the age of fourteen years, is responsible for determining whether the person designated by the minor as successor custodian has been duly designated, or is obliged to inquire into the validity or propriety under this act of the instrument designation.

Section 7. Resignation, Death or Removal of Custodian; Bond. Designation of Successor Custodian. (a) Only an adult member of the minor's family, a guardian of the minor or a trust company is eligible to become successor custodian. A custodian may designate his successor by executing and dating an instrument of designation before a subscribing witness other than the successor; the instrument of designation may but need not contain the resignation of the custodian. If the custodian does not so designate his successor before he dies or becomes legally incapacitated and the minor has attained the age of fourteen years, the minor may designate a successor custodian by executing an instrument of designation before a subscribing witness other than the successor. A successor custodian has all the rights, powers, duties and immunities of a custodian designated in a manner prescribed by this act.

(b) The designation of a successor custodian as provided in Subsection (a) takes effect as to each item of the custodial property when the custodian resigns, dies or becomes legally incapacitated and the custodian or his legal representative:

(1) causes the item, if it is a security in registered form or a life insruance policy or annuity contract, to be registered, with the issuing insurance company in the case of a life insurance policy or annuity contract, in the name of the successor custodian followed, in substance, by the words:

as custodian for _____ under the [name of enacting
[name of minor]
state] Uniform Gifts to Minors Act.

and

(2) delivers or causes to be delivered to the successor custodian any other item of the custodial property, together with the instrument of designation of the successor custodian or a true copy thereof and any additional instruments required for the transfer thereof to the successor custodian.

(c) A custodian who executes an instrument of designation of his successor containing the custodian's resignation as provided in Subsection (a) shall promptly do all things within his power to put each item of the custodial property in the possession and control of the successor custodian named in the instrument. The legal representative of a custodian who dies or becomes legally incapacitated shall promptly do all things within his power to put each item of the custodial property in the possession and control of the successor custodian named in an instrument of designation executed as provided in Subsection (a) by the custodian or, if none, by the minor if he has no guardian and has attained the age of fourteen years, or in the possession and control of the guardian of the minor if he has a guardian. If the custodian has executed as provided in Subsection (a) more than one instrument of designation, his legal representative shall treat the instrument dated on an earlier date as having been revoked by the instrument dated on a later date.

(d) If a person designated as custodian or as successor custodian by the custodian as provided in Subsection (a) is not eligible, dies or becomes legally incapacitated before the minor attains the age of twenty-one years and if the minor has a guardian, the guardian of the minor shall be successor custodian. If the minor has no guardian and if no successor custodian who is eligible and has not died or become legally incapacitated has been designated as provided in Subsection (a), a donor, his legal representative, the legal representative of the custodian or an adult member of the minor's family may petition the court for the designation of a successor custodian.

(e) A donor, the legal representative of a donor, a successor custodian, an adult member of the minor's family, a guardian of the minor or the minor, if he has attained the age of fourteen years, may petition the court that, for cause shown in the petition, the custodian be removed and a successor custodian be designated or, in the alternative, that the custodian be required to give bond for the performance of his duties.

(f) Upon the filing of a petition as provided in this Section, [the court shall grant an order, directed to the persons and returnable on such notice as the court may require, to show cause why the relief prayed for in the petition should not be granted and, in due course, grant such relief as the court finds to be in the best interests of the minor].

Section 8. Accounting by Custodian. (a) The minor if he has attained the age of fourteen years, or the legal representative of the minor, an adult member of the minor's family, or a donor or his legal representative may petition the court for an accounting by the custodian or his legal representative.

(b) the Court, in a proceeding under this act or otherwise, may require or permit the custodian or his legal representative to account and, if the custodian is removed, shall so require and order delivery of all custodial property to the successor custodian and the execution of all instruments required for the transfer thereof.

Section 9. Construction. (a) This act shall be so construed as to effectuate its general purpose to make uniform the law of those states which enact it.

(b) This act shall not be construed as providing an inclusive method for making gifts to minors.

Section 10. Short Title. This act may be cited as the "[name of enacting state] Uniform Gifts to Minors Act."

Section 11. Severability. If any provision of this act or the application thereof to any person or circumstances is held invalid, the invalidity shall not affect other provisions or applications of the act which can be given effect without the invalid provision or application, and to this end the provisions of this act are severable.

UNIFORM TRANSFERS TO MINORS ACT

The following is the complete text of the Uniform Transfers to Minors Act adopted by most states.

Section 1. Definitions. In this [Act]:

(1) "Adult" means an individual who has attained the age of 21 years.

(2) "Benefit plan" means an employer's plan for the benefit of an employee or partner.

(3) "Broker" means a person lawfully engaged in the business of effecting transactions in securities or commodities for the person's own account or for the account of others.

(4) "Conservator" means a person appointed or qualified by a court to act as general, limited, or temporary guardian of a minor's property or a person legally authorized to perform substantially the same functions.

(5) "Court" means [_____ court].

(6) "Custodial property" means (i) any interest in property transferred to a custodian under this [Act] and (ii) the income from and proceeds of that interest in property.

(7) "Custodian" means a person so designated under Section 9 or a successor or substitute custodian designated under Section 18.

(8) "Financial institution" means a bank, trust company, savings institution, or credit union, chartered and supervised under state or federal law.

(9) "Legal representative" means an individual's personal representative or conservator.

(10) "Member of the minor's family" means the minor's parent, stepparent, spouse, grandparent, brother, sister, uncle, or aunt, whether of the whole or half blood or by adoption.

(11) "Minor" means an individual who has not attained the age of 21 years.

(12) "Person" means an individual, corporation, organization, or other legal entity.

(13) "Personal representative" means an executor, administrator, successor personal representative, or special administrator of a decedent's estate or a person legally authorized to perform substantially the same functions.

(14) "State" includes any state of the United States, the District of Columbia, the Commonwealth of Puerto Rico, and any territory or possession subject to the legislative authority of the United States.

(15) "Transfer" means a transaction that creates custodial property under Section 9.

(16) "Transferor" means a person who makes a transfer under this [Act].

(17) "Trust company" means a financial institution, corporation, or other legal entity, authorized to exercise general trust powers.

Section 2. Scope and Jurisdiction. (a) This [Act] applies to a transfer that refers to this [Act] in the designation under Section 9(a) by which the transfer is made if at the time of the transfer, the transferor, the minor, or the custodian is a resident of this State or the custodial property is located in this State. The custodianship so created remains subject to this [Act] despite a subsequent change in residence of a transferor, the minor, or the custodian, or the removal of custodial property from this State.

(b) A person designated as custodian under this [Act] is subject to personal jurisdiction in this State with respect to any matter relating to the custodianship.

(c) A transfer that purports to be made and which is valid under the Uniform Transfers to Minors Act, the Uniform Gifts to Minors Act, or a substantially similar act, of another state is governed by the law of the designated state and may be executed and is enforceable in this State if at the time of the transfer, the transferor, the minor, or the custodian is a resident of the designated state or the custodial property is located in the designated state.

Section 3. Nomination of Custodian. (a) A person having the right to designate the recipient of property transferable upon the occurrence of a future event may revocably nominate a custodian to receive the property for a minor beneficiary upon the occurrence of the event by naming the custodian followed in substance by the words: "as custodian for _____ (name of minor) under the [name of Enacting State] Uniform Transfers to Minors Act." The nomination may name one or more persons as substitute custodians to whom the property must be transferred, in the order named, if the first nominated custodian dies before the transfer or is unable, declines, or is ineligible to serve. The nomination may be made in a will, a trust, a deed, an instrument exercising a power of appointment, or in a writing designating a beneficiary of contractual rights which is registered with or delivered to the payor, issuer, or other obligor of the contractual rights.

(b) A custodian nominated under this section must be a person to whom a transfer of property of that kind may be made under Section 9(a).

(c) The nomination of a custodian under this section does not create custodial property until the nominating instrument becomes irrevocable or a transfer to the nominated custodian is completed under Section 9. Unless the nomination of a custodian has been revoked, upon the occurrence of the future event the custodianship becomes effective and the custodian shall enforce a transfer of the custodial property pursuant to Section 9.

Section 4. Transfer by Gift or Exercise of Power of Appointment. A person may make a transfer by irrevocable gift to, or the irrevocable exercise of a power of appointment in favor of, a custodian for the benefit of a minor pursuant to Section 9.

Section 5. Transfer Authorized by Will or Trust. (a) A personal representative or trustee may make an irrevocable transfer pursuant to Section 9 to a custodian for the benefit of a minor as authorized in the governing will or trust.

(b) If the testator or settlor has nominated a custodian under Section 3 to receive the custodial property, the transfer must be made to that person.

(c) If the testator or settlor has not nominated a custodian under Section 3, or all persons so nominated as custodian die before the transfer or are unable, decline, or are ineligible to serve, the personal representative or the trustee, as the case may be, shall designate the custodian from among those eligible to serve as custodian for property of that kind under Section 9(a).

Section 6. Other Transfer by Fiduciary. (a) Subject to subsection (c), a personal representative or trustee may make an irrevocable transfer to another adult or trust company as custodian for the benefit of a minor pursuant to Section 9, in the absence of a will or under a will or trust that does not contain an authorization to do so.

(b) Subject to subsection (c), a conservator may make an irrevocable transfer to another adult or trust company as custodian for the benefit of the minor pursuant to Section 9.

(c) A transfer under subsection (a) or (b) may be made only if (i) the personal representative, trustee, or conservator considers the transfer to be in the best interest of the minor, (ii) the transfer is not prohibited by or inconsistent with provisions of the applicable will, trust agreement, or other governing instrument, and (iii) the transfer is authorized by the court if it exceeds [$10,000] in value.

Section 7. Transfer by Obligor. (a) Subject to subsections (b) and (c), a person not subject to Section 5 or 6 who holds property of or owes a liquidated debt to a minor not having a conservator may make an irrevocable transfer to a custodian for the benefit of the minor pursuant to Section 9.

(b) If a person having the right to do so under Section 3 has nominated a custodian under that section to receive the custodial property, the transfer must be made to that person.

(c) If no custodian has been nominated under Section 3, or all persons so nominated as custodian die before the transfer or are unable, decline, or are ineligible to serve, a transfer under this section may be made to an adult member of the minor's family or to a trust company unless the property exceeds [$10,000] in value.

Section 8. Receipt for Custodial Property. A written acknowledgement of delivery by a custodian constitutes a sufficient receipt and discharge for custodial property transferred to the custodian pursuant to this [Act].

Section 9. Manner of Creating Custodial Property and Effecting Transfer; Designation of Initial Custodian; Control. (a) Custodial property is created and a transfer is made whenever:

(1) an uncertificated security or a certificated security in registered form is either:

(i) registered in the name of the transferor, an adult other than the transferor, or a trust company, followed in substance by the words: "as custodian for _____ (name of minor) under the [Name of Enacting State] Uniform Transfers to Minors Act"; or

(ii) delivered if in certificated form, or any document necessary for the transfer of an uncertificated security is delivered, together with any necessary endorsement to an adult other than the transferor or to a trust company as custodian, accompanied by an instrument in substantially the form set forth in subsection (b);

(2) money is paid or delivered to a broker or financial institution for credit to an account in the name of the transferor, an adult other than the transferor, or a trust company, followed in substance by the words: "as custodian for _____ (name of minor) under the [Name of Enacting State] Uniform Transfers to Minors Act";

(3) the ownership of a life or endowment insurance policy or annuity contract is either:

(i) registered with the issuer in the name of the transferor, an adult other than the transferor, or a trust company, followed in substance by the words: "as custodian for _____ (name of minor) under the [Name of Enacting State] Uniform Transfers to Minors Act"; or

(ii) assigned in a writing delivered to an adult other than the transferor or to a trust company whose name in the assignment is followed in substance by the words: "as custodian for _____ (name of minor) under the [Name of Enacting State] Uniform Transfers to Minors Act";

(4) an irrevocable exercise of a power of appointment or an irrevocable present right to future payment under a contract is the subject of a written notification delivered to the payor, issuer, or other obligor that the right is transferred to the transferor, an adult other than the transferor, or a trust company, whose name in the notification is followed in substance by the words: "as custodian for _____ (name of minor) under the [Name of Enacting State] Uniform Transfers to Minors Act";

(5) an interest in real property is recorded in the name of the transferor, an adult other than the transferor, or a trust company, followed in substance by the words: "as custodian for _____ (name of minor) under the [Name of Enacting State] Uniform Transfers to Minors Act";

(6) a certificate of title issued by a department or agency of a state or of the United States which evidences title to tangible personal property is either:

(i) issued in the name of the transferor, an adult other than the transferor, or a trust company, followed in substance by the words: "as custodian for _____ (name of minor) under the [Name of Enacting State] Uniform Transfers to Minors Act"; or

(ii) delivered to an adult other than the transferor or to a trust company, endorsed to that person followed in substance by the words: "as custodian for _____ (name of minor) under the [Name of Enacting State] Uniform Transfers to Minors Act"; or

(7) an interest in any property not described in paragraphs (1) through (6) is transferred to an adult other than the transferor or to a trust company by a

written instrument in substantially the form set forth in subsection (b).

(b) An instrument in the following form satisfies the requirements of paragraphs (1)(ii) and (7) of subsection (a):

"TRANSFER UNDER THE
[NAME OF ENACTING STATE]
UNIFORM TRANSFERS TO MINORS ACT

I, _____ (name of transferor or name and representative capacity if a fiduciary) hereby transfer to_____ (name of custodian), as custodian for _____ (name of minor) under the [Name of Enacting State] Uniform Transfers to Minors Act, the following: (insert a description of the custodial property sufficient to identify it).
Dated: _____

_____
(Signature)

_____ (name of custodian) acknowledges receipt of the property described above as custodian for the minor named above under the [Name of Enacting State] Uniform Transfers to Minors Act.
Dated: _____

_____ ."
(Signature of Custodian)

(c) A transferor shall place the custodian in control of the custodial property as soon as practicable.

Section 10. Single Custodianship. A transfer may be made only for one minor, and only one person may be the custodian. All custodial property held under this [Act] by the same custodian for the benefit of the same minor constitutes a single custodianship.

Section 11. Validity and Effect of Transfer. (a) The validity of a transfer made in a manner prescribed in this [Act] is not affected by:

(1) failure of the transferor to comply with Section 9(c) concerning possession and control;

(2) designation of an ineligible custodian, except designation of the transferor in the case of property for which the transferor is ineligible to serve as custodian under Section 9(a); or

(3) death or incapacity of a person nominated under Section 3 or designated under Section 9 as custodian or the disclaimer of the office by that person.

(b) A transfer made pursuant to Section 9 is irrevocable, and the custodial property is indefeasibly vested in the minor, but the custodian has all the

Securities Transfer

rights, powers, duties, and authority provided in this [Act], and neither the minor nor the minor's legal representative has any right, power, duty, or authority with respect to the custodial property except as provided in this [Act].

(c) By making a transfer the transferor incorporates in the disposition all the provisions of this [Act] and grants to the custodian, and to any third person dealing with a person designated as custodian, the respective powers, rights, and immunities provided in this [Act].

Section 12. Care of Custodial Property. (a) A custodian shall:

(1) take control of custodial property;

(2) register or record title to custodial property if appropriate; and

(3) collect, hold, manage, invest, and reinvest custodial property.

(b) In dealing with custodial property, a custodian shall observe the standard of care that would be observed by a prudent person dealing with property of another and is not limited by any other statute restricting investments by fiduciaries. If a custodian has a special skill or expertise or is named custodian on the basis of representations of a special skill or expertise, the custodian shall use that skill or expertise. However, a custodian, in the custodian's discretion and without liability to the minor or the minor's estate, may retain any custodial property received from a transferor.

(c) A custodian may invest in or pay premiums on life insurance or endowment policies on (i) the life of the minor only if the minor or the minor's estate is the sole beneficiary, or (ii) the life of another person in whom the minor has an insurable interest only to the extent that the minor, the minor's estate, or the custodian in the capacity of custodian, is the irrevocable beneficiary.

(d) A custodian at all times shall keep custodial property separate and distinct from all other property in a manner sufficient to identify it clearly as custodial property of the minor. Custodial property consisting of an undivided interest is so identified if the minor's interest is held as a tenant in common and is fixed. Custodial property subject to recordation is so identified if it is recorded, and custodial property subject to registration is so identified if it is either registered, or held in account designated, in the name of the custodian, followed in substance by the words: "as a custodian for _____ (name of minor) under the [Name of Enacting State] Uniform Transfers to Minors Act."

(e) A custodian shall keep records of all transactions with respect to custodial property, including information necessary for the preparation of the minor's tax returns, and shall make them available for inspection at reasonable intervals by a parent or legal representative of the minor or by the minor if the minor has attained the age of 14 years.

Section 13. Powers of Custodian. (a) A custodian, acting in a custodial capacity, has all the rights, powers, and authority over custodial property that unmarried adult owners have over their own property, but a custodian may exercise those rights, powers, and authority in that capacity only.

(b) This section does not relieve a custodian from liability for breach of Section 12.

Section 14. Use of Custodial Property. (a) A custodian may deliver or pay to the minor or expend for the minor's benefit so much of the custodial property as the custodian considers advisable for the use and benefit of the minor, without court order and without regard to (i) the duty or ability of the custodian personally or of any other person to support the minor, or (ii) any other income or property of the minor which may be applicable or available for that purpose.

(b) On petition of an interested person or the minor if the minor has attained the age of 14 years, the court may order the custodian to deliver or pay to the minor or expend for the minor's benefit so much of the custodial property as the court considers advisable for the use and benefit of the minor.

(c) A delivery, payment, or expenditure under this section is in addition to, not in substitution for, and does not affect any obligation of a person to support the minor.

Section 15. Custodian's Expenses, Compensation, and Bond. (a) A custodian is entitled to reimbursement from custodial property for reasonable expenses incurred in the performance of the custodian's duties.

(b) Except for one who is a transferor under Section 4, a custodian has a non-cumulative election during each calendar year to charge reasonable compensation for services performed during that year.

(c) Except as provided in Section 18(f), a custodian need not give a bond.

Section 16. Exemption of Third Person from Liability. A third person in good faith and without court order may act on the instructions of or otherwise deal with any person purporting to make a transfer or purporting to act in the capacity of a custodian and, in the absence of knowledge, is not responsible for determining:

(1) the validity of the purported custodian's designation;

(2) the propriety of, or the authority under this [Act] for, any act of the purported custodian;

(3) the validity or propriety under this [Act] of any instrument or instructions executed or given either by the person purporting to make a transfer or by the purported custodian; or

(4) the propriety of the application of any property of the minor delivered to the purported custodian.

Section 17. Liability to Third Persons. (a) A claim based on (i) a contract entered into by a custodian acting in a custodial capacity, (ii) an obligation arising from the ownership or control of custodial property, or (iii) a tort committed during the custodianship, may be asserted against the custodial property by proceeding against the custodian in the custodial capacity, whether or not the custodian or the minor is personally liable therefor.

(b) A custodian is not personally liable:

(1) on a contract properly entered into in the custodial capacity unless the custodian fails to reveal that capacity and to identify the custodianship in the contract; or

(2) for an obligation arising from control of custodial property or for a tort committed during the custodianship unless the custodian is personally at fault.

Section 18. Renunciation, Resignation, Death, or Removal of Custodian; Designation of Successor Custodian. (a) A person nominated under Section 3 or designated under Section 9 as custodian may decline to serve by delivering a valid disclaimer [under the Uniform Disclaimer of Property Interests Act of the Enacting State] to the person who made the nomination or to the transferor or the transferor's legal representative. If the event giving rise to a transfer has not occurred and no substitute custodian able, willing, and eligible to serve was nominated under Section 3, the person who made the nomination may nominate a substitute custodian under Section 3; otherwise the transferor or the transferor's legal representative shall designate a substitute custodian at the time of the transfer, in either case from among the persons eligible to serve as custodian for that kind of property under Section 9(a). The custodian so designated has the rights of a successor custodian.

(b) A custodian at any time may designate a trust company or an adult other than a transferor under Section 4 as successor custodian by executing and dating an instrument of designation before a subscribing witness other than the successor. If the instrument of designation does not contain or is not accompanied by the resignation of the custodian, the designation of the successor does not take effect until the custodian resigns, dies, becomes incapacitated, or is removed.

(c) A custodian may resign at any time by delivering written notice to the minor if the minor has attained the age of 14 years and to the successor custodian and by delivering the custodial property to the successor custodian.

(d) If a custodian is ineligible, dies, or becomes incapacitated without having effectively designated a successor and the minor has attained the age of 14 years, the minor may designate as successor custodian, in the manner prescribed in subsection (b), an adult member of the minor's family, a conservator of the minor, or a trust company. If the minor has not attained the age of 14 years or fails to act within 60 days after the ineligibility, death, or incapacity, the conservator of the minor becomes successor custodian. If the minor has no conservator or the conservator declines to act, the transferor, the legal representative of the transferor or of the custodian, an adult member of the minor's family, or any other interested person may petition the court to designate a successor custodian.

(e) A custodian who declines to serve under subsection (a) or resigns under subsection (c), or the legal representative of a deceased or incapacitated custodian, as soon as practicable, shall put the custodial property and records in the possession and control of the successor custodian. The successor custodian by action may enforce the obligation to deliver custodial property and records and becomes responsible for each item as received.

(f) A transferor, the legal representative of a transferor, an adult member of the minor's family, a guardian of the person of the minor, the conservator of the minor, or the minor if the minor has attained the age of 14 years may petition the court to remove the custodian for cause and to designate a successor custodian other than a transferor under Section 4 or to require the custodian to give appropriate bond.

Section 19. Accounting by and Determination of Liability of Custodian. (a) A minor who has attained the age of 14 years, the minor's guardian of the person or legal representative, an adult member of the minor's family, a transferor, or a transferor's legal representative may petition the court (i) for an accounting by the custodian or the custodian's legal representative; or (ii) for a determination of responsibility, as between the custodial property and the custodian personally, for claims against the custodial property unless the responsibility has been adjudicated in an action under Section 17 to which the minor or the minor's legal representative was a party.

(b) A successor custodian may petition the court for an accounting by the predecessor custodian.

(c) The court, in a proceeding under this [Act] or in any other proceeding, may require or permit the custodian or the custodian's legal representative to account.

(d) If a custodian is removed under Section 18(f), the court shall require an accounting and order delivery of the custodial property and records to the successor custodian and the execution of all instruments required for transfer of the custodial property.

Section 20. Termination of Custodianship. The custodian shall transfer in an appropriate manner the custodial property to the minor or to the minor's estate upon the earlier of:

(1) the minor's attainment of 21 years of age with respect to custodial property transferred under Section 4 or 5;

(2) the minor's attainment of [majority under the laws of this State other than this [Act]] [age 18 or other statutory age of majority of Enacting State] with respect to custodial property transferred under Section 6 or 7; or

(3) the minor's death.

Section 21. Applicability. This [Act] applies to a transfer within the scope of Section 2 made after its effective date if:

(1) the transfer purports to have been made under [the Uniform Gifts to Minors Act of the Enacting State]; or

(2) the instrument by which the transfer purports to have been made uses in substance the designation "as custodian under the Uniform Gifts to Minors Act" or "as custodian under the Uniform Transfers to Minors Act" of any other state, and the application of this [Act] is necessary to validate the transfer.

Section 22. Effect on Existing Custodianships. (a) Any transfer of custodial property as now defined in this [Act] made before [the effective date of this Act] is validated notwithstanding that there was no specific authority in [the Uniform Gifts to Minors Act of the Enacting State] for the coverage of custodial property of that kind or for a transfer from that source at the time the transfer was made.

(b) This [Act] applies to all transfers made before the effective date of this [Act] in a manner and form prescribed in [the Uniform Gifts to Minors Act of the Enacting State] except insofar as the application impairs constitutionally vested rights or extends the duration of custodianships in existence on the effective date of this [Act].

[(c) Sections 1 and 20 with respect to the age of a minor for whom custodial property is held under this [Act] do not apply to custodial property held in a custodianship that terminated because of the minor's attainment of the age of [18] after [date prior Act was amended to specify [18] as age of majority] and before [the effective date of this Act].]

Section 23. Uniformity of Application and Construction. This [Act] shall be applied and construed to effectuate its general purpose to make uniform the law with respect to the subject of this [Act] among states enacting it.

Section 24. Short Title. This [Act] may be cited as the "[Name of Enacting State] Uniform Transfers to Minors Act."

Section 25. Severability. If any provisions of this [Act] or its application to any person or circumstance is held invalid, the invalidity does not affect other provisions or applications of this [Act] which can be given effect without the invalid provision or application, and to this end provisions of this [Act] are severable.

Section 26. Effective Date. This [Act] takes effect _____ .

Section 27. Repeals. [Insert appropriate reference to the existing Gifts to Minors Act of the Enacting State or other jurisdiction] is hereby repealed. To the extent that this [Act], by virtue of Section 22(b), does not apply to transfers made in a manner prescribed in [the Gifts to Minors Act of the Enacting State] or to the powers, duties, and immunities conferred by transfers in that manner upon custodians and persons dealing with custodians, the repeal of [the Gifts to Minors Act of the Enacting State] does not affect those transfers or those powers, duties, and immunities.

CHAPTER 5

Types of Legal Entities

SOLE PROPRIETORSHIPS

An instrument evidencing sole proprietorship is submitted to the securities firm at the opening of the account. Since only one person comprises this entity, the transfer agent is generally satisfied with a certification by the broker that "The registered holder is a sole proprietorship and the person signing is the sole proprietor with full authority to sign."

Transfer of stock from the name of a sole proprietorship to the individual name of the sole proprietor is not considered fraudulent, and the transfer should not be refused.

Death of a Sole Proprietor

At the death of the sole proprietor, the securities constitute a part of the estate. The requirements are:

1. assignment by the executor or administrator,
2. a certified copy of the certificate of appointment of the fiduciary, dated within sixty days of the submission of the stock to the transfer agent,
3. an affidavit of domicile (see Figure 5-1 on page 63), and
4. resident and/or nonresident inheritance tax waivers if required by state.

PARTNERSHIPS

A partnership agreement is submitted to the brokerage firm at the initiation of the account, and it should be kept on file at all times. Transfers of stock registered in the name of a legally organized partnership do not require documentation, nor are transfer agents under any duty of inquiry about the transferor or the transferee. It is advisable, therefore, to designate the account a partnership on the face of the certificate to enable subsequent transfers without supporting documentation.

Unlike officers of a corporation, general partners (but not limited partners) exercise full power and authority; therefore, an assignment executed by any one of them is sufficient proof of authorization to effect a transfer of stock.

Sale of Stock in the Name of a Partnership

Required documents are:

1. an assignment executed by a general partner, such as "Smith & Co., John Doe, general partner" and
2. certification: "It is hereby certified that the registered stockholder is a partnership and the person signing is a general partner with authority to sign."

Transfer of Stock from the Partnership to the Name of a Partner

Required documents are:

1. an assignment executed by all partners, and
2. a complete list of the names of all general partners.

Change in Name of the Partnership

Documents required for this transaction include:

1. an assignment by a general partner, and
2. an instrument evidencing the change of name.

Death of a Partner

The sale or transfer of the security should be in accordance with the partnership agreement. When the partnership is composed of two partners, both of them deceased, the following documents are required:

1. an assignment by the legal representative of the partner last deceased,
2. a court-certified copy of appointment evidencing the fiduciary capacity of the assignor,
3. affidavits of domicile of both decedents (Figure 5-1), and
4. inheritance tax waivers of both estates if required from the state of residence of the decedents or from the state of incorporation of the security.

INVESTMENT CLUBS

Legal Aspects

Investment clubs are not legally organized entities. The formation of these clubs has acquired tremendous popularity in recent years. It is a common mis-

Figure 5-1. Affidavit of Domicile

AFFIDAVIT OF DOMICILE

STATE OF .... }
COUNTY OF .... } ss:

..................................., being duly sworn, deposes and says:
I reside at ...., Street, City of ....,
County of ...., State of ....,
and am Executor/Administrator/survivor of ....,
deceased, who died on the ...... day of ...., 19..... .
At the time of death the legal residence of said decedent was....
.... Street, City of .... County of ....
State of .... He/She resided in the State of ....
for .... years prior to death, and was not a resident of
.... or any State (other than that of
(State of Incorporation of the Stock)
his/her Domicile) within the United States of America, at the time death.

This affidavit is made for the purpose of securing the transfer of the following described securities owned by said decedent at the time of death.

.... Shares ....
.... Shares ....
.... Shares ....

That the said securities were physically located in the City of
..................., State of .... at the date of
the death of decedent. ....

Sworn to or affirmed
before me this ....
day of .... 19........
My Commission expires...............
Affix Seal

X..
(Signature of Deponent)

take, however, to organize the clubs on a purely speculative basis, confining their interest to social objectives and neglecting the fundamental principles of investment education.

Investment clubs often lack proper organizational structure, a charter, or a constitution; and their authority is not vested in a governing body or a committee. Because of this very nature, they create certain complications in the field of securities transfers. Transfer agents are therefore usually reluctant to register stocks in the name of an investment club. It is advisable, therefore, to hold the stocks in "street name" or in the name of a nominee to avoid inconvenience and delay.

Investment Clubs as Partnerships

To eliminate these complications and to encourage the organization of these clubs, the National Association of Investment Clubs advises that investment clubs should be organized as partnerships and that the stocks should be registered as "XYZ Investment Club (a partnership)." Here, the requirements are the same as those of a partnership.

Investment Clubs Organized in Other Ways

When an investment club is not organized as a partnership, transactions are handled in the following ways:

Documents required for sale of stock:

1. assignment by an authorized member,
2. a certified copy of the club's charter,
3. a certified copy of the bylaws, and
4. a club resolution signed by the secretary.

In certain cases, depending on the judgment of the transfer agent, the transaction may also require:

1. assignment by all the members of the club, and
2. certification by the secretary that the entire membership has executed the assignment.

Transfer of Stock into the Name of a Member

Required documents for this transaction include:

1. assignment by an authorized member,
2. a certified copy of the charter,
3. a certified copy of the bylaws, and

4. a club resolution specifically authorizing the transfer to the name of the member as an individual.

Disbandment of the Club

Required documents are:

1. assignment by an authorized member,
2. a certified copy of the instrument of disbandment signed by all the members, and
3. certification by the secretary that the entire membership has executed the instrument of disbandment.

EXONERATION STATUTES

By common law, a corporation had limited responsibility in verifying the propriety of transfers. According to this law, it was not the issuer's concern to check whether the person requesting the transfer of shares was authorized to do so. For the purposes of transfer, fiduciaries whose names were recorded in the books of the corporation were the only authorized stockholders to request transfer of shares. The corporation assumed no responsibility to protect the rights and interests of the beneficial owners as long as they were represented by fiduciaries.

By English common law, imposing a responsibility of this type upon the joint stock company was found to be impractical. The opinion of Lord Coleridge, written in the nineteenth century, is of particular interest:

> Companies have nothing whatever to do with the relations between trustees and their beneficiaries in respect of the shares of the company. If a trustee is on the company's register as the holder of shares, the relation which he may have with some other person in respect of the shares are matters with which the company has nothing whatever to do. They can look only to the man whose name is upon the register. It seems to me that, if we were to throw any doubt upon that rule, we should make the carrying on of their business by joint stock companies extremely difficult, and might involve those companies in very serious questions, and the ultimate result would be anything but beneficial to the holders of shares in such companies themselves.

This English law was not taken as precedent, however, in America when in 1848 a court ruled that corporations were responsible for the propriety of transfers by fiduciaries. In *Lowry v. Commercial Farmers' Bank*, the judge ruled that:

> A corporation was the custodian of the shares of stock, and clothed with power sufficient to protect the rights of everyone interested, from unauthorized transfers; it is a trust placed in the hands of the corporation for the pro-

tection of individual interests, and like every other trustee, it is bound to execute the trust with proper diligence and care, and is responsible for any injury sustained by its negligence and misconduct.

This was a deviation from common law. Under this ruling, the issuers had the obligation to protect the rights and interests of beneficial owners. The corporation was required:

1. to verify that the fiduciary was legally appointed,
2. to verify that the fiduciary was incumbent on the date of transfer, and
3. to make inquiry as to the authority of the fiduciary to make the transfer.

Failure to make this inquiry made the issuer liable to the beneficial owner. At this time the corporations, in order to protect themselves from this liability, demanded full documentation before effecting a transfer of stock. Full documentation meant court-certified copies of the will, letters of probate, trust instruments, court orders, and so on. Each supporting document had to be examined by the transfer agent before a transfer of shares was safely entered into the books of the corporation. This became a cumbersome procedure.

To simplify the requirements and at the same time to continue to insulate the corporations from liability, various simplification statutes were enacted by several states. Under these statutes it was necessary for the issuer and the transfer agent only to verify the fiduciary's endorsement, appointment, and incumbency. There was no need to examine copies of the will, trust indentures, or court orders authorizing the distribution of shares.

At present, there are two exoneration statutes enacted by all states and the District of Columbia: (1) The Uniform Act for Simplification of Fiduciary Security Transfers, published in 1957, and (2) the Uniform Commercial Code—Article 8, published in 1951 and subsequently amended in 1958. These statutes have simplified the procedures and requirements of securities transfers.

Article 8 of the Uniform Commercial Code reduces the liability of the corporation and the transfer agent. If a fiduciary transfer is completed without a court approval or an examination of a supporting document, the issuer's liability is minimal. The Code places total responsibility on authorized endorsements. Under the code, the issuer and its transfer agent are protected by proof that the endorsement of the stockholder is genuine and effective. The procedure of signature guarantee, therefore, plays an important role.

The Uniform Act for Simplification of Fiduciary Security Transfers simplifies the procedures of securities processing by eliminating unnecessary and expensive transfer requirements.

Under the Act, the transfer agent need not inquire into the propriety of the transfer. Neither is it necessary to submit copies of the will, court orders, trust instruments, or affidavits of debt. The Act, however, requires the transfer agent to verify the appointment of the fiduciary by requesting letters of administration or testamentary, dated within sixty days. The transfer agent must also be certain of the authority of the person making the transfer. Further, various inheritance tax, estate, or succession duty requirements must be complied with before a transfer is safely recorded in the books of the corporation.

CORPORATIONS

At initiation of the account, the securities firm is furnished with a corporate trading authorization to effect transactions in accord with the bylaws of the corporation.

Transfers involving securities registered in the name of a corporation should be accompanied by a corporate resolution (see Figure 5-2 on page 68)—an instrument evidencing the power and the authority of the officer assigning the certificates. The secretary, as custodian of corporate records, is generally the officer who signs the resolution. The resolution should specifically indicate the authority of the assigning officer to sell, assign, and transfer securities or other corporate property standing in the name of the corporation. It should not be signed by the same officer who has assigned the certificates. The corporate seal should be affixed, and the resolution dated within thirty days of the submission of the stock to the transfer agent. If dated earlier, a certification made by the secretary that the resolution is still in full force and effect will be acceptable.

Sale of Stock in a Corporate Name

Required documentation includes:

1. an endorsement by an officer, such as "A. B. Cee Corp. John Brown, President," and
2. a resolution under the corporate seal signed by an officer other than the president. If the resolution indicates that the assignment should be executed under the corporate seal, the transfer agent should be furnished this document.

Transfer of Stock from a Corporate Name into the Name of an Officer

Care should be exercised in handling this type of transfer. The broker should be certain that the transfer is in accordance with the bylaws of the corporation and that the assignment is not fraudulent. Requirements are:

1. an assignment executed by an officer other than the transferee,
2. a resolution under the corporate seal by another officer, not the transferee, specifically authorizing the transfer to the transferee as an individual.

Only One Officer in the Corporation. When there is only one officer in the corporation, he or she may execute both the assignment and the resolution, provided that the latter is certified by the majority of the members of the board of directors.

Figure 5-2. Corporate Resolution

CORPORATION RESOLUTION

BE IT RESOLVED, that the President ....
                                                              (Name)

Vice President ....   Treasurer ....
              (Name)   (Name)

and .... or any one of them acting
        (Name & Title)

individually, be and they are hereby authorized to sell, assign, transfer and/or deliver any and all stocks, bonds or other securities now or hereafter registered in the name of this Corporation.

I, ... Secretary of

....
(Name of Corporation)

hereby certify that the foregoing is a true and complete copy of a resolution duly adopted by the Board of Directors of the said corporation at a meeting duly held on the   day of   , 19 , at which a quorum was present and voting throughout, and that same has not been repealed or amended, and remains in full force and effect and does not conflict with the by-laws of said corporation.

Date...........................   X..
                                                              Secretary

(CORPORATE SEAL)   (must be signed by an officer other than the officer endorsing the certificates)

SIGNATURE GUARANTEED

....

Corporate Committee Authorized to Make Transactions. When a committee of a corporation, in accordance with its bylaws, is authorized to make transactions under the supervision of the board of directors, the broker should be furnished with:

1. an assignment by the officer(s) mentioned in the resolution of the committee,
2. a certified copy of the bylaws of the corporation,
3. a resolution of the committee, and
4. a resolution of the board of directors under corporate seal.

Change of Corporate Name

Transfer of stock from the old corporate name to its new name requires:

1. an assignment by an authorizing officer,
2. a resolution under corporate seal by another officer (Figure 5-2),
3. a letter from the secretary of the state of incorporation, indicating the change of name.

Dissolution of a Corporation

Dissolution of a corporation requires the following documents:

1. an assignment by an authorizing officer,
2. a resolution by another officer (Figure 5-2), and
3. a certified copy of the instrument of dissolution.

UNINCORPORATED ASSOCIATIONS

The requirements of stock registered in the name of an unincorporated association are similar to those for a corporation. The broker should secure a copy of the articles or extracts of the bylaws of the association at the opening of the account.

Unincorporated Association with Governing Body

If the association has a governing body, the transfer will not be difficult to effect. The usual requirements are:

1. an assignment executed by an authorized person, and
2. a resolution of the governing body certified by someone other than the one assigning the certificates.

Chapter 5

CHURCHES AND RELIGIOUS ORDERS

Requirements of stocks registered in the name of a church or religious organization depend largely on the statutes of the state in which the church is organized.

Care should be exercised to have the stock properly registered in the name of the church to avoid misleading interpretations of ownership. Registrations such as "Rev. John Brown, pastor of A. B. Cee Church" might create complications on subsequent transfers, as the ownership of the security is not properly defined.

Stock Registered in the Name of the Church's Board of Trustees

When the stock is registered in the name of the board of trustees of the church, the requirements are:

1. an assignment executed by an authorized trustee, and
2. a resolution signed by another trustee.

Stock Registered in the Name of a Church

General requirements of stocks registered in the name of a church are:

1. an assignment executed by a bishop or rector of the church, and
2. a resolution by the governing body of the church signed by someone other than the one assigning the certificates.

CHAPTER **6**

Fiduciary Transfers

POWER OF ATTORNEY

A securities account should be opened for the principal only, and requests for registrations such as "John Brown, agent for Mary Brown" should be refused. There cannot be an agency relationship in ownership of the share. The property belongs to the principal, and the agent's authority is purely representative. The agent makes transactions and assigns certificates in behalf of the stockholder without a personal interest in the transaction.

Initiation of the Account

At the initiation of the account, a power of attorney is submitted to the securities firm. This is a document signed by the principal empowering the agent to sell, assign, and transfer securities registered in his or her name, as well as to execute and deliver all instruments, deeds, and contracts. The power of attorney should be carefully examined by the broker in order to:

1. be certain that the principal is still alive and mentally competent,
2. verify that the agent has authority to assign, transfer, and sell the securities, and
3. examine all the provisions of the power of attorney to see whether the agent's authority is restricted to certain representations or if it is broad enough to include such actions as using the securities for collateral.

An unauthorized action by the agent imperils the brokerage house. The firm is held responsible by the principal or his/her heirs for a transfer of money or securities contrary to the provisions of the power of attorney.

Sale of Stocks

When the shares are sold, the following documentation is necessary:

1. an assignment by the attorney,
2. an original or certified copy of the power of attorney, and
3. a certification affixed to the power of attorney: "It is hereby certified that the foregoing power of attorney is a true and accurate copy of the original, is still in full force and effect and unamended as of the present date and that the maker is still alive as of [date]."

Transfer of Stocks

The transfer of stocks from the name of the registered holder to the name of the attorney-in-fact or to any other individual cannot be effected unless a specific provision is made in the power of attorney to do so.

Revocation

A power of attorney may be revoked by the principal at any time. It is immediately revoked, of course, upon the death of the principal: the agent's authority terminates, and stocks held by the broker constitute part of the principal's estate.

Discretionary Power of Attorney

A broker may hold a discretionary power of attorney, commonly referred to as a "trading authorization," for a customer. Extreme care should be exercised, however, in handling the account. Initiation of the account must be approved by a general partner or by an officer who is a voting stockholder of the brokerage firm.

BANKRUPTCY AND RECEIVERSHIP

A court order authorizing the transfer of securities registered in the name of a bankrupt is required. A trustee in bankruptcy, or receiver, is appointed by the court, and his or her duties are performed in accord with court authorization: the trustee cannot sell, assign, deliver, or transfer the bankrupt's property without the express approval of the court.

At the initiation of the account, the broker should be furnished with a court-certified copy of the certificate of appointment of the trustee in bankruptcy, and subsequent transactions should be authorized by a court order.

Sale of Stock in the Name of a Bankrupt

Such a sale requires:

1. an assignment executed by the receiver, and
2. a court-certified copy of the certificate of appointment of receivership, dated within sixty days.

Transfer from the Name of a Bankrupt into the Name of a Receiver

This type of transfer calls for:

1. an assignment by the bankrupt, and
2. a court-certified copy of the certificate of appointment of receivership, dated within sixty days.

Transfer from the Name of a Bankrupt into the Name of a Third Party

Transfer into the name of a third party requires:

1. an assignment by the receiver,
2. a court-certified copy of appointment of receivership, dated within sixty days, and
3. a certified copy of a court order authorizing the transfer.

TRUSTS

A trust is a legal entity managed by a trustee for the benefit of the beneficiaries. The trust is created by a trustor. A trust, therefore, has three persons: the trustor, the trustee, and the beneficiary. Two or more of these roles can be filled by the same person. Care must be exercised, however, in preparing a trust in which all three are one and the same person.

Types of Trusts

1. *Living trust:* (also called inter vivos trust) created during the lifetime of the trustor.
2. *Testamentary trust:* created by the last will and testament of the trustor.
3. *Court trust:* subject to the jurisdiction of the court.
4. *Non-court trust:* not subject to court jurisdiction.

5. *Revocable trust:* can be revoked or amended any time.
6. *Irrevocable trust:* cannot be changed or revoked by the trustee.
7. *Pour-over trust:* the property of the living trust is "poured over" from the trustor's last will and testament.
8. *Life insurance trust:* the living trust receives the proceeds of life insurance.
9. *Clifford trust:* created for tax purposes with a life just over ten years.
10. *Charitable trust:* the beneficiary is a charity.
11. *Support trust:* supports the beneficiary.
12. *Accumulation trust:* the income is retained, not distributed.
13. *Discretionary trust:* the trustee has the power to retain or pay out the income of the trust.
14. *Spend-thrift trust:* the principal is protected from a beneficiary's creditors.

LIVING TRUSTS

A certified or plain copy of the trust agreement is submitted to the securities firm upon opening the account. It is the broker's responsibility to scrutinize the provisions and articles of the trust, especially as they define the powers of the trustees, to see whether one of the trustees is given sufficient authority to invest in securities on behalf of all the trustees, or whether the authority is vested in the majority of the trustees.

The trustees of a living trust hold and administer the property of the trust according to their judgment and discretion. Their power is derived solely from the articles of the trust instrument made by the settlor. Since they are not court-appointed fiduciaries, they do not seek the intervention of the court for their resignation and appointment or for the administration of the trust fund.

Transfer into the Name of a Trust

To avoid complications and delay on subsequent transfers, furnish complete disclosure of the trust when requesting a stock registration:

1. the name(s) of the trustee(s),
2. the nature of the trust,
3. the maker of the trust,
4. the date of the trust, and
5. the beneficiary(s) of the trust.

Transfer from the Name of a Trust

An assignment by all trustees registered on the face of the certificate is required.

If the trustees' names are not inscribed in the registration, the following are required:

1. an assignment by all trustees,
2. a copy of the trust instrument (the entire deed of trust should be submitted rather than extracts of the agreement), and
3. a certification affixed to the trust agreement:

It is certified that the within instrument is a true and correct copy of the original instrument and is still in full force and effect as of _____ .
[date]

Some transfer agents accept a certification by the broker such as:

The person(s) signing has (have) been duly appointed and is (are) presently the sole acting trustee(s) of the within described trust and that the situs of the trust is the state of _____ .
[name of state]

This certification may be given in lieu of the trust indenture. The broker should be cautious, however, in its application. Certifications of this kind should always accord with the terms of the trust agreement.

Resignation of a Trustee

In the case of a certificate bearing the names of trustees, one of whom has resigned, the requirements are:

1. an assignment by all presently acting trustees, and
2. a copy of the instrument (provided a provision is in the deed by which a trustee may resign and a successor appointed).

Death of a Trustee

In the case of a certificate bearing the names of trustees, one of them deceased, the requirements are:

1. an assignment by all presently acting trustees,
2. a certified copy of the death certificate of the deceased trustee, and
3. a copy of the trust agreement (provided a term is in the instrument by which a successor trustee is appointed at the death of a trustee).

Delegation of Authority

A trustee of a living trust may not delegate the authority to sell, assign, and transfer securities held in the name of the trust to a third party acting as an attorney-in-fact.

Revocation of the Trust

A trust agreement may be revoked if it is a revocable agreement and if there is a provision to that effect. The broker should receive an instrument of revocation signed by the settlor.

TESTAMENTARY TRUSTS

Testamentary trusts are created by the last will and testament. The broker is furnished with a certified or plain copy of the will for the permanent file.

A testamentary trustee holds and administers the trust estate in accord with the will. His or her authority to sell, assign, and transfer securities is derived from the will. A court-appointed fiduciary, he or she remains responsible to the court at all times. Under the simplification statutes, the requirements of a transfer by a trustee have been minimized, and the broker should exercise only reasonable care in presenting a transfer of stock requested by a testamentary trustee.

Transfer into the Name of a Trust

No documentation is required.

Transfer from the Name of a Trust

An assignment executed by all trustees registered on the face of the certificate is required.

Resignation of a Trustee

When a certificate has the names of the trustees, one of them resigned, the necessary documentation includes:

1. an assignment made by the remaining trustees and the successor trustee, and

2. a certified copy of the will creating the trust, or a certified copy of the certificate of appointment of the successor trustee, dated within sixty days of the entry of transfer.

Death of a Trustee

A certificate bearing the names of the trustees, one of them deceased, requires the following documents for transfer:

1. an assignment executed by all presently acting trustees,
2. a certified copy of the death certificate of the deceased trustee, and
3. a certified copy of the certificate of appointment of the successor trustee.

Delegation of Authority

A testamentary trustee may not delegate the authority to assign certificates to an agent as an attorney-in-fact.

GUARDIANSHIP

A guardian holds and administers the property of a minor until the minor reaches majority. Therefore, guardianship is a tentative arrangement based on the statutes of the state of domicile until the disabilities of the ward are removed and the securities are transferred to the individual name of the minor.

The broker should exercise due care in initiating a guardianship account or in requesting a transfer of security. He or she should be furnished with a court-certified copy of the certificate of appointment of the guardian, issued within a recent date, as further evidence of the existence of the guardianship.

A guardian has the authority and power to invest, sell, assign, and transfer securities registered in the name of the minor, holding the minor, however, as the beneficial owner of the shares at all times.

Transfer into the Name of a Guardian

No documentation is required.

Transfer from the Name of a Guardian

An assignment by the guardian is required.

Termination of the Guardianship

At termination of guardianship, the broker is furnished with court-certified letters evidencing the termination. Powers and duties of the guardian cease, and securities are transferred to the name of the minor. The broker should not request a transfer of stock to a third party without the consent of the ward. The guardianship account is closed, and the securities held in the account are transferred to the individual account of the minor.

In addition to the instrument of termination, the broker is furnished with a certified copy of the minor's birth certificate before proceeding with a transfer to the minor's name.

Death of the Guardian

Required documents are:

1. an assignment by successor guardian,
2. a certified copy of the death certificate of the deceased guardian, and
3. a certificate of appointment of the successor guardian.

Death of the Ward

Upon the death of a ward, the stocks constitute a part of the ward's estate, and the guardianship is terminated. Required documentation includes:

1. an assignment by the executor or the administrator of the ward,
2. a certificate of appointment of the fiduciary,
3. an affidavit of domicile (refer to Figure 5-1), and
4. a resident and/or nonresident inheritance tax waiver, if required by statute.

Stocks Issued in the Name of a Minor

Securities erroneously registered in the name of a minor may be corrected by a special letter of indemnity executed and guaranteed by the broker who has requested the transfer. The certificate, however, should be presented to the transfer agent within a reasonable time after the issuance. Stocks held in a minor's name over a period of time necessitate an issuance of letters of appointment of guardian by the court.

COMMITTEE AND CONSERVATORSHIP

Transfers involving committeeship or conservatorship are governed by the same principles as those of guardianship. The broker should require proof of the authority of the committee or conservator in the form of a recently issued certificate of appointment. The committee has the same authority and power as the guardian in the regular course of investing, selling, and transferring securities held in the name of an incompetent. The ward must be kept as the beneficial owner of the property at all times.

Transfer into the Name of a Committee or Conservator

No documentation is required for these transfers.

Transfer from the Name of a Committee or Conservator

An assignment by the committee or conservator is required.

Transfer into the Individual Name of the Ward

Upon termination of the committeeship, securities may be transferred to the name of the ward. The broker is furnished with a certified copy of a court order evidencing the competence of the ward. Securities should not be transferred to a third party without the express approval of the ward.

Delegation of Authority

An attorney-in-fact, under a power of attorney, may not execute assignments on behalf of a committee, since the authority of a committee, originated by the court, may not be delegated.

CHAPTER 7

Joint Ownership

JOINT TENANCY WITH RIGHT OF SURVIVORSHIP

The creation of this type of account is evidenced by the execution of a joint tenancy agreement. Probably this is the most widely used joint account, especially for spouses. However, any two parties may create a joint tenancy. The tenants agree, jointly or severally, that each one of them shall have authority in behalf of the joint account to deal in securities. Each party owns an undivided one-half interest. The broker may follow instructions from either one in every respect concerning the account. In the transfer of securities, however, the endorsement of all tenants is an indispensable requirement. Upon the death of one party, the survivor, as a matter of law even if there is a will, takes title to all the property in the account. During the lifetime of the parties, neither participant can force the other to divide the account; nor can a third party, such as a creditor, attach the account for the debts of one party and force the division of the account to satisfy the judgment. If, however, a judgment is obtained against both parties, the account can be attached.

In addition to flexibility, this type of joint ownership has another major advantage. Upon the death of one tenant, the property does not have to pass through probate. The effect is twofold: (1) the expenses of probate are avoided; and (2) the surviving party takes title immediately without the necessity of court orders or letters of probate.

Prior to 1981, the Internal Revenue Service assumed that the decedent had total ownership of the account; that is, the account belonged solely to the decedent. Unless the surviving party could prove that part of the funds in the account were his or hers, the entire amount became part of the decedent's taxable estate. This was changed under the Economic Recovery Act of 1981. Under this law, when one of the tenants dies after 1981, the estate of the first decedent will include one-half the value of the joint property, regardless of which spouse paid for the property.

Joint tenancy is governed by the statutes of the state of domicile of the tenants.

Types of Joint Ownership in Fifty States and District of Columbia

Table 7-1 below is a summary of laws regarding joint ownership of securities adopted by fifty states and District of Columbia.

Table 7-1

Alabama	Joint tenants with right of survivorship is allowed. Upon the death of one joint tenant the interests of the decedent will pass to the surviving joint tenant or tenants.
Alaska	There are no statutory provisions in Alaska regarding the creation of joint tenancy. Although it is common practice to register securities in Alaska as *John Doe* or *Mary Doe* to indicate joint ownership, care must be exercised to avoid this form of registration and use the acceptable format of JT TEN or TEN COM.
Arizona	The statutes recognize joint tenants with right of survivorship and community property.
Arkansas	Joint tenants with right of survivorship is recognized.
California	Community property statutes are recognized. Joint interest is one owned by two or more persons in equal shares.
Colorado	Joint tenants with right of survivorship is recognized.
Connecticut	Joint tenants with right of survivorship is generally applied.
Delaware	Even though there are no statutory requirements for joint ownership in investment shares, joint tenants with right of survivorship or tenants in common can be applied as long as they are clearly stated as such.
District of Columbia	Joint tenants with right of survivorship and tenants in common are recognized.
Florida	Tenancy by entirety is recognized in this state. Upon divorce, tenants by entirety become tenants in common.
Georgia	Tenancy in common and joint tenants with right of survivorship are recognized.
Hawaii	Tenants by entirety, tenants in common, and joint tenants with right of survivorship are recognized.
Idaho	Joint tenants with right of survivorship is recognized, as well as community property.
Illinois	Tenants in common and joint tenants with right of survivorship are recognized.
Indiana	Tenants in common and joint tenants with right of survivorship are recognized.
Kansas	Tenants in common and joint tenants with right of survivorship are recognized.
Kentucky	Tenants in common and joint tenants with right of survivorship are recognized.

Table 7-1 (cont'd.)

Louisiana	The statutes in this state do not have any provision regarding joint tenancy with right of survivorship. Tenants in common is recognized here. The usual form of joint ownership is an old Napoleonic law called *usufructuary*, from the Latin words *uses fructus*, "the use of the fruit." A certificate is registered in the name of John Doe, usufruct for Mary Doe, a naked owner. Mary Doe is the owner of the instrument but the dividends will go to the usufruct.
Maine	Tenants in common and joint tenants with right of survivorship are recognized.
Maryland	Joint tenants with right of survivorship and tenants by entirety are recognized.
Massachusetts	Joint tenants with right of survivorship and tanants in common are recognized.
Michigan	Joint tenants with right of survivorship and tenants in common are recognized.
Minnesota	Joint tenants with right of survivorship and tenants in common are recognized.
Mississippi	Tenants in common and joint tenants with right of survivorship are recognized.
Missouri	Tenants in common and joint tenants with right of survivorship are recognized.
Montana	Tenants in common and joint tenants with right of survivorship may be applied.
Nebraska	Tenants in common and joint tenants with right of survivorship may be applied.
Nevada	Tenants in common, joint tenants with right of survivorship may be applied, and community property.
New Hampshire	Joint tenants with right of suvivorship is applied.
New Jersey	Tenants in common and joint tenants with right of survivorship may be applied.
New Mexico	Tenants in common, joint tenants with right of survivorship may be applied, and community property.
New York	Tenants in common and joint tenants with right of survivorship are recognized.
North Carolina	Tenants in common and joint tenants with right of survivorship may be applied.
North Dakota	Tenants in common and joint tenants with right of survivorship may be applied.
Ohio	Tenants in common and joint tenants with right of survivorship may be applied.
Oklahoma	Tenants in common and joint tenants with right of survivorship may be applied.
Oregon	Tenants in common and joint tenants with right of survivorship may be applied.
Pennsylvania	Tenants in common, joint tenants with right of survivorship, and tenants by entirety between spouses are rec-

Table 7-1 (cont'd.)

	ognized. Tenancy by entirety can be terminated by death of one spouse, by amicable separation, or by conveyance. In the event of a divorce, tenancy by entirety is automatically converted into tenancy in common.
Rhode Island	Tenants in common and joint tenants with right of survivorship may be applied.
South Carolina	Tenants in common and joint tenants with right of survivorship may be applied.
South Dakota	Tenants in common and joint tenants with right of survivorship may be applied.
Tennessee	Joint tenancy with right of survivorship may be conferred by will, deed, or other instrument. The right of survivorship is retained in tenancies by the entirety.
Texas	Tenants in common, community property, and joint tenants with right of survivorship may be applied. In the event of a simultaneous death in a joint tenancy with right of survivorship, fifty percent of the property will go to one estate and fifty percent to the other.
Utah	There are no statutes of joint ownership in this state. Tenants in common or joint tenants with right of survivorship may be applied.
Vermont	Tenants in common and joint tenants with right of survivorship may be applied.
Virginia	Tenants in common and joint tenants with right of survivorship are applied.
Washington	Tenants in common, joint tenants with right of survivorship, and community property may be applied.
West Virginia	Tenants in common, tenants by entirety, and joint tenants with right of survivorship may be applied.
Wisconsin	Tenants in common and joint tenants with right of survivorship may be applied.
Wyoming	Tenants in common and joint tenants with right of survivorship may be applied.

Death of a Tenant

Required documents upon the death of a tenant are:

1. an assignment by the surviving tenant and
2. a certified copy of the death certificate.

Death of Both Tenants

When both tenants are deceased, documentation required is:

1. an assignment by the legal representative of the last decedent,
2. a certified copy of the death certificate of the first decedent,
3. an affidavit of domicile (refer to Figure 5-1) signed by the legal representative of the last decedent,

4. a certified copy of the certificate of appointment of the fiduciary of the last decedent, and
5. a resident and/or nonresident inheritance tax waiver of last decedent, if required.

TENANCY IN COMMON

Tenancy in common is another popular form of joint ownership consisting of two or more tenants. It is effectively a partnership account.

There are three distinctions between tenancy in common and joint tenants with right of survivorship. First, there can be any number of tenants in a tenancy in common, but there are usually only two in joint tenancy. Second, the division of the account in tenancy in common need not be fifty-fifty, whereas in joint tenancy it must be. Last, and most important, each party in a tenancy in common owns a divisible interest; if a husband and wife have a tenancy in common with one-half interest, each owns one-half. On the death of the husband, the wife's one-half interest is still hers and is not part of the decedent's taxable or probatable estate. Upon the death of a tenant in common, therefore, the surviving tenant does not take the account outright. The will may provide for a distribution of the decedent's interest to a third party.

Death of a Tenant in Common

Requirements are:

1. an assignment by the surviving tenant,
2. an assignment by the legal representative of the deceased tenant,
3. a certified copy of the certificate of appointment of the fiduciary,
4. an affidavit of domicile (refer to Figure 5-1) by the legal representative of the deceased tenant, and
5. a resident and/or nonresident inheritance tax waiver, if required.

Death of Both Tenants in Common

Requirements are:

1. an assignment by the legal representatives of both tenants,
2. affidavits of domicile (refer to Figure 5-1), one for each deceased tenant,
3. two certified copies of the certificate of appointment of fiduciaries of both tenants, and
4. resident and/or nonresident tax waivers, one for each decedent, if required.

Registration without Tenancy Clause

In the event that a certificate is registered without tenancy designation (simply "John Brown and Mary Brown"), the transfer agent considers this as tenancy in common. At the death of a tenant, transfer requirements of tenancy in common are observed.

TENANTS BY ENTIRETY

In this type of joint ownership, each tenant has full interest in the securities. Upon the death of one, the entire asset is transferred to the survivor. Tenancies by entirety may be created only between husband and wife. Transfer requirements are the same as those in joint tenancy with right of survivorship.

LIFE TENANCY

The broker is furnished with a certified or plain copy of the will to establish the validity of the account and the authority of the life tenant.

For a life tenant there is always a remainderman. The broker should recognize their proper relationship and exercise reasonable care in requesting a registration of stock to either one of them. The interest of the remainderman should not be jeopardized by unauthorized transfers.

Transfer into the Name of a Life Tenant

Transfers to the individual name of the life tenant should not be permitted without proper authorization by the remainderman. This authorization is usually given in the form of a stock power. Transfers into the name of a life tenant may be entered, however, if the will creating the tenancy has a provision to that effect.

No documents are required.

Transfer from the Name of a Life Tenant

The following documents are required:

1. an assignment by the life tenant, and
2. a certified copy of the will.

Death of a Life Tenant

Transfer should be effected in accordance with the will of the first decedent. The required documents are:

1. an assignment executed by the administrator c.t.a. of the estate of the first decedent,
2. a certified copy of the life tenant's death certificate, and
3. a certified copy of certificate of appointment of administrator c.t.a.

COMMUNITY PROPERTY

Upon opening the account, the broker is furnished with a community property agreement (see Figure 7-1 on page 88) signed by the parties. Transfer of securities into community property designation requires the submission of the agreement to the transfer agent.

To speak in generalities about community property is difficult, as the laws vary considerably from state to state. Under the old law, the marriage contract was also considered a business arrangement and the parties entering into the contract retained title to their own property acquired prior to marriage; hence the "husband's separate property" and the "wife's separate property." Any property acquired after marriage became community property, including income derived from the separate property. For example, a dividend on stock owned by the wife as separate property becomes community property.

In community property each has a divisible one-half interest in the account. Upon the death of either, the survivor takes half, and the remaining half is probated and taxable. Essentially, therefore, community property is a tenancy in common between husband and wife.

Although under the present law property acquired by the wife before or after marriage by gift or devise is her separate property, the husband has the right to control and administer it. In most states, however, the wife has the right to manage her own separate property with some limited exceptions.

Transfer requirements are similar to those of tenancy in common.

The following are the community property states:

Arizona, California, Idaho, Louisiana, Nevada, New Mexico, Texas, and Washington.

Figure 7-1. Community Property Agreement

COMMUNITY PROPERTY AGREEMENT
(State of California)

Gentlemen:

    In support of our request (to you) for the transfer by you of .... shares of .... stock of .... into the names of " .... and .... as their Community Property", and in consideration of your so doing on behalf of said corporation, we hereby declare and agree that wheresoever said property is situated and regardless of the state of residence of either of us, our respective rights in said property, irrespective of the location or legal situs thereof, shall be determined solely under and in accordance with the laws of the State of California relating to Community Property, and any right of management and control thereof by either of us is hereby modified to the extent that the transfer, sale or exchange of the shares so held as Community Property shall require the written assignment executed by both of us, or, in the event of the death of either, by his or her personal representative approved or authorized by the Court having jurisdiction.

                       Sincerely yours,

                    ....

                    ....

CHAPTER 8

Estates

DECEDENTS WITH LAST WILL AND TESTAMENT

As part of estate planning, it is important to prepare a last will and testament to protect the distribution of one's properties. The will is a formal instrument. It provides the medium for the decedent to leave his or her properties to his or her heirs.

There are basically three types of wills: oral, handwritten, and witnessed. The first two are not commonly used, but certain states consider them legal documents. The oral will, also called *noncupative will*, is made by individuals wishing to make oral statements a few days before death as to the proper disposition of their properties. In certain states the total value of the property cannot exceed $100 under this arrangement. The handwritten will, also called *holographic will*, is considered a valid document by most states. It is a handwritten statement signed by the decedent before death. This will does not have to be witnessed. The only requirements are the date and the person's signature. Although it is considered a valid instrument in most states, care must be exercised as to the proper wording of the document. There have been cases where the courts have questioned the authenticity of the document.

The third and the most widely used will is the formal witnessed will. There are certain requirements in preparing a witnessed will.

1. If a person cannot sign the will, another person can do so in his or her presence, provided the signing takes place in the presence of witnesses.

2. It is not necessary for the witnesses to read the will. Some states require two witnesses and some require three. Their signatures usually appear at the end of the document. Selection of witnesses is important. Certain states do not allow beneficiaries mentioned in the will to witness the will.

3. The writer of the will must have legal capacity to write the will. The contesting of wills is avoided if their preparation is supervised by an attorney. The requisites for legal capacity are many. First is the age of the writer of the will—whether he or she is a minor or an adult in his or her state of domicile. Second, he or she must be of sound mind while writing the will. Third, the preparation of the will must be free from undue influence or duress.

A will can be amended any time before the person's death. This is done by simply attaching a codicil to the existing will. The person can even revoke the will by simply writing a new one. To avoid the contesting of a will, it is important to destroy the first one once the second will is completed. The court will only probate the "last" will and testament of the decedent.

In preparing a will, clarity is extremely important.

The disposition of one's properties can be done in several ways. If the writer of the will owns the property outright, he or she can bequeath this to his or her heirs on a permanent basis, or he or she can control the future ownership of property through a procedure called *life estates and remainders.* Temporary ownership interest in one's property can be bequeathed to an heir for a period of time: a week, a month, several years, or a time period measured by somebody's lifetime. The term *life estate* is used if the time period is measured by the recipient's life. Here the recipient is called the life tenant. In a temporary disposition of this type, it is important for the writer to state the final distribution of his or her property once this time period has expired. He or she can state the name of another heir to be the final beneficiary of this property. The property at this point is called a *remainder* and the person receiving the property is called the *remainderman.*

A last will and testament can also create a trust. The writer appoints a trustee to act for the best interest of the beneficiaries of the will. Called *testamentary trust,* such a bequest becomes operative only after the person's death.

A final element of a will is the appointment of one executor or several co-executors. An individual or a bank can be an executor.

HOW THE WILL IS PROBATED

After the person dies, the attorney of the estate submits the decedent's will for probate. This is the period of court administration to insure that all legal requirements have been satisfied. During the probate period, all disputes are resolved and the accuracy of the will is established. Once this is done, the properties are distributed to the heirs as mentioned in the will. The court issues a final decree of distribution, and the heirs receive the properties.

The expense of probate is generally born by the heirs. Probate fees to the court and the estate's attorney vary from state to state. Most states have set up fees by statutes. These fees are generally based on the percentage of the value of the estate to provide reasonable compensation to the attorneys and executors. In California it is four percent of the first $15,000 of the value of the estate; three percent of the next $85,000; two percent of the next $900,000; and one percent of the balance of $1 million. In New York, the fee is four percent of the first $25,000; three-and-one-half percent of the next $125,000; three percent of the next $150,000; and two percent on the remainder. The statutes of other states simply require reasonable compensation.

The probation of the will includes all the properties of the decedent with the exception of properties held in joint tenancy with right of survivorship, properties placed in a trust, and the proceeds of life insurance policies or other contractual agreements.

The probate process is rather complicated and cumbersome. Procedures vary in different jurisdictions, but the following is typical.

1. The attorney of the estate files the will with the probate court, generally within thirty days after the person's death.
2. The attorney petitions the court to have an executor appointed. If an executor is mentioned in the will, the judge usually appoints that person. If no executors are mentioned in the will or if the person died without a will, the court appoints an administrator.
3. Generally within 30 days after the executor or administrator is appointed, the attorney petitions the court to open the estate. This petition admits the estate to probate.
4. After the opening of the estate, the executor has sixty days to file an inventory of all estate properties. If properties are difficult to locate, extensions are usually granted.
5. After the itemized accounting is completed, creditors file their claims against the estate. This is usually done within six months after completion of the inventory.
6. The executor must prepare a final balance sheet of all monies paid to heirs and creditors, generally within six months after the filing of the claims by creditors. Extensions are granted for difficulties in preparing this final accounting statement.
7. The estate is declared closed.

Typically, probate continues between twelve to eighteen months after the person's death, though the procedure and schedule vary in different jurisdictions.

EXECUTOR OF ESTATE

At initiation of the account, the broker is furnished with a recently dated court-certified copy of the certificate of appointment of an executor to prove the validity of the account and the authority of the fiduciary. Court documents should always be certified by the clerk or the judge of the court. Certifications by other persons are not acceptable.

Transfer into the Name of an Executor

Documentation is usually not required to transfer the estate name if the purchase is made by the executor after the decedent's death. A certification should be given to the transfer agent that the transfer does not constitute part of the decedent's estate.

If the stock was purchased before the decedent's death, the following documents are required before transfer:

1. a certified copy of the certificate of appointment of the executor, dated within sixty days of transfer, and
2. a resident inheritance tax waiver, if required by statute.

Transfer from the Name of an Executor

Requirements to effect the transfer include an assignment by the executor.

Death of an Executor

Required documents are:

1. an assignment by the administrator c.t.a. of the first decedent, and
2. a certified copy of the certificate of appointment of the administrator c.t.a.

Delegation of Authority

An assignment executed by an attorney-in-fact acting in behalf of an executor is not acceptable, since the authority and power of the fiduciary may not be delegated.

Decedents with No Will

A person who dies without a last will and testament is called *intestate*; one leaving a will is called *testate*. The administration of estates with no will is very involved and may include not only the decedent's state of domicile but also the state where real properties are located. The decedent's real estate is administered in the state where it is located, and the tangible and intangible personal properties are handled in the state of domicile. During the course of this administration, the court appoints an administrator to take care of the distribution of the properties to various beneficiaries. The distribution is based on the statutes of the state. A typical schedule is as follows, though it varies from state to state.

1. A surviving spouse receives one third of the decedent's estate, and a child or descendants of the child receive two thirds.

2. When there are no surviving children, a surviving spouse receives the entire estate.
3. When there is no surviving spouse, the descendant children receive the entire property.
4. When there are no surviving spouse or descendant children, the decedent's parent, brother, sister, or the descendants of a brother or sister receive the entire property.
5. When there are none of those named in item 4, the entire property goes to the grandparents of the decedent. If the grandparents are deceased, the property goes to the descendants of the grandparents.
6. The very last priority is given to any other kin of the decedent.
7. If no relatives can be found, the properties go to the state. This is called *escheat*.

ADMINISTRATOR OF ESTATE

The securities firm is furnished with a court-certified copy of the certificate of appointment of an administrator, dated within sixty days, as evidence of the court appointment. Court appointments or letters of administration should be examined by the broker to see if they stipulate any limitations of authority.

Transfer into the Name of an Administrator

If the purchase of the security is made after the death of the decedent, documentation is usually not required. If it is purchased before the death, the following documents should be presented to the transfer agent:

1. a certified copy of the administrator's certificate of appointment, and
2. a resident inheritance tax waiver, if required.

Transfer from the Name of an Administrator

An assignment by the administrator is required.

Delegation of Authority

The authority of an administrator may not be delegated. Therefore, an assignment by an attorney-in-fact acting in behalf of an administrator is not acceptable.

DECEDENT

Upon the death of the client, the brokerage account is changed to indicate the proper designation of the authority of the fiduciary. The broker should be furnished with evidence of the appointment of the legal representative, an affidavit of domicile, and inheritance tax waivers, if required by statute of the state of domicile. Transactions in the account should not be effected until the authority of the fiduciary has been established.

Transfer into the Name of a Decedent

Transfers cannot be effected into the individual name of the decedent.

Transfer from the Name of a Decedent

Transfer is effected by providing:

1. an assignment executed by the fiduciary (executor or administrator),
2. a certified copy of the certificate of appointment of the fiduciary,
3. an affidavit of domicile (refer to Figure 5-1) signed by the fiduciary and duly notarized, and
4. a resident and/or nonresident inheritance tax waiver, if required by statute.

Transfer to Beneficiary

The distribution of the property of the decedent should be in accordance with the provisions of the last will and testament.

The broker should be furnished with a copy of the will and a written authorization by the fiduciary before proceeding with the transfers of securities. He or she should be certain that the transferees are named in the will as legatees and that the number of shares transferred is in pursuance to the express approval of the fiduciary. Unauthorized transfers to persons other than legatees or distributees are done at the peril of the securities firm. Since transfer agents do not make inquiry as to the propriety of the transfer, the presentation of the will to the agent is unnecessary.

Distribution and Sale under a Court Order

If a court order authorizes the distribution of shares to various beneficiaries and if the proposed transfer is to the name of only one beneficiary, stock powers signed by all the other beneficiaries relinquishing their interests in the shares are required before a transfer.

Settlement of Small Estates without Administration

Court administration of an estate may be dispensed with if the entire property of the decedent does not exceed a certain amount, depending on the statutes of the state of domicile. In certain instances, however, a court order is necessary before a security is liquidated or transferred to the name of a legatee. The statutes of the following states have such provisions:

Alabama	Michigan
Alaska	Minnesota
Arizona	Montana
Arkansas	Nebraska
California	Nevada
Colorado	New Hampshire
Connecticut	New Jersey
Delaware	New Mexico
District of Columbia	New York
Florida	Ohio
Georgia	Oregon
Hawaii	Pennsylvania
Idaho	Rhode Island
Illinois	South Carolina
Indiana	South Dakota
Iowa	Tennessee
Kentucky	Texas
Louisiana	Vermont
Maryland	Washington
Massachusetts	Wisconsin

Stock Dividends

Shares, in the form of stock dividends or stock split that are issued after the death of the decedent, do not require inheritance tax waivers for transfer. But they do require:

1. an assignment by the fiduciary (executor or administrator),
2. a certified copy of certificate of the appointment of the fiduciary,
3. an affidavit of domicile (refer to Figure 5-1), and
4. notice to the transfer agent that the inheritance tax waiver covering the original shares is on file.

Death of a Beneficiary

The broker is furnished with evidence of the beneficiary's death before a transfer to the names of the remaining beneficiaries.

More than One Executor or Administrator

When there are two or more executors or administrators of an estate, the assignment by any one of them is sufficient for a transfer if the situs of the estate is located in any of the following states:

Alaska	Minnesota
Arizona	Montana
Arkansas	Nevada
California	New Jersey
Colorado	New Mexico
District of Columbia	New York
Florida	North Carolina
Georgia	North Dakota
Hawaii	Oklahoma
Idaho	Oregon
Indiana	South Dakota
Iowa	Texas
Kentucky	Utah
Louisiana	Washington
Maine	Wisconsin
Maryland	Wyoming

In the remaining states, there are some provisions for an executor to act on behalf of all the other executors. Proof should be submitted, however, that the other executors are unable to execute the assignment, for such reasons as absence from the state or illness.

Delegation of Authority

An attorney-in-fact, under a power of attorney, may not execute an assignment for a fiduciary.

ESTATE AND GIFT TAX PROVISIONS UNDER ECONOMIC RECOVERY ACT OF 1981

Increase in Unified Credit

Under the Economic Recovery Act of 1981, individuals can increase the amount of property that can pass to heirs free from estate and gift tax from $175,625 to $600,000 by 1987. This increase is effected by gradually increasing the unified credit against estate and gift taxes from $47,000 to $192,800 as follows:

Year	Unified Tax Credit	Exemption Equivalent
1982	$ 62,800	$225,000
1983	79,300	275,000
1984	96,300	325,000
1985	121,800	400,000
1986	155,800	500,000
1987 and on	192,800	600,000

Reduction in Maximum Tax Rate

The maximum gift and tax rates will be gradually reduced from seventy percent on transfers in excess of $5 million to fifty percent in five percent decrements over a four-year period. The highest transfer tax rate beginning in 1985 will be fifty percent on transfers in excess of $2.5 million.

Marital Deduction

Effective for decedents dying and gifts made after 1981, the new law removes the limits on the marital deductions. All qualifying transfers between spouses pass free of both gift and estate taxes.

Under certain conditions, the Act permits a life estate transferred to a spouse to qualify for the unlimited marital deduction. In such a case, the spouse or the spouse's estate is subject to transfer taxes at the earlier of the date on which the spouse disposes of the qualifying income interest or the date of the spouse's death. Previously, a transfer of a life estate to a spouse, with the remainder to the decedent's children, did not qualify for the marital deduction.

Joint Tenancy

Effective for decedents dying after 1981, the estate of the first decedent will include one-half the value of the jointly held property, regardless of which spouse paid for the property.

Increase in Annual Gift Tax Exclusion

The Act increases the annual gift tax exclusion from $3,000 per donee per year to $10,000 per donee per year. The Act also provides an unlimited exclusion for gift tax purposes for amounts paid on behalf of a donee for medical care and school tuition regardless of the donee's relationship to the donor. Payments must be made directly to the providor of health care or to the educational institution.

Highlights of the Tax Reform Act of 1986

1. Repeal of the Investment Tax Credit.
2. Interest cost on consumer loans is not a tax deductible item. The interest cost on home and vacation home mortgages is a tax deductible item if the amount of the mortgage does not exceed the original purchase cost of the house plus improvements. The cost on house equity loans is a tax deductible item, if the funds are used to pay for medical and educational expenses. This does not apply for homes purchased before August 17, 1986.

   Interest cost on securities margin debit is a tax deductible item up to the amount of interest or dividends received.

3. The unemployment compensation is a taxable item.
4. A child under 14 is taxed under the parent's tax bracket for unearned income in excess of $1,000. Unearned income for children above 14 is taxed under the child's tax bracket. The same applies for trust income.
5. Medical expenses are deductible for amounts exceeding 7.5% of adjusted gross income (AGI).
6. Miscellaneous itemized deductions, such as safe deposit box rentals and tax accountant's fees, are deductible only if they exceed 2% of adjusted gross income.
7. Contributions to IRA accounts are limited only to those who are not active participants in their employer's pension plan. People filing a single tax return may deposit up to $2,000 a year in their IRA if their income is less than $25,000. Two working spouses filing a joint return may deposit up to $2,000 each in their respective IRA's if the combined income is less than $40,000 a year. Single filers earning income between $25,000 and $35,000 a year must reduce the $2,000 IRA limitation by $20 for every $100 in excess of $25,000. Individuals filing a joint return earning income between $40,000 and $50,000 must reduce the $2,000 IRA limitation by $20 for every $100 in excess of $40,000. For example, two working spouses with a combined income of $43,000 may deposit up to $1,400 each in their respective IRA's. A reminder: There is no such a thing as a joint IRA.
8. Expenses from tax shelters are deductible only up to the investment income received from the venture. Exception: People earning less than $100,000 a year may deduct expenses from investment properties from their ordinary income up to $25,000 a year.
9. Annual contribution to a 401 (K) pay deferral is limited to $7,000 a year.
10. Preferential treatment for long term capital gains is repealed.
11. Income averaging is repealed.
12. Joint return deduction for two wage earners is repealed.
13. Dividends are fully taxable.
14. Sales tax is not a deductible item.
15. Credit for political contributions is repealed.
16. Only 80% of business meals is deductible.
17. Interest on municipal bonds issued for non-governmental purposes is generally taxable.

CHAPTER 9

Foreign Securities Transfer

CANADA

Transfers of Canadian securities involve many complicated problems of law, since Canada, as a foreign jurisdiction, is not within the scope of any one of the protective simplification statutes. Therefore, transfer agents require full documentation before a transfer is safely entered into the books of a corporation.

Inter Vivos Trust

Documents required:

1. an assignment by all the trustees, and
2. a certified copy of the trust instrument.

Testamentary Trust

Documents required:

1. an assignment by all trustees,
2. a certified copy of the will, and
3. a certified copy of the certificate of appointment of the trustee.

Executor or Administrator of Estate

Documents required:

1. an assignment by all fiduciaries,
2. a certified copy of the certificate of appointment of the fiduciary, and
3. a certified copy of the will.

Decedent

Documents required:

1. an assignment by the fiduciary,
2. a certified copy of the certificate of appointment of fiduciary,
3. a certified copy of the will,
4. a declaration of transmission (see Figure 9-1 on page 101),
5. provincial waiver: if the corporation is organized in a province that requires a waiver, or if the location of the transfer agent is in a province that requires a waiver, or if the principal place of business is in a province that requires a waiver (see chart of inheritance tax waivers), and
6. an inheritance tax waiver from the state of residence, if required by statute.

REQUIREMENTS FOR TRANSFER

Following is a summary of stock transfer laws in each province and in England.

Alberta

1. *Guardianship to a minor.* A guardian to a minor does not have authority to sell personal property without a court order.
2. *Executor or administrator to an estate.* No court orders are required for an executor or an administrator to sell personal property of an estate.
3. *Guardianship to a person declared incompetent.* A court order is required for the sale of personal property.
4. *Joint ownership.* Alberta is a common law province, and it has no statutes of joint tenants with right of survivorship.

British Columbia

1. *Guardianship to a minor.* A guardian to a minor does not have authority to sell personal property without a court order.
2. *Executor or administrator to an estate.* No court orders are required for an executor or an administrator to sell personal property of an estate.
3. *Guardianship to a person declared incompetent.* A court order is required for a guardian to sell personal property of an incompetent.
4. *Joint ownership.* Common law prevails in British Columbia. Creation of joint ownership is generally indicated by inscriptions such as

Figure 9-1. Declaration of Transmission

DECLARATION OF TRANSMISSION

IN THE MATTER OF THE Estate of

....
(Full name of Deceased)

late of..

STATE OF
} S.S.
COUNTY OF

We/I,..
(Full name(s) of Executor(s) or Administrator(s))

being duly sworn depose(s) and say(s) that we/I are/am the executor(s) administrator(s) of the said Deceased and THAT:

(1) Said Deceased died at..

on the........day of..............., 19......, testate (or intestate) and at the date of death was domiciled in

....

(2) Letters Probate of the Will (or Letters of Administration with Will annexed or Letters of Administration to the estate) of said Deceased were granted to the declarant(s)..

....on the...............day of..............., 19......,

by the..................................Court of..................................
(Full name of court)

(3) Said Deceased was not at the date of death, nor is the estate now, indebted to any person, firm or corporation residing or having its chief place of business in the Provinces of Ontario or Quebec, or British Columbia.

(4) Said Deceased at date of death was the owner of..shares of the

..................................Capital Stock of..................................
(If Common or Preferred state which)   (Name of Company)

represented by certificate(s) numbered..
                                                                            (Certificate Numbers)

registered in the name of..
                                        (Name on certificate(s))

(5) Said Deceased and..
                              (Name on certificate(s))

named in the said certificate(s) was one and the same person.

(6) The aforementioned certificate(s) was/were at the death of the Deceased physically situated

at..
(Give full particulars as to actual situs of shares)

(7) By virtue of the foregoing the said shares have devolved upon and become vested in the Executor(s) and Administrator(s) as aforesaid who desire(s) to have the same recorded in the name(s) of the Executor(s) and Administrator(s) as aforesaid upon the books of the said Company (and immediately thereafter transferred as follows:

....
(If issue of new certificate in name(s) other than that of Executor(s)

....)
or Administrator(s) is desired insert particulars)

Sworn to before me this

..........day of..............., 19......   ....
                                              Executor(s) Administrator(s)

....
(Signature and title of official administering oath)

My commission expires..
                                                (Affix seal of officer administering oath)

"John Doe and Mary Doe," "Joint Tenants," or "Joint owners," or simply by the word "jointly."

Manitoba

1. *Guardianship to a minor.* A guardian to a minor does not have authority to sell personal property without a court order.
2. *Executor or administrator to an estate.* An executor may sell personal property of an estate without a court order if it is necessary to do so to pay estate debts. An administrator may sell property without a court order.
3. *Guardianship to a person declared incompetent.* A guardian to an incompetent person does not have authority to sell personal property without a court order.
4. *Joint ownership.* Common law rules apply in Manitoba.

New Brunswick

1. *Guardianship to a minor.* A guardian to a minor does not have authority to sell personal property without a court order.
2. *Executor or administrator to an estate.* No court orders are required to sell personal property of an estate.
3. *Guardianship to a person declared incompetent.* A court order is required to sell personal property.
4. *Joint ownership.* Common law rules apply in New Brunswick.

Newfoundland

1. *Guardianship to a minor.* A guardian to a minor does not have authority to sell personal property without a court order.
2. *Executor or administrator to an estate.* No court orders are required.
3. *Guardianship to a person declared incompetent.* A court order is required to sell personal property.
4. *Joint ownership.* Common law rules apply in Newfoundland.

Nova Scotia

1. *Guardianship to a minor.* A court order is required for a guardian to sell personal property.
2. *Executor or administrator to an estate.* No court orders are required.
3. *Guardianship to a person declared incompetent.* No court orders are required for a guardian to sell personal property.

4. *Joint ownership.* There must be specific agreement signed between the parties as to the creation of joint tenancy with right of survivorship.

Ontario

1. *Guardianship to a minor.* A court order is required for a guardian to sell personal property.
2. *Executor or administrator to an estate.* No court orders are required.
3. *Guardianship to a person declared incompetent.* A court order is required to sell personal property.
4. *Joint ownership.* Common law rules apply in Ontario. Securities registered in the name of two or more tenants may be considered as joint ownership with right of survivorship. Upon the death of one tenant, the surviving tenant receives full ownership of the security.

Prince Edward Island

1. *Guardianship to a minor.* A court order is required for a guardian to sell personal property.
2. *Executor or administrator to an estate.* No court orders are required.
3. *Guardianship to a person declared incompetent.* A court order is required to sell personal property. The sale is generally done by a committee appointed to manage the property of a mentally incompetent person.
4. *Joint ownership.* Common law rules apply in Prince Edward Island.

Quebec

1. *Guardianship to a minor.* A court order is required for a guardian to sell personal property. A guardian to a minor is known in this province as a *tutor*.
2. *Executor or administrator to an estate.* Generally a court order is required for an executor to sell personal property.
3. *Guardianship to a person declared incompetent.* Here the guardian to a mentally incompetent person is known as a *curator*. A court order is required to sell personal property.
4. *Joint ownership.* The usual method of owning securities jointly is tenancy in common. Tenancy with right of survivorship may be created if there is a specific agreement signed by the tenants.

Saskatchewan

1. *Guardianship to a minor.* A court order is required to sell personal property.
2. *Executor or administrator to an estate.* No court orders are required.
3. *Guardianship to a person declared incompetent.* Court orders are required to sell personal property.
4. *Joint ownership.* Common law rules apply in Saskatchewan.

Yukon Territory

1. *Guardianship to a minor.* Court orders are required to sell personal property.
2. *Executor or administrator to an estate.* No court orders are required.
3. *Guardianship to a person declared incompetent.* No court orders are required.
4. *Joint ownership.* Common law rules apply in the Yukon.

ENGLAND

1. *Guardianship to a minor.* Generally a court order is required to sell personal property of a minor. However, a guardian to a minor, who is known in England as *trustee to a minor*, can sell one half the property without a court order if the sale is done for the advancement of the minor.
2. *Executor or administrator to an estate.* No court orders are required to sell personal property of an estate. An executor may also distribute the decedent's properties to the heirs without court orders.
3. *Guardianship to a person declared incompetent.* Court orders from the Court of Protection are required to sell personal property of a mentally incompetent person.
4. *Joint ownership.* There are no statutory provisions in England as to joint ownership of securities. Joint ownership is generally recognized as partnership between parties.

CHAPTER 10

Stock Transfer Taxation

Tax on securities transactions and transfer has been in effect in the state of New York since 1905. New legislation provides a 100-percent rebate of these taxes effective October 1, 1981. The impact of New York State stock transfer tax, therefore, has been phased out. Effective with trades occurring on and after October 1, 1981, all taxpayers are eligible to receive this rebate. The following is the rebate procedure devised by New York State Tax Commission:

PLAN OF OPERATION

1. Daily brokers must record individual transactions on the purchase-and-sale blotter indicating the amount of tax liability for each transaction. Daily, they must summarize this category on the purchase-sale blotter and record the rebatable portion of the tax. This rebatable position is the same amount as the tax liability.

The amount of stock transfer tax must be recorded for each taxable transaction on the purchase-and-sale blotter. The daily tax liability must also be recorded in a separate account in the general ledger. This is required even though the tax liability may only be a "memo charge" on the blotter and not part of settlement calculation.

Failure to comply with these record-keeping requirements shall constitute evidence of nonpayment of the tax, and the transactions shall be subject to the penalties imposed by Article 12 of the tax law. Penalties are not rebatable. In addition to the penalties, a broker may be required to pay the tax liability weekly to the State Tax Commission.

2. From the information recorded above, the broker must prepare in duplicate a weekly return on Form MT-651 called "Weekly Return of Stock Transfer Taxes." This report will summarize the tax liability during the calendar week for each day. The broker will file the report with the Stock Transfer Tax Section in Albany, no later than the second business day of the following week.

3. Quarterly, the broker must prepare, in duplicate, Form MT–650, called "Quarterly Return of Stock Transfer Taxes Withheld." This report will sum-

marize the rebatable portion of taxes withheld each week during the quarter. The broker will submit this return and remittance with the regular weekly return to the Stock Transfer Tax Section in Albany, no later than the second business day of the week following the first full business week in the last month of the quarter.

4. By the first business day of the next quarter, when the statutory procedures allowing the rebate payment are completed, New York State Division of the Treasury will be authorized to release rebate checks that represent the aggregate amount of rebates reported during the preceding quarter.

5. Any discrepancies that might occur will be carried forward and resolved in the next quarterly report.

NEW YORK STATE TRANSFER TAX RATES

1. The rate for transfers not involving a sale is $2^1/_2$ ¢ a share.
2. Tax on sale of stock:

Selling Price per Share	Tax Rate per 100 Shares
$20 and over	$5.00
$10–$19.99	$3.75
$5–$9.99	$2.50
Under $5	$1.25

MAXIMUM TAX

Effective July 1, 1973, the maximum tax on a single taxable sale of shares of the same class issued by the same issuer is $350.

TAXABLE TRANSACTIONS

The following transfers are taxable:

1. the transfer of shares, whether represented by certificates or not,
2. the transfer of temporary or interim certificates,
3. the transfer of certificates representing a subscriber's interest,
4. the transfer of voting trust certificates,
5. the transfer of stock in dissolved corporations,
6. the transfer of stock on the books of the corporation within the

State of New York, regardless of where the other acts in connection with the sale or transfer of the stock were done,
7. the transfer of stock by gift,
8. the transfer of stock from or to a partnership,
9. the purchase, redemption, or other reacquisition by a corporation of its shares of stock and the transfers or retransfers of its own stock by a corporation,
10. the distribution by a corporation to its stockholders of stock in another corporation,
11. the transfer of stock of a corporation to be merged, to the merging corporation, prior to the actual merger and as a condition precedent to the merger,
12. transfers to and by trustees,
13. the transfer of stock from an individual to himself as trustee,
14. the transfer of stock by an executor or an administrator, whether to trustees, legatees, or other persons,
15. transfers from tenants in common to themselves as individuals, or to one of them,
16. transfers from individuals to themselves as joint tenants with right of survivorship,
17. transfers from joint tenants to either one of them,
18. the delivery of a certificate by the transferor, or by his or her agent, to the transferee or agent,
19. transfers by fiduciaries of certificates issued in the name of anyone other than themselves to their nominees,
20. transfers by owners of certificates issued in the name of anyone other than themselves to their custodians,
21. the transfer from a broker to the customer for whom the securities were purchased,
22. the transfer to a broker as the owner,
23. transfers by or to brokers for their own accounts,
24. transfers of stock by brokers at a price different from that at which they account to their selling customers.
25. transfers of stock dividends by brokers to customers,
26. the transfer from a nominee of one fiduciary to the nominee of another fiduciary, and
27. the transfer of the shares of an investment trust of the management type, such as sales by one dealer to another or by one investor to another.

NONTAXABLE TRANSACTIONS

1. A change of the stockholder's name,
2. the exchange of single certificate for several,
3. the exchange of several certificates for one,
4. the transfer of a fraction of a share,
5. the transfer of preferred stock in exchange for common, or vice versa, issued in the same name,
6. the mere registration in the State of New York, by a registrar, of a transfer already made by the corporation or its transfer agent outside of New York,
7. the execution or the endorsement within the state where all other acts connected with the transfer are done outside of New York,
8. transfers by trustees where no change of ownership is involved,
9. the surrender of stock of a merged corporation in exchange for stock of a corporation merging at the time and as part of a statutory merger,
10. the surrender of stock of a consolidated corporation in exchange for stock in the resulting corporation in the case of the consolidation of two or more corporations, and
11. transfer to a surviving joint tenant.

EXEMPT TRANSACTIONS

The following transactions are specifically exempted by the provisions of Section 270 of the New York State Tax Law. The following exemptions are allowed if accompanied by proper exemption certificates (except where noted):

1. odd lot sales on an exchange within the State of New York,
2. transfers of collateral security,
3. transfers pursuant to some statutory provisions,
4. transfers between fiduciary and nominee,
5. transfers between the owner and a custodian or between a custodian and its nominee,
6. loans of stock or the return of stock loan,
7. broker and customer transfers,
8. transfers between a corporation and a nominee, or between two registered nominees of the same corporation,
9. transfer from the owner to a custodian's nominee,
10. transfer from a custodian to a new custodian or nominees,
11. the transfer of stock by a custodian for the owner to a broker,
12. transfers between a purchaser and seller with the same broker,

13. the transfer of stock from the name of a decedent to the executor or administrator (no need to present an exemption certificate),
14. a transfer by an ancillary to a domiciliary executor (no need to present exemption certificate),
15. a transfer by an ancillary to a domiciliary guardian,
16. transfers between trustees, and
17. the sale or transfer of stock by a transferor that is an organization or a governmental entity normally exempt from tax.

CHAPTER **11**

Inheritance Tax Waivers

To comply with the statutes of most states, the issuers and their transfer agents must request consent to transfer shares registered in the name of decedents. Notice must be filed with the tax authorities of the state that the stockholder is deceased and that a transfer will be made by the legal representative of the estate. If inheritance taxes are due, the estate must pay them before the transfer is effected in the books of the corporation. The usual requirement of the transfer agent is a document called the "inheritance tax waiver," issued by the tax officials of the state in question.

Fines and penalties are provided by the statutes. If the transfer is completed without the required tax waiver, the transfer agent is fined by the state. The fine is usually the amount of tax due the state or a nominal amount of $1,000. The statutes do not provide exemptions. A waiver must be obtained even if a court authorizes the transfer. Four factors determine the necessity of an inheritance waiver in a particular transfer:

1. the domicile of the decedent,
2. the state of the incorporation of the security,
3. the situs of the transfer agent, and
4. the situs of the stock certificate at the time of death.

The transfer agent must consider the statutes of each state before a transfer. The explicit questions are:

1. Was the stockholder a resident of a state that requires a waiver?
2. Is the issue in question incorporated in a state that requires a waiver?
3. Is the transfer agent located in a state that requires a waiver?
4. Finally, was the location of the stock certificate at the time of death in a state that requires a waiver?

SPECIAL AFFIDAVITS

Thirteen states require special affidavits in lieu of waivers: California, Illinois, Iowa, Kentucky, Michigan, Minnesota, New Jersey, New York, Ohio, Oregon, Pennsylvania, Utah, and Wisconsin.

FEDERAL TRANSFER CERTIFICATE

Transfers involving securities held in the name of a decedent who was a nonresident of the United States at the time of death require a federal transfer release before the stock is safely entered into the books of the corporation (see Table 11-1 below). Application for the release is made to the Director of the Office of International Operations, Internal Revenue Service, P.O. Box 19007, Washington, D.C. 20236.

INHERITANCE TAX OFFICES

See Table 11-2 on pages 114–116 for listings of offices that issue inheritance tax waivers or consents to transfer shares

BIRTH AND DEATH CERTIFICATES

See Table 11-3 on pages 117–122 for a listing of offices that issue birth and death certificates.

Table 11-1. State and Canadian Provinces That Require Inheritance Tax Waivers

Domestic Corporation Resident Decedents

Alabama
Arizona
  Connecticut (unless administration has been taken out)
District of Columbia (waivers not necessary for transfers upon the order of a court appointed fiduciary)
Indiana
Iowa
Kansas
Kentucky
Louisiana
Montana
New Hampshire
New Jersey (if gross estate of decedent exceeds $200 or in case of transfer to spouse exceeding $1,500)

New York (if stocks exceed $30,000 in value)
North Carolina
Ohio
Oklahoma
Oregon
Puerto Rico
Quebec
Rhode Island
South Carolina
South Dakota
Tennessee
Wisconsin (waivers may not be necessary except for jointly held securities)

Table 11-1 (cont'd.)

Foreign Corporations Resident Decedents

Alabama
Connecticut (unless administration has been taken out)
District of Columbia (waivers not necessary for transfers upon the order of a court appointed fiduciary)
Iowa
Indiana
Kansas
Kentucky
Louisiana (unless transfer takes place outside state)
Montana
New Hampshire
New York (if stock exceed $10,000 in value and transfer takes place outside state)
North Carolina (if corporation domesticated in state and stock exceeds $200 in value)
Ohio
Oklahoma (if corporation does business in state)
Oregon
Puerto Rico
Quebec
Rhode Island (unless transfer takes place outside state)
South Carolina
South Dakota
Tennessee
Wisconsin (waivers may not be required except for jointly held securities)

Domestic Corporation Nonresident Decedents

Alabama
Kentucky
New Hampshire
Puerto Rico
Quebec
South Carolina
Tennessee

Foreign Corporations Nonresident Decedents

Puerto Rico
Quebec
Tennessee (unless transfer takes place outside state)

Note: 1. The Dominion of Canada inheritance tax has been eliminated. The estate tax waiver is no longer required if the decedent died after December 31, 1971.
2. In California in lieu of waiver, special affidavit of domicile may be required.

Table 11-2. Offices Issuing Inheritance Tax Waivers or Consents to Transfer Shares Registered in the Name of Decedents

Alabama	State Department of Revenue Estate Tax Division Montgomery	Illinois	Attorney General Inheritance Tax Department Springfield
Alaska	Estate Tax Commissioner Department of Revenue Juneau	Indiana	Inheritance Tax Division Department of State Revenue Indianapolis
Arizona	Estate Tax Commissioner State Capital Building Phoenix	Iowa	Department of Revenue Inheritance Tax Division Des Moines
Arkansas	Department of Finance and Administration Little Rock	Kansas	Inheritance Tax Division Department of Revenue Topeka
California	Inheritance Tax Department State Controller's Office Sacramento	Kentucky	Department of Revenue Property and Inheritance Tax Division Inheritance and Estate Section Frankfort
Colorado	Department of Revenue Inheritance Tax Division Denver	Louisiana	Department of Revenue Baton Rouge
Connecticut	State Tax Department Inheritance Tax Division Hartford	Maine	Supervisor of Inheritance Tax State Bureau of Taxation Augusta
Delaware	Department of Finance Wilmington	Maryland	Attorney General of Maryland Baltimore
District of Columbia	Finance Office Government of D.C. Inheritance & Estate Tax Section Washington, D.C.	Massachusetts	Commissioner of Corporations and Taxation Division of Inheritance Taxes Boston
Florida	Department of Revenue Tallahassee	Michigan	Department of Treasury Revenue Division Lansing
Georgia	Department of Revenue Estate Tax Unit Atlanta	Minnesota	Commissioner of Revenue Inheritance Division St. Paul
Hawaii	Department of Taxation Inheritance Tax Unit Honolulu	Mississippi	State Tax Commission Jackson
Idaho	State Tax Commission Inheritance Tax Division Boise	Missouri	Inheritance Tax Department Department of Revenue Jefferson City

Table 11-2 (cont'd.)

State	Agency	State	Agency
Montana	Department of Revenue Helena	Oregon	Inheritance and Gift Tax Division Department of Revenue Salem
Nebraska	Supervisor of Inheritance Tax Office of the State Tax Commissioner Lincoln	Pennsylvania	Department of Revenue Bureau of County Collections Inheritance Tax Division Harrisburg
Nevada	No inheritance tax law		
New Hampshire	Department of Revenue Administration Inheritance Tax Division Concord	Puerto Rico	Secretary of the Treasury San Juan
New Jersey	Division of Taxation Transfer Inheritance Tax Bureau Trenton	Rhode Island	State Division of Taxation Inheritance and Gift Tax Section Providence
New Mexico	Bureau of Revenue Estate Tax Division Santa Fe	South Carolina	State Tax Commission Inheritance Tax Division Columbia
New York	Department of Taxation and Finance Miscellaneous Tax Bureau Transfer and Estate Tax Section Albany	South Dakota	State Department of Revenue Division of Taxation Inheritance Tax Department Pierre
North Carolina	State Department of Revenue Inheritance Tax Division Raleigh	Tennessee	State Department of Revenue Inheritance, Estate and Gift Tax Division Nashville
North Dakota	Office of State Tax Commissioner Estate Tax Deputy Bismarck	Texas	Office of the Comptroller of Public Accounts Inheritance Tax Division Austin
Ohio	State Department of Taxation Estate Tax Division Columbus	Utah	State Tax Commission Inheritance Tax Division Salt Lake City
		Vermont	Commissioner of Taxes Department of Taxes Montpelier
Oklahoma	Estate Tax Division Oklahoma Tax Commission Oklahoma City	Virginia	Department of Taxation Division of Inheritance and Gift Taxes Richmond

Table 11-2 (cont'd.)

Washington	Supervisor of Inheritance Tax Department of Revenue Olympia	Alberta	Collector of Succession Duties Edmonton
West Virginia	Office of the State Tax Commissioner Inheritance Tax Division Charleston	British Columbia	Director—Taxation Vancouver
		Manitoba	Director—Taxation Winnipeg
		New Brunswick	Director—Taxation St. John
Wisconsin	Department of Revenue and Taxation Director of Inheritance and Gift Tax Division Madison	Newfoundland	Director—Taxation St. John's
		Nova Scotia	Director—Taxation Halifax
		Ontario	Director—Taxation Toronto
Wyoming	Department of Revenue Insurance and Inheritance Tax Division Cheyenne	Prince Edward Island	Provincial Treasurer Charlottetown
		Quebec	Collector of Succession Duties for the Province Quebec
Canadian Provinces			
		Saskatchewan	Director—Taxation Regina
Dominion of Canada	Minister of National Revenue Administrator, Estate Tax Branch Department of National Revenue Ottawa, Ont.	Yukon Territory	Territorial Treasurer Dawson

Table 11-3. How To Get Birth and Death Certificates

Place of Birth or Death	Addresses of Offices of Vital Statistics
Alabama	Bureau of Vital Statistics State Department of Public Health Montgomery, Alabama 36104
Alaska	Bureau of Vital Statistics Department of Health and Welfare Pouch "H" Juneau, Alaska 99801
Arizona	Division of Vital Records State Department of Health P.O. Box 3887 Phoenix, Arizona 85030
Arkansas	Division of Vital Records Arkansas Department of Health 4815 West Markham Street Little Rock, Arkansas 72201
California	Vital Statistics Section State Department of Health 410 N. Street Sacramento, California 95814
Colorado	Records and Statistics Section Colorado Department of Health 4210 East 11th Avenue Denver, Colorado 80220
Connecticut	Public Health Statistics Section Statement of Health 79 Elm Street Hartford, Connecticut 06115
Delaware	Bureau of Vital Statistics Division of Public Health Department of Health and Social Services Jesse S. Cooper Memorial Building Dover, Delaware 19901
District of Columbia	Department of Human Resources Vital Records Section Room 1022 300 Indiana Ave., N.W. Washington, D.C. 20001
Florida	Department of Health and Rehabilitative Services Division of Health Bureau of Vital Statistics P.O. Box 210 Jacksonville, Florida 32201

Table 11-3 (cont'd.)

Georgia	Vital Records Unit State Department of Human Resources Room 217-H 47 Trinity Avenue, S.W. Atlanta, Georgia 30334
Hawaii	Research and Statistics Office State Department of Health P.O. No. 3378 Honolulu, Hawaii 96801
Idaho	Bureau of Vital Statistics State Department of Health and Welfare Statehouse Boise, Idaho 83720
Illinois	Office of Vital Records State Department of Public Health 535 W. Jefferson Street Springfield, Illinois 62761
Indiana	Division of Vital Records State Board of Health 1330 West Michigan Street Indianapolis, Indiana 46206
Iowa	Division of Records and Statistics State Department of Health Des Moines, Iowa 50319
Kansas	Bureau of Registration and Health Statistics 6700 S. Topeka Avenue Topeka, Kansas 66620
Kentucky	Office of Vital Statistics State Department of Health 275 East Main Street Frankfort, Kentucky 40601
Louisiana	Office of Vital Records State Department of Health P.O. Box 60630 New Orleans, Louisiana 70160
Maine	Office of Vital Records State Department of Health and Welfare State House Augusta, Maine 04333
Maryland	Division of Vital Records State Department of Health State Office Building 201 West Preston Street P.O. Box 13146 Baltimore, Maryland 21203

Table 11-3 (cont'd.)

Massachusetts	Registrar of Vital Statistics Room 103 McCormack Building 1 Ashburton Place Boston, Massachusetts 02108
Michigan	Office of Vital and Health Statistics Michigan Department of Public Health 3500 North Logan Street Lansing, Michigan 48914
Minnesota	Minnesota Department of Health Section of Vital Statistics 717 Delaware Street, S.E. Minneapolis, Minnesota 55440
Mississippi	Vital Records Registration Unit State Board of Health P.O. Box 1700 Jackson, Mississippi 39205
Missouri	Bureau of Vital Records Division of Health State Department of Public Health and Welfare Jefferson City, Missouri 65101
Montana	Bureau of Records and Statistics State Department of Health and Environmental Sciences Helena, Montana 59601
Nebraska	Bureau of Vital Statistics State Department of Health Lincoln Building 1003 "O" Street Lincoln, Nebraska 68508
Nevada	Department of Human Resources Division of Health—Vital Statistics Capitol Complex Carson City, Nevada 89710
New Hampshire	Department of Health and Welfare Division of Public Health Bureau of Vital Statistics 61 South Spring Street Concord, New Hampshire 03301
New Jersey	State Department of Health Bureau of Vital Statistics Box 1540 Trenton, New Jersey 08625
New Mexico	Vital Records New Mexico Health and Social Services Department PERA Building Room 118 Santa Fe, New Mexico 87501

Table 11-3 (cont'd.)

New York (except New York City)	Bureau of Vital Records State Department of Health Empire State Plaza Tower Building Albany, New York 12237
New York City (All boroughs)	Bureau of Records and Statistics Department of Health of New York City 125 Worth Street New York, N.Y. 10013
North Carolina	Department of Human Resources Division of Health Services Vital Records Branch P.O. Box 2091 Raleigh, North Carolina 27602
North Dakota	Division of Vital Records Office of Statistical Services State Department of Health Bismarck, North Dakota
Ohio	Division of Vital Statistics Ohio Department of Health G-20 Ohio Departments Building 65 S. Front Street Columbus, Ohio
Oklahoma	Vital Records Section State Department of Health Northeast 10th Street & Stonewall P.O. Box 53551 Oklahoma City, Oklahoma 73105
Oregon	Vital Statistics Section Oregon State Health Division P.O. Box 231 Portland, Oregon 97207
Pennsylvania	Division of Vital Statistics State Department of Health Central Building 101 South Mercer Street P.O. Box 1528 Newcastle, Pennsylvania 16103
Rhode Island	Division of Vital Statistics State Department of Health Room 101 Health Building Davis Street Providence, Rhode Island 02908
South Carolina	Division of Vital Records Bureau of Health Measurement S.C. Department of Health and Analysis Environmental Control 2600 Bull Street Columbia, South Carolina 29201

Table 11-3 (cont'd.)

South Dakota	Division of Public Health Statistics State Department of Health Pierre, South Dakota 57501
Tennessee	Division of Vital Statistics State Department of Public Health Cordell Hull Building Nashville, Tennessee 37219
Texas	Bureau of Vital Statistics Texas Department of Health Resources 410 East 5th Street Austin, Texas 78701
Utah	Division of Vital Statistics Utah State Department of Health 554 South Third East Salt Lake City, Utah 84113
Vermont	Secretary of State Vital Records Department State House Montpelier, Vermont 05602 Public Health Statistics Division Department of Health Burlington, Vermont 05401
Virginia	Bureau of Vital Records and Health Statistics State Department of Health James Madison Building Box 1000 Richmond, Virginia 23208
Washington	Bureau of Vital Statistics Health Services Division Department of Social and Health Services P.O. Box 709 Olympia, Washington 98504
West Virginia	Division of Vital Statistics State Department of Health State Office Building No. 3 Charleston, West Virginia 25305
Wisconsin	Bureau of Health Statistics Wisconsin Division of Health P.O. Box 309 Madison, Wisconsin 53701
Wyoming	Vital Records Services Division of Health and Medical Services State Office Building West Cheyenne, Wyoming 82002

Table 11-3 (cont'd.)

U.S. Possessions

American Samoa	Office of the Territorial Registrar Government of American Samoa Pago Pago American Samoa 96799
Guam	Office of Vital Statistics Department of Public Health and Social Services Government of Guam P.O. Box 2716 Agana, Guam, M.I. 96910
Puerto Rico	Division of Demographic Registry and Vital Statistics Department of Health San Juan, Puerto Rico 00908

Virgin Islands

St. Thomas	Registrar of Vital Statistics Charlotte Amalie St. Thomas, Virgin Islands 00802
St. Croix	Registrar of Vital Statistics Charles Harwood Memorial Hospital St. Croix, Virgin Islands

CHAPTER **12**

Rules of Delivery

TYPES OF DELIVERIES

Principally there are three types of deliveries to satisfy an exchange contract:

1. for cash transactions,
2. for regular way contracts, and
3. for seller's option.

Cash Contracts

Deliveries of securities to honor a cash transaction must be made before 2:30 P.M. if the transaction is made at or before 2:00 P.M. Deliveries against transactions made for "cash" after 2:00 P.M. are due within thirty minutes. Cash transactions are generally made in unusual circumstances—a buyer wants immediate delivery of a certificate, or a seller sells to dispose of his or her ownership. Reasons for this emergency procedure are many—taxes, tender offers, conversions, rights, privileges, and so on.

Regular Way Contracts

A majority of securities transactions are made in a regular way. This is the standard type of delivery where the securities sold in the securities market must be delivered on the fifth business day after the transaction. If the trade is executed on Monday, the delivery must be made on the following Monday, assuming that there are no holidays between trade date and settlement date. The trade settles regular way on T + 5. All contracts that would otherwise fall due on a holiday mature on the succeeding business day unless otherwise directed by the stock exchange.

Seller's Option

Seller's option is a special contract that allows the seller to deliver the security on a delayed basis. The delivery is made on the expiration day of the option. It can also be made prior to the expiration date if the seller submits one day's written notice to the buyer.

Under this arrangement the seller has up to sixty calendar days to effect a delivery. If the expiration day falls on a non-business day, the delivery is made on the succeeding business day.

Unless otherwise directed by the clearing corporation, broker to broker securities deliveries must be made before 11:30 A.M., or the selling broker will fail to deliver and the buying broker will fail to receive. Rule 180 of the New York Stock Exchange is very specific about consequences of unaccomplished deliveries. The contract may be closed by the buyer as provided by the rules. If the buyer chooses not to close the contract, he or she will continue without interest until the security is delivered. In every case of nondelivery, the party in default is liable for any damages.

ACCEPTABLE DENOMINATIONS FOR DELIVERY

For Stocks

To settle an exchange contract, stock certificates must be in the exact amount of the trading unit if the trading unit is 100 shares, or in any multiple of the trading unit or smaller amounts aggregating the trading unit. If the unit of trading is less than 100 shares, the delivery must be in the exact amount of the stock sold or for smaller amounts aggregating the amount sold.

For Bonds

If the unit of trading is $1,000, the denominations of the bonds must be either $1,000 or $500. Bonds in lower denominations are also acceptable if they are exchangeable without charge for $1,000 or $500 pieces.

If the unit of trading is more than $1,000, the delivery must be made in the denominations of the trading unit. Bonds in larger denominations are acceptable if they can be exchangeable without charge for bonds in the unit of trading.

Contracts in bonds may be settled by delivering bonds in coupon or registered form, provided that these bonds are interchangeable without charge and are prepared in accord with the engraving requirements of the New York Stock Exchange.

In all cases, the buyer must accept partial deliveries from the seller if delivered in lots of one trading unit or in multiples of the unit.

All certificates must be in good deliverable form when used for delivery. A temporary certificate is not a good delivery when permanent certificates are available. All certificates and registered bonds must have proper assignments.

Securities Transfer

If the name of an individual or a member organization is inserted in the assignments as attorney, a Power of Substitution executed by the individual or the member organization in blank must be obtained.

Generally, securities requiring documents to effect transfer are not good delivery. Care must be exercised to differentiate items "good for transfer" from items "good for delivery." A certificate accompanied by a proper document may be considered as "good for transfer," but under the rules of the New York Stock Exchange and the NASD it is not "good for delivery." The NYSE, the American Stock Exchange and the NASD have amended their rules to accept securities registered in fiduciary names as good delivery items provided that documentation is not necessary to effect transfers. This would be certificates registered in the names of executors, administrators, trustees, guardians, etc.

Rule 201 of the New York Stock Exchange states that a certificate shall not be a good delivery with an assignment executed by:

1. the person since deceased,
2. the trustee or trustees,
3. the guardian,
4. the infant,
5. the executor,
6. the administrator,
7. the receiver in bankruptcy,
8. the agent, and
9. the attorney.

Exceptions to this rule are the following:

1. If the securities are registered in the name of a domestic executor or an administrator and properly endorsed.
2. If the securities are registered in the name of a domestic living (inter vivos) or testamentary trustee and properly endorsed.
3. If the securities are registered in the names of a domestic guardian, committees, conservators or curators and properly endorsed, they are considered as good deliverable items to accomplish a delivery provided that the securities are for domestic issuers—organized under the laws of any state of the United States or the District of Columbia.

As discussed elsewhere in this book, these securities do not require documentation to effect transfer.

CHAPTER **13**

Beneficial Ownership

Securities are either registered in the name of the stockholder, evidencing his or her proportionate ownership in the corporation, or in the name of a nominee acting as agent for the stockholder. In the first case, the investor is a direct shareholder of the corporation with ownership properly recorded in the books of the corporation. In the second case, he or she is the beneficial owner of the security with ownership masked behind the name of the nominee.

While nominee or street registrations facilitate securities transactions, their widespread use makes communications between corporations and shareholders difficult: it is difficult for a corporate secretary to ascertain the extent of share ownership when securities are registered in nominee or street name over a record date.

Nominee registration is an old arrangement primarily used by insurance companies, mutual funds, brokerage houses, banks, and trust companies. The practice was begun to avoid requirements of registrations and to facilitate securities delivery. The securities exchanges have specific requirements with respect to the condition of the certificates when they are delivered to satisfy an exchange contract.

Generally securities registered in the name of fiduciaries that require documentation for transfer are not considered to be in good deliverable form to settle a contract. The selling broker, therefore, must transfer the shares into his or her nominee name before delivery. To avoid this double transfer and extensive documentation, financial institutions adopted the practice of leaving the securities in their nominee name. Although this was contrary to English common law, most states enacted statutes to permit the practice.

A nominee is a partnership formed to facilitate securities transactions. Each general partner is authorized to make transfers on behalf of the nominee partnership. The name may be derived from the name of the organization; but frequently it has no relation to the name of the parent entity. American Society of Corporate Secretaries publishes an annual list of nominee names employed by major institutions. Some institutions use different nominee names for various purposes. Following is a list of fiduciary relationships using nominee registrations.

1. Estates
2. Living and testamentary trusts
3. Pension trusts
4. Investment management accounts
5. Corporate trust accounts
6. Safekeeping or custody accounts
7. Legal and common trust funds
8. Self-employed retirement accounts
9. Individual Retirement Act accounts
10. Profit sharing or pension plans

There is widespread use of nominee ownership in American corporations. The New York Stock Exchange periodically prepares a census of shareowners of most publicly held corporations. The reports indicate that the percentage of securities held by nominees has increased substantially since 1952.

There are three factors recognized in the definition of beneficial ownership: (1) the right to exercise investment discretion over securities, (2) the right to vote, and (3) the right to receive benefits. A person is a beneficial owner if he or she is entitled to any one of these rights. In many cases, however, securities are registered in other than the name of beneficial owners even though one person possesses all three rights of ownership.

Under SEC rules, a corporation is obligated to inquire with respect to securities held in nominee name by brokers and banks. Before a record date, the corporation sends a "search letter" to ascertain the number of beneficial owners of its securities.

Under the rules of various securities exchanges, a broker may vote its customers' securities only under certain conditions. In general, a broker may vote only after the customer has been given notice to indicate a voting preference. Brokers are not permitted, however, to vote on mergers and acquisitions without instructions from their customers.

In addition to brokers and banks, the development of depositories where certificates are left in the name of the depository's nominee has created another layer of beneficial ownership. On record date, the depository furnishes the corporation with a report indicating the number of shares held in the accounts of the depository's participants. The depository submits an omnibus proxy with the report assigning its voting rights to its participants.

PURPOSE OF STREET NAME REGISTRATION

The main purpose of street name registration is to facilitate securities transactions. Double transfers are eliminated. The selling broker is able to deliver securities to the buying broker without transferring the securities first to his or her nominee name. The certificates, even though registered in different street names, are fungible in nature—100 shares of the stock is equal to another 100 shares of the same stock.

This practice has contributed significantly to the rise and the eventual development of securities depositories and clearing organizations. It is one of the most important facets of their operations. In fact, their securities processing is dependent on street name registrations. Certificates registered in nominee name at central depositories are immobilized while transfers of title are accomplished through bookkeeping entries.

In a brokerage account, the street name arrangement preserves the customer's anonymity with respect to his or her investments. Collection of dividends is performed by the broker and credited to the customer's account.

With this arrangement, the broker is able to retain his or her interest in the shares where securities are bought on margin. Furthermore, it gives him or her the ability to rehypothecate the securities to finance the customer's indebtedness in the margin account. For fiduciary or corporate accounts, it has eliminated the need to submit evidence of authority or appointment of the fiduciary to make the item a deliverable instrument.

If, on one hand, street registrations have facilitated securities processing, on the other hand the practice has not eliminated the temptation by brokers to use fully paid customer securities for their own purposes. There is, therefore, the risk of broker misconduct and wrongdoing. In the event of brokerage insolvency, the customer whose securities are held in street name bears the risk. These customers may experience delays in settling claims, and their security positions may stay frozen until final settlement is reached. This risk has, in recent years, been somewhat mitigated by the Securities Investor Protection Act of 1970, where each account is insured to the extent of $100,000 in cash and $400,000 in securities. A bank's custody department provides a similar service. Here the certificates are registered in the name of the bank's nominee and kept for the account of the customer.

There are no accurate figures on the total market value of securities held in nominee name, but estimated are approximately $600 billion worth of securities in bank trust accounts and $3000 billion in securities depositories.

Even though issuer-shareowner communication is made difficult by this arrangement, there are no easy alternatives to the practice. Keeping all securities registered in the names of beneficial owners would seriously hamper the processing of securities transactions. The Securities and Exchange Commission has adopted several rules in an effort to retain the practice of nominee registrations while facilitating issuer-stockholder communications.

DISCLOSURE OF BENEFICIAL OWNERSHIP

Various sections of the Securities Exchange Act of 1934 require that any person owning more than 5 percent of any stock in a corporation must disclose the amount of beneficial holdings of that corporation's equity securities. The following are some of the highlights of this regulation:

SEC Regulation 13D

240. 13d-1. SEC rules require that any person, after acquiring, directly, or indirectly, over 5 percent of beneficial ownership of any equity security, file a report with the Commission within ten days after such acquisition.

For the purposes of this section, "equity security" is defined as equity security of a class of stock that is registered pursuant to Section 12 of the Act, or any equity security issued by a closed-end mutual fund registered under the Investment Company Act of 1940.

240. 13d-2. If any material change occurs in the percentage of beneficial ownership, the person is required to file an amendment disclosing such change.

240. 13d-3. Determination of beneficial owner. For the purposes of this section, a beneficial owner is defined as a person who, directly or indirectly, has the power to vote the subject securities, or to direct to vote, and the power to dispose of the securities, or to direct their disposition.

240.13d-4. Disclaimer of beneficial ownership. This section permits any person to expressly declare that the filing of a statement shall not be construed as an admission that the person is the beneficial owner of the securities.

240. 13d-5. Acquisition of securities. This section defines the manner in which the securities are acquired. Donees, executors, trustees, and legatees who become beneficial owners of securities will be deemed to have "acquired" such securities even though they had no intention to do so.

240. 13d-6. Exemption of certain acquisitions. This section cites certain exemptions to acquisition of securities.

240. 13d-7. Fees for Filing Schedules 13D or 13G. This rule establishes a uniform fee schedule for acquisition statements filed with the SEC. The fee is $100, to be accompanied with the first schedule. All amendments reflecting an increase in ownership above 5 percent do not require an additional fee.

CHAPTER **14**

SEC Rule 144

Rule 144 adopted by the Securities and Exchange Commission under the Securities Act of 1933 provides the mechanics by which restricted securities may be sold or transferred.

The following are required of the customer, the brokerage firm, and the transfer agent in processing securities under this rule.

1. To sell a security under Rule 144, the broker must make certain that the issuing corporation has filed reports pursuant to Section 13 or 15 (d) of the Securities Exchange Act of 1934 at least ninety days prior to the sale.
2. The broker must make sure that the customer had owned the security for a period of at least two years prior to the sale.
3. The customer, under this rule, cannot sell more than one percent of the total outstanding shares of the corporation in the over-the-counter market within a three-month period, or if the security is listed at an exchange, he or she cannot sell more than the average weekly volume of the security traded in all exchanges during four consecutive weeks prior to the sale.
4. The sale must be executed by the broker on an agency basis. The broker cannot solicit or arrange for the solicitation of buy orders.
5. Brokerage firms require Form 144, a Certificate of Facts, to be completed by the selling customer, as well as a letter transmitting Form 144 to the SEC.
6. The transfer agent must require an opinion of the attorney representing the issuer and the seller.
7. The broker and the transfer agent must exercise extreme care that the sale does not exceed one percent of total shares in an over-the-counter transaction within a three-month period. The rule defines the selling customer as a beneficial owner of the security. All shares beneficially owned by the customer cannot exceed one percent of the total outstand-

ing shares of the corporation. These shares may be part of a partnership, owned by relatives, or held in street name. The one percent calculation includes all these shares. The text of SEC Rule 144 follows.

SEC Rule 144

Rule 144 is designed to implement the fundamental purposes of the Act, as expressed in its preamble, "To provide full and fair disclosure of the character of the securities sold in interstate commerce and through the mails and to prevent fraud in the sale thereof . . ." The rule is designed to prohibit the creation of public markets in securities of issuers concerning which adequate current information is not available to the public. At the same time, where adequate current information concerning the issuer is available to the public, the rule permits the public sale in ordinary trading transactions of limited amounts of securities owned by persons controlling, controlled by, or under common control with the issuer and by persons who have acquired restricted securities of the issuer.

Certain basic principles are essential to an understanding of the requirement of registration in the Act:

1. If any person utilized the jurisdictional means to sell any nonexempt security to any other person, the security must be registered unless a statutory exemption can be found for the transaction.
2. In addition to the exemptions found in section 3, four exemptions applicable to transactions in securities are contained in section 4. Three of these section 4 exemptions are clearly not available to anyone acting as an "underwriter" of securities. (The fourth, found in section 4(4), is available only to those who act as brokers under certain limited circumstances.) An understanding of the term "underwriter" is therefore important to anyone who wishes to determine whether or not an exemption from registration is available for his sale of securities.

The term underwriter is broadly defined in section 2(11) of the Act to mean any person who has purchased from an issuer with a view to, or offers or sells for an issuer in connection with, the distribution of any security, or participates, or has a direct or indirect participation in any such undertaking, or participates or has a participation in the direct or indirect underwriting of any such undertaking. The interpretation of this definition has traditionally focused on the words "with a view to" in the phrase "purchased from an issuer with a view to . . . distribution." Thus an investment banking firm which arranges with an issuer for the public sale of its securities is clearly an "underwriter" under that section. Individual investors who are not professionals in the securities business may also be "underwriters" within the meaning of that term as used in the Act if they act as links in a chain of transactions through which securities move from an issuer to the public. Since it is difficult to ascertain the mental state of the purchaser at the time of his acquisition, subsequent acts and circumstances have been considered to determine whether such person took with a view to distribution at the time of his acquisition. Emphasis has been placed on factors such as the length of time the person has held the securities and whether there has been an unforeseeable change in circumstances of the holder. Experience has shown, however, that reliance upon such factors as the above has not assured adequate protection of investors through the maintenance of informed trading markets and has led to uncertainty in the application of the registration provision of the Act.

It should be noted that the statutory language of section 2(11) is in the disjunctive. Thus, it is insufficient to conclude that a person is not an underwriter solely because he did not purchase securities from an issuer with a view to their distribution. It must also be established that the person is not offering or selling for an issuer in connection with the distribution of the securities, does not participate or have a direct or indirect participation in any such undertaking, and does not participate or have a participation in the direct or indirect underwriting of such an undertaking.

In determining when a person is deemed not to be engaged in a distribution several factors must be considered.

First, the purpose and underlying policy of the Act to protect investors requires that there be adequate current information concerning the issuer, whether the resales of securities by persons result in a distribution or are effected in trading transactions. Accordingly, the availability of the rule is conditioned on the existence of adequate current public information.

Secondly, a holding period prior to resale is essential, among other reasons to assure that those persons who buy under a claim of a section 4(2) exemption have assumed the economic risks of investment, and therefore are not acting as conduits for sale to the public of unregistered securities, directly or indirectly, on behalf of an issuer. It should be noted that nothing in section 2(11) places a time limit on a person's status as an underwriter. The public has the same need for protection afforded by registration whether the securities are distributed shortly after their purchase or after a considerable length of time.

A third factor, which must be considered in determining what is deemed not to constitute a "distribution," is the impact of the particular transaction or transactions on the trading markets. Section 4(1) was intended to exempt only routine trading transactions between individual investors with respect to securities already issued and not to exempt distributions by issuers or acts of other individuals who engage in steps necessary to such distributions. Therefore, a person reselling securities under section 4(1) of the Act must sell the securities in such limited quantities and in such a manner as not to disrupt the trading markets. The larger the amount of securities involved, the more likely it is that such resales may involve methods of offering and amounts of compensation usually associated with a distribution rather than routine trading transactions. Thus, solicitation of buy orders or the payment of extra compensation is not permitted by the rule.

In summary, if the sale in question is made in accordance with all the provisions of the section as set forth below, any person who sells restricted securities shall be deemed not to be engaged in a distribution of such securities and therefore not an underwriter thereof. The rule also provides that any person who sells restricted or other securities on behalf of a person in a control relationship with the issuer shall be deemed not to be engaged in a distribution of such securities and therefore not to be an underwriter thereof if the sale is made in accordance with all the conditions of the section.

(a) Definitions. The following definitions shall apply for the purposes of this section.

(1) An "affiliate" of an issuer is a person that directly, or indirectly through one or more intermediaries, controls, or is controlled by, or is under common control with, such issuer.

(2) The term "person" when used with reference to a person for whose account securities are to be sold in reliance upon this section includes, in addition to such person, all of the following persons:

(i) Any relative or spouse of such person, or any relative of such spouse, any one of whom has the same home as such person:

(ii) Any trust or estate in which such person or any of the persons specified in paragraph (a)(2)(i) of this section collectively own ten percent or more of the total beneficial interest or of which any of such persons serve as trustee, executor, or in any similar capacity; and

(iii) Any corporation or other organization (other than the issuer in which such person or any of the persons specified in paragraph (a)(2)(i) of this section are the beneficial owners collectively of 10 percent or more of any class of equity securities or 10 percent or more of the equity interest.

(3) The term "restricted securities" means securities acquired directly or indirectly from the issuer thereof, or from an affiliate of the issuer in a transaction or chain of transactions not involving any public offering or from the issuer in a transaction in reliance on Rule 240 or Rule 242 under the Act or which were issued by an issuer in a transaction in reliance on Rule 240 or Rule 242 and were acquired in the transaction or chain of transactions not involving any public offering.

(b) Conditions to be met. Any affiliate or other person who sells restricted securities of an issuer for his own account, or any person who sells restricted or any other securities for the account of an affiliate of the issuer of such securities, shall be deemed not to be engaged in a distribution of such securities and therefore not to be an underwriter thereof within the meaning of section 2(11) of the Act if all of the conditions of this section are met.

(c) Current public information. There shall be available adequate current public information with respect to the issuer of the securities. Such information shall be deemed to be available only if either of the following conditions is met.

(1) Filing of reports. The issuer has securities registered pursuant to section 12 of the Securities Exchange Act of 1934, has been subject to the reporting requirements of section 13 of that Act for a period of at least ninety days immediately preceding the sale of the securities and has filed all the reports required to be filed thereunder during the 12 months preceding such sale (or for such shorter period that the issuer was required to file such reports); or has securities registered pursuant to the Securities Act of 1933, has been subject to the reporting requirements of section 15(d) of the Securities Exchange Act of 1934 for a period of at least 90 days immediately preceding the sale of the securities and has filed all the reports required to be filed thereunder during the 12 months preceding such sale (or for such shorter period that the issuer was required to file such reports). The person for whose account the securities are to be sold shall be entitled to rely upon a statement in whichever is the most recent report, quarterly or annual, required to be filed and filed by the issuer that such issuer has filed all reports required to be filed by section 13 or 15(d) of the Securities Exchange Act of 1934 during the preceding 12 months (or for such shorter period that the issuer was required to file such reports) and has been subject to such filing requirements for the past 90 days, unless he knows or has reason to believe that the issuer has not complied with such requirements. Such person shall also be entitled to rely upon a written statement from the issuer that it has complied with such reporting requirements unless he knows or has reasons to believe that the issuer has not complied with such requirements.

(2) Other public information. If the issuer is not subject to section 13 or 15(d) of the Securities Exchange Act of 1934, there is publicly available the information concerning the issuer specified in subdivision (i) or (xiv), inclusive, and subdivision (xvi) of paragraph (a)(4) of 240.15c2-11 of this chapter or, if the issuer is an insurance company, the information specified in section 12(g)(2)(G)(i) of that Act.

(d) Holding period for restricted securities. If the securities sold are restricted securities, the following provisions apply:

(1) General rule. The person for whose account the securities are sold shall have been the beneficial owner of the securities for a period of at least 2 years prior to the sale and, if the securities were purchased, the full purchase price or other consideration shall have been paid or given at least 2 years prior to the sale.

(2) Promissory notes, other obligations or installment contracts. Giving the person from whom the securities were purchased a promissory note or other obligation to pay the purchase price, or entering

into an installment purchase contract with such person, shall not be deemed full payment of the purchase price unless the promissory note, obligation or contract—

(i) Provides for full recourse against the purchaser of the securities;

(ii) Is secured by collateral, other than the securities purchased, having a fair market value at least equal to the purchase price of the securities purchased; and

(iii) Shall have been discharged by payment in full prior to the sale of the securities.

(3) Short sales, puts or other options to sell securities. In computing the 2-year holding period the following periods shall be excluded:

(i) If the securities sold are equity securities, there shall be excluded any period during which the person for whose account they are sold had a short position in, or any put or other option to dispose of, any equity securities of the same class or any securities convertible into securities of such class; and

(ii) If the securities sold are nonconvertible debt securities, there shall be excluded any period during which the person for whose account they are sold had a short position in or any put or other option to dispose of, any non-convertible debt securities of the same issuer.

(4) Determination of holding period. The following provisions shall apply for the purpose of determining the period securities have been held:

(i) Stock dividends, splits and recapitalizations. Securities acquired from the issuer as a dividend or pursuant to a stock split, reverse split or recapitalization shall be deemed to have been acquired at the same time as the securities on which the dividend or, if more than one, the initial dividend was paid, the securities involved in the split or reverse split, or the securities surrendered in connection with the recapitalization;

(ii) Conversions. If the securities sold were acquired from the issuer for a consideration consisting solely of other securities of the same issuer surrendered for conversion, the securities so acquired shall be deemed to have been acquired at the same time as the securities surrendered for conversion;

(iii) Contingent issuance of securities. Securities acquired as a contingent payment of the purchase price of an equity interest in a business, or the assets of a business, sold to the issuer or an affiliate of the issuer shall be deemed to have been acquired at the time of such sale if the issuer or affiliate was then committed to issue the securities subject only to conditions other than the payment of further consideration for such securities. An agreement entered into in connection with any such purchase to remain in the employment of, or not to compete with, the issuer or affiliate or the rendering of services pursuant to such agreement shall not be deemed to be the payment of further consideration for such securities.

(iv) Pledged securities. Securities which are bona fide pledged by any person other than the issuer when sold by the pledgee, or by a purchaser, after a default in the obligation secured by the pledge, shall be deemed to have been acquired when they were acquired by the pledgor, except that if the securities were pledged without recourse they shall be deemed to have been acquired by the pledgee at the time of the pledge or by the purchaser at the time of purchase.

Note: Securities sold by the pledgee shall be aggregated with those sold by the pledgor, as provided in paragraph (e)(3)(ii) of this section.

(v) Gifts of securities. Securities acquired from any person, other than the issuer, by gift shall be deemed to have been acquired by the donee when they were acquired by the donor;

Note: Securities sold by the donee shall be aggregated with those sold by the donor, as provided in paragraph (e)(3)(iii) of this section.

(vi) Trusts. Securities acquired from the settlor of a trust by the trust or acquired from the trust by the beneficiaries thereof shall be deemed to have been acquired when they were acquired by the settlor;

Note: Securities sold by the trust shall be aggregated with those sold by the settlor of the trust, as provided in paragraph (e)(3)(iv) of this section.

(vii) Estates. Securities held by the estate of a deceased person or acquired from such an estate by the beneficiaries thereof shall be deemed to have been by the deceased person, except that no holding period is required if the estate is not an affiliate of the issuer or if the securities are sold by a beneficiary of the estate who is not such an affiliate.

Notes: (a) Securities sold by the estate shall be aggregated with those sold by the deceased person, as provided in paragraph (e)(3)(v) of this section, if the estate is an affiliate of the issuer.

(b) While there is no holding period or amount limitation for estates and beneficiaries thereof, which are not affiliates of the issuer, paragraphs (c), (f), (g), (h), and (i) of the section apply to securities sold by such persons in reliance upon the section.

(e) Limitation on amount of securities sold. Except as hereinafter provided, the amount of securities which may be sold in reliance upon this rule shall be determined as follows:

(1) Sales by affiliates. If restricted or other securities are sold for the account of an affiliate of the issuer, the amount of securities sold, together with all sales of restricted and other securities of the same class for the account of such person within the preceding three months, shall not exceed the greater of (i) one percent of the shares or other units of the class outstanding as shown by the most recent report or statement published by the issuer, or (ii) the average weekly reported volume of trading in such securities on all national securities exchanges and/or reported through the automated quotation system of a registered securities association during the four calendar weeks preceding the filing of notice required by paragraph (h), or if no such notice is required the date of receipt of the order to execute the transaction by the broker or the date of execution of the transaction directly with a

market maker, or (iii) the average weekly volume of trading in such securities reported through the consolidated transaction reporting system contemplated by Rule 11Aa3-1 under the Securities Exchange Act of 1934 (240.11A301) during the four-week period specified in paragraph (e)(1)(ii) of this section.

(2) Sales by persons other than affiliates. The amount of restricted securities sold for the account of any person other than an affiliate of the issuer, together with all other sales of restricted securities of the same class for the account of such person within the preceding three months, shall not exceed the amount specified in paragraphs (e)(1)(i), (1)(ii) or (1)(iii) of this section, whichever is applicable, unless the conditions of paragraph (k) of this rule are satisfied.

(3) Determination of amount. For the purpose of determining the amount of securities specified in paragraphs (e) (1) and (2) of this section, the following provisions shall apply:

(i) Where both convertible securities and securities of the class into which they are convertible are sold, the amount of convertible securities sold shall be deemed to be the amount of securities of the class into which they are convertible for the purpose of determining the aggregate amount of securities of both classes sold;

(ii) The amount of securities sold for the account of a pledgee thereof, or for the account of a purchaser of the pledged securities, during any period of 3 months within 2 years after a default in the obligation secured by the pledge, and the amount of securities sold during the same 3-month period for the account of the pledgor shall not exceed, in the aggregate, the amount specified in paragraph (e)(1) or (2) of this section, whichever is applicable.

(iii) The amount of securities sold for the account of a donee thereof during any period of 3 months within 2 years after the donation, and the amount of securities sold during the same three-month period for the account of the donor, shall not exceed, in the aggregate, the amount specified in paragraph (e)(1) or (2) of this section, whichever is applicable.

(iv) Where securities were acquired by a trust from the settlor of the trust, the amount of such securities sold for the account of the trust during any period of 3 months within 2 years after the acquisition of the securities by the trust, and the amount of securities sold during the same 3 month period for the account of the settlor, shall not exceed, in the aggregate, the amount specified in paragraph (e)(1) or (2) of this section, whichever is applicable;

(v) The amount of securities sold for the account of the estate of a deceased person, or for the account of a beneficiary of such estate, during any period of 3 months and the amount of securities sold during the same period for the account of the deceased person prior to his death shall not exceed, in the aggregate, the amount specified in paragraph (e)(1) or (2) of this section, whichever is applicable: Provided, That no limitation on amount shall apply if the estate or beneficiary thereof is not an affiliate of the issuer;

(vi) When two or more affiliates or other persons agree to act in concert for the purpose of selling securities of an issuer, all securities of the same class sold for the account of all such persons during any period of 3 months shall be aggregated for the purpose of determining the limitation on the amount of securities sold;

(vii) Securities sold pursuant to an effective registration statement under the Act or pursuant to an exemption provided by Regulation A under the Act or in a transaction exempt pursuant to section 4 of the Act and not involving any public offering need not be included in determining the amount of securities sold in reliance upon this rule.

(f) Manner of sale. The securities shall be sold in "brokers' transactions" within the meaning of section 4(4) of the Act or in transactions directly with a "market maker," as that term is defined in section 3(a) (38) of the Securities Exchange Act of 1934, and the person selling the securities shall not (1) solicit or arrange for the solicitation of orders to buy the securities in anticipation of or in connection with such transaction, or (2) make any payment in connection with the offer or sale of the securities to any person other than the broker who executes an order to sell the securities. The requirements of this paragraph, however, shall not apply to securities sold for the account of the estate of a deceased person or for the account of a beneficiary of such estate provided the estate or beneficiary thereof is not an affiliate of the issuer; nor shall they apply to securities sold for the account of any person other than an affiliate of the issuer provided the conditions of paragraph (k) of this rule are satisfied.

(g) Brokers' transactions. The term "brokers' transactions" in section 4(4) of the Act shall for the purposes of this rule be deemed to include transactions by a broker in which such broker—

(1) Does no more than execute the order or orders to sell the securities as agent for the person for whose account the securities are sold; and receives no more than the usual and customary broker's commission;

(2) Neither solicits nor arranges for the solicitation of customers' orders to buy the securities in anticipation of or in connection with the transaction; provided, that the foregoing shall not preclude (i) inquiries by the broker of other brokers or dealers who have indicated an interest in the securities within the preceding 60 days, (ii) inquiries by the broker of his customers who have indicated an unsolicited bona fide interest in the securities within the preceding 10 business days; or (iii) the publication by the broker of bid and ask quotations for the security in an inter-dealer quotation system provided that such quotations are incident to the maintenance of a bona fide inter-dealer market for the security for the broker's own account and that the broker has published bona fide bid and ask quotations for the security in an inter-dealer quotation system on each of at least twelve days within the preceding thirty calendar days with no more than four business days in succession without such two-way quotations;

Note to paragraph (g)(2)(ii): The broker should obtain and retain in his files written evidence of indications of bona fide unsolicited interest by his customers in the securities at the time such indications are received.

(3) After reasonable inquiry is not aware of circumstances indicating that the person for whose account the securities are sold is an underwriter with respect to the securities or that the transaction is a part of a distribution of securities of the issuer. Without limiting the foregoing, the broker shall be deemed to be aware of any facts or statements contained in the notice required by paragraph (h) of this section.

Notes: (i) The broker, for his own protection, should obtain and retain in his files a copy of the notice required by paragraph (h) of this section.

(ii) The reasonable inquiry required by paragraph (g) (3) of this section should include, but not necessarily be limited to, inquiry as to the following matters:

(a) The length of time the securities have been held by the person for whose account they are to be sold. If practicable, the inquiry should include physical inspection of the securities;

(b) The nature of the transaction in which the securities were acquired by such person;

(c) The amount of securities of the same class sold during the past 3 months by all persons whose sales are required to be taken into consideration pursuant to paragraph (e) of this section;

(d) Whether such person intends to sell additional securities of the same class through any other means;

(e) Whether such person has solicited or made any arrangement for the solicitation of buy orders in connection with the proposed sale of securities;

(f) Whether such person has made any payment to any other person in connection with the proposed sale of the securities; and

(g) The number of shares or other units of the class outstanding, or the relevant trading volume.

(h) Notice of proposed sale. If the amount of securities to be sold in reliance upon the rule during any period of three months exceeds 500 shares or other units or has an aggregate sale price in excess of $10,000, three copies of a notice on Form 144 shall be filed with the Commission at its principal office in Washington, D.C.; and if such securities are admitted to trading on any national securities exchange, one copy of such notice shall also be transmitted to the principal exchange on which such securities are so admitted. The Form 144 shall be signed by the person for whose account the securities are to be sold and shall be transmitted for filing concurrently with either the placing with a broker of an order to execute a sale of securities in reliance upon this rule or the execution directly with a market maker of such a sale. Neither the filing of such notice nor the failure of the Commission to comment thereon shall be deemed to preclude the Commission from taking any action it deems necessary or appropriate with respect to the sale of the securities referred to in such notice. The requirements of this paragraph, however, shall not apply to securities sold for the account of any person other than an affiliate of the issuer, provided the conditions of paragraph (k) of this rule are satisfied.

(i) Bona fide intention to sell. The person filing the notice required by paragraph (h) of this section shall have a bona fide intention to sell the securities referred to therein within a reasonable time after the filing of such notice.

(j) Non-exclusive rule. Although this rule provides a means for reselling restricted securities and securities held by affiliates without registration, it is not the exclusive means for reselling such securities in that manner. Therefore, it does not eliminate or otherwise affect the availability of any exemption for resales under the Securities Act that a person or entity may be able to rely upon.

(k) Termination of certain restrictions on sales of restricted securities by persons other than affiliates. The requirements of paragraphs (e), (f) and (h) of this rule shall not apply to restricted securities sold for the account of a person who is not an affiliate of the issuer at the time of the sale and has not been an affiliate during the preceding three months, providing the securities have been beneficially owned by the person for a period of at least three years prior to their sale. In computing the period for which securities have been beneficially owned for purposes of this provision, reference should be made to paragraph (d) of this section.

CHAPTER 15

Stock Transfer Turnaround

Rules of the securities exchanges and state governments, rules of the Securities and Exchange Commission, and various codes and statutes govern the registration of securities. Transfer agents, in the main, have been able to effectively employ these requirements in providing registration services to the public in general and to the investing community in particular.

The Securities and Exchange Commission has adopted several rules which provide a national standard of performance for transfer agents in cancelling, issuing and registering certificates of ownership. The rules require promptness and accuracy, early warnings of inadequate performance, prompt response to inquiries about the status of transfer items, and limits on expansion of transfer agents' activities. Designed to protect the investing public throughout the country, these are the first substantive rules applicable to transfer agents adopted pursuant to Section 17A of the Securities and Exchange Act of 1934.

The SEC turnaround rules do not supersede similar rules imposed by self-regulatory organizations, notably the New York Stock Exchange, which require that transfer agents acting for certain issues effect turnaround within 48 hours.

OPERATION OF THE RULES 240.17 Ad-1 THROUGH 17 Ad-7

SEC Turnaround Rules

The rules became effective on October 3, 1977, and January 2, 1978. Following is a detailed description of the operation of these rules.

1. *Turnaround and Processing of Transfer Items*

   a. Each month, transfer agents must turn around at least ninety percent of all routine transfer items within three business days of receipt. Items

received at or before noon on a business day are considered received at noon on that day. Items received after noon on a business day or received on a non-business day are considered received at noon on the next business day.
b. Transfer agents acting as outside registrars must process at least ninety percent of all items received during a month.
c. Transfer agents failing to comply with the turnaround schedule are required to file notice with the Securities and Exchange Commission within ten business days following the end of the month. This notice states the number of routine and non-routine items received for transfer during the month, the number of routine items that the transfer agent failed to turn around, the reasons for such failures, and the steps taken to prevent a future failure.
d. The rules require continuous attention to all routine items not turned around within three business days for processing as soon as possible.

2. Limitations on Expansion

a. Transfer agents required to file notices of noncompliance for each of three consecutive months are prevented from expanding their business activities so that they can bring their performance into compliance with the rules. These limitations remain in effect for at least three consecutive months, starting on the fifth business day following the end of the three-month period during which notices of noncompliance were filed with the Commission.

During this period, a transfer agent may not add new issues for transfer, nor can it expand its activity for issues already on the list.
b. The limitations also apply to those transfer agents failing to turnaround at least seventy-five percent of all routine items for each of two consecutive months. These transfer agents are required to send a copy of the notice of noncompliance to the chief executive officer of each corporation on the list with the transfer agent.

3. Applicability of the Rules and Exceptions

The SEC turnaround rules do not apply to transfer agents receiving fewer than 500 items for transfer during any six consecutive months. Notice must be filed with the SEC to classify them as exempt transfer agents. Exemption is removed if volume expands beyond the 500 figure.

The Commission has also determined that the turnaround rules do not apply to open-end, redeemable securities of investment companies. Transfer of these shares is significantly different from the transfer of ownership of stocks and bonds.

Securities Transfer

4. Written Inquiries and Requests

a. All written inquiries about the status of transfer items must be answered by the transfer agent within five business days of receipt of the inquiry. The inquiry must include complete data—registered name, certificate numbers, name of stock, and so on. No further response is necessary from the transfer agent if the new certificate is mailed to the presentor within five business days following receipt of the inquiry.

b. When a broker-dealer requests in writing that a transfer agent acknowledge a transfer instruction or revalidate a window ticket with respect to a security presented for transfer, the transfer agent is required to respond in writing within five business days following receipt of the request. If a new certificate is en route to the presentor, no further response is necessary.

c. If a request is made that a transfer agent confirm possession as of a given date of a certificate presented for transfer during the preceding thirty days, the transfer agent must respond within ten business days following receipt of the request. The transfer agent may charge a fee for honoring the request.

d. If a request is made for a transcript of a person's account with respect to a particular issue, the transfer agent must respond to the request within twenty business days following receipt of the request. The transfer agent may charge a fee.

5. Recordkeeping

a. Transfer agents are required to maintain all receipts, tickets, schedules and logs showing the date each routine and non-routine item is received from the presentor.

b. They are required to maintain monthly records for all items turned around within three business days, and also the number of routine items that were not turned around within three business days—for both routine and non-routine items.

c. A transfer agent is required to record the number of routine items in its possession for more than four business days.

d. If the transfer agent is an outside registrar, it must maintain all records and tickets showing receipt of items from presenting transfer agents and monthly records showing number of items processed within the prescribed time and number of items not processed.

e. Transfer agents must maintain a file of all written inquiries and responses to the inquiries as well as a file of inquiries received during the month but not responded to.

f. All documents, resolutions, and appointments of transfer agents must be kept in a permanent file. A file must also be maintained for stop orders, notices of adverse claims, transfer restrictions, and so on.

g. Transfer agents must retain all cancelled certificates and accompanying documentation.

6. Record Retention

The SEC rules provide a schedule of retention by transfer agents of all records, logs, and documents. The period, generally two years, is considered necessary for an agency to monitor compliance with the turnaround rules. These records must be available for examination by regulatory authorities.

RULE 496 OF THE NEW YORK STOCK EXCHANGE

Turnaround rules also apply to securities listed on the New York and American Stock Exchanges. Rules 496 of the New York Stock Exchange and 891 of the American Stock Exchange provide turnaround schedules for independent agents acting as or in lieu of New York City transfer agents.

Rule 496 of the New York Stock Exchange, adopted in June 1971, has specific requirements for transfer agents located outside New York City.

1. The transfer agent must have an office located south of Chambers Street in New York to receive and redeliver securities.
2. Routine transfers are to be processed and available for pick-up at the office under normal conditions within forty-eight hours.
3. The transfer agency must assume total responsibility and liability for securities from the time of deposit until they are redelivered at the window. For this purpose, the transfer agent must have capital and capital reserves aggregating to at least $10 million.
4. Out of town transfer agents are allowed drop facilities in New York. Appropriate arrangements must be made, however, to operate within a forty-eight-hour framework.
5. The staff must have sufficient knowledge and experience to respond to inquiries regarding routine and legal items.
6. Securities received at the office before the record date must be recorded as of that date to establish the transferee's right and interests.
7. Facilities should be available to provide rapid transfer service. The transfer agent may charge a reasonable fee for this service.
8. An out of town transfer agent having a New York office or a drop must maintain insurance coverage of at least $25 million to protect securities while in transit or in process.

Securities Transfer

9. In the event of the failure of a transfer agent to comply with these requirements, the New York Stock Exchange may request the termination of the service.

Ever since its implementation, and particularly after the enactment of SEC Turnaround Rules, the out of town transfer agents have commented on Rule 496. They find both rules of the New York and American Stock Exchanges discriminatory. According to them, the continued operation of Rule 496 enhances the competitive position of the New York financial community. In view of the SEC rules, the out of town transfer agents feel the turnaround standard required by Rule 496 is no longer necessary and that both Rules should be eliminated.

The New York Stock Exchange has suggested that the Securities and Exchange Commission delay a consideration of the forty-eight-hour turnaround provision of Rule 496 until the results of turnaround reporting can be examined.

TRANSFER AGENT DROP FACILITY IN NEW YORK

There are several organizations that provide drop locations for out of town transfer agents. These offices are located south of Chambers Street in Manhattan in accordance with Rule 496. Agreements between the transfer agent and the drop facility must be approved by the New York and American Stock Exchanges before system implementation.

The following is a schedule of services provided by the "drop" organization:

1. Maintain an office in New York south of Chambers Street, where securities for which the transfer agent is qualified may be received for transfer and redelivered.
2. Provide for the receipt, inspection, and redelivery of securities over the window through the ASECC Envelope Service or from the Depository Trust Company.
3. Provide personnel qualified to answer inquiries relative to legal transfer items and advise on other transfer problems. In cases where a further interpretation of legal requirements is necessary, the drop organization will initiate communication directly with the transfer agent.
4. Provide facilities in New York for a safekeeping of securities in its possession.
5. Initiate communication with the transfer agent to provide details of rush transfers.
6. Maintain all records of securities received for transfer and surrender the securities to the courier service employed by the transfer agent.

The transfer agent, on its part, will provide the following service to the drop organization:

1. Arrange for the shipment of securities to and from the drop facility.
2. Designate a qualified individual within the transfer department to be authorized to accept calls from the drop facility, answer inquiries, and initiate action on rush transfers.
3. Supply the drop organization with a complete list of securities for which the transfer agent is qualified to effect transfer.
4. Inform the drop facility in writing of a record date prior to the record date and request special handling.

CHAPTER 16

Stock Transfer Services

There are various services provided by several organizations to aid the processing of securities transfers. One of the most important is the distribution service of the American Stock Exchange Clearing Corporation. The Amex has operated a central location for brokers, bank trust departments, and transfer agents since 1947, and was developed primarily to speed up transfer turnaround and reduce operating costs. Its initial objective was to aid the New York financial community. In recent years, however, it has been expanded to include other metropolitan areas working in conjunction with various clearing corporations. This out of town distribution is done through the National Transfer Service.

As compensation for these services, the American Stock Exchange Clearing Corporation charges each participant $15 a week and 15¢ for each envelope received or delivered in the New York area. This includes upper Manhattan, Newark, and Jersey City. Charges for the National Transfer Service vary. They are established by each area center, and participants are charged accordingly.

NATIONAL TRANSFER SERVICE (NTS)

The participant prepares securities to be transferred in New York City or other financial centers, attaches a transfer instruction and a "broker originated window ticket" (BOWT) to each item, sorts the items by agent, and places them in a special designated envelope addressed to the agent. The envelopes and the accompanying control tickets are then delivered to respective clearing organizations for distribution. Each clearing corporation sorts the envelopes by city and transfer agent. Messengers and insured couriers deliver the envelopes to individual transfer agents.

Liability for lost certificates is generally handled by the participating member or transfer agent. The clearing corporation and its agents provide only a limited coverage for processing claims. The delivering broker or bank assumes responsibility for lost certificates prior to completion of the transfer, and the transfer agent assumes responsibility for certificates lost subsequent to transfer. The following is the standard operating procedure for transfers to participating out of town area centers.

1. Participating member prepares items for transfer.

   a. Prepares certificates, transfer instructions, and BOWT.
   b. Places certificates in preaddressed envelopes to the transfer agent.
   c. Prepares the Transfer Control Form indicating total number of envelopes being delivered to each agent and the grand total of all envelopes.
   d. Attaches the Transfer Control Form to the envelopes and delivers them to the area center for distribution.

2. The area center receives packages of envelopes.

   a. Counts the number of envelopes received, signs the Transfer Control Form, and returns one copy to the participating broker.
   b. Places the envelopes in containers grouped by transfer agent for delivery to out of town area center.
   c. Prepares two-part receipt indicating total number of containers.
   d. Locks containers of envelopes.

3. Envelope containers are dispatched to appropriate out of town area center. These are generally transported by armored air courier messengers.

4. The out of town area center receives envelopes from delivering area center.

   a. Counts number of containers.
   b. Unlocks the containers.
   c. Prepares transfer agent receipt for number of envelopes to be delivered to each agent.
   d. Delivers envelopes to the transfer agent.

5. Transfer agent receives envelopes from area center.

   a. Counts envelopes and signs receipt after verification.
   b. Opens envelopes and processes items for transfer.
   c. Files one copy of BOWT with the debit certificate. Issues the credit certificate and attaches the other copy of BOWT to the credit certificate for broker identification.

Securities Transfer 151

    d. Places the new certificates in envelopes addressed to broker.

    e. Prepares receipt for area center.

    f. Delivers envelopes to area center for return to the participant.

6. Area center receives envelopes from delivering transfer agent.

    a. Counts number of envelopes.

    b. Signs agent's receipt and sorts all envelopes by participating out of town members.

    c. Places envelopes in containers, locks containers and prepares two-part receipt indicating total number of containers and total envelopes being delivered to the out of town area center.

7. Envelope containers are dispatched to appropriate area center.

8. Out of town area center receives envelopes from delivering area center.

    a. Counts number of containers, unlocks containers, signs two-part receipt, removes envelopes from containers and prepares member firm receipts to be delivered to each participating member.

    b. Delivers envelopes to participant via member messenger pick up.

9. Member receives the new certificates from area center.

PROCEDURE FOR RECORD DATE TRANSFERS IN NEW YORK THROUGH THE NTS

All record date transfers should be identified as such on their corresponding BOWTs. The procedure does not call for separate envelopes for legal and record date items. Similarly, transferred new certificates need not be separated from regular items when being delivered to the initiating participant.

Record date items, however, must be submitted under a separate Transfer Agent List, form CC63, marked "Record Date" or "Bank Closing."

Record date transfers received in the afternoon at the American Stock Exchange Clearing Corporation are delivered to downtown New York transfer agents on the same day of the receipt.

Regular transfers received in the afternoon are delivered to those transfer agents in New York accepting night drops. These envelopes are delivered between 4:00 P.M. and 5:30 P.M. The transfers are delivered the following day.

Following is the schedule of the transfer service:

1. 8:30–9:30 A.M.   Members deliver all transfer envelopes to the clearing corporation for transfer.

2. 12:30–1:30 P.M. Record date envelopes are accepted for delivery to the New York area transfer agents.
3. 12:30–2:00 P.M. Record date items for delivery to downtown New York agents are accepted.
4. 1:00–5:30 P.M. Members may begin picking up completed transfers. (Out of town envelopes are available after 3:00 P.M.)
5. 3:30–5:30 P.M. Bond envelopes are delivered to Amex for delivery to transfer agents accepting night drops.

AGENT-ORIGINATED ENVELOPE

Agent-originated envelopes are specially designated envelopes used by transfer agents to return completed or rejected transfer items to the participating broker. These envelopes are initiated when a regular transfer envelope is not available and are delivered to the area center along with regular envelopes for processing.

BROKER-ORIGINATED WINDOW TICKET (BOWT)

The use of broker-originated window tickets started in 1968 to facilitate securities transfer and eliminate, in most cases, the necessity of window receipts issued by transfer agents.

These tickets are used for transfer items presented through the Amex transfer service. Some transfer agents in New York continue to issue receipts for items received "over the window," BOWTs are standard tickets in three parts with the following data:

1. Six digit preprinted control number with broker's clearing number as prefix.
2. Number of shares represented.
3. Full security description.
4. Legal items must be so indicated on the ticket.
5. Broker name.
6. Optional data that may be included on the ticket by originating broker, such as transfer agent's name or number and date securities were sent to the transfer agent.

FAST AND TRANSFER AGENT CUSTODIAN (TAC)

A major step that can be taken to facilitate securities processing is to remove certificates from circulation and place them into depositories where transactions can be handled by bookkeeping entries. There are, at present, several depositories throughout the country that perform this function. To further immobilize the stock certificate, a program called "transfer agent custodian" (TAC), was developed some years ago. The program calls for the storage of the stock at the transfer agent of the security for the account of the participating depository organization or the brokerage house. The certificates are delivered based on broker instructions. The importance of this program is the fact that the securities are retained at their source—at the transfer agents—and the movement of certificates is minimized. Full implementation of TAC could solve the operational problems of the securities industry, particularly when the program is integrated with a nationwide system of securities clearing and settlement.

To initiate the program, a custodian agreement is signed by the participating organization and the transfer agent. The certificates are deposited at TAC in good deliverable form and withdrawn on written instructions of an authorized person. The shares are kept by the transfer agent in large denominational form usually registered in the nominee name of the participating organization. Some transfer agents require that a legend be placed on the balance certificate. The following is standard:

"This certificate, the property of Abeecee Trust Company, is issued under an agreement dated October 6, 1975 between Abeecee Trust Company and the transfer agent, and is transferable only when properly authorized by Abeecee Trust Company in accordance with the provisions of said agreement, or as otherwise authorized by Abeecee Trust Company. It is not a negotiable instrument for trading purposes and may not be used as settlement for a business transaction or as collateral for any reason."

The TAC arrangement is advantageous to both the transfer agent and the participating organization.

APPENDIX: SEC RULES FOR REGISTRATION OF TRANSFER AGENTS

240.17 Ac2-1 Application for registration of transfer agents.

(a) An application for registration, pursuant to section 17(c) of the Act, of a transfer agent for which the Commission is the appropriate regulatory agency, as defined in section 3(a)(34)(B) of the Act, shall be filed with the Commission on Form TA-1, in accordance with the instructions contained therein and shall become effective on the thirtieth day following the date on which the application is filed, unless the Commission takes affirmative action to accelerate, deny, or postpone such registration in accordance with the provisions of section 17A(c) of the Act.

(b) The filing of any amendment to an application for registration as a transfer agent pursuant to paragraph (a) of this section, which registration has not become effective, shall postpone the effective date of the registration until the thirtieth day following the date on which the amendment is filed, unless the Commission takes affirmative action to accelerate, deny, or postpone the registration in accordance with the provisions of section 17A(c) of the Act.

(c) Within twenty-one calendar days following the date on which any information reported at items 1-6 of Form TA-1 becomes inaccurate, misleading, or incomplete, the registrant shall file an amendment on Form TA-1 correcting the inaccurate, misleading, or incomplete information.

(d) Every registration and amendment filed pursuant to this section shall constitute a "report" or "application" within the meaning of sections 17, 17A(c), and 32(a) of the Act.

240.17Ac301 Withdrawal from registration with the Commission.

(a) Notice of withdrawal from registration as a transfer agent with the Commission pursuant to section 17A(c)(3)(C) of the Act shall be filed on Form TA-W in accordance with the instructions contained thereon.

(b) Except as hereinafter provided, a notice to withdraw from registration filed by a transfer agent pursuant to section 17A(c)(3)(C) of the Act shall become effective on the sixtieth day after the filing thereof with the Commission or within such shorter period of time as the Commission may determine. If a notice to withdraw from registration is filed with the Commission at any time subsequent to the date of issuance of a Commission order instituting proceedings pursuant to section 17A(c)(3)(A) of the Act, or if prior to the effective date of the notice of withdrawal the Commission institutes such a proceeding or a proceeding to impose terms and conditions upon such withdrawal, the notice of withdrawal shall not become effective except at such time and upon such terms and conditions as the Commission deems necessary or appropriate in the public interest, for the protection of Investors, or in furtherance of the purposes of section 17A.

(c) Every notice of withdrawal filed pursuant to this rule shall constitute a "report" within the meaning of sections 17 and 32(a) of the Act.

CHAPTER **17**

Missing, Lost, or Stolen Securities

The business of securities theft has flourished with increasing sophistication over the past several years. The value of securities thefts can be measured in hundreds of millions of dollars per year.

Stock certificates have always been attractive targets for criminals. The business of securities theft and counterfeiting has reached the proportions of an industry, not only in the United States but throughout the world. After a series of Congressional hearings, the Securities and Exchange Commission issued a study, "Unsafe and Unsound Practices of Brokers and Dealers." The report's recommendation, published in 1970, was to establish a legislative framework for the receipt of reports and inquiries concerning missing, lost, stolen, and counterfeit securities.

Pursuant to this report, the Commission has adopted Rule 17f-1, effective October 3, 1977, and January 2, 1978. The rule requires all brokers, dealers, registered transfer agents, clearing organizations, securities, exchanges, and banks to report and make inquiries with respect to missing, lost, counterfeit or stolen securities. The Securities Information Center, Inc. (SIC) is the Commission's designee for the operation of the rule.

OPERATION OF RULE 17f-1

Reporting Institutions

For purposes of the rule, SEC considers the following as reporting institutions:

1. National Securities Exchange
2. Members of stock exchanges
3. Registered securities associations
4. Brokers, dealers

5. Registered transfer agents
6. Registered clearing organizations
7. Participants of clearing organizations
8. Members of Federal Reserve System
9. Banks whose deposits are insured by the FDIC

Reporting Requirements

1. *Stolen securities.* If there is reason to believe that criminal activity is involved, the reporting institution shall report the discovery of the theft to SIC and to the transfer agent within one business day. Appropriate law enforcement agencies must also be notified.
2. *Missing or lost securities.* All missing or lost securities must be reported to SIC and to the transfer agent within two business days of the discovery of the loss.
3. *Securities lost in transit.* Securities lost in transit to customers, transfer agents, banks, brokers or dealers must be reported by the delivering institution no later than two business days after notice of non-receipt or as soon as the certificate numbers of the securities can be ascertained.
4. *Securities considered lost or missing as a result of audit counts.* These losses must be reported no later than ten business days after completion of the audit or as soon as the certificate numbers of the securities can be ascertained.
5. *Delivery through a clearing corporation.* If the securities are not received during the completion of a delivery, the delivering participant must supply the receiving institution with the certificate numbers of the missing securities within two business days after notice of non-receipt. The receiving institution, in turn, must notify SIC and the transfer agent within one business day.
6. *Delivery over the window.* The delivery institution must supply the receiving institution with the certificate numbers of the missing security within two business days after notice of non-receipt. The receiving institution, in turn, must notify SIC and the transfer agent within one business day.
7. *Delivery by mail or via draft.* If payment for these securities is not received within ten business days, the delivering institution must receive a confirmation of non-receipt. The delivering institution, in turn, must notify SIC and the transfer agent within two business days of such confirmation.
8. *Counterfeit securities.* A reporting institution must report to SIC, the transfer agent, and the law enforcement agency the discovery of any counterfeit securities within one business day of such discovery.

Securities Transfer

9. *Recovery*. Recovery of previously reported lost, missing, or stolen securities must be reported to SIC and to the transfer agent within one business day of such recovery or finding. The law enforcement agency must also be notified of the recovery if a report of the stolen security was previously made to the agency.

Method of Reporting

Rule 17f-1 requires the reporting institutions to report on Form X-17F-1A, a form specially designed for this purpose. The form must be signed by an authorized person whose signature is on file. The report must have the following data with respect to each security:

1. Issuer
2. Type of security and series
3. Date of issue
4. Maturity date
5. Denomination
6. Interest rate
7. Certificate number
8. Name of registered holder
9. Distinguishing characteristics if counterfeit
10. Date of discovery of loss or recovery
11. CUSIP and FINS number

A reporting institution may wish to make a preliminary report by telephone or Telex. The preliminary report should include all pertinent data. In all cases, it must be followed by a written report on Form X-17F-1A. SIC will respond by sending a confirmation to the reporting institution.

Requirement for Inquiry

All reporting institutions must ascertain whether any security that comes into their possession has been reported as missing, lost, counterfeit, or stolen. No inquiry is necessary if the security is received directly from the issuer or issuing agent at the time of the issuance of the security, if the security is received from another reporting institution, or if the security is received from a customer of the reporting institution and is registered in the name of the customer or the customer's nominee.

Method of Inquiry

A reporting institution can either be a direct inquirer or an indirect inquirer of the system. Direct inquirers make inquiries by using telephone, Telex, mail, or magnetic tape. An indirect inquirer uses the facility through a direct inquirer. Direct inquirers are assigned appropriate access codes. The code is used to insure that only authorized direct inquirers have access to the system.

Immediately after the inquiry is submitted to the system, SIC will search the file to determine if there is a match of the certificate numbers in the inquiry. If so, the institution is notified immediately of the match and all other pertinent data.

Recordkeeping

The Rule requires that all records and copies of Form X-17F-1A be kept by reporting institutions for three years.

Exceptions to the Rule

The following securities are not subject to provisions of the Rule relating to reporting and inquiry.

1. Registered securities of the United States Government, any agency of the United States Government, the International Bank for Reconstruction and Development, the Inter-American Development Bank or the Asian Development Bank.
2. Counterfeit securities of such organizations.

Replacement of Lost Certificates

The replacement of lost securities is one of the most important functions of stock transfer. There are statutory provisions for the issuance of new certificates replacing those that are lost, stolen or destroyed.

The term "lost" as applied to a security covers physical disappearance of any sort—whether lost in the mail, destroyed by fire or flood, misplaced, embezzled, and so on. It is an inherent right of the stockholder to receive a duplicate certificate after the requirements are satisfied and sufficient indemnity bonds are furnished. Under the Uniform Commercial Code, the issuer is required to issue a new certificate in place of a lost, destroyed, or stolen one without a court order. It cannot refuse to issue a duplicate on the ground that its by-laws contain no authority for such issuance. The by-laws of corporations usually have the following article with respect to lost, stolen, or destroyed certificates:

"Lost, stolen or destroyed certificates may be replaced by the corporation with new certificates of the same number of shares, provided however, that the Corporation shall have received due and prompt notice of the loss, theft, or destruction and provided, further, that the Corporation shall have been furnished with satisfactory evidence of such loss, theft, or destruction or with security sufficient, in the determination of the Board of Directors, to indemnify the Corporation against any claim which might be made by reason of the issue of new certificates for the same shares."

This practice is deeply embedded in corporation law. Section 8–405 of the Uniform Commercial Code states:

1. Where a security has been lost, apparently destroyed, or wrongfully taken and the owner fails to notify the issuer of that fact within a reasonable time after he has notice of it and the issuer registers a transfer of the security before receiving such a notification, the owner is precluded from asserting against the issuer any claim for registering the transfer under the preceding section or any claim to a new security under this section.
2. Where the owner of a security claims that the security has been lost, destroyed or wrongfully taken, the issuer must issue a new security in place of the original security if the owner (a) so requests before the issuer has notice that the security has been acquired by a bona fide purchaser, and (b) files with the issuer a sufficient indemnity bond, and (c) satisfies any other reasonable requirements imposed by the issuer.
3. If, after the issue of the new security, a bona fide purchaser of the original security presents it for registration of transfer, the issuer must register the transfer unless registration would result in over-issue, in which event the issuer's liability is governed by Section 8–104. In addition to any rights on the indemnity bond, the issuer may recover the new security from the person to whom it was issued.

Procedure to Replace Lost Instruments

According to statutes, it is the owner's responsibility to notify the issuer that his certificates are lost. The statute further states that this notification be done within a reasonable time after the owner has discovered the loss.

There are no specific requirements as to form of notification. The stockholder may contact the transfer agent by telephone to place the necessary stop. Most transfer agents insist, however, that the oral communication is confirmed in writing. If the replacement of the security is being sought by the individual stockholder, the owner will apply for an indemnity bond. This involves expense for the premium of the bond, usually between three to five percent of the market value of the security.

If the replacement has been requested by a broker, it will be the broker's responsibility to furnish necessary indemnity bonds. Brokerage houses have blanket insurance coverage for this purpose.

The indemnity bond runs to the issuer, the transfer agent, the registrar, indenture trustees, depositories, fiscal or disbursing agents, and to any other person possibly subject to risk by reason of the issuance of the replacement security. They are all indemnified against any liability or expense to which they may be subjected by reason of the recovery of the original certificates.

The corporation may refuse to issue a new certificate without indemnity. Before the bond is posted it is customary for the owner to execute an affidavit of loss or non-receipt. The affidavit will have statements as to:

1. the ownership of the security,
2. circumstances under which the "loss" occurred,
3. a statement that the security has not been transferred, hypothecated, pledged, or otherwise disposed of,
4. the condition of the security at the time of loss, and
5. an agreement to surrender the original shares, should they reappear.

In these proceedings, it is customary for transfer agents to require a bond with an unlimited penalty. These are called "open penalty bonds." Personal indemnity agreements executed by the stockholder are generally not acceptable to the transfer agent.

Mutilated certificates are often replaced without the necessity of a bond of indemnity. The transfer agent makes the determination based on the condition of the certificate being replaced. If the distinguishing marks, such as certificate numbers, company name, signature, and seal are not destroyed, the transfer agent effects the replacement without a bond.

APPENDIX A

Glossary

A-B Trust: A single trust divided into two portions, *A* and *B*.

Abbreviations: Acceptable and standard abbreviations used in security registrations recommended by the New York Clearing House Association.

Account Executive: A representative of a brokerage firm assigned to handle customers' accounts: broker, customer's broker, customer's man, registered representative.

Accumulation Trust: The income of this trust may be retained in whole or in part instead of being distributed to the beneficiaries.

Administrator: A court-appointed fiduciary who handles the administration of an estate where there is no will.

Affidavit of Domicile: A notarized affidavit executed by the legal representative of an estate reciting the residence of the decedent at the time of death.

Alteration Guarantee: Certification by an authorized person used in an altered assignment.

American Depository Receipts (ADRs): Certificates of deposit issued by an American trust company against the actual foreign shares deposited with the European correspondent of the bank.

Appointment Section: The space on a stock power or on the reverse side of a stock certificate for designation of a power of attorney.

Assigned in Blank: Assignment does not contain the name of the transferee.

Assignment Section: The space on a stock power or on the reverse side of a stock certificate used to designate the name of the transferee or the new owner of the stock in preparation for transfer.

Assignment Separate from Certificate: A stock power or a bond power.

Attorney-in-Fact: Transfer by an agent acting for the stockholder under a power of attorney.

Automatic Transfer: The use of electronic data processing in the security transfer operation. Complete reliance of forms and records generated and issued by the computer.

Bad Delivery: A delivery of securities that does not fulfill the requirements to honor an exchange contract.

Balance Order: A net balance order issued by a clearing house directing a brokerage firm to receive or deliver securities on the trade settlement date.

Bearer Securities: Usually bonds. The instrument does not indicate any registration of ownership.

Beneficiary: The recipient of trust income, benefit plans, or gifts in a will.

Big Board: The New York Stock Exchange.

Blue Chip: Stock in a company known nationally for the quality and wide acceptance of its products and/or services.

Bond: An instrument of debt issued by a corporation, government or municipality.

Bond Power: An assignment separate from certificate used for bonds.

Book-closing Item: See *Record Date*.

Box: The physical location in a brokerage house where securities are kept. These securities are used to meet immediate obligations. Also known as *active box*.

Bring-down: In the transfer of securities in a private name, the change of shares coming back in the name of the brokerage firm.

Buy-in: The procedure through which an exchange contract is closed out by purchasing the security for the seller's account.

Cage: The Cashier's Department of a brokerage house. See also *Cashier's Department*.

Callable: A bond issue all or part of which may be redeemed under definite conditions before maturity. The term also applies to preferred shares.

Cancellation of Certificates: Before issuance of a new certificate, the old certificate, presented to the transfer agent, is cancelled. The cancelled certificates are eventually destroyed after a number of years.

Capital Stock: Generally, the same as common stock. Usually used when the corporation does not have preferred stock.

Cash Account: Purchases and sales of securities at a brokerage firm are handled on a cash basis.

Cash Dividend: Dividends paid in cash to stockholders of record.

Cash Sale or Purchase: The purchase or sale of a security with identical trade and settlement dates.

Cashier's Department: The department in a brokerage firm responsible for securities processing, transfer, receipt and delivery, and control of cash.

Certificate: An instrument that evidences ownership in a corporation or debt of the issuer.

Classes of Stock:
   Common: Represents the principal ownership of the corporation, the first class to be issued and the last to be retired.
   Classified Common Stock: Division of the common stock usually into two classes, class A and class B, to differentiate controlling or voting power.
   Preferred: A cross between a common stock and a bond. Holders receive dividends before profits are distributed to holders of common stock.

Cumulative Preferred: Dividends, if not paid to stockholders, are accumulated and paid at a future date.
Noncumulative Preferred: The stockholder is paid dividends if they are earned, without any cumulative provision.
Participating Preferred: The stockholder will receive a specified dividend. He or she may also be entitled to additional earnings generally available to common stockholders.
Classified Preferred Stock: 4.25 PFD, Class A PFD, Class B PFD, etc. This distinction usually relates to different dividend rates or voting privileges.
Convertible Preferred: This class carries a provision giving a privilege to the stockholder to convert his or her stock into common shares.
Clearing Corporation: A clearing organization affiliated with a securities exchange that expedites the clearance and settlement of securities purchased or sold by members of that exchange.
Clearing Member: A firm entitled to use the full services of a clearing organization.
Clifford Trust: A trust where the original creator gets the property back after a period of time.
Codicil: A document changing or supplementing a last will and testament.
Collateral: Securities or other property pledged by a borrower to secure a loan.
Commingling: When the properties in a community property and separate properties are mixed in one account.
Common Law State: A group of states that take their marital property law from English common law.
Community Property: Properties acquired after marriage are divisible by two between two spouses.
Confirmation: A statement confirming the transaction between a brokerage firm and its clients for the purchase or sale of securities.
Convertible Bond: A bond with privilege of conversion into common shares if the bondholder so desires.
Co-registrar: As in the case of transfer agents, a corporation may employ co-registrars in different cities.
Co-transfer Agents: A corporation may employ co-agents in various cities.
Coupon Bond: A bond with coupons attached. The interest on the bond is collected by detaching the coupons as they become due.
Court Trust: A trust under the jurisdiction of a probate court.
Creation of Stock Certificates: The creation of the stock is authorized by the charter of the corporation and generally empowered by the board of directors.
Credit Department: The department in a brokerage firm that oversees the customer's cash and margin activities.
Crummey Trust: An income trust where the minor has the right to withdraw money.
Curb: The American Stock Exchange.

Custodian to Minor: Under Uniform Gifts to Minors Act, a supervisor of the custodial property acting for the interests of the minor.

D.K.: An abbreviation for "don't know." The term is applied to a delivery of securities between two brokerage firms or used to indicate an invalid comparison.

Date of Assignment: The date when the certificate is endorsed.

Debenture: A form of bond issued without collateral.

Discretionary Trust: A trust in which the trustee has the power to distribute trust income to specified persons as he or she sees fit.

Dividend: The payment authorized by the Board of Directors of a corporation to be distributed to stockholders of record.

Dividend Disbursing Agent: A commercial bank or a professional agency that disburses dividends to the stockholders.

Domicile: The resident state of the decedent or the legal resident state of a stockholder.

Donee: The person to whom a property is given.

Donor: The person who donates a property.

Due Bill: A promissory note issued by a financial organization that promises to pay a dividend upon its receipt from a company. It is payable to the holder on or after the payable date of the dividend.

Duplicate Security: A security issued as a replacement of a lost or stolen certificate.

Endorsement: The signature of the stockholder or an appropriate person on the reverse side of the certificate or on a stock power.

Endorsement by X Mark: An alternate endorsement by a person who is unable to sign his or her name.

Engraved Security: Securities engraved with steel plates using various colors, a requirement by the New York Stock Exchange for listed securities.

Equity: The ownership interest of common and preferred stockholders in a company.

Erasure Guarantee: A guarantee of any irregularity in the assignment by the broker or the commercial bank before a transfer can be effected.

Escheat: The property escheats to the state when a person dies without a will and there are no heirs. The term is also applied to unclaimed properties in a financial institution. After a period of time the institution must turn over the properties to the state.

Estate Tax: Tax imposed by federal and state governments on the estate of a decedent.

Estate Trust: A trust in which a surviving spouse does not receive all the income of the trust. The trust property goes to the decedent's estate.

Execution Date Guarantee: A certification as to the correct date of execution in cases where the date previously affixed is altered.

Executor: A fiduciary named in a will and appointed by the court to handle the administration of an estate.

Exemption Statutes: Statutes governing the fiduciary transfers exonerating the transfer agent in requesting documents otherwise necessary under the common law.

Facsimile Signature: A machine signature acceptable only for members of national securities exchanges.

Fail: An unfulfilled exchange contract. A selling broker fails to deliver the security to the buying broker on the trade settlement date.

Fiduciary: A person acting for another person for the best interest of that person.

Fractional Share: A portion of a share of stock.

Gift Tax: An excise tax on gifts.

Good Delivery: A delivery of securities that fulfills the delivery requirement to honor an exchange contract.

Grantor: See *Trustor*.

Heir: A beneficiary under a will.

Holder of Record: The person whose name appears in the records of the corporation.

Holographic Will: A handwritten will permissible in certain states.

House Account: An account used to maintain trading or security positions of a brokerage firm.

Hypothecation: Pledging of securities as collateral for a loan.

In-and-Out Transfers: A rapid transfer of security. The transfer of the stock is accomplished in one day.

Indenture: An agreement or a statement that includes all the terms of a bond issue or the articles of a trust.

Inheritance Tax Waiver: A document procured from the tax bureau of a state consenting to the transfer of the certificate registered in the name of a decedent.

Inter-Vivos: A living trust, established during the grantor's lifetime. See also *Grantor*.

Interest: The charge made for the use of money. Payments received by a bondholder.

Intestate: A decedent who leaves no will.

Interim Certificate: A temporary certificate issued by the transfer agent.

Irrevocable Trust: A trust that may never be revoked.

Investment Banker: An institution involved primarily in underwriting securities.

Investment Stock: Securities issued under an investment letter. Restriction, in the form of a legend, usually appears on the certificate restricting the security against sale or transfer.

Issuer: Issuer of stock; the corporation.

Joint Tenants with Right of Survivorship: Joint ownership. Upon the death of one party, the survivor takes title of all the shares.

Joint Will: A single will signed by both husband and wife.

Legal Transfer: Transfer of securities registered in the name of decedents, fiduciaries, trusts, bankrupts, corporations, partnerships, clubs, institutions, and so on. Transfer of items not generally recognized as good delivery items.

Letters of Administration: A certificate issued by the court evidencing the appointment of the administrator of an estate.

Letter of Erasure: Letter signed by an authorized person indemnifying the transfer agent and the corporation against liability in effecting a transfer on an erased or altered assignment.

Letter of Indemnity: Letter signed by an authorized person indemnifying the transfer agent and the corporation against liability in correcting the registration of a stock certificate.

Letters Testamentary: A certificate issued by the court evidencing the appointment of the executor of an estate.

Letter of Transmittal: A form used in transmitting securities to the transfer agent. Generally used for exchanges and tenders.

Letter of Trusteeship: A certificate issued by the court evidencing the appointment of the trustee of an estate.

Life Estate: The right to use property for a period of time.

Life Tenant: A person having possession of a life estate.

Listed Security: A security listed on an exchange.

Location of the Transfer Agent: A corporation may employ a trust company to act as its transfer agent located in any city. Certain corporations, such as General Motors and Cities Service, handle their own transfers.

Long: A term used by brokerage firms to indicate ownership of securities.

Making a Market: A broker's activity that establishes and maintains the price on a security.

Margin: In the purchase of securities, margin is the cash or securities that a customer is required to submit to the broker as collateral.

Margin Call: A request to the customer to put up additional cash or securities to meet the margin requirements.

Margin Department: The Credit Department of a brokerage firm.

Maturity: The date on which a loan or a bond comes due.

Member Firm: A brokerage firm that owns a seat on the exchange.

Midwest Stock Exchange: A regional securities auction market located in Chicago.

Minor: In the security industries usage, a minor is a person under twenty-one years of age.

Municipal Bond: A certificate evidencing a portion of a debt of a municipality.

National Association of Securities Dealers (NASD): An association that regulates the over-the-counter securities market.

Negotiable: The condition of a certificate that requires no additional certifications for delivery or transfer.

New York Stock Exchange: The largest securities auction market in the United States.

Nonnegotiable: The condition of a certificate that requires additional certifications or documents to effect a delivery or transfer.

Nuncupative Will: An oral will made a few days before the decedent's death, considered legal in certain states.

O.T.C.: The over-the-counter market.

Odd-Lot: Number of shares less than 100 shares in stocks and below $1,000 value in bonds.

Omnibus Waiver: A waiver affixed to a certificate when the transfer is a nontaxable transaction.
One-and-the-Same Guarantee: A certification used in the event that the signature of the stockholder differs slightly from the name appearing on the face of the certificate.
Option: A contract that grants the holder the right to buy or sell before the expiration date a specified number of shares of a security at a predetermined price.
Optional Dividend: A dividend payable in either stock or cash.
Order Room: A department in a brokerage firm that receives all orders to buy or sell securities.
Orphan's Court: The term for probate court in certain states.
Out-of-Town Bank Guarantee: Assignment guaranteed by an out-of-town bank or trust company not having a local correspondent.
Over-the-Counter Market: Market for unlisted securities.
Over-the-Window: Direct delivery of a security made to the receiving window of a brokerage house.
P & S: See *Purchase and Sales Department.*
Par Value: The face value of a stock; par value has no relation to market value.
Payable Date: The date for payment of a dividend to the stockholder of record.
Payment Order: An order for the payment of dividends to another person, signed by the registered holder of the security.
Power of Attorney: An agent handling the transfer representing the stockholder.
Private Placement: An arrangement made through an investment banker for a sale of a block of securities to a single investor or a group of investors.
Probate: Administration of a decedent's property under the jurisdiction of the court.
Proxy: An authorization that allows a person to act for another.
Purchase and Sales Department: The department in a brokerage firm responsible for trade and customer confirmation, and the liaison with clearing corporations for clearance and settlement activities. Also known as P & S.
Qualitative One-and-the-Same Guarantee: Certification to the effect that the person signing is the same person whose name appears on the certificate.
Receipt: Issued by the transfer agent against the security presented to them, either over-the-window or through the clearing corporation.
Receive and Deliver: The department in a brokerage firm responsible for receipt and delivery of securities.
Record Date: The date when the books of the corporation are closed and stockholders recorded in the books as of the close of that day receive dividends, proxies, rights, or other benefits elected by the board of directors.
Redemption Date: The payment that a company makes under the terms stated on a bond or an indenture. See also *Indenture.*

Registered Bond: A bond with ownership recorded on the face of the certificate.

Registered Owner: The stockholder whose name appears in the registration of the security and in the corporation books.

Registered Representative: See *Account Executive.*

Registrar: An agency employed by a corporation to guard against over-issuance of corporate stock. Cancellations and issuance of certificates by the transfer agent are verified by the registrar.

Regular Way: Regular method of securities delivery on the normal settlement date, five business days after the trade.

Regulation T: A Federal Reserve Board regulation that governs the extension of credit by brokers and securities dealers.

Rejection of Transfer: An incomplete transfer rejected by the transfer agent.

Remainder: The property passing to a new owner after the termination of a life estate.

Remainderman: A person acquiring property known as the *remainder.* See *Remainder.*

Reorganization Department: The department in a brokerage firm responsible for processing mergers, conversions, tenders, and corporate reorganization. Also known as the Exchange Reorganization Department.

Restricted Transfer: The transfer of the security is restricted by reason of a prior notification to the transfer agent; lost or stolen securities, control or investment stock, etc.

Revocable Trust: A trust that may be revoked any time.

Rights: An instrument that allows a stockholder to purchase or to subscribe to additional shares at a price usually lower than the market price.

Round Lot: A full lot: 100 shares in stocks and $1,000 value in bonds.

SEC: The Securities and Exchange Commission.

Safekeeping: A procedure by which securities registered in the name of a customer are kept in safekeeping at a brokerage firm.

Scrip Certificate: A fractional share of a stock issued by a corporation.

Secondary Issue: The sale of a block of stock on a secondary underwriting, usually arranged by an investment banker.

Securities: Instruments representing evidence of ownership.

Segregation: A brokerage firm procedure to safeguard customers' fully paid securities.

Separate Property: In a community property state, a property acquired before marriage.

Settlement Date: The date on which the purchase or sale of a security is settled.

Settlor: See *Trustor.*

Short: A term used to indicate that a customer owes securities to the brokerage firm.

Short Sale: Selling a security without owning it.

Signature Guarantee: Guarantee of the signature of the stockholder by a member of the New York Stock Exchange or a commercial bank in the financial district of New York City.
Situs Certification: A certification by an authorized person reciting the residence of the fiduciary or the physical location of a certificate at the time of death.
Small Estate Statutes: Transfer of securities by fiduciaries without probate proceedings.
Specialist: A member of a securities exchange responsible for maintaining an orderly market in one or more securities.
Sprinkling Trust: A discretionary trust. The trustee can distribute (sprinkle) the income among various beneficiaries.
Stock Certificate: An instrument indicating a stockholder's proportional ownership in a corporation.
Stock Dividend: A dividend paid in stock to stockholders of record.
Stock Power or Fly Power: An assignment separate from certificate.
Stock Record Department: The department in a brokerage firm that reviews and keeps in balance all security positions.
Stock Split: A form of stock dividend.
Stock Transfer Tax: Transfer tax imposed by certain states.
Stop Transfers: A stop order placed on the certificate.
Street: The New York financial community in the Wall Street area.
Street Name: Securities held in the name of the brokerage firm; or securities held in a name other than the owner's.
Subscription: The procedure of buying securities by exercising rights or warrants.
Surety Bond: A bond from a surety company by which the replacement of a lost or stolen security is made possible.
Surrogate Court: Probate court.
Syndicate: A group of brokers involved in underwriting a security issue. See also *Underwriter*.
Tax Stamp: A stamp affixed to certificates to indicate that transfer tax on the security has been paid.
Ten-Year Trust: Clifford Trust.
Tenants by Entirety: A joint ownership acceptable only in certain states, generally based on the marital status of the husband and wife.
Tenants in Common: Effectively, a partnership account, each tenant having a divisible interest.
Testate: Dying with a will.
Testator: The person writing a will.
Totten Trusts: A bank account "in trust for" someone else in which the depositor retains sole ownership of the funds.
Trade Date: The execution date of the trade.
Transfer Agent: A professional agency employed by a corporation to handle the transfer of certificates, conversion of securities, mailings to

stockholders, payments of dividends, stock subscriptions, and maintaining the books of the corporation.

Transfer Fanfold: A transfer instruction form generally used by brokerage office personnel.

Transferee: The assignee.

Transferor: The assignor.

Treasury Stock: Stock issued by a company but held in the company's treasury indefinitely.

True-copy Certification: A certification affixed to a copy of a document to the effect that the document is a true copy of the original and is still in full force and effect.

Trust: A legal entity wherein one or more persons manage properties for the best interest of someone else.

Trustee: The person who manages a trust property. See also *Trustor*.

Trustor: The creator of a trust; settlor, grantor.

Underwriter: A broker who distributes large blocks of securities on a wholesale basis.

Uniform Gifts to Minors Act: A statute adopted by many states to standardize a convenient arrangement for making a gift, often of securities, to a minor.

Uniform Probate Code: A uniform court procedure adopted by certain states to simplify proceedings in the probation of a will.

Unlisted Securities: Securities that are not listed on a national exchange.

Validation Certification: A certification used in cases where the stockholder's signature is placed on the wrong line.

Voting Trust Certificate: A certificate issued in accordance with the terms of the voting trust agreement of a corporation.

Warrant: A certificate entitling the holder to purchase additional shares at a specified price.

When Issued: A term to describe transaction of an unissued security. The security is authorized but at the time of the trade is not issued yet. The trade will be made on a "when, as, and if issued" basis.

Will: A formal instrument giving instructions for the disposal of one's property after death.

Will Contest: Procedure to overturn a decedent's will.

Wire House: A brokerage firm with a branch office network; branches linked together by various communications devices.

Wire Rooms: The order room or the communications center of a brokerage firm.

Witness: A person who witnesses the endorsement of the stockholder.

APPENDIX B

Certifications in Securities Transfer

1. SIGNATURE GUARANTEED

   _____
   A.B. CEE & CO.
   MEMBERS NEW YORK STOCK EXCHANGE

2. We hereby certify that this transaction represents a transfer of assets from the name of a fiduciary covered by the laws of the State of _____ under which the trust/estate is being administered.

   Dated _____

   _____
   Authorized Signature

3. A minor under Uniform Gifts to Minor Act.

4. ERASURE GUARANTEED

   _____
   Authorized Signature

5. We hereby certify that the assignors of the within _____ shares constitute all of the presently acting and authorized trustees.

   _____
   Authorized Signature

6. As joint tenants with right of survivorship but not as tenants in common.

7. TRANSFER ONLY AS DIRECTED ON ATTACHED INSTRUCTIONS OF A.B. CEE & CO.

8. We hereby certify that the registered holder is a partnership and the person endorsing is a general partner with full authority to sell and assign.

   _____
   Authorized Signature

9. It is hereby certified that the delivery and transfer of the attached certificate is not subject to the New York Stock Transfer Tax under Section 28(d) of the Securities Exchange Act of 1934 and no transaction subject to the tax has occurred.

   _____
   Authorized Signature

10. It is hereby certified that the transfer of the accompanying instrument(s) is made under such circumstances as to come

within one of the exceptions specified in section 270(5) of the Tax Law of the State of New York, and that evidence in proof of the exception is maintained by the undersigned and is available for inspection by representatives of the New York State Tax Commission.

Authorized Signature

11. Client insists on registration exactly as shown. Do not alter in any manner.

12. We hereby guarantee the above signature to be a valid endorsement.

Authorized Signature

13.   DELIVERED BY
N.Y. TAX DUE PAID
THRU STK. CLN. CPN.
DEC. 5, 1974
A.B.CEE & CO

14. We certify that the stock shares were purchased after the death of the decedent.

Authorized Signature

15. We hereby guarantee this signature to be that of the person whose name appears on the face of this certificate.

Authorized Signature

16. WE CERTIFY THAT _____ AND _____
ARE ONE AND THE SAME PERSON

Authorized Signature

17. We certify _____ is the legal given name of the transferee.

Authorized Signature

18. We certify that _____ is a Corporation and that this is its complete legal name.

Authorized Signature

19. STOCK POWER ATTACHED TO CTF. NO. ____

20. We hereby certify that the within represents a true and correct copy of the original and is still in full force and effect as of the day _____

Authorized Signature

21. WE CERTIFY THAT

IS NOW BY MARRIAGE

Authorized Signature

22. We guarantee this to be a true copy of the original power of attorney of _____ and the maker is still alive and this power of attorney is in full force and effect as of _____ _____ .

Authorized Signature

23. We certify that _____ is the duly appointed Guardian for _____

Authorized Signature

24. We hereby irrevocably constitute and appoint _____ _____ substitute to transfer the within named stock under the foregoing power of attorney, with like power of substitution.

A. B. CEE & CO.

_____
Authorized Signature

APPENDIX C

SEC Rules of Transfer Agents Turnaround

TEXT OF §§ 240.17Ad-1 THROUGH 17Ad-7

§ 240.17Ad-1 *Definitions.*

As used in this section and §§ 240.17Ad-2, 240.17Ad-3, 240.17Ad-4, 240.17Ad-5, 240.17Ad-6, and 240.17Ad-7:

(a) The term "item" means a certificate or certificates of the same issue of securities covered by one ticket (or, if there is no ticket, presented by one presentor) presented for transfer, or an instruction to a transfer agent which holds securities registered in the name of the presentor to transfer or to make available all or a portion of those securities. In the case of an outside registrar each certificate to be countersigned is an item.

(b) The term "outside registrar" with respect to a transfer item means a transfer agent which performs only the registrar function for the certificate or certificates presented for transfer and includes the persons performing similar functions with respect to debt issues.

(c) An item is "made available" when

(1) In the case of an item for which the services of an outside registrar are not required, or which has been received from an outside registrar after processing, the transfer agent dispatches or mails the item to, or the item is awaiting pick-up by, the presentor or a person designated by the presentor, or

(2) In the case of an item for which the services of an outside registrar are required, the transfer agent dispatches or mails the item to, or the item is awaiting pick-up by, the outside registrar, or

(3) In the case of an item for which an outside registrar has completed processing, the outside registrar dispatches or mails the item to, or the item is awaiting pick-up by, the presenting transfer agent.

(d) The "transfer" of an item is accomplished when, in accordance with the presentor's instructions, all acts necessary to cancel the certificate or certificates presented for transfer and to issue a new certificate or certificates, including the performance of the registrar function, are completed and the item is made available to the presentor by the transfer agent, or when, in accordance with the presentor's instructions, a transfer agent which holds securities registered in the name of the presentor completes all acts necessary to issue a new certificate or certificates representing all or a portion of those securities and makes available the new certificate or certificates to the presentor or a person designated by the presentor or, with respect to those transfers of record ownership to be accomplished without the physical issuance of certificates, completes registration of change in ownership of all or a portion of those securities.

(e) The "turnaround" of an item is completed when transfer is accomplished or, when an outside registrar is involved, the transfer agent in accordance with the presentor's instructions completes all acts necessary to cancel the certificate or certificates presented for transfer and to issue a new certificate or certificates, and the item is made available to an outside registrar.

(f) The term "process" means the accomplishing by an outside registrar of all acts necessary to perform the registrar function and to make available to the presenting transfer agent the completed certificate or certificates or to advise the presenting transfer agent, orally or in writing, why performance of the registrar function is delayed or may not be completed.

(g) The "receipt" of an item or a written inquiry or request occurs when the item or written inquiry or request arrives at the premises at which the transfer agent performs transfer agent functions, as defined in Section 3(a) (25) of the Act.

(h) A "business day" is any day during which the transfer agent is normally open for business and excludes Saturdays, Sundays, and legal holidays, or other holidays normally observed by the transfer agent.

(i) An item is "routine" if it does not (1) require requisitioning certificates of an issue for which the transfer agent, under the terms of its agency, does not maintain a supply of certificates; (2) include a certificate as to which the transfer agent has received notice of a stop order, adverse claim, or any other restriction on transfer; (3) require any additional certificates, documentation, instructions, assignments, guarantees, endorsements, explanations, or opinions of counsel before transfer may be effected; (4) require review of supporting documentation other than assignments, endorsements or stock powers, certified corporate resolutions, signatures, or other common and ordinary guarantees, or appropriate tax, or tax waivers; (5) involve a transfer in connection with a reorganization, tender offer, exchange, redemption, or liquidation; (6) include a warrant, right, or convertible security presented for transfer of record ownership within five business days before any day upon which exercise or conversion privileges lapse or change; (7) include a warrant, right, or convertible security presented for exercise or conversion; or (8) include a security of an issue which within the previous fifteen business days was offered to the public, pursuant to a registration statement effective under the Securities Act of 1933, in an offering not of a continuing nature.

Securities Transfer 177

§ 240.17Ad-2 *Turnaround, processing, and forwarding of items.*

(a) Every registered transfer agent (except when acting as an outside registrar) shall turnaround within three business days of receipt of at least 90 percent of all routine items received for transfer during a month. For the purposes of this paragraph, items received at or before noon on a business day shall be deemed to have been received at noon on that day, and items received after noon on a business day or received on a day not a business day shall be deemed to have been received at noon on the next business day.

(b) Every registered transfer agent acting as an outside registrar shall process at least ninety percent of all items received during a month (1) by the opening of business on the next business day, in the case of items received at or before noon on a business day, and (2) by noon of the next business day, in the case of items received after noon on a business day. For the purposes of paragraphs (b) and (d) of this section, "items received" shall not include any item enumerated in §240.17Ad-1(i) (5), (6), (7), or (8) or any item which is not accompanied by a debit or cancelled certificate. For the purposes of this paragraph, items received on a day not a business day shall be deemed to have been received before noon on the next business day.

(c) Any registered transfer agent which fails to comply with paragraph (a) of this section with respect to any month shall, within ten business days following the end of such month, file with the Commission and the transfer agent's appropriate regulatory agency, if it is not the Commission, a written notice in accordance with paragraph (h) of this section. Such notice shall state the number of routine items and the number of non-routine items received for transfer during the month, the number of routine items which the registered transfer agent failed to turn around in accordance with the requirements of paragraph (a) of this section, the percentage that such routine items represent of all routine items received during the month, the reasons for such failure, the steps which have been taken, are being taken or will be taken to prevent a future failure and the number of routine items, aged in increments of one business day, which as of the close of business on the last business day of the month have been in its possession for more than four business days and have not been turned around.

(d) Any registered transfer agent which fails to comply with paragraph (b) of this section with respect to any month shall, within ten business days following the end of such month, file with the Commission and the transfer agent's appropriate regulatory agency, if it is not the Commission, a written notice in accordance with paragraph (h) of this section. Such notice shall state the number of items received for processing during the month, the number of items which the registered transfer agent failed to process in accordance with the requirements of paragraph (b) of this section, the percentage that such items represent of all items received during the month, the reasons for such failure and the steps which have been taken, are being taken or will be taken to prevent a future failure, and the number of items which as of the close of business on the last business day of the month have been in the transfer agent's possession for more than the time allowed for processing and have not been processed.

(e) All routine items not turned around within three business days of receipt and all items not processed within the periods prescribed by paragraph (b) of this section shall be turned around or processed promptly, and all non-routine items shall receive diligent and continuous attention and shall be turned around as soon as possible.

(f) A registered transfer agent which receives items at locations other than the premises at which it performs transfer agent functions shall have appropriate procedures to assure, and shall assure, that items are forwarded to such premises promptly.

(g) A registered transfer agent which receives processed items from an outside registrar shall have appropriate procedures to assure, and shall assure, that such items are made available promptly to the presentor.

(h) Any notice required by this section or § 240.17Ad-4 shall be filed as follows:

(1) Any notice required to be filed with the Commission shall be filed in triplicate with the principal office of the Commission in Washington, D.C. 20549 and, in the case of a registered transfer agent for which the Commission is the appropriate regulatory agency, an additional copy shall be filed with the Regional Office of the Commission for the region in which the registered transfer agent has its principal office for transfer agent activities.

(2) Any notice required to be filed with the Comptroller of the Currency shall be filed with the Office of the Comptroller of the Currency, Administrator of National Banks, Washington, D.C. 20219.

(3) Any notice required to be filed with the Board of Governors of the Federal Reserve System shall be filed with the Board of Governors of the Federal Reserve System, Washington, D.C. 20251 and with the Federal Reserve Bank of the district in which the registered transfer agent's principal banking operations are conducted.

(4) Any notice required to be filed with the Federal Deposit Insurance Corporation shall be filed with the Federal Deposit Insurance Corporation Washington, D.C. 20249.

§ 240.17Ad-3 *Limitations on expansion.*

(a) Any registered transfer agent which is required to file any notice pursuant to § 240.17Ad-2 (d) or (d) for each of three consecutive months shall not, from the fifth business day after the end of the third such month until the end of the next following period of three successive months during which no such notices have been required:

(1) Initiate the performance of any transfer agent function or activity for an issue for which the transfer agent does not perform, or is not under agreement to perform, transfer agent functions prior to such fifth business day; and

(2) With respect to an issue for which transfer agent functions are being performed on such fifth business day, initiate for that issue the performance of an additional transfer agent function or activity which the transfer agent does not perform, or is not under agreement to perform, prior to such fifth business day.

(b) Any registered transfer agent which for each of two consecutive months fails to turn around at least seventy-five percent of all routine items in accordance with the requirements of § 240.17Ad-2(a) or to process at least seventy-five percent of all items in accordance with the requirements of § 240.17Ad-2 (b) shall be subject to the limitations imposed by paragraph (a) of this section and further shall, within twenty business days after the close of the second such month, send to the chief executive officer of each issuer for which such registered transfer agent acts a copy of the written notice filed pursuant to § 240.17Ad-2(c) or (d) with respect to the second such month.

§ 240.17Ad-4 *Applicability of §§ 240.17Ad-2, 240.17Ad-3 and 240.17Ad-6 (a) (1) through (7) and (11).*

(a) Sections 240.17Ad-2, 240.17Ad-3 and 240.17Ad-6(a) (1) through (7) and (11) shall not apply to interests in limited partnerships, to redeemable securities of investment companies registered under Section 8 of the Investment Company Act of 1940, or to interests in dividend reinvestment programs.

(b) Except as provided in paragraph (c) of this section, §§ 240.17Ad-2 (a), (b), (c), (d) and (h), 240.17Ad-3 and 240.17Ad-6 (a) (2) through (7) and (11) shall not apply to any registered transfer agent which during any six consecutive months shall have received fewer than 500 items for transfer and fewer than 500 items for processing and which, within ten business days following the close of the sixth such consecutive month, shall have filed with its appropriate regulatory agency a notice certifying to that effect (hereinafter an "exempt transfer agent").

(c) Within five business days following the close of each month, every exempt transfer agent shall calculate the number of items which it received during the preceding six months. Whenever any exempt transfer agent receives 500 or more items for transfer or 500 or more items for processing during any six consecutive months, it shall, within ten business days after the end of such month, file with its appropriate regulatory agency notice to that effect. Thereafter, beginning with the first month following the month in which such notice is required to be filed, the registered transfer agent shall no longer be exempt under paragraph (b) of this section from the requirements of §§ 240.17Ad-2 (a), (b), (c), (d) and (h), 240. 17Ad-3 and 240.17Ad-6(a) (2) through (7) and (11). Any registered transfer agent which has ceased to be an exempt transfer agent shall not qualify again for exemption until it has conducted its transfer agent operations pursuant to the foregoing sections for six consecutive months following the month in which it filed the notice required by this paragraph.

§ 240.17Ad-5 *Written inquiries and requests.*

(a) When any person makes a written inquiry to a registered transfer agent concerning the status of an item presented for transfer during the preceding six months by such person or anyone acting on his behalf, which inquiry identifies the issue, the number of shares (or principal amount of debt securities or number of units if relating to any other kind of security) presented, the approximate date of presentment and the name in which it is registered, the registered transfer agent shall, within five business days following receipt of the inquiry, respond, stating whether the item has been received; if received, whether it has been transferred; if received and not transferred, the reason for the delay and what additional matter, if any, is necessary before transfer may be effected; and, if received and transferred, the date and manner in which the completed item was made available, the addressee and address to which it was made available and the number of any new certificate which was registered and the name in which it was registered. If a new certificate is dispatched or mailed to the presentor within five business days following receipt of an inquiry pertaining to that certificate, no further response to the inquiry shall be required pursuant to this paragraph.

(b) When any broker-dealer requests in writing that a registered transfer agent acknowledge the transfer instructions and the possession of a security presented for transfer by such broker-dealer or revalidate a window ticket with respect to such security and the request identifies the issue, the number of shares (or principal amount of debt securities or number of units if relating to any other kind of security), the approximate date of presentment, the certificate number and the name in which it is registered, every registered transfer agent shall, within five business days following receipt of the request, in writing, confirm or deny possession of the security, and if the registered transfer agent has possession (1) acknowledge the transfer instructions or (2) revalidate the window ticket. If a new certificate is dispatched or mailed to the presentor within five business days following receipt of a request pertaining to that certificate, no further response to the inquiry shall be required pursuant to this paragraph.

(c) When any person, or anyone acting under his authority, requests in writing that a transfer agent confirm possession as of a given date of a certificate presented by such person during the thirty days before the date the inquiry is received and the request identifies the issue, the number of shares (or principal amount of debt securities or number of units if relating to any other kind of security), the approximate date of presentment, the certificate number and the name in which the certificate was registered, every registered transfer agent shall, within ten business days following receipt of the request and upon assurance of payment of a reasonable fee if required by such transfer agent, make available a written response to such person, or anyone acting under his authority, confirming or denying possession of such security as of such given date.

(d) When any person requests in writing a transcript of such person's account with respect to a particular issue, either as the account appears currently or as it appeared on a specific date not more than six months prior to the date

Securities Transfer 181

the registered transfer agent receives the request, every registered transfer agent shall, within twenty business days following receipt of the request and upon assurance of payment of a reasonable fee if required by such transfer agent, make available to such person a transcript, ledger or statement of account in sufficient detail to permit reconstruction of such account as of the date for which the transcript was requested.

§ 240.17Ad-6 *Recordkeeping.*

(a) Every registered transfer agent shall make and keep current the following:

(1) A receipt, ticket, schedule, log or other record showing the business day each routine item and each non-routine item is (i) received from the presentor and, if applicable, from the outside registrar and (ii) made available to the presentor and, if applicable, to the outside registrar;

(2) A log, tally, journal, schedule or other record showing for each month:
(i) The number of routine items received;
(ii) The number of routine items received during the month that were turned around within three business days of receipt;
(iii) The number of routine items received during the month that were not turned around within three business days of receipt;
(iv) The number of non-routine items received during the month;
(v) The number of non-routine items received during the month that were turned around;
(vi) The number of routine items that, as of the close of business on the last business day of each month, have been in such registered transfer agent's possession for more than four business days, aged in increments of one business day (beginning on the fifth business day); and
(vii) The number of non-routine items in such registered transfer agent's possession as of the close of business on the last business day of each month;

(3) With respect to items for which the registered transfer agent acts as an outside registrar;
(i) A receipt, ticket, schedule, log or other record showing the date and time:
(A) Each item is (*1*) received from the presenting transfer agent and (*2*) made available to the presenting transfer agent;
(B) Each written or oral notice of refusal to perform the registrar function is made available to the presenting transfer agent (and the substance of the notice); and
(ii) A log, tally, journal schedule or other record showing for each month:
(A) The number of items received;
(B) The number of items processed within the time required by § 240.17Ad-2(b); and
(C) The number of items not processed within the time required by § 240.17Ad-2(b);

(4) A record of calculations demonstrating the registered transfer agent's monitoring of its performance under § 240.17Ad-2(a) and (b);

(5) A copy of any written notice filed pursuant to § 240.17Ad-2;

(6) Any written inquiry or request, including those not subject to the requirements of § 240.17Ad-5, concerning an item, showing the date received; a copy of any written response to an inquiry or request, showing the date dispatched or mailed to the presentor; if no response to an inquiry or request was made, the date the certificate involved was made available to the presentor; or, in the case of an inquiry or request under § 240.17Ad-5(a) responded to by telephone, a telephone log or memorandum showing the date and substance of any telephone response to the inquiry;

(7) A log, journal, schedule or other record showing the number of inquiries subject to § 240.17Ad-5 (a), (b), (c) and (d) received during each month but not responded to within the required time frames and the number of such inquiries pending as of the close of business on the last business day of each month;

(8) Any document, resolution, contract, appointment or other writing, and any supporting document, concerning the appointment and the termination of such appointment of such registered transfer agent to act in any capacity for any issue on behalf of the issuer, on behalf of itself as the issuer or on behalf of any person who was engaged by the issuer to act on behalf of the issuer;

(9) Any record of an active (i.e., unreleased) stop order, notice of adverse claim or any other restriction on transfer;

(10) A copy of any transfer journal and registrar journal prepared by such registered transfer agent; and

(11) Any document upon which the transfer agent bases its determination that an item received for transfer was received in connection with a reorganization, tender offer, exchange, redemption, liquidation, conversion or the sale of securities registered pursuant to the Securities Act of 1933 and, accordingly, was not routine under § 240.17Ad-1(i) (5) or (8).

(b) Every registered transfer agent which, under the terms of its agency, maintains securityholder records for an issue or which acts as a registrar for an issue shall, with respect to such issue, obtain from the issuer or its transfer agent and retain documentation setting forth the total number of shares or principal amount of debt securities or total number of units if relating to any other kind of security authorized and the total issued and outstanding pursuant to issuer authorization.

(c) Every registered transfer agent which, under the terms of its agency, maintains securityholder records for an issue shall, with respect to such issue, retain each cancelled registered bond, debenture, share, warrant or right, other registered evidence of indebtedness, or other certificate of ownership and all accompanying documentation, except legal papers returned to the presentor.

Securities Transfer

§ 240.17Ad-7 Record retention.

(a) The records required by § 240.17-Ad-6(a), (1), (3)(i), (6) or (11) shall be maintained for a period of not less than two years, the first six months in an easily accessible place.

(b) The records required by § 240.17Ad-6(a) (2), (3)(ii), (4), (5) or (7) shall be maintained for a period of not less than two years, the first year in an easily accessible place.

(c) The records required by § 240.17Ad-6(a) (8), (9) and (10) and (b) shall be maintained in an easily accessible place during the continuance of the transfer agency and shall be maintained for one year after termination of the transfer agency.

(d) The records required by § 240.17Ad-6(c) shall be maintained for a period of not less than six years, the first six months in an easily accessible place.

(e) Every registered transfer agent shall maintain in an easily accessible place:

(1) All records required under § 240.17f-2(d) until at least three years after the termination of employment of those persons required by § 240.17f-2 to be fingerprinted; and

(2) All records required pursuant to § 240.17f-2(e) for three years.

(f) The records required to be maintained pursuant to § 240.17Ad-6 may be produced or reproduced on microfilm and be preserved in that form for the time required by § 240.17Ad-7. If such microfilm substitution for hard copy is made by a registered transfer agent, it shall:

(1) At all times have available for examination by the Commission and the appropriate regulatory agency for such transfer agent, facilities for immediate, easily readable projection of the microfilm and for producing easily readable facsimile enlargements;

(2) Arrange the records and index and file the films in such a manner as to permit the immediate location of any particular record;

(3) Be ready at all times to provide, and immediately provide, any facsimile enlargement which the Commission and the appropriate regulatory agency by their examiners or other representatives may request; and

(4) For the period for which the microfilmed records are required to be maintained, store separately from the original microfilm records a copy of the microfilm records.

(g) If the records required to be maintained and preserved by a registered transfer agent pursuant to the requirements of §§ 240.17Ad-6 and 240.17Ad-7 are maintained and preserved on behalf of the registered transfer agent by an outside service bureau, other recordkeeping service or the issuer, the registered transfer agent shall obtain, from such outside service bureau, other recordkeeping service or the issuer, an agreement, in writing, to the effect that:

(1) Such records are subject at any time, or from time to time, to reasona-

ble periodic, special, or other examinations by representatives of the Commission and the appropriate regulatory agency for such registered transfer agent, if it is not the Commission; and

(2) The outside service bureau, recordkeeping service, or issuer will furnish to the Commission and the appropriate regulatory agency, upon demand, at either the principal office or at any regional office, complete, correct and current hard copies of any and all such records.

(h) When a registered transfer agent ceases to perform transfer agent functions for an issue, the responsibility of such transfer agent under § 240.17Ad-7 to retain the records required to be made and kept current under § 240.17Ad-6(a) (1), (6), (9), (10) and (11), (b) and (c) shall end upon the delivery of such records to the successor transfer agent.

Accordingly, the Commission hereby adopts §§ 240.17Ad-1, 240.17Ad-2, 240.17Ad-3, 240.17Ad-4, 240.17Ad-5, 240.17Ad-6 and 240.17Ad-7.

APPENDIX D

SEC Lost and Stolen Securities Program

§ 240.17f-1 *Requirements for reporting and inquiry with respect to missing, lost, counterfeit or stolen securities.*

(a) *Definitions*—(1) *Reporting institution.* For purposes of this section, the term "reporting institution" shall include every national securities exchange, member thereof, registered securities association, broker, dealer, municipal securities dealer, registered transfer agent, registered clearing agency, participant therein, member of the Federal Reserve System and bank whose deposits are insured by the Federal Deposit Insurance Corporation.

(2) *Appropriate instrumentality.* For purposes of this section the term "appropriate instrumentality" shall mean:

(i) Any Federal Reserve Bank or Branch thereof with respect to securities issued by:

(A) The United States Government,

(B) Any agency of instrumentality of the United States Government,

(C) The International Bank for Reconstruction and Development,

(D) The Inter-American Bank, or

(E) The Asian Development Bank, and

(ii) The Securities and Exchange Commission with respect to all other securities.

(b) *Reporting requirements*—(1) *Stolen securities.* (i) Every reporting institution shall report to the appropriate instrumentality and to a registered transfer agent for the issue the discovery of the theft or loss of any security where there is substantial basis for believing that criminal activity was involved. Such report shall be made within one business day of the discovery and, if the certificate numbers of the securities cannot be ascertained at that time, they shall be reported as soon thereafter as possible.

(ii) Every reporting institution shall promptly report to the appropriate law enforcement agency upon the discovery of the theft or loss of any security where there is substantial basis for believing that criminal activity was involved.

(2) *Missing or lost securities.* Every reporting institution shall report to the appropriate instrumentality and to a registered transfer agent for the issue the discovery of the loss of any security where criminal actions are not suspected when the security has been missing or lost for a period of two business days. Such report shall be made within one business day of the end of such period except that:

(i) Securities lost in transit to customers, transfer agents, banks, brokers or dealers shall be reported by the delivering institution no later than two business days after notice of non-receipt or as soon after such notice as the certificate numbers of the securities can be ascertained.

(ii) Securities considered lost or missing as a result of securities counts or verifications required by rule, regulation or otherwise (e.g. dividend record date verification made as a result of firm policy or internal audit function report) shall be reported no later than ten business days after completion of such securities count or verification or as soon after such count or verification as the certificate numbers of the securities can be ascertained.

(iii) Securities not received during the completion of a delivery, deposit or withdrawal shall be reported in the following manner:

(A) Where delivery of securities is through clearing agency, the delivering institution shall supply the receiving institution the certificate number of the security within two business days from the date of request from the receiving institution. The receiving institution shall report within one business day of notification of the certificate number;

(B) Where the delivery of securities is over the window and where the delivering institution has a receipt, the delivering institution shall supply the receiving institution the certificate numbers of the securities within two business days from the date of request from the receiving institution. The receiving institution shall report within one business day of notification of the certificate number;

(C) Where the delivery of securities is over the window and where the delivering institution has no receipt, the delivering institution shall report within two business days of notification of non-receipt by the receiving institution; or

(D) Where delivery of securities is made by mail or via draft, if payment is not received within ten business days, the delivering institution shall confirm with the receiving institution the failure to receive such delivery; if confirmation shows non-receipt, the delivering institution shall report within two business days of such confirmation.

(3) *Counterfeit securities.* Every reporting institution shall report the discovery of any counterfeit security to the appropriate instrumentality and the appropriate law enforcement agency within one business day of such discovery.

(4) *Recovery.* Every reporting institution shall report the recovery or finding of any security previously reported missing, lost or stolen pursuant to this section to the appropriate instrumentality and to a registered transfer agent for the issue within one business day of such recovery or finding. If a report of stolen securities was made to the appropriate law enforcement agency, a report of

such recovery shall also be made to such agency. Recovery may only be reported by the institution which reported the security as missing, lost or stolen.

(5) *Information to be reported.* All reports made pursuant to this section shall include, if applicable or available, the following information with respect to each security:

(i) Issuer;
(ii) Type of security and series;
(iii) Date of issue;
(iv) Maturity date;
(v) Denomination;
(vi) Interest rate;
(vii) Certificate number, including alphabetical prefix or suffix;
(viii) Name in which registered;
(ix) Distinguishing characteristics, if counterfeit;
(x) Date of discovery of loss or recovery;
(xi) CUSIP number; and
(xii) FINS number.

(6) *Forms.* All reports made pursuant to this section shall be made on Form X-17F-1A.

(c) *Required inquiries.* (1) Every reporting institution shall inquire of the appropriate instrumentality with respect to every security which comes into its possession or keeping, whether by pledge, transfer or otherwise, to ascertain whether such security has been reported as missing, lost, counterfeit or stolen, unless

(i) The security is received directly from the issuer or issuing agent at issuance:

(ii) The security is received from another reporting institution or Federal Reserve Bank in its capacity as fiscal agent;

(iii) The security is received from a customer of the reporting institution and is registered in the name of such customer or its nominee.

(2) *Form of inquiry.* Inquiries shall be made in such manner as prescribed by the appropriate instrumentality.

(d) *Permissive reports and inquiries.* Every reporting institution may report to or inquire of the appropriate instrumentality with respect to any security not otherwise required by this section to be the subject of a report or inquiry. The Commission on written request or upon its own motion may permit reports to and inquiries of the system by any other person or entity upon such terms and conditions as it deems appropriate and necessary in the public interest and for the protection of investors.

(e) *Exemptions.* Registered securities of the United States Government, any agency or instrumentality of the United States Government, the International Bank for Reconstruction and Development, the Inter-American Development Bank, or the Asian Development Bank, and counterfeit securities of such entities are not subject to the provisions of this section relating to reporting and inquiry with the appropriate instrumentality.

(f) *Recordkeeping.* Every reporting institution shall maintain and preserve in an easily accessible place for three years copies of all Forms X-17F-1A filed pursuant to this section and all confirmations or other information received from the appropriate instrumentality or its designee as a result of inquiry.

APPENDIX E

Uniform Commercial Code

ARTICLE 8
INVESTMENT SECURITIES

Part 1 Short Title and General Matters

Short Title
Sec. 8–101. This Article shall be known and may be cited as Uniform Commercial Code—Investment Securities.

Definitions and Index of Definitions
Sec. 8–102. (1) In this Article unless the context otherwise requires

(a) A "Security" is an instrument which

(i) is issued in bearer or registered form; and

(ii) is of a type commonly dealt in upon securities exchanges or markets or commonly recognized in any area in which it is issued or dealt in as a medium for investment; and

(iii) is either one of a class or series or by its terms is divisible into a class or series of instruments; and

(iv) evidences a share, participation or other interest in property or in an enterprise or evidences an obligation of the issuer.

(b) A writing which is a security is governed by this Article and not by Uniform Commercial Code-Commercial Paper even though it also meets the requirements of that Article. This Article does not apply to money.

(c) A security is in "registered form" when it specifies a person entitled to the security or to the rights it evidences and when its transfer may be registered upon books maintained for that purpose by or on behalf of an issuer or the security so states.

(d) A security is in "bearer form" when it runs to bearer according to its terms and not by reason of any indorsement.

(2) A "subsequent purchaser" is a person who takes other than by original issue.

(3) A "clearing corporation" is a corporation all of the capital stock of which is held by or for a national securities exchange or association registered under a statute of the United States such as the Securities Exchange Act of 1934.

(4) A "custodian bank" is any bank or trust company which is supervised and examined by state or federal authority having supervision over banks and which is acting as custodian for a clearing corporation.

(5) Other definitions applying to this Article or to specified Parts thereof and the sections in which they appear are:

Adverse claim	Section 8-301.
Bona fide purchaser	Section 8-302.
Broker	Section 8-303.
Guarantee of the signature	Section 8-402.
Intermediary bank	Section 4-105.
Issuer	Section 8-201.
Overissue	Section 8-104.

(6) In addition Article 1 contains general definitions and principles of construction and interpretation applicable throughout this Article.

Issuer's Lien

Sec. 8–103. A lien upon a security in favor of an issuer thereof is valid against a purchaser only if the right of the issuer to such lien is noted conspicuously on the security.

Effect of Overissue; "Overissue"

Sec. 8–104. (1) The provisions of this Article which validate a security or compel its issue or reissue do not apply to the extent that validation, issue or reissue would result in overissue; but

(a) if an identical security which does not constitute an overissue is reasonably available for purchase, the person entitled to issue or validation may compel the issuer to purchase and deliver such a security to him against surrender of the security, if any, which he holds; or

(b) if a security is not so available for purchase, the person entitled to issue or validation may recover from the issuer the price he or the last purchaser for value paid for it with interest from the date of his demand.

(2) "Overissue" means the issuer of securities in excess of the amount which the issuer has corporate power to issue.

Securities Transfer

Securities Negotiable; Presumptions
Sec. 8–105. (1) Securities governed by this Article are negotiable instruments.

(2) In any action on a security

(a) unless specifically denied in the pleadings, each signature on the security or in a necessary indorsement is admitted;

(b) when the effectiveness of a signature is put in issue the burden of establishing it is on the party claiming under the signature but the signature is presumed to be genuine or authorized;

(c) when signatures are admitted or established production of the instrument entitles a holder to recover on it unless the defendant establishes a defense or a defect going to the validity of the security; and

(d) after it is shown that a defense or defect exists the plaintiff has the burden of establishing that he or some person under whom he claims is a person against whom the defense or defect is ineffective (Section 8–202).

Applicability
Sec. 8–106. The validity of a security and the rights and duties of the issuer with respect to registration of transfer are governed by the law (including the conflict of laws rules) of the jurisdiction of organization of the issuer.

Securities Deliverable; Action for Price
Sec. 8–107. (1) Unless otherwise agreed and subject to any applicable law or regulation respecting short sales, a person obligated to deliver securities may deliver any security of the specified issue in bearer form or registered in the name of the transferee or endorsed to him or in blank.

(2) When the buyer fails to pay the price as it comes due under a contract of sale the seller may recover the price

(a) of securities accepted by the buyer; and

(b) of other securities if efforts at their resale would be unduly burdensome or if there is no readily available market for their resale.

Part 2 Issue—Issuer

"Issuer"
Sec. 8–201. (1) With respect to obligations or defenses to a security "issuer" includes a person who

(a) places or authorizes the placing of his name on a security (otherwise than as authenticating trustee, registrar, transfer agent or the like) to evidence that it represents a share, participation or other interest in his property or in an enterprise or to evidence his duty to perform an obligation evidenced by the security; or

(b) directly or indirectly creates fractional interests in his rights or property which fractional interests are evidenced by securities; or

(c) becomes responsible for or in place of any other person described as an issuer in this section.

(2) With respect to obligations on or defenses to a security a guarantor is an issuer to the extent of his guaranty whether or not his obligation is noted on the security.

(3) With respect to registration of transfer (Part 4 of this Article) "issuer" means a person on whose behalf transfer books are maintained.

Issuer's Responsibility and Defenses; Notice of Defect or Defense
Sec. 8–202. (1) Even against a purchaser for value and without notice, the terms of a security include those stated on the security and those made part of the security by reference to another instrument, indenture or document or to a constitution, statute, ordinance, rule, regulation, order or the like to the extent that the terms so referred to do not conflict with the stated terms. Such a reference does not of itself charge a purchaser for value with notice of a defect going to the validity of the security even though the security expressly states that a person accepting it admits such notice.

(2) (a) A security other than one issued by a government or governmental agency or unit even though issued with a defect going to its validity is valid in the hands of a purchaser for value and without notice of the particular defect unless the defect involves a violation of constitutional provisions in which case the security is valid in the hands of a subsequent purchaser for value and without notice of the defect.

(b) The rule of subparagraph (a) applies to an issuer which is a government or governmental agency or unit only if either there has been substantial compliance with the legal requirements governing the issue or the issuer has received a substantial consideration for the issue as a whole or for the particular security and a stated purpose of the issue is one for which the issuer has power to borrow money or issue the security.

(3) Except as otherwise provided in the case of certain unauthorized signatures on issue (Section 8–205), lack of genuineness of a security is a complete defense even against a purchaser for value and without notice.

(4) All other defenses of the issuer including nondelivery and conditional delivery of the security are ineffective against a purchaser for value who has taken without notice of the particular defense.

(5) Nothing in this section shall be construed to affect the right of a party to a "when, as, and if issued" or a "when distributed" contract to cancel the contract in the event of a material change in the character of the security which is the subject of the contract or in the plan or arrangement pursuant to which such security is to be issued or distributed.

Staleness as Notice of Defects or Defenses
Sec. 8–203. (1) After an act or event which creates a right to immediate performance of the principal obligation evidenced by the security or which sets a date on or after which the security is to be presented or surrendered for redemption or exchange, a purchaser is charged with notice of any defect in its issue or defense of the issuer

(a) if the act or event is one requiring the payment of money or the delivery of securities or both on presentation or surrender of the security and such funds or securities are available on the date set for payment or exchange and he takes the security more than one year after that date; and

(b) if the act or event is not covered by paragraph (a) and he takes the security more than two years after the date set for surrender or presentation or the date on which such performance became due.

(2) A call which has been revoked is not without subsection (1).

Effect of Issuer's Restrictions on Transfer
Sec. 8–204. Unless noted conspicuously on the security a restriction on transfer imposed by the issuer even though otherwise lawful is ineffective except against a person with actual knowledge of it.

Effect of Unauthorized Signature on Issue
Sec. 8–205. An unauthorized signature placed on a security prior to or in the course of issue is ineffective except that the signature is effective in favor of a purchaser for value and without notice of the lack of authority if the signing has been done by

(a) an authenticating trustee, registrar, transfer agent or other person entrusted by the issuer with the signing of the security or of similar securities or their immediate preparation for signing; or

(b) an employee of the issuer or of any of the foregoing entrusted with responsible handling of the security.

Completion or Alteration of Instrument
Sec. 8–206. (1) Where a security contains the signatures necessary to its issue or transfer but is incomplete in any other respect

(a) any person may complete it by filling in the blanks as authorized; and

(b) even though the blanks are incorrectly filled in, the security as completed is enforceable by a purchaser who took it for value and without notice of such incorrectness.

(2) A complete security which has been improperly altered even though fraudulently remains enforceable but only according to its original terms.

Rights of Issuer with Respect to Registered Owners
Sec. 8–207. (1) Prior to due presentment for registration of transfer of a security in registered form the issuer or indenture trustee may treat the regis-

tered owner as the person exclusively entitled to vote, to receive notifications and otherwise to exercise all the rights and powers of an owner.

(2) Nothing in this Article shall be construed to affect the liability of the registered owner of a security for calls, assessments or the like.

Effect of Signature of Authenticating Trustee, Registrar or Transfer Agent
Sec. 8–208. (1) A person placing his signature upon a security as authenticating trustee, registrar, transfer agent or the like warrants to a purchaser for value without notice of the particular defect that

(a) the security is genuine; and

(b) his own participation in the issue of the security is within his capacity and within the scope of the authorization received by him from the issuer; and

(c) he has reasonable grounds to believe that the security is in the form and within the amount the issuer is authorized to issue.

(2) Unless otherwise agreed, a person by so placing his signature does not assume responsibility for the validity of the security in other respects.

Part 3 Purchase

Rights Acquired by Purchaser; "Adverse Claim";
Title Acquired by Bona Fide Purchaser
Sec. 8–301. (1) Upon delivery of a security the purchaser acquires the rights in the security which his transferor had or had actual authority to convey except that a purchaser who has himself been a party to any fraud or illegality affecting the security or who as a prior holder had notice of an adverse claim cannot improve his position by taking from a later bona fide purchaser. "Adverse claim" includes a claim that a transfer was or would be wrongful or that a particular adverse person is the owner of or has an interest in the security.

(2) A bona fide purchaser in addition to acquiring the rights of a purchaser who acquires the security free of any adverse claim.

(3) A purchaser of a limited interest acquires rights only to the extent of the interest purchased.

" 'Bona Fide' Purchaser"
Sec. 8–302. A "bona fide purchaser" is a purchaser for value in good faith and without notice of any adverse claim who takes delivery of a security in bearer form or of one in registered form issued to him or indorsed to him or in blank.

"Broker"
Sec. 8–303. "Broker" means a person engaged for all or part of his time in the business of buying and selling securities, who in the transaction concerned acts for, or buys a security from or sells a security to a customer.

Nothing in this Article determines the capacity in which a person acts for purposes of any other statute or rule to which such person is subject.

Notice to Purchaser of Adverse Claims

Sec. 8–304. (1) A purchaser (including a broker for the seller or buyer but excluding an intermediary bank) of a security is charged with notice of adverse claims if

(a) the security whether in bearer or registered form has been indorsed "for collection" or "for surrender" or for some other purpose not involving transfer; or

(b) the security is in bearer form and has on it an unambiguous statement that it is the property of a person other than the transferor. The mere writing of a name on a security is not such a statement.

(2) The fact that the purchaser (including a broker for the seller or buyer) has notice that the security is held for a third person or is registered in the name of or indorsed by a fiduciary does not create a duty of inquiry into the rightfulness of the transfer or constitute notice of adverse claims. If, however, the purchaser (excluding an intermediary bank) has knowledge that the proceeds are being used or that the transaction is for the individual benefit of the fiduciary or otherwise in breach of duty, the purchaser is charged with notice of adverse claims.

Staleness as Notice of Adverse Claims

Sec. 8–305. An act or event which creates a right to immediate performance of the principal obligation evidenced by the security or which sets a date on or after which the security is to be presented or surrendered for redemption or exchange does not of itself constitute any notice of adverse claims except in the case of a purchase

(a) after one year from any date set for such presentment or surrender for redemption or exchange; or

(b) after six months from any date set for payment of money against presentation or surrender of the security if funds are available for payment on that date.

Warranties on Presentment and Transfer

Sec. 8–306. (1) A person who presents a security for registration of transfer or for payment or exchange warrants to the issuer that he is entitled to the registration, payment or exchange. But a purchaser for value without notice of adverse claims who receives a new, reissued or re-registered security on registration of transfer warrants only that he has no knowledge of any unauthorized signature (Section 8–311) in a necessary indorsement.

(2) A person by transferring a security to a purchaser for value warrants only that

(a) his transfer is effective and rightful; and

(b) the security is genuine and has not been materially altered; and

(c) he knows no fact which might impair the validity of the security.

(3) Where a security is delivered by an intermediary known to be entrusted with delivery of the security on behalf of another or with collection of a draft or other claim against such delivery, the intermediary by such delivery warrants only his own good faith and authority even though he has purchased or made advances against the claim to be collected against the delivery.

(4) A pledgee or other holder for security who redelivers the security received, or after payment and on order of the debtor delivers that security to a third person makes only the warranties of an intermediary under subsection (3).

(5) A broker gives to his customer and to the issuer and a purchaser the warranties provided in this section and has the rights and privileges of a purchaser under this section. The warranties of and in favor of the broker acting as an agent are in addition to applicable warranties given by and in favor of his customer.

Effect of Delivery Without Indorsement; Right to Compel Indorsement
Section 8–307. Where a security in registered form has been delivered to a purchaser without a necessary indorsement he may become a bona fide purchaser only as of the time the indorsement is supplied, but against the transferor the transfer is complete upon delivery and the purchaser has a specifically enforceable right to have any necessary indorsement supplied.

Indorsement, How Made; Special Indorsement;
Indorser Not a Guarantor; Partial Assignment
Sec. 8–308. (1) An indorsement of a security in registered form is made when an appropriate person signs on it or on a separate document an assignment or transfer of the security or a power to assign or transfer it or when the signature of such person is written without more upon the back of the security.

(2) An indorsement may be in blank or special. An indorsement in blank includes an indorsement to bearer. A special indorsement specifies the person to whom the security is to be transferred, or who has power to transfer it. A holder may convert a blank indorsement into a special indorsement.

(3) "An appropriate person" in subsection (1) means

(a) the person specified by the security or by special indorsement to be entitled to the security; or

(b) where the person so specified is described as a fiduciary but is no longer serving in the described capacity,—either that person or his successor; or

(c) where the security or indorsement so specifies more than one person as fiduciaries and one or more are no longer serving in the described capacity,— the remaining fiduciary or fiduciaries, whether or not a successor has been appointed or qualified; or

(d) where the person so specified is an individual and is without capacity to act by virtue of death, incompetence, infancy or otherwise—his executor, administrator, guardian or like fiduciary; or

(e) where the security or indorsement so specifies more than one person as tenants by the entirety or with right of survivorship and by reason of death all cannot sign,—the survivor or survivors; or

(f) a person having power to sign under applicable law or controlling instrument; or

(g) to the extent that any of the foregoing persons may act through an agent,—his authorized agent.

(4) Unless otherwise agreed the indorser by his indorsement assumes no obligation that the security will be honored by the issuer.

(5) An indorsement purporting to be only of part of a security representing units intended by the issuer to be separately transferable is effective to the extent of the indorsement.

(6) Whether the person signing is appropriate is determined as of the date of signing and an indorsement by such a person does not become unauthorized for the purposes of this Article by virtue of any subsequent change of circumstances.

(7) Failure of a fiduciary to comply with a controlling instrument or with the law of the state having jurisdiction of the fiduciary relationship, including any law requiring the fiduciary to obtain court approval of the transfer, does not render his indorsement unauthorized for the purposes of this Article.

Effect of Indorsement Without Delivery
Sec. 8–309. An indorsement of a security whether special or in blank does not constitute a transfer until delivery of the security on which it appears or if the indorsement is on a separate document until delivery of both the document and the security.

Indorsement of Security in Bearer Form
Sec. 8–310. An indorsement of a security in bearer form may give notice of adverse claims (Section 8–304) but does not otherwise affect any right to registration the holder may possess.

Effect of Unauthorized Indorsement
Sec. 8–311. Unless the owner has ratified an unauthorized indorsement or is otherwise precluded from asserting its ineffectiveness

(a) he may assert its ineffectiveness against the issuer or any purchaser other than a purchaser for value and without notice of adverse claims who has in good faith received a new, reissued or re-registered security on registration of transfer; and

(b) an issuer who registers the transfer of a security upon the unauthorized indorsement is subject to liability for improper registration (Section 8–404).

Effect of Guaranteeing Signature or Indorsement
Sec. 8–312. (1) Any person guaranteeing a signature of an indorser of a security warrants that at the time of signing

(a) the signature was genuine; and

(b) the signer was an appropriate person to indorse (Section 8-308); and

(c) the signer has legal capacity to sign. But the guarantor does not otherwise warrant the rightfulness of the particular transfer.

(2) Any person may guarantee an indorsement of a security and by so doing warrants not only the signature (subsection 1) but also the rightfulness of the particular transfer in all respects. But no issuer may require a guarantee of indorsement as a condition to registration of transfer.

(3) The foregoing warranties are made to any person taking or dealing with the security in reliance on the guarantee and the guarantor is liable to such person for any loss resulting from breach of the warranties.

When Delivery to the Purchaser Occurs; Purchaser's Broker as Holder
Sec. 8-313. (1) Delivery to a purchaser occurs when

(a) he or a person designated by him acquires possession of a security; or

(b) his broker acquires possession of a security specially indorsed to or issued in the name of the purchaser; or

(c) his broker sends him confirmation of the purchase and also by book entry or otherwise identifies a specific security in the broker's possession as belonging to the purchaser; or

(d) with respect to an identified security to be delivered while still in the possession of a third person when that person acknowledges that he holds for the purchaser; or

(e) appropriate entries on the books of a clearing corporation are made under Section 8-320.

(2) The purchaser is the owner of a security held for him by his broker, but is not the holder except as specified in subparagraphs (b), (c) and (e) of subsection (1). Where a security is part of a fungible bulk the purchaser is the owner of a proportionate property interest in the fungible bulk.

(3) Notice of an adverse claim received by the broker or by the purchaser after the broker takes delivery as a holder for value is not effective either as to the broker or as to the purchaser. However, as between the broker and the purchaser the purchaser may demand delivery of an equivalent security as to which no notice of an adverse claim has been received.

Duty to Deliver, When Completed
Sec. 8-314. (1) Unless otherwise agreed where a sale of a security is made on an exchange or otherwise through brokers

(a) the selling customer fulfills his duty to deliver when he places such a security in the possession of the selling broker or of a person designated by the broker or if requested causes an acknowledgment to be made to the selling broker that it is held for him; and

(b) the selling broker including a correspondent broker acting for a selling customer fulfills his duty to deliver by placing the security or a like security in the possession of the buying broker or a person designated by him or by effecting clearance of the sale in accordance with the rules of the exchange on which the transaction took place.

(2) Except as otherwise provided in this section and unless otherwise agreed, a transferor's duty to deliver a security under a contract of purchase is not fulfilled until he places the security in form to be negotiated by the purchaser in the possession of the purchaser or of a person designated by him or at the purchaser's request causes an acknowledgement to be made to the purchaser that it is held for him. Unless made on an exchange a sale to a broker purchasing for his own account is within this subsection and not within subsection (1).

Action Against Purchaser Based upon Wrongful Transfer
Sec. 8–315. (1) Any person against whom the transfer of a security is wrongful for any reason, including his incapacity, may against anyone except a bona fide purchaser reclaim possession of the security or obtain possession of any new security evidencing all or part of the same rights or have damages.

(2) If the transfer is wrongful because of an unauthorized indorsement, the owner may also reclaim or obtain possession of the security or new security even from a bona fide purchaser if the ineffectiveness of the purported indorsement can be asserted against him under the provisions of this Article on unauthorized indorsements (Section 8–311).

(3) The right to obtain or reclaim possession of a security may be specifically enforced and its transfer enjoined and the security impounded pending the litigation.

Purchaser's Right to Requisites for Registration of Transfer on Books
Sec. 8–316. Unless otherwise agreed the transferor must on due demand supply his purchaser with any proof of his authority to transfer or with any other requisite which may be necessary to obtain registration of the transfer of the security but if the transfer is not for value a transferor need not do so unless the purchaser furnishes the necessary expenses. Failure to comply with a demand made within a reasonable time gives the purchaser the right to reject or rescind the transfer.

Attachment of Levy Upon Security
Sec. 8–317. (1) No attachment or levy upon a security or any share or other interest evidenced thereby which is outstanding shall be valid until the security is actually seized by the officer making the attachment or levy but a security which has been surrendered to the issuer may be attached or levied upon at the source.

(2) A creditor whose debtor is the owner of a security shall be entitled to such aid from courts of appropriate jurisdiction, by injunction or otherwise, in reaching such security or in satisfying the claim by means thereof as is al-

lowed at law or in equity in regard to property which cannot readily be attached or levied upon by ordinary legal process.

No Conversion by Good Faith Delivery

Sec. 8–318. An agent or bailee who in good faith (including observance of reasonable commercial standards if he is in the business of buying, selling or otherwise dealing with securities) has received securities and sold, pledged or delivered them according to the instructions of his principal is not liable for conversion or for participation in breach of fiduciary duty although the principal had no right to dispose of them.

Statute of Frauds

Sec. 8–319. A contract for the sale of securities is not enforceable by way of action or defense unless

(a) there is some writing signed by the party against whom enforcement is sought or by his authorized agent or broker sufficient to indicate that a contract has been made for sale of a stated quantity of described securities at a defined or stated price; or

(b) delivery of the security has been accepted or payment has been made but the contract is enforceable under this provision only to the extent of such delivery or payment; or

(c) within a reasonable time a writing in confirmation of the sale or purchase and sufficient against the sender under paragraph (a) has been received by the party against whom enforcement is sought and he has failed to send written objection to its contents within ten days after its receipt; or

(d) the party against whom enforcement is sought admits in his pleading, testimony or otherwise in court that a contract was made for sale of a stated quantity of described securities at a defined or stated price.

Transfer or Pledge Within a Central Depository System

Sec. 8–320. (1) If a security

(a) is in the custody of a clearing corporation or of a custodian bank or a nominee of either subject to the instructions of the clearing corporation; and

(b) is in bearer form or indorsed in blank by an appropriate person or registered in the name of the clearing corporation or custodian bank or a nominee of either; and

(c) is shown on the account of a transferor or pledgor on the books of the clearing corporation;

then, in addition to other methods, a transfer or pledge of the security or any interest therein may be effected by the making of appropriate entries on the books of the clearing corporation reducing the account of the transferor or pledgor and increasing the account of the transferee or pledgee by the amount of the obligation or the number of shares or rights transferred or pledged.

(2) Under this section entries may be with respect to like securities or interests therein as a part of a fungible bulk and may refer merely to a quantity

of a particular security without reference to the name of the registered owner, certificate or bond number or the like and, in appropriate cases, may be on a net basis taking into account other transfers or pledges of the same security.

(3) A transfer or pledge under this section has the effect of a delivery of a security in bearer form or duly indorsed in blank (Section 8–301) representing the amount of the obligation or the number of shares or rights transferred or pledged. If a pledge or the creation of a security interest is intended, the making of entries has the effect of a taking of delivery by the pledgee or a security party (Sections 9–304 and 9–305). A transferee or pledgee under this section is a holder.

(4) A transfer or pledge under this section does not constitute a registration of transfer under Part 4 of this Article.

(5) That entries made on the books of the clearing corporation as provided in subsection (1) are not appropriate does not affect the validity or effect of the entries nor the liabilities or obligations of the clearing corporation to any person adversely affected thereby.

Part 4 Registration

Duty of Issuer to Register Transfer
Sec. 8–401. (1) Where a security in registered form is presented to the issuer with a request to register transfer, the issuer is under a duty to register the transfer as requested if

(a) the security is indorsed by the appropriate person or persons (Section 8–308); and

(b) reasonable assurance is given that those indorsements are genuine and effective (Section 8–402); and

(c) the issuer has no duty to inquire into adverse claims or has discharged any such duty (Section 8–403); and

(d) any applicable law relating to the collection of taxes has been complied with; and

(e) the transfer is in fact rightful or is to a bona fide purchaser.

(2) Where an issuer is under a duty to register a transfer of a security the issuer is also liable to the person presenting it for registration or his principal for loss resulting from any unreasonable delay in registration or from failure or refusal to register the transfer.

Assurance that Indorsements Are Effective
Sec. 8–402. (1) The issuer may require the following assurance that each necessary indorsement (Section 8–308) is genuine and effective

(a) in all cases, a guarantee of the signature (subsection (1) of Section 8–312) of the person indorsing; and

(b) where the indorsement is by an agent, appropriate assurance of authority to sign;

(c) where the indorsement is by a fiduciary, appropriate evidence of appointment or incumbency;

(d) where there is more than one fiduciary, reasonable assurance that all who are required to sign have done so;

(e) where the indorsement is by a person not covered by any of the foregoing, assurance appropriate to the case corresponding as nearly as may be to the foregoing.

(2) A "guarantee of the signature" in subsection (1) means a guarantee signed by or on behalf of a person reasonably believed by the issuer to be responsible. The issuer may adopt standards with respect to responsibility provided such standards are not manifestly unreasonable.

(3) "Appropriate evidence or appointment or incumbency" in subsection (1) means

(a) in the case of a fiduciary appointed or qualified by a court, a certificate issued by or under the direction or supervision of that court or an officer thereof and dated within sixty days before the date of presentation for transfer; or

(b) in any other case, a copy of a document showing the appointment or a certificate issued by or on behalf of a person reasonably believed by the issuer to be responsible or, in the absence of such a document or certificate, other evidence reasonably deemed by the issuer to be appropriate. The issuer may adopt standards with respect to such evidence provided such standards are not manifestly unreasonable. The issuer is not charged with notice of the contents of any document obtained pursuant to this paragraph (b) except to the extent that the contents relate directly to the appointment or incumbency.

(4) The issuer may elect to require reasonable assurance beyond that specified in this section but if it does so and for a purpose other than that specified in subsection 3(b) both requires and obtains a copy of a will, trust, indenture, articles of co-partnership, by-laws or other controlling instrument it is charged with notice of all matters contained therein affecting the transfer.

Limited Duty of Inquiry

Sec. 8–403. (1) An issuer to whom a security is presented for registration is under a duty to inquire into adverse claims if

(a) a written notification of an adverse claim is received at a time and in a manner which affords the issuer a reasonable opportunity to act on it prior to the issuance of a new, reissued or re-registered security and the notification identifies the claimant, the registered owner and the issue of which the security is a part and provides an address for communication directed to the claimant; or

(b) the issuer is charged with notice of an adverse claim from a controlling instrument which it has elected to require under subsection (4) of Section 8–402.

(2) The issuer may discharge any duty of inquiry by any reasonable means, including notifying an adverse claimant by registered or certified mail at the address furnished by him or if there be no such address at his residence or regular place of business that the security has been presented for registration of transfer by a named person, and that the transfer will be registered unless within thirty days from the date of mailing the notification, either

(a) an appropriate restraining order, injunction or other process issues from a court of competent jurisdiction; or

(b) an indemnity bond sufficient in the issuer's judgment to protect the issuer and any transfer agent, registrar or other agent of the issuer involved, from any loss which it or they may suffer by complying with the adverse claim is filed with the issuer.

(3) Unless an issuer is charged with notice of an adverse claim from a controlling instrument which it has elected to require under subsection (4) of Section 8–402 or receives notification of an adverse claim under subsection (1) of this section, where a security presented for registration is indorsed by the appropriate person or persons the issuer is under no duty to inquire into adverse claims. In particular

(a) an issuer registering a security in the name of a person who is a fiduciary or who is described as a fiduciary is not bound to inquire into the existence, extent, or correct description of the fiduciary relationship and thereafter the issuer may assume without inquiry that the newly registered owner continues to be the fiduciary until the issuer receives written notice that the fiduciary is no longer acting as such with respect to the particular security;

(b) an issuer registering transfer on an indorsement by a fiduciary is not bound to inquire whether the transfer is made in compliance with a controlling instrument or with the law of the state having jurisdiction of the fiduciary relationship, including any law requiring the fiduciary to obtain court approval of the transfer; and

(c) the issuer is not charged with notice of the contents of any court record or file or other recorded or unrecorded document even though the document is in its possession and even though the transfer is made on the indorsement of a fiduciary to the fiduciary himself or to his nominee.

Liability and Non-liability for Registration
Sec. 8–404. (1) Except as otherwise provided in any law relating to the collection of taxes, the issuer is not liable to the owner or any other person suffering loss as a result of the registration of a transfer of a security if

(a) there were on or with the security the necessary indorsements (Section 8–308); and

(b) the issuer had no duty to inquire into adverse claims or has discharged any such duty (Section 8–403).

(2) Where an issuer has registered a transfer of a security to a person not entitled to it the issuer on demand must deliver a like security to the true owner unless

(a) the registration was pursuant to subsection (1); or

(b) the owner is precluded from asserting any claim for registering the transfer under subsection (1) of the following section; or

(c) such delivery would result in overissue, in which case the issuer's liability is governed by Section 8–104.

Lost, Destroyed and Stolen Securities
Sec. 8–405. (1) Where a security has been lost, apparently destroyed or wrongfully taken and the owner fails to notify the issuer of that fact within a reasonable time after he has notice of it and the issuer registers a transfer of the security before receiving such a notification, the owner is precluded from asserting against the issuer any claim for registering the transfer under the preceding section or any claim to a new security under this section.

(2) Where the owner of a security claims that the security has been lost, destroyed or wrongfully taken, the issuer must issue a new security in place of the original security if the owner

(a) so requests before the issuer has notice that the security has been acquired by a bona fide purchaser; and

(b) files with the issuer a sufficient indemnity bond; and

(c) satisfies any other reasonable requirements imposed by the issuer.

(3) If, after the issue of the new security, a bona fide purchaser of the original security presents it for registration of transfer, the issuer must register the transfer unless registration would result in overissue, in which event the issuer's liability is governed by *Section 8–104*. In addition to any rights on the indemnity bond, the issuer may recover the new security from the person to whom it was issued or any person taking under him except a bona fide purchaser.

Duty of Authenticating Trustee, Transfer Agent or Registrar
Sec. 8–406. (1) Where a person acts as authenticating trustee, transfer agent, registrar, or other agent for an issuer in the registration of transfers of its securities or in the issue of new securities or in the cancellation of surrendered securities

(a) he is under a duty to the issuer to exercise good faith and due diligence in performing his functions; and

(b) he has with regard to the particular functions he performs the same obligation to the holder or owner of the security and has the same rights and privileges as the issuer has in regard to those functions.

(2) Notice to an authenticating trustee, transfer agent, registrar or other such agent is notice to the issuer with respect to the functions performed by the agent.

APPENDIX F

Participant Operating Procedures at Depository Trust Company Pertaining to Securities Processing and Transfer

DEPOSITS

How to Make a Deposit

- Check DTC's Eligible Securities booklet to determine if the security to be deposited is eligible for deposit in DTC.
- Be sure DTC's nominee name (Cede & Co.) has been entered in the assignment area on the back of the certificate and, where applicable, the appropriate New York State tax waiver stamp has been affixed to the back of the certificate.
- A participant may use a stock power for deposits of more than one certificate of the same security and the same registration.
- Be sure the back of the certificate has been properly endorsed, that is, that it contains all necessary signature and/or erasure guarantees, as well as power of attorney releases, whenever applicable.
- Prepare a DTC deposit ticket limiting one form to one security issue, making sure the security description, quantity (odd and round lots of the same security issue may be combined), CUSIP number, and DTC participant number are correct.

    Bonds: Quantity of bonds is entered in factors of 1,000: 1 for $1,000, etc.

    "Baby" bonds (less than $1,000) are not accepted.

- Attach by a paper clip or a staple copies 1, 2, and 3 to the left side of the securities, making sure that the clip or staple is also at the left side of the deposit ticket forms.
- Retain copy 5 for the participant's records.
    If the participant requires a receipt, the participant must request one from DTC at the time of the deposit. DTC will then receipt copy 4 and forward the receipted copy to the participant via its Central Delivery Department the following business day.
- Forward by DTC plastic envelope the securities and deposit ticket copies to the deposit window at DTC.
    TIME SCHEDULE (NEW YORK TIME)
    Same day credit: 7:30 A.M. to 11:30 A.M.
    Next day credit: 4:00 P.M. to 6:00 P.M.

ADR Deposits

A participant depositing American Depositary Receipts (ADRs) must include the acronym ADR in the security description portion of the deposit ticket and must write the name of the depositary that issued the ADR in the upper right-hand corner of the deposit ticket.

Note: In certain instances there is more than one depositary for the same security. In this event, the participant is required to prepare a separate deposit ticket for each depositary, even though the security being deposited is identical in all other respects.

CNS Deposits

A continuous-net-settlement deposit (CNS) can be made by broker participants to make securities available first to the CNS system of certain clearing corporations. Using a DTC CNS deposit ticket, follow the aforementioned deposit procedures. In other words, except for the form to be used and the requirement for separate submission, the procedures and requirements for a CNS deposit are exactly the same as for a non-CNS deposit.

After CNS processing has been completed, any remaining position is credited to the participant's general or interim free accounts in accordance with the procedures described in this section.

Legal Deposits

Certain registrations requiring legal documentation for sale or transfer will be accepted provided that, among other things, each submission is limited to a separate deposit ticket and accompanied by appropriate documentation authorizing the sale or transfer of the security.

- *Same Day Processing.* Legal deposits made for same day processing must be segregated from all other deposits and delivered by hand to DTC's Central Delivery Department.
- *Next Day Processing.* Legal deposits made for next day processing may be commingled with other types of deposits and delivered to DTC in the manner described in this section.

The participant must: Prepare a DTC legal deposit ticket and follow the preceding deposit procedures. In other words, except for the form to be used and the requirement of accompanying documentation as well as the necessity for separate submission, the procedures and requirements for legal deposit are exactly the same as for a non-legal deposit.

Special Considerations—All Deposits

Record Securities. Securities being deposited that are recorded for dividends or other distributions are accepted. However, to assure proper servicing of the participant's account, the participant is requested to identify those securities by attaching a DTC stock record tag.

Reorganization Item. Securities that become DTC ineligible (based on merger, corporate reorganization, change in state of incorporation, etc.) are not accepted for deposit on the day prior to the effective date of DTC ineligibility.

However, if a participant is making a deposit in a DTC-ineligible security to cover a short position, the deposit ticket must be marked "Reorg-Short." If those words do not clearly appear, the deposit will be rejected.

How Deposits Are Credited. Deposited securities are credited to the participant's general free account except when DTC's interim accounting procedures are in effect.

Participant should check the activity statement carefully, noting any discrepancy on a DTC notification of participant activity difference list.

When Deposits Are Rejected. DTC will make every effort to correct deposits that cannot be accepted in the form submitted. However, since a rejected deposit deprives the participant of use of the securities and in some cases may result in a short position while the cause for rejection is being resolved, the participant should take every precaution to avoid deposit rejects.

The following are the most frequent causes of deposit rejects:

- Certificates are not properly prepared.
- Security being deposited is not DTC eligible or is in the process of reorganization.

- Deposit tickets are not properly completed.
- CUSIP number does not agree with the security being deposited.
- Quantity or security description listed on the deposit ticket differs from the securities being deposited.

DTC may correct participant's error in the following manner:

Correctable: If upon examination of the securities and forms, DTC determines a deposit is unacceptable and DTC is able to make the correction, DTC makes the correction, completing a deposit reject notice forwarding the completed notice to the participant via DTC's Central Delivery Department.

Not correctable: If upon examination of the securities and forms, DTC determines a deposit is unacceptable and DTC is unable to make the correction, DTC automatically debits the participant's account to the extent it was credited by the deposit. After debiting the participant's account, DTC will complete a deposit reject notice, forwarding the notice, together with the securities, to the participant via DTC's Central Delivery Department.

Should DTC determine that the deposit is unacceptable and the reason for rejection cannot be immediately corrected, DTC debits the participant's account to the full extent of the deposit. If this debit drives the participant's account into a short (or negative) position, DTC automatically debits the participant's settlement account by 130 percent of the current market value of the securities used. This debit remains in effect until the matter has been resolved.

Should the transfer agent determine a deposit is unacceptable, the transfer agent returns the securities to DTC, together with a transfer agent's reject notice. DTC then follows the procedures outlined above.

Procedures for Deposit of Coupon Bonds

1. Check carefully the most recently published DTC Eligible Securities booklet and DTC reorganization notices to make certain that the coupon bonds you wish to deposit qualify for deposit with DTC under these procedures.

   From time to time, DTC notifies participants by reorganization notice of additions and deletions to the list of coupon bonds eligible for deposit. The DTC Eligible Securities booklet, published periodically, contains a cumulative list of coupon bonds eligible for deposit.

   Not all DTC-eligible interchangeable bond issues are eligible for the coupon bond deposit service. Participants are urged to exercise extreme caution in checking the eligibility of a bond issue against the cumulative list of coupon bonds eligible for deposit and reorganization notices before stamping the required restrictive legend on the bonds and coupons. The process for rectifying stamping errors, which may involve letters of indemnity and other special paperwork, is cumbersome, costly, and time consuming for both participants and DTC. Where bonds

Securities Transfer

stamped in error are available in coupon form only, substantial costs may be incurred by participants in obtaining replacement certificates.

2. Determine that the last coupon affixed to each bond is for the proper interest payment date. With one exception, the last affixed coupon must be the coupon for interest payable on the next interest payment date after the date of deposit.

    The one exception occurs when the date of deposit is between the day after record date (or cut-off date) and the day before payment date for interest on the registered form of the bond issue. In that event, clip the coupon for the next interest payment date, because the bonds will be credited to the participant's interim account at DTC, excluding them from the DTC interest collection and distribution process for that payment.

3. Examine all coupons to make certain that none is missing for an interest payment date subsequent to that of the last proper affixed coupon (as determined in item 2, above).

4. Examine all coupons to make certain that none is mutilated.

5. Only after steps 1 through 4 above have been carefully completed stamp the legend:

    THIS SECURITY IS THE PROPERTY OF THE DEPOSITORY TRUST COMPANY OF 55 WATER ST., N.Y., N.Y., FOR DEPOSIT ONLY WITH THE BOND/DEBENTURE REGISTRAR FOR EXCHANGE INTO FULLY REGISTERED BONDS/DEBENTURES

    and your participant number on the face of each bond and on the last coupon affixed to each bond. The purpose of the restrictive legend is to inhibit unauthorized usage of the bonds and coupons.

6. Prepare a deposit ticket in accordance with the procedures for other deposits. In addition, type or print clearly on the ticket the following information:

    1. The word "Coupon"
    2. The payment date of the last affixed coupons, followed by the letters "SCA," meaning subsequent coupons attached

    Participants are reminded to enter the number of bonds in the quantity box on the deposit ticket (that is, enter "10" for a $10,000 deposit quantity, "25" for $25,000, etc.).

7. Package the coupon bond deposits separately from deposits of registered securities.

8. Deliver by hand the coupon bond deposits, between 8:00 A.M. and 11:00 A.M. only, to the coupon bond deposit window #1 in the DTC Central Delivery Department.

9. Deposits meeting the requirements specified above and the requirements of DTC's Rules and Procedures are credited on the same day to the par-

ticipant's general free account except, as indicated in item 2 above, coupon deposits made between the day after record date (or cut-off date) and the day before payment date for interest on the registered form are credited to the participant's interim free account.

Long positions created by deposits of coupon bonds are available for the full range of depository services, including book-entry deliveries and collateral loans and withdrawals of registered securities in nominee name (CODs) and by transfer (WTs). Withdrawal of bonds in coupon form cannot, however, be effected. Deposits and subsequent transactions appear as usual in the Participants' Daily Activity Statement distributed the following morning.

10. Rejected deposits are processed in accordance with the procedures for other rejected deposits. Participants' messengers pick up and sign for rejected bonds between 11:00 A.M. and 1:00 P.M. at the coupon bond window #1 in the DTC Central Delivery Department.

MUNICIPAL BEARER BOND DEPOSITS

Participants may deposit the bearer form of debt securities issued by state and local governments (municipal bearer bonds) directly at DTC.

Procedures for Deposit of Municipal Bearer Bonds

Check carefully the most recently published DTC Eligible Securities booklet and DTC notices to make certain that the municipal bearer bonds to be deposited qualify for deposit with DTC under these procedures.

From time to time, DTC distributes notices to participants of additions and deletions to the list of municipal bearer bonds eligible for deposit. The DTC Eligible Securities Booklet, published monthly, contains a cumulative list of municipal bearer bonds eligible for deposit. The cumulative list includes the municipal bearer bonds that were previously identified in DTC notices as qualifying for deposit and that were still qualified at the time the booklet was printed.

Do not commingle deposits of the bearer form with the registered form of the same issue of interchangeable municipal bonds.

Do not deposit called bonds.

Some DTC depository facilities accept deposits of municipal bearer bonds.

Determine that the last coupon affixed to each municipal bearer bond is for the proper interest payment date. With one exception, the last coupon affixed must be the coupon for interest payable on the next interest payment date after the date of deposit.

Exception. The one exception occurs when the deposit is made between the day after record date set by the issuer or DTC or the day after the DTC cut-off date and the day before payment date for interest. In that event, clip the coupon for the next interest payment date, because the municipal bearer bonds will be credited to your interim account at DTC, excluding them from the DTC interest collection and distribution process for that payment.

Examine all coupons to make certain that none is missing for an interest payment date subsequent to that of the last properly affixed coupon (as determined in the preceding step).

Examine all coupons to make certain that none is mutilated.

Prepare a DTC municipal bearer bond (MBB) deposit ticket for each DTC-eligible issue, making sure the participant number, quantity, CUSIP number, security description, and coupon date are correct.

Participants are reminded to enter the number of municipal bearer bonds in the quantity box on the MBB deposit ticket (that is, enter "10" for a $10,000 deposit quantity, "25" for $25,000, etc.).

Participants are required to indicate in the box so titled the number of certificates attached to each deposit when the deposit includes more than 10 certificates.

Under "Participant Coordinator," enter the name and telephone number of the person that DTC can contact if it is necessary to correct a deposit error or reject the deposited certificates.

Attach with a staple copies 1, 2, and 3 of the MBB deposit ticket to the left side of the securities, making sure that the staple is also at the left side of the MBB deposit ticket form.

Retain copy 4 for your records.

Package the municipal bearer bond deposits separately from deposits of registered securities by using a separate DTC plastic envelope.

Do not stamp any legend or participant number on the face of any bond or on any coupon affixed to the bond.

A CNS (continuous-net-settlement) deposit can be made by broker participants to make securities available to the CNS system of the National Securities Clearing Corporation. Securities deposited as a CNS deposit are first tapped by DTC to cover any CNS short position before being used to cover any other instructions submitted by the participant. Using a DTC municipal bearer bond (MBB) CNS deposit ticket, follow the preceding deposit procedures. In other words, except for the form to be used and the requirement for submission in a separate envelope, the procedures and requirements for a CNS deposit are exactly the same as for a non-CNS deposit.

If a participant is making a deposit in a DTC-ineligible security to cover a short position, which arose prior to the security becoming ineligible, the MBB deposit ticket must be marked "Reorg-Short." If those words do not clearly appear, the deposit will be rejected. Deliver the municipal bearer bond deposits to the coupon bond deposit window #1 in the DTC Central Delivery Department between 4:00 P.M. and 6:00 P.M. (Eastern time) in the evening prior to the transaction day or between 7:30 A.M. and noon (Eastern time) on the transaction day.

Deposits meeting the requirements specified above and the requirements of DTC's Rules and Procedures will be credited on the same day to the participant's general free account except that, as previously indicated, municipal bearer bond deposits made between the day after record date or cut-off date and the day before payment date for interest will be credited to the participant's interim free account.

Long positions created by deposits of municipal bearer bonds are available for the full range of depository services, including book-entry deliveries and collateral loans. Deposits and subsequent transactions appear as usual in the participant's statement (Daily Activity Statement) distributed the following morning, except that bearer deposits are identified by the letter *B* in parentheses (**B**).

Activity Verification

Participants should check the activity statement carefully, noting any discrepancy on a DTC Notification of Participant Activity Difference form. The notification must be received by DTC no later than noon on the day the statement was made available for participant pick-up.

Rejected Deposits

DTC will make its best efforts to correct deposit errors where:

1. The CUSIP number on the MBB deposit ticket disagrees with the certificates; or
2. in the case of a large deposit only, where the quantity entered on the MBB deposit ticket differs from the certificates being deposited.

    Since a rejected deposit deprives the participant of use of the securities, the participant should take every precaution to avoid deposit errors. The following are common reasons for rejecting deposits:

    Last coupon affixed to municipal bearer bond is not for proper interest payment date.

    Security being deposited is not DTC eligible.

    MBB deposit tickets are not properly completed.

    CUSIP number entered on the MBB deposit ticket does not agree with the securities being deposited.

    Quantity entered on the MBB deposit ticket differs from the securities being deposited.

Note: A fee is assessed for excessive deposit rejects. Rejected deposits must be picked up by the participant at DTC, in accordance with the procedures for municipal bearer bond withdrawals. DTC completes and attaches to rejected certificates a Municipal Bearer Bond Deposit Rejection/Adjustment Notice indicating the reason for rejection, together with copy 2 of the MBB deposit ticket stamped "REJECTED." If the MBB deposit ticket contains an incorrect CUSIP number or quantity and DTC is able to adjust it, DTC makes available for participant pickup a Deposit Rejection/Adjustment Notice indicating the adjustment made. The participant's messenger is required to receipt copy 5 of the notice for both rejected and adjusted deposits.

Institutional Delivery System (ID)

Trade Date. The broker-dealer furnishes DTC with trade data.

The broker-dealer: Submits trade data to DTC by means of hard copy, facsimile transmission, punched cards, or magnetic tape, giving DTC all information necessary to describe the trade, including security name, CUSIP number, price, quantity, commission, etc.

DTC: Begins processing trade data furnished by the broker-dealer.

Trade Date +1. DTC furnishes each institution with its confirmations and forwards a listing of unacceptable trades as well as printed confirmations to the broker-dealer.

DTC:

- Forwards printed confirmations and Broker Trade Error Report to the broker-dealer. The Broker Trade Error Report indicates any transaction not acceptable for processing through the ID system and the reason for its rejection (missing settlement date, non-numeric data in a numeric field, etc.).
- Forwards confirmations to the institution and/or, if authorized by the institution, to the agent bank via a form of transmission previously arranged between the institution (or its agent bank) and DTC. These forms of transmission include:
    —Hard copy
    —Participant Terminal System (PTS)
    —Dial-in teletype-compatible terminal
    —Tape transmission
    —Facsimile

A broker-dealer may execute a large order in a given security in two or more trades (partials). Each partial is considered as a separate ID confirmation for billing purposes.

The broker-dealer: Receives by 9:00 A.M. (Eastern time) printed confirmation and a Broker Trade Error Report—a listing of all trades containing edit errors—via its DTC distribution box or via some other form of transmission previously arranged.

After examining its printed confirmations and Broker Trade Error Report, the broker-dealer may submit data on additional trades or corrections of existing trades. In each instance the broker-dealer should use the special instruction field of its input to provide any detail the institution may require to identify the trade.

The institution: Receives by 9:00 A.M. (Eastern time) confirmations via its DTC distribution box or via some other form of transmission previously arranged.

May submit acknowledgments to DTC by means of hard copy, facsimile transmission, tape transmission, or via the participant terminal system, giving the DTC trade identification number of each trade to which it agrees, the total number of acknowledged trades, etc. This information will be accepted up to the night of trade date +3 and is to be delivered via:

Hard Copy: Use DTC Acknowledgment Form to list acknowledgments. Forward completed forms to DTC's Central Delivery Department—2:00 P.M.– 5:00 P.M. (Eastern time).

An institution may, in lieu of using this form, deliver one copy of the confirmation with the word "acknowledge" stamped below the identification number ("DTC IDENT") of those trades it accepts.

Facsimile: Use DTC Acknowledgment Form to list acknowledgments. Transmit completed forms over telecopier machines to DTC's Interface Department between 2:00 P.M. and 5:00 P.M. (Eastern time).

Tape transmission: Transmit tape directly to DTC Data Processing throughout the day up to 7:00 P.M. (Eastern time).

Participant terminal system: Institutions that use DTC's participant terminal system may key in their acknowledgments over their online terminals between 12:30 P.M. and 7:00 P.M. (Eastern time).

DTC: Processes acknowledgments and any additional trade input.

Trade Date +2. The institution may acknowledge trades to which it agrees, forwarding the acknowledgments to DTC. The broker-dealer may submit additional trade data to DTC.

The institution: Receives confirmations by 9:00 A.M. for any additional or corrected trades submitted by the broker/dealer on trade date + 1. May submit acknowledgments to DTC as previously described.

The broker-dealer: May submit additional or corrected trade data to DTC as previously described.

Receives printed confirmations and a Broker Trade Error Report for any additional trade data submitted on Trade Date + 1.

DTC: Processes the additional trade data and acknowledgments.

Trade Date +3. Agent bank and broker-dealer receive Eligible Trade Reports and Deliver and Receive Instructions from DTC for those trades acknowledged on either trade date + 1 or trade date + 2. In addition, the broker-dealer receives a listing of all trades that the institution did not acknowledge by trade date + 2.

ID-PDQ Processing

DTC: Forwards the ID/PDQ Eligible Trade Report to the broker-dealer and agent bank for those trades that are eligible for ID-PDQ settlement processing and have been acknowledged on either trade date + 1 or trade date + 2.

Securities Transfer

DTC performs a final eligibility check on those trades that have been acknowledged by trade date + 2 in order to verify that the security is still eligible for depository services.

The broker-dealer: Receives by 9:00 A.M. (Eastern time) the ID/PDQ Eligible Trade Report (a listing of those trades that have been acknowledged by trade date + 2 and are ID/PDQ-eligible) via its DTC distribution box or via some other form of transmission previously arranged.

Receives printed confirmations and a Broker Trade Error Report for any additional trade data submitted on trade date + 2.

The agent bank: Receives by 9:00 A.M. (Eastern time) the ID/PDQ Eligible Trade Report (a listing of all trades that have been acknowledged by trade date + 2 and are ID/PDQ-eligible) via its DTC distribution box or via some other form of transmission previously arranged.

The institution: Receives confirmations by 9:00 A.M. for any additional or corrected trades submitted by the broker-dealer on trade date + 2. May submit acknowledgments to DTC as previously described (See Trade Date + 1).

Trades not acknowledged by trade date + 3 are automatically dropped from the ID system and no further processing occurs.

ID/CNS Processing. ID users have the option to have acknowledged trades entered into the Continuous Net Settlement (CNS) system of the National Securities Clearing Corporation (NSCC). This is permissible where the security is CNS eligible and the broker-dealer, the institution, and the agent bank subscribe to the ID/CNS interface. Arrangements to participate in this program must be made through the Participant Services Representative and NSCC.

DTC: Forwards ID/CNS Eligible Trade Report to the broker-dealer and the agent bank for those trades that are CNS eligible and have been acknowledged on either trade date + 1 or trade date + 2.

Releases CNS-eligible trades to the CNS system for settlement processing.

The broker-dealer: Receives by 9:00 A.M. (Eastern time) the ID/CNS Eligible Trade Report (a listing of those trades that are CNS eligible and have been acknowledged on either trade date + 1 or trade date + 2 and are to be released for CNS processing) via its DTC distribution box or via some other form of transmission previously arranged.

The agent bank: Receives by 9:00 A.M. (Eastern time) the ID/CNS Eligible Trade Report (a listing of those trades that are CNS eligible and have been acknowledged on either trade date + 1 or trade date + 2 and are to be released for CNS processing) via its DTC distribution box or via some other form of transmission previously arranged.

From this point on, these transactions are not processed through the ID system; they are processed and completed within the CNS system.

Settlement Outside DTC

DTC: Forwards Deliver and Receive Instruction Forms for those trades that have been acknowledged on either trade date + 1 or trade date + 2 and in which the security is ineligible for delivery through DTC to the broker-dealer and agent bank.

The broker-dealer: Receives by 9:00 A.M. (Eastern time) Deliver and Receive Instruction Forms for DTC-ineligible trades (those not meeting the eligibility requirements for either the CNS or PDQ systems) that have been acknowledged on either trade date + 1 or trade date + 2 via its DTC distribution box or via some other form of transmission previously arranged.

The agent bank: Receives by 9:00 A.M. (Eastern time) Deliver and Receive Instruction Forms for DTC-ineligible trades (those not meeting the eligibility requirements for either the CNS or PDQ systems) that have been acknowledged on either trade date + 1 or trade date + 2 via its DTC distribution box or via some other form of transmission previously arranged.

From this point on, these DTC-ineligible trades are not processed through DTC; they are to be settled outside DTC.

Unacknowledged Trades

DTC: Forwards the Unaffirmed Report to the broker-dealer for any trade not acknowledged by the institution as of the close of business on trade date + 2.

The broker-dealer: Receives by 9:00 A.M. (Eastern time) the Unaffirmed Report (a listing of all trades that have not yet been acknowledged) via its DTC distribution box or via some other form of transmission previously arranged.

The broker-dealer should review the Unaffirmed Report received on the morning of trade date + 3 and contact the respective institutions regarding acknowledgment. Institutions, as previously stated, may acknowledge trades prior to the close of business on trade date + 3, enabling DTC to process their trades through the ID/PDQ System.

DTC: Processes any acknowledgments received from an institution on trade date + 3.

Conducts a final eligibility check prior to releasing acknowledged trades for either PDQ or CNS processing.

Trade Date + 4. Delivering party prepares to comply with settlement requirements.

The broker-dealer:

- Receives a supplementary ID/PDQ Eligible Trade Report listing those trades acknowledged on trade date + 3.
- Receives a supplementary ID/CNS Eligible Trade Report listing those trades acknowledged on trade date + 3.
- Receives Deliver and Receive Instruction Forms for those DTC-ineligible trades acknowledged on trade date + 3.

The agent bank:

- Receives a supplementary ID/PDQ Eligible Trade Report listing those trades acknowledged on trade date + 3.
- Receives a supplementary ID/CNS Eligible Trade Report listing those trades acknowledged on trade date + 3.

Securities Transfer

- Receives Deliver and Receive Instruction Forms for those DTC-ineligible trades acknowledged on trade date + 3.

Preparing for Delivery

ID/PDQ-Non-Segregated Position Option
The delivering party: Compares its ID/PDQ Eligible Trade Report with its free long position (securities on deposit) in DTC.

In the event that the delivering party's position is insufficient, the delivering party must increase its position in one or more of the following ways: depositing securities to its DTC account, arranging for a stock loan, or utilizing DTC's conditional deliver order (CDO) procedure as outlined in Section C, Deliveries. These deposits, stock loans, or conditional deliver orders must be made sufficient to DTC by 6:00 P.M. (Eastern time).

Deliveries that are not to be made are to be noted either by listing on DTC's PDQ Daily Authorization/Exception Notice.

ID/PDQ:
ID/PDQ-Segregated Position Option
The delivering party may segregate a portion of a position that should not be used to complete ID deliveries and attempt delivery based only upon the remaining available position by entering the segregated position on the PDQ Daily Authorization/Exception Notice or the ID/PDQ Eligible Trade Report.

ID/PDQ:
Recycling Option
Participating ID users may elect to recycle deliveries and/or receives to day-side processing. Recycling is applicable only to trades in which both the deliver and receiver subscribe to this feature. It allows those ID trades that do not contain a segregated quantity and that fail to settle during PDQ to be added to a day-side recycling file. Day-side processing then attempts to make settlement throughout the day.

All trades that are recycling appear on the PDQ Deliver Balance Order List-Not Delivered-Recycling (for the deliverer). This list contains item count, security quantity, and net amount grand totals for recycling trades and those trades not delivered on the PDQ Deliver Balance Order List-Not Delivered. All trades that are recycling appear on the PDQ Deliver Balance Order List-Recycling Debits (for the receiver).

At the completion of recycle processing, all trades that have been updated are eliminated from the system and appear on the Dropped Receive/Deliver List, which is produced and distributed along with the Participants' Preliminary Settlement Statement.

ID/PDQ:
Compression Option
A broker-dealer may execute an order in two or more trades (partials). When this occurs, the ID system processes each partial as a separate trade and,

if acknowledged by the institution, each partial appears on the ID/PDQ Eligible Trade Report as a separate deliver/receive instruction. However, upon prior arrangement with DTC, an institution may instruct DTC to utilize the ID/PDQ compression option to "consolidate" its partial trades. In this event, DTC automatically combines the partials of all trades it processes for the institution for a given order in the same security by settlement date and produces one deliver/receive instruction on the ID/PDQ Eligible Trade Report.

Settlement Date. DTC settles all non-excepted eligible trades that have been acknowledged by the institution and forwards reports to the concerned parties.

DTC: Furnishes reports and completes money settlement.

The broker-dealer and the agent bank: Receive by 9:00 A.M. (Eastern time) the following reports via the DTC distribution box or via some other form of transmission previously arranged:

1. ID deliveries made—PDQ Deliver Balance Order List—Credit
2. ID deliveries not made—PDQ Deliver Balance Order List—Not Delivered
3. ID deliveries received—PDQ Deliver Balance Order List—Debit
4. ID recycling trades—PDQ Deliver Balance Order List—Not Delivered—Recycling
5. ID recycling trades—PDQ Deliver Balance Order List—Recycling Debits

   Money settlement will be netted in the DTC Settlement System

An item excepted from PDQ processing may be delivered on settlement date or any day thereafter by preparing a miscellaneous deliver order (MDO).

Conditional Deliver Order. The conditional deliver order (CDO) program, by facilitating the return of borrowed securities, enables all participants to complete automatically and economically all or most of their institutional deliveries on settlement day.

Participants needing securities to make deliveries through the Institutional Delivery (ID) system arrange to borrow the securities on the afternoon before settlement day, specifying to the lender or lenders of their choice that CDO procedures are to be used. The lenders prepare CDO forms for the securities to be loaned from their DTC accounts and submit them to DTC that afternoon. DTC processes and stores these CDOs in its computer for the PDQ night cycle of the ID system. Towards the end of the night cycle, DTC matches open ID deliveries against the stored CDOs and releases for processing the CDOs and the ID deliveries.

Then, DTC analyzes the borrowing participant's securities free position, instructions contained in the CDO, and any segregation quantity specified in the ID deliver order to determine if any of the securities borrowed can be returned to the lender in full or in part. If so, DTC generates and releases for processing an appropriate return-deliver order. Exceptions to a partial return

Securities Transfer

occur where (1) the CDO indicates no partial return, (2) the CDO indicates round-lot partial return and only an odd-lot quantity of securities is available, or (3) multiple CDOs are on hand from different lenders for the same issue of securities. A CDO not matched against an open ID delivery is normally returned in full. All CDO activity is reported to the borrower and lender early in the morning of settlement day. Thus, with the CDO program, borrowing participants do not have to analyze their settlement morning positions to return securities not needed and do not have to prepare miscellaneous deliver orders (MDOs) for their return, while lending participants do not have to handle these return-deliver MDOs and do not receive the securities in their accounts too late for re-lending that day. The CDO service, by reducing processing tasks and costs, provides incentives beyond those inherent in the normal lender/borrower relationship to use lendable securities for completion of all ID deliveries on settlement day.

Deliveries

Deliveries Between Participants. DTC receives and processes delivery instructions submitted in three forms.

1. *Hardcopy instruction submitted by participants, which includes* deliver balance orders (DBOs) issued by the National Securities Clearing Corporation (NSCC) for securities to be delivered against payment, from one participant to another. DBOs are produced for settlement of trades in securities that are ineligible for the Continuous Net Settlement (CNS) system of NSCC or for settlement of trades that participants wish excluded from CNS processing.

   Miscellaneous deliver orders (MDOs) are used by a participant for a variety of reasons, including a delivery between a participant broker and a participant bank that is the broker's customer or is acting as agent for the broker's customer; a partial delivery of a non-CNS NSCC transaction; a stock loan; a return of stock borrowed; or a transfer of a customer account to another participant.

   A delivery using an MDO may be "valued" (for money) or "free" (without money).

2. *A computerized delivery instruction submitted by* clearing corporations, including NSCC and the Stock Clearing Corporation of Philadelphia (SCCP); and depositories, including Midwest Securities Trust Company (MSTC) and Pacific Securities Depository Trust Company (PSDTC).

3. *A computerized delivery instruction submitted by a participant through* participation in DTC's Institutional Delivery (ID) system. PDQ automated deliveries.

For either deliver balance order and miscellaneous deliver order processing the participant must: Determine that the required securities are available in its general and/or interim free accounts.

Prepare the appropriate delivery instruction (DBO or MDO) by:

Completing all required information.

Inserting copy 1 of the instruction into a credit list envelope after entering the receiving participants' numbers and dollar amounts on the face of the credit list envelope.

Inserting copies 2 and 3 of the instruction with any related documentation into a delivery envelope after entering the receiving participant's number on the envelope.

Retaining copies 4 and 5 for its own records.

> Each credit list envelope must be imprinted with the participant's facsimile signature when presented to DTC. If participant does not have machine-imprinted facsimile, a rubber stamp must be used.

Compare the individual delivery envelopes to the entries on the related credit list envelopes. There must be one delivery envelope for each entry on the credit list envelope. A maximum of 20 delivery envelopes may be attached to each credit list envelope.

Forward the credit list envelopes with the delivery envelopes attached to the NSCC Central Delivery Department between 8:00 A.M. and 11:00 A.M. (New York time) for same day credit or 4:00 P.M. and 6:00 P.M. (New York time) for next day credit.

Additional time is provided until 12:30 P.M. (New York time) for participants to make corporate bond deliveries with a net value of $95,000 or more to the ten New York clearing house banks. A clearing house bank accepts a delivery of this type only if the bank is retaining the delivery (not acting as agent for a put-away account). Any other deliveries of corporate bonds to the clearing house banks should be made within the normal time schedule.

Separate credit list envelopes must be used for deliver balance orders and miscellaneous deliver balance orders. Record the dollar value of all deliveries and enter that total in the appropriate box on the participant's settlement statement.

A participant may receive a Dropped Delivery Report indicating that certain deliveries could not be completed. Both the delivery and receiving participants receive Dropped Delivery Reports. The value of these deliveries must be subtracted from the participant's settlement statement and not included in money settlement figures.

DTC will verify: The deliverer's security position in its general and/or interim free accounts, deduct the securities, and credit the receiver's account. If the delivery is valued (for money), DTC will credit the account of the deliverer with the money value specified on the delivery instruction and debit the account of the receiver.

To continue processing (recycle) the delivery if the deliverer does not initially have a sufficient position, DTC will recycle the delivery until the early afternoon—approximately 2:00 P.M. (New York time). At that time, if the deliverer's account is still deficient, the delivery will be "dropped." The receiver

Securities Transfer 221

will not receive the securities and will not be charged the money value of the delivery.

DTC may: Delete a delivery instruction it deems invalid for various reasons (e.g., missing, incomplete, or incorrect data). Pursuant to the execution of an authorization agreement with the participant and for a special charge per correction, DTC will correct and reinstate a delivery instruction which might otherwise be rejected.

Reclamations. In case of an irregularity in a DTC delivery, the receiving participant may reclaim (return) the delivery up to 12:30 P.M. (New York time) on the day of the delivery.

To reclaim a delivery the participant must:

- Prepare an MDO and a credit list envelope, stamping all copies of both documents with the legend "Reclamation."
- Complete all required information.
- Insert copy 1 of the reclamation MDO into the reclamation credit list envelope.
- Insert copies 2 and 3 of the reclamation MDO and copy 3 of the original delivery instruction being reclaimed into a reclamation delivery envelope.
- Retain copies 4 and 5 for its own records.
- Forward the reclamation credit list envelope with reclamation delivery envelope attached to NSCC Central Delivery before 12:30 P.M. (New York time).

Reclamations of erroneous corporate bond deliveries with a net value of $95,000 or more from the ten New York clearing house banks are accepted between 12:30 P.M. and 2:00 P.M. (New York time).

Receiving a DTC Delivery
The receiving participant must:

- Instruct its messenger(s) to make pick-ups at the NSCC Central Delivery Department throughout the course of the processing day.
- Examine information its messenger has picked up, including the 2 and 3 copies of all MDOs or DBOs and any receiver notifications produced by the ID system, PDQ, CNS, or the clearing corporations.
- Enter the dollar value of all valued receipts in the appropriate box on the participant's settlement statement.

A receiving participant may receive a Dropped Receive/Deliver List indicating certain deliveries were not made. The value of these deliveries should not be included in the related debits in that day's money settlement figures.

A participant may receive a Dropped Delivery Report indicating that certain deliveries could not be completed. Both the delivering and receiving participants receive Dropped Delivery Reports. The value of these deliveries must be subtracted from the participant's settlement statement and not included in money settlement figures.

Money Settlement. Each participant is required to calculate the amount of its daily money settlement obligation with DTC.

The participant must:

- Prepare a participant's settlement statement furnished by DTC. Part I will indicate the amount of money due to or from DTC.
- Submit participant's settlement statement, accompanied by an appropriate check or draft to DTC's Settlement Department prior to 3:00 P.M. (New York time) each day.
- Pay balances due to DTC as a result of the day's settlement activities with a check drawn on an approved New York clearing house bank. The check must be certified (if the amount is over $5,000), unless this requirement is waived by DTC.
- Present a draft to the Settlement Department for balances due from DTC as a result of the day's settlement activities. DTC will sign the draft for the amount due to the participant.

Settlement forms and the accompanying check or draft must be submitted prior to 3:00 P.M. (New York time) each business day.

DTC and the National Securities Clearing Corporation have a pre-endorsement arrangement, whereby a participant may pre-endorse its draft against either corporation to satisfy (in part or in full) a payment obligation with the other corporation.

Dividends and Interest. Cash dividends and bond interest are credited to participants through the daily settlement system. Credits for dividends and/or interest appear as a separate line and activity code on the participant's settlement statement.

Monthly Charges. On a daily basis, DTC levies transaction charges and other fees for services rendered. DTC accumulates these charges and fees during the course of a month. Several business days after the last business day of the month, DTC debits the participant's settlement account for the total of the accumulated charges and fees. The monthly charges and fees appear as a separate line item and activity code on the participant's settlement statement. A monthly bill detailing all charges and fees is forwarded to the participant on the day the participant's settlement account is debited.

Penalties. During the course of business, a participant may erroneously use securities it does not have on deposit at DTC. This results in a short position in the participant's account. A penalty charge is assessed without regard to whether an error or omission by the participant has caused the short position. The penalty charge is calculated at 130 percent of the market value of the securities used but not on deposit. The value of the securities is marked to the market on a daily basis. The penalty charge is debited from the participant's settlement account and appears on the participant's settlement statement on the business day after the short position has occurred. The penalty is returned the business day after the short position has been covered. A Short Position Report detailing any deficient security position is available to the participant on the morning the participant's settlement account is to be debited.

Fines. DTC may impose a fine on a participant for a violation of DTC rules, or the procedures, or for errors, delays, or other conduct detrimental to the operations of DTC, provided, however, that no fine for any given offense shall exceed the sum of $1,000.

Suspenses. On a daily basis, any settlement balances that have not been paid or collected by 6:00 P.M. (New York time) are suspensed (offset) by DTC to balance the participant's settlement statement for that day. On the morning of the next business day, DTC will re-establish the suspensed balances in the participant's settlement account. The previous day's suspense will appear as a separate line item and activity code on that day's participant's settlement statement.

Pre-Authorized Delivery System (PDQ). The Pre-Authorized Delivery System (PDQ) is a method of delivery without use of delivery instructions, envelopes, or credit lists. Deliver balance orders and ID system deliveries settle through PDQ.

The participant must: Prepare deliver balance orders or ID system delivery requirements to its related DTC account balances.

Separate any deliveries it cannot make due to unavailable position.

Determine if it wishes to increase its account balances by borrowing securities (and requesting the lender to submit an MDO before 6:00 P.M., New York time, on the night before settlement day or by depositing additional securities before 6:00 P.M., New York time).

Exclude any remaining deliveries that cannot be made by completing a PDQ Daily Authorization/Exception Notice and listing the control numbers of the deliveries it does not wish to make. The notice must be submitted to the NSCC Central Delivery by 6:00 P.M. (New York time) on the night before settlement day.

A PDQ Daily Authorization/Exception Notice must be submitted each day, even if there are no exceptions. If there are none, the box marked "No Exceptions" on the notice should be checked. Failure to submit the notice will result in no deliveries being made.

The notice also provides a participant with the ability to exclude a portion of its position due to segregation requirements. This segregation capability exists only for night processing and only for the ID system.

DTC will, subject to payment, automatically complete all deliveries that had not been excepted and for which the participant has sufficient position. The following reports are produced and available at 8:00 A.M. (New York time) on the next business day:

- Deliveries made by PDQ.
- Deliveries not made by PDQ.
- Deliveries received by PDQ. This report is produced for all participants receiving securities via PDQ.

Participant Statements. DTC will forward the following reports daily to those participants whose accounts have been affected by delivery instructions:

1. Preliminary settlement statement, which provides a summary by activity type of the debits and credits for a given business day. The report includes a net dollar position either owed to DTC or owed by DTC. A participant may be telephoned by DTC settlement personnel if any adjustments are to be made to this statement.
2. Debit and Credit Listing, which details the debits and credits resulting from a given business day's deliver and receive transactions.
3. Drop Notices for any deliveries that have been recycled throughout the day and are to be excluded from the day's final settlement.
4. Final settlement statement, which lists additional debit or credit adjustment entries not included on the preliminary statement.
5. Participant's statement (daily activity), which lists the delivery and receive transactions (stating the security, quantity, and contra party) that have affected a participant's position on the previous day.

Discrepancies. If there are any discrepancies between the participant's internal records and its participant statement, the participant must submit: A Notification of Participant Activity Difference List noting the security, type of error, and activity date the difference was incurred.

Withdrawal of Nominee Certificates

Regular CODs, Fast CODs. Participants may, from time to time, need to make rapid withdrawals of physical stock or bond certificates from the depository. To satisfy this need, DTC permits participants to withdraw securities in round lots, registered in the name of and endorsed by Cede & Co. (DTC's nominee name) with the name of the participant entered as attorney on the reverse side of each certificate. On some occasions when DTC is unable to satisfy participant requests for COD withdrawals of Cede & Co. nominee-registered certificates, DTC will provide certificates that have been assigned to Cede & Co. and reassigned to the withdrawing participant.

Certain issues are included in the depository's FAST program, enabling participants (for those issues only) to withdraw certificates in round lots, odd

Securities Transfer

lots, or mixed lots, registered in a standard name specified previously by the participant (usually the participant's street name).

Procedures—Regular CODs

The participant must: Prepare DTC Withdrawal of Nominee Stock form, limiting the form to one issue, the quantity to round lots, and making sure the firm's facsimile signature has been affixed to copy 4 of the form.

- Retain copy 5 for a permanent record.
- Forward copies 1, 2, 3, and 4 (day CODs) or copies 1, 2, and 3 (night CODs) to DTC.

Time Schedule (New York Time)

- *Day withdrawal,* 7:30 A.M. through 4:00 P.M. Day withdrawals are processed immediately through the participant's account and securities are available for participant pick-up the same day.
- *Night withdrawal,* 4:00 P.M. through 6:00 P.M. Night withdrawals are processed through the participant's account overnight and securities are available for participant pick-up the following business day. Night withdrawals will be considered as activity in the participant's account the following business day.

DTC will: Retain copies 1, 2, and 3 for its own internal processing. For day CODs, DTC will time-stamp copy 4, returning the time-stamped copy to the participant's messenger.

The participant will: Return to DTC's Central Delivery Department, where the messenger must present copy 4 bearing the DTC time-stamp.

DTC will then: Deliver the securities, together with copy 2 of DTC's Remote Output Reply form, retaining copy 4 of the Withdrawal of Nominee Stock form as its receipt and for its own internal processing.

Special Considerations

- *Recycling* (day CODs only): Whenever a withdrawal request cannot be filled initially due to insufficient participant position, the withdrawal request is automatically recycled until all same-day account update processing (deposits, deliveries, etc.) is completed. Should the participant's position remain insufficient, the withdrawal request will be rejected.
- *Expediting Group:* Whenever a participant anticipates an unusually large withdrawal request or has a COD withdrawal problem, the participant should notify DTC's Expediting Group.

How Withdrawals Are Debited. If securities are available, the general free account will be reduced, except during an interim period, when the interim free account will be reduced.

When Withdrawals Are Rejected

DTC will: Depending on the time of submission as well as the reason for rejection, return the following to the participant via DTC's Central Delivery Department:

- *Day CODs*
- *Insufficient Participant Position/DTC-ineligibility*
  Copy 1 of the Withdrawal of Nominee Stock form stating the reason for rejection.
- *Denominations Not Available*
  Copy 2 of DTC's Remote Output Reply stating the reason for rejection.
- *Night CODs*
- *Insufficient Participant Position/DTC-ineligibility*
  Dropped Withdrawal List listing the withdrawals rejected and stating the reason for rejection.
- *Denominations Not Available*
  Copy 2 of DTC's Remote Output Reply stating the reason for rejection.

Inquiries/Errors/Discrepancies. The participant should note any discrepancy on a DTC Notification of Participant Activity Difference List, forwarding the completed form to DTC.

Procedures for FAST CODs. These procedures are applicable only to those issues currently included in the depository's FAST COD service.

The significant differences, aside from the forms to be used and the time schedule to be followed, between a FAST COD withdrawal and a regular COD withdrawal are as follows:

- Certificates are registered in a name previously specific by the participant (usually the participant's street name).
- Withdrawals may be made in round lots, odd lots, or mixed lots (e.g., 257 shares).
- Any appropriate New York stock transfer tax waiver stamp must be applied to the face of copy 1 of the withdrawal request.

The participant must: Prepare DTC Transfer Control form, limiting the form to one issue, one denominational request, and making sure copy 5 bears the firm's facsimile signature and all copies have been stamped with the legend "FAST." Also, be sure an appropriate New York stock transfer tax waiver stamp has been applied to copy 1 of the Transfer Control form.

Note: Due to DTC program limitations, the participant must limit the quantity field for FAST COD withdrawals to no more than five digits, e.g., 99,999. Any quantity submitted in excess of five digits will be rejected.

Retain copy 6 for a permanent record.

Forward copies 0 through 5 (day CODs) or copies 0 through 3 (night CODs) to DTC.

DTC will: Retain copies 0, 1, 2, 3, and 4 for its own internal processing; for same day CODs time-stamp copy 5, returning the time-stamped copy to the participant's messenger.

The participant will: Return to DTC's Central Delivery Department, where the messenger must present copy 5 bearing the DTC time-stamp.

DTC will then: Deliver the securities together with copy 2 of DTC's Remote Output Reply form, retaining copy 5 of the Transfer Control form as its receipt and for its own internal processing.

Municipal Bearer Bond Withdrawals

Participants may, from time to time, need to withdraw from their DTC accounts the bearer form of debt securities issued by state and local governments (municipal bearer bonds).

Procedures. Prepare a DTC Municipal Bearer Bond (MBB) withdrawal ticket, limiting the form to one issue and making sure copy 2 bears the participant's facsimile signature or the rubber stamp impression currently on file with DTC.

- Participants are reminded to enter the number of municipal bearer bonds in the quantity box on the withdrawal ticket (that is, enter "10" for a $10,000 withdrawal quantity, "25" for $25,000, etc.).
- Instead of preparing a MBB withdrawal ticket, participants subscribing to the Participant Terminal System (PTS) may request withdrawals of municipal bearer bonds by specifying the function "CODB." Accepted requests produce PTS MBB terminal tickets.

Hold copy 2 of the MBB withdrawal ticket or copy 1 of the PTS MBB terminal ticket for pick-up of the securities.

Retain copy 3 of the MBB withdrawal ticket or copies 2 and 3 of the PTS MBB terminal ticket for participant's records.

Forward copy 1 of the MBB withdrawal ticket to DTC.

Time schedule (Eastern time). Participants may submit withdrawal requests to DTC according to the following time schedule.

- *Day withdrawal,* 7:30 A.M. to 4:00 P.M. Day withdrawals are processed immediately against the participant's account and securities are available for participant pick-up the same day.
- *Night withdrawal,* 4:00 P.M. to 6:00 P.M. Night withdrawals are processed overnight and securities are available for participant pick-up the following business day. Night withdrawals are included as activity in the participant's account the following business day.

If the participant's securities position is sufficient, the general free account will be reduced, except during the interim accounting period for bond interest, when the interim free account will be reduced.

- Whenever a withdrawal request for day withdrawals cannot be filled initially due to insufficient participant position, the withdrawal request is automatically recycled until all account update processing (deposits, deliveries, etc.) is completed. Should the participant's position remain insufficient, the withdrawal request will be rejected.
- Night withdrawal requests are processed only in DTC's night cycle. They are not carried over to the following day cycle. Since such requests may be rejected in the night cycle for insufficient position, participants are reminded to compare their night MBB withdrawal tickets or night PTS MBB terminal tickets against the list of withdrawal rejects distributed by DTC the next day before attempting to pick up the bonds.
- Municipal bearer bonds withdrawn during the interim accounting period will not have the current coupon attached. Participants will receive credit for the interest payment through DTC's interest collection and distribution process on payment date.

Activity verification. The transaction(s) are reflected on the participant's statement (daily activity statement) available for participant pick-up at DTC at the opening of business on the following business day. The participant should note any discrepancy on a DTC Notification of Participant Activity Difference form and forward the completed form to DTC.

The notification must be received by DTC no later than noon on the day the statement was made available for pick-up.

Picking up bearer bonds at DTC. Present copy 2 of the MBB withdrawal ticket or copy 1 of the PTS MBB terminal ticket, bearing the participant's facsimile signature or the rubber stamp impression currently on file with DTC, to window 2 in the Central Delivery Department, beginning at 7:15 A.M. (Eastern time) for night withdrawal requests, submitted the prior evening, and three hours after submitting day withdrawal requests to DTC, but no later than 6:00 P.M. (Eastern time).

Rejected withdrawals. Depending on the reason for rejection, DTC will return to the participant via DTC's Central Delivery Department either copy 1 of the withdrawal ticket or a Withdrawal Drop Notice stating the reason for rejection.

The following are the most frequent causes for withdrawal request rejects:

- *Insufficient Position:* Long position must be checked before making a withdrawal request.
- *Incomplete Data:* CUSIP number and all other data must be correct.
- *Illegible Data:* All information must be legible.

DIVIDENDS AND INTEREST PAYMENTS

Cash and/or stock dividends and bond interest payments received by DTC are credited to participants' accounts.

Record Date Notification

A participant maintaining a position in any DTC account, with the exception of withdrawal by transfer, in a security record for dividend or interest payment will receive prompt notification of impending dividends or payments by means of a DTC Dividend Record Date Notice.

This notice, forwarded automatically to the participant via DTC's Central Delivery Department, names the security for which the dividend or interest payment is being declared and lists all the pertinent information, including the total number of shares or number of bonds held by the participant, the dividend or interest rate, and the record and payable dates. In addition, it displays adjustments to previously announced dividends or interest payments.

Whenever a security is record for dividend or interest payment and is in the process of being registered in the name of the participant or the participant's nominee—withdrawal of transfer—the disbursing agent will send the dividend directly to the registered holder.

Discrepancies/Inquiries. When a participant's records differ from those of DTC and the payment date has not passed, the participant is required to prepare a DTC Notification of Participant Activity Difference, forwarding the completed form immediately to DTC.

A participant's inquiries are researched and the results noted on the original copy of the inquiry; the annotated form is returned to the participant. Depending on the outcome of the research, DTC may make adjustments to the participant's record date position so that the proper disbursement will be made on payable date.

Interim Accounting for Distributions

When necessary, DTC applies interim accounting procedures between record date and payable date so that stock distributions and interest payments will be allocated to participants properly.

Interim accounting is used when:

There is a stock distribution that would require trades to settle with due bills attached. Rather than require due bills, DTC will open on the day after record date a separate account (an interim free account) for all deposit and withdrawal activities.

Deliveries and collateral loan pledges and releases are the only activities that are allocated to affect a participant's general free account during the interim period. The interim period ends at the close of business on the last day that trades settle with due bills, that is, the day prior to payable date for bond interest and at due-bill redemption date for stock distributions.

Bond settlement takes place with interest accrued. Interim accounting for bond interest generally parallels interim accounting for stock distributions.

When securities are transferred outside New York City, DTC may establish a cut-off day in advance of record date for the start of a modified interim account processing. When a cut-off date is used, DTC opens an interim account on the day after cut-off date and closes the interim account at the close of business on record date. In addition to deliveries and collateral loan activity, during the modified interim period DTC deducts withdrawals of nominee stock (CODs) from the participant's general free account. If the participant does not effect a transfer of the withdrawn Cede & Co. Cede certificate(s) by record date and does not receive special dividend protection from the transfer agent, the participant should make a dividend claim on DTC.

Credits for Cash Dividends and Interest Payments

Cash dividends and interest payments are credited to the participant's settlement account on the day of receipt, or if received by DTC too late in the day for inclusion in the day's money settlement, on the business day following receipt.

Participants are notified of cash dividends and interest payments by means of DTC's Dividend Cash Settlement List forwarded automatically to the participant via DTC's Central Delivery Department. The Dividend Cash Settlement List describes the security and lists the total amount being paid, as well as identifying the credit with a unique code. Explanations of the codes appear on the Dividend Cash Settlement List.

Credits for Stock Dividends

Stock dividends are credited to the participant's account by increasing the participant's position in the security for which a stock dividend has been declared. The increase is reflected on the participant's statement (daily activity) forwarded automatically to the participant via DTC's Central Delivery Department the following business day and on the Record Date Notice.

- Regular stock dividends are credited automatically to the participant's general free account at the start of business on payment date.
- Stock splits/distributions (interim accounting): For stock splits/distributions that are trading with due bills, DTC uses interim accounting, which eliminates the need for participants to issue due bills for an activity that is delivered or settled through DTC in an applicable security. Stock splits/distributions are allocated to all general accounts on the business day following the close of the interim period. Shares allocated to pledged accounts automatically become additional collateral for the loan, without requiring any action on the part of the participant.
- Cash in lieu of fractional shares resulting from a stock distribution is reflected on the DTC Cash Settlement List, as previously detailed.

Securities Transfer

When a corporation declares a stock dividend payable in DTC-ineligible securities, after allocating shares to the participant's account, DTC will generate and forward to the participant an Important Notice detailing DTC's procedures regarding this allocation, including pick-up arrangements.

All share withdrawals will be in COD form (registered in the name of and endorsed by Cede & Co., naming the participant as attorney).

Dividends/Interest Claims

Participants possessing or controlling certificates registered in the name of Cede & Co., DTC's nominee, over record date for a cash and/or stock dividend or interest payment, and having missed the record date by failing to transfer the certificates, and wishing to claim the dividend are required to prepare a DTC Dividend/Interest Claim form, forwarding the completed form and the securities being claimed on or facsimiles thereof to DTC.

The participant must: Prepare a DTC Dividend/Interest Claim form, checking to be sure that all the requested information is entered.

Retain copies 1 and 3 for the participant's records.

Attach by a paper clip or a staple in the upper left-hand corner, copies 1 and 2 of the Dividend/Interest Claim form to the securities (or facsimiles).

Forward in a DTC plastic envelope copies 1 and 2 of the Dividend/Interest Claim form and the securities (or facsimiles) to DTC.

Dividend Reinvestment Service

In recent years numerous issuers of DTC-eligible securities have implemented plans for the automatic reinvestment of dividends paid on securities issued by them. DTC has instituted a dividend reinvestment service (DRS) that will permit DTC to utilize certain of these plans on behalf of participants and their customers. Under the DRS, DTC, acting pursuant to a participant's instruction and the issuer's plan, will arrange for the reinvestment of dividends on qualifying securities. DRS will permit participants to maintain qualifying securities on deposit with DTC without losing the benefits available under such plans and will encourage further immobilization of certificates.

DTC determines those securities that qualify for DRS and notifies participants of that determination by Important Notice approximately three weeks prior to each cash dividend record date for a qualifying security.

A participant that has qualifying securities on deposit may authorize through DTC reinvestment of the cash dividends on all or a portion of the record date position in such securities. In accordance with its authorization and in order to insure that the cash dividends that are to be reinvested are not paid, DTC decreases the participant record date position for the cash dividend by the quantity of the security on which dividends paid are to be reinvested. DTC then notifies the administrator of the issuer's dividend reinvestment plan to effect such reinvestment. When DTC receives the dividend reinvestment plan payment (full shares plus cash in lieu of any fractional shares), it credits the shares to the participant's DTC account by book-entry and credits the cash to the participant's money account through the dividend settlement system. The dividend reinvestment plan payment date normally occurs approximately three weeks afer the cash dividend payment date.

DRS does not permit participants to make optional cash payments to purchase securities, and, depending upon the nature of the issuer's plan, may not permit participants to avail themselves of all beneficial features of the plan.

Dividend Reinvestment Option Announced. DTC will determine that a security qualifies for DRS if such a security is DTC eligible, the dividend reinvestment plan permits the utilization of these procedures, and the plan administrator agrees to act in accordance with these procedures. All provisions of the dividend reinvestment plan except as otherwise provided herein or in a DTC notice to participants will govern all action taken under these procedures.

Approximately three weeks prior to the dividend record date for a qualifying security, DTC notifies participants that these procedures apply to acceptances of the dividend reinvestment option. The notice includes a general description of the dividend reinvestment plan based upon information made available by the plan administrator. The notice also contains information relevant to processing dividend reinvestment instructions under these procedures, as follows:

- Time period during which participants must submit to DTC their reinvestment instructions on DRS Instructions forms. DTC generally accepts DRS instructions only on the business day after the dividend record date.
- The approximate date on which DTC will receive and allocate the dividend reinvestment plan payment of full shares plus cash in lieu of any fractional shares. This date is usually about three weeks after the cash dividend payment date.
- The plan's withdrawal cut-off date (normally one day prior to the purchase date) and the date and time by which participants must submit written notification to DTC if they elect to cancel DRS instructions previously submitted.
- The DRS position description and CUSIP number reserved by DTC to record by participant the quantity of securities on which the dividend is to be reinvested.

Notes for participants:

1. Reserve for internal processing the same CUSIP number reserved by DTC for the DRS position.
2. The DRS position is a memorandum position. It does not affect the participant's position in the underlying issue of qualifying securities that can be delivered, pledged or withdrawn in the usual manner, as the participant chooses. The DRS position represents the participant's rights through DTC to securities and cash in lieu of any fractional shares (the dividend reinvestment plan payment) in place of the cash dividend on a quantity of securities equal to the DRS position, in accordance with

Securities Transfer 233

these procedures and the terms of the dividend reinvestment plan as amended in order for the securities to qualify for these procedures.

Acceptance of the Dividend Reinvestment Option. After receiving DTC's notice that these procedures will apply to a dividend reinvestment option, a participant that has a dividend record date position in the qualifying security may reinvest the dividend on all or a portion of that position in the manner set forth below, with the time period specified by DTC's notice.

1. Type or print clearly on the DRS Instructions form the following information:

    a. At the top of the form, enter the firm name of the participant, participant number, and "today's" date.
    b. Under the "Security Identification," enter the quantity of the security equal to or less than the dividend record date position on which the dividend is to be reinvested. Also enter the CUSIP number, description of the security qualifying for DRS, and the dividend record date.
    c. Under "DRS Position Identification," enter the CUSIP number and security description exactly as assigned by DTC.

2. Retain copy 4 of the DRS Instructions form and forward copies 1, 2, and 3 to the DTC Dividend Department between the hours of 9:00 A.M. and 4:00 P.M. (New York time) on the day(s) specified by DTC's notice.
3. DTC acknowledges receipt of DRS instructions by time-stamping copy 3 of the form and returning it to the waiting participant messenger.
4. DTC prepares an Adjustment to Pending Dividend Notice and decreases the participant's dividend record date position by the quantity of securities on which the dividend is to be reinvested as specified in the DRS Instructions form. The Adjustment to Pending Dividend Notice specifies the reason for adjustment as "Participant DRS Instructions." DTC sends copy 2 of this notice to the participant via the DD Box.
5. DTC adds to the participant's DRS position the quantity of securities on which the dividend is to be reinvested. This activity appears in the daily participant activity statement.
6. DTC notifies the dividend reinvestment plan administrator to reinvest the dividend on the quantity of securities specified by the participant.

Withdrawal of Acceptance. A participant that has accepted a dividend reinvestment option under these procedures may withdraw its acceptance, if withdrawal is permitted by the terms of the plan, in the manner set forth below before the withdrawal date and time specified by DTC's notice.

1. Submit written notification to DTC's Dividend Department to cancel all or a portion of the dividend reinvestment instructions previously submitted.

2. Upon receipt of the withdrawal instructions, DTC notifies the dividend reinvestment plan administrator and deducts the withdrawn quantity from the participant's DRS position.
3. The plan administrator should issue a check for the dividend on the withdrawn quantity approximately three weeks after the cash dividend payment date. When the check is received, DTC prepares a Cash Dividend Adjustment Notice and distributes copy 2 of this notice and the cash to the participant through its dividend settlement system.

DRS Payment. Normally, the DRS payment date is approximately three weeks after the cash dividend payment date. When payment is received, DTC processes the payment as follows:

1. Allocates to each participant full shares and cash for any fractional interest as calculated by the dividend reinvestment plan administrator.
2. Closes out participants' DRS positions on its books. This activity appears in the daily participant activity statement

COLLATERAL LOAN

A participant may pledge securities credited to his own free accounts as collateral for a loan with any pledgee bank participating in DTC's Collateral Loan Program.

Pledge of Collateral

The following procedures are to be used when making a new loan, increasing an existing loan, or supplying additional collateral.

The participant must: Make customary arrangements with the pledgee bank, then prepare a Pledge of Collateral form.

- *Note:* A separate Pledge of Collateral form must be used in connection with each loan transaction for each different loan date.
- *Note:* In the event a bond or U.S. Government Treasury note is pledged as collateral, enter quantity in multiples of 1,000, e.g., "10" for $10,000, "50" for $50,000, etc.
  Retain copy 3 for participant's records.
  Forward signed copies 1 and 2 to DTC. For same day processing, they must reach DTC's Collateral Loan Department by 4:00 P.M. New York time.

DTC will then:

- Debit (reduce) participant's general or interim free accounts and credit (increase) participant's general or interim pledged accounts.

Securities Transfer 235

- Countersign copy 1, forwarding the signed copy to the pledgee bank as confirmation. Pledgee bank retains copy 1 for its records. In cases of pledgee banks located out of New York City, DTC will facsimile-transmit the forms bearing all the signatures described and subsequently mail the original to the out-of-town pledgee bank.

Other considerations:

1. When a stock distribution requiring due bills is declared on securities pledged as collateral, the distribution automatically becomes additional collateral.
2. A pledgee bank can at any time direct DTC to deliver securities pledged to it.
3. Securities pledged may not be from mixed accounts; that is, in the event 1,000 shares are pledged, the shares must either be totally in the general free account or totally in the interim free account. All transactions are reflected on the participant's statement.

Release of Collateral (Full or Partial)

The participant must: Prepare a Release of Collateral form. A separate Release of Collateral form must be used for each loan date. In the event a bond of U.S. Government Treasury Note is pledged as collateral, enter the quantity in multiples of 1,000, e.g., "10" for $10,000, "50" for $50,000, etc. Retain copy 3 for participant's records. Forward signed copies 1 and 2 to the pledgee bank. For same day processing, they must reach the bank by 3:15 P.M. New York time. In the event the pledgee bank is located out of town, the participant must forward copies 1 and 2 to DTC's Collateral Loan Department in time for DTC to transmit the release instructions to the out-of-town pledgee bank.

The pledgee bank will: Countersign copy 2 and forward it to DTC.

DTC will: Receive signed copy 2 from the pledgee bank, make the appropriate bookkeeping entries to release the securities from the participant's general or interim pledged accounts, and move them to the participant's general or interim free account. Though a telecopier is used between pledgee banks and DTC, the original copy 2 must be forwarded to DTC by the pledgee bank, with a note that it was previously transmitted. All transactions are reflected on the participant's statement.

CNS Release of Collateral

Participants may offset or lift a CNS Level II Exemption, which permits settlement of an outstanding CNS short obligation, by submitting a CNS Release of Collateral form. Procedures for a CNS release of collateral are the same as the preceding release of collateral procedures, except for the form used and an important time difference: CNS Release of Collateral form copy 2 signed by the pledgee bank must be received by DTC no later than 12:30 P.M.

New York time. After CNS processing has been completed, any remaining position is credited to the participant's general or interim free accounts in accordance with the procedures previously described in this section.

Substitution of Collateral

When a participant and pledgee bank agree to substitution of collateral— *The participant must:*

- Pledge the new securities, following the procedures detailed under the section Pledge of Collateral.
- Release securities previously pledged, following the procedures detailed for release of collateral.

In other words, for each security being substituted, the participant must pledge the new security and release the security previously pledged.

All transactions are reflected on the participant's statement.

OVERNIGHT LOAN

The DTC overnight collateral loan service gives participants the opportunity to pledge securities for an overnight bank loan while anticipating their automatic release from pledge the next morning in time for book-entry deliveries to other participants.

The overnight collateral loan program supplements basic DTC collateral loan services. The automatic release feature eliminates preparation and processing of separate regular release forms of CNS release forms for overnight loans and facilitates timely completion of book-entry deliveries dependent upon the released securities.

To make an overnight collateral loan, the participant prepares a special DTC Pledge/Release of Collateral (Overnight Loan) form, which is signed by the pledgee before it is processed by DTC. The form provides for automatic release of securities from pledge at 9:30 A.M. New York time on the next business day unless the pledgee cancels the automatic release before that time.

Securities released from pledge are used automatically to fill any recycling deliveries. Recycling deliveries may include:

- Deliveries to cover short positions in Stock Clearing's and AMEX Clearing's Continuous Net Settlement (CNS) system, recycling because no exemptions were submitted by the participant to those clearing entities the previous evening.
- Deliveries to cover CNS short positions, recycling because Level II exemptions were submitted by the participants to those clearing entities the previous evening. Note that the securities released from pledge are used automatically to cover the CNS short positions because overnight loan releases are always treated as qualifying CNS releases.

Securities Transfer 237

- Deliver Balance Orders (DBOs) submitted by the participant to DTC the previous evening or the same morning as the automatic release from pledge.
- Miscellaneous Deliver Orders (MDOs) submitted by the participant to DTC the previous evening or the same morning as the automatic release from pledge, including any MDOs overriding Level I CNS exemptions submitted the previous evening.

Procedures, Day 1

The participant (pledgor) must:

- Arrange overnight loan with the pledgee.
- Prepare special DTC Pledge of Collateral/Release of Collateral (Overnight Loan). Be sure that at least the quantity of each security pledged is credited to the participant's (pledgor's) DTC general or interim free account and that the securities may properly be pledged. Hereafter the Pledge of Collateral/Release of Collateral (Overnight Loan) form is referred to as the "pledge/release form."
- Use one pledge/release form for each overnight loan (multi-page loans are not permitted). Be sure not to combine securities in general and interim free accounts on the same form.
- Sign all copies of pledge/release form.
- Forward copies 1, 2, 4, and 5 of pledge/release form to pledgee (not to DTC).
- Retain copy 3.

If any of the securities pledged are to be used the next day to cover CNS short positions or for deliveries by DBO or MDO, anticipate automatic release of the securities from pledge in time to be available for the day cycle when preparing the delivery instructions for submission to the clearing entities and/or DTC. Remember that the pledgee has the right to cancel the automatic release of the pledged securities.

The pledgee will:

- Arrange overnight loan and repayment with participant (pledgor).
- Receive copies 1, 2, 4, and 5 of pledge/release form from participant (pledgor).
- Sign copies 1, 2, 4, and 5 of pledge/release form.
- Forward copies 1, 2, and 5 to DTC.
- Retain copy 4.

DTC will:

- Receive copies 1, 2, and 5 of pledge/release form from pledgee.

- Follow normal pledge processing routines, making the necessary bookkeeping entries to effect the movement of securities to pledged accounts, subject to the participant's (the pledgor's) having sufficient positions in general or interim free accounts.
- Sign copies 1, 2, and 5 of pledge/release form.
- Forward copy 2 of pledge/release form to pledgee, copy 5 to participant (pledgor).
- Retain copy 1.

The pledgee will then:

- Receive copy 2 from DTC (with DTC signature verifying pledge).
- Disburse loan proceeds to participant (pledgor).

Procedures, Day 2

The participant (pledgor) will: Pay pledgee directly or effect a day loan, new pledge of securities, or other repayment arrangements previously agreed to with pledgee.

The pledgee will: Receive payment from participant (pledgor) or put into effect other repayment arrangements previously agreed to with participant (pledgor).

DTC will:

- Release securities from pledge at 9:30 A.M. on the business day (i.e., the day on which DTC is open for business) following the day of pledge (the time of the preauthorized release), unless directed otherwise by pledgee before that time.
  —*Participant's (pledgor's) note:* The released securities will be used to fill any recycling CNS, DBO, or MDO deliveries in accordance with the participant's (pledgor's) instructions.
  —*Pledgee's note:* To prevent automatic release of securities from pledge: Notify DTC in writing to cancel the automatic release. Identify the release to be cancelled by the serial number, name of pledgee, and name of participant (pledgor) appearing on the pledge/release form. Be sure the notification carries an authorized signature of the pledgee.
- Deliver the notification to DTC at window 7 in DTC's Central Delivery Department before 9:30 A.M. New York time on the business day (i.e., the day on which DTC is open for business) following the day of pledge.

Notification to cancel the automatic release may be given to DTC by telephone or by such other means as DTC may permit at the time. DTC will use its best efforts to cancel the release but takes no responsibility for the cancellation of the release except where written notification is given in accordance with the procedures described above.

Telephone notification may be given by calling the manager, Collateral Loan Section, before 9:30 A.M. New York time on the business day (i.e., the day on which DTC is open for business) following the day of pledge. The caller must identify him- or herself and the release to be cancelled by the serial number, name of pledgee, and name of participant (pledgor) appearing on the pledge/release form. Subsequently, written notification is to be delivered promply to DTC at window 7 in DTC's Central Delivery Department.

Pledge/Release of Collateral With Banks Using Facsimile Transmission

In preparing the pledge/release form all items in the upper portion must be completed, and all securities should be listed in order by CUSIP number. All data entered on the form must be typed.

Procedures, Day 1
The participant (pledgor) must:

- Arrange overnight loan with pledgee.
- Prepare DTC pledge/release form. Be sure that at least the quantity of each security pledged is credited to the participant's (pledgor's) DTC general or interim free account and that the securities may properly be pledged.
- Use one pledge/release form for each overnight loan (multi-page loans are not permitted). Be sure not to combine securities in general and interim free accounts on the same form.
- Sign all copies of the pledge/release form.
- Forward copies 1, 2, 4, and 5 of the pledge/release form to DTC for facsimile transmission to pledgee.
- Retain copy 3. If any of the securities pledged are to be used the next day to cover CNS short positions or for deliveries by DBO or MDO, anticipate automatic release of the securities from pledge in time to be available for the day cycle when preparing the delivery instructions for submission to the clearing entities and/or DTC. Remember that the pledgee has the right to cancel the automatic release of the pledged securities.

DTC will:

- Receive copies 1, 2, 4, and 5 of pledge/release form from participant (pledgor).
- Facsimile-transmit copy 1 to pledgee for signature authorizing the pledge/release.

The pledgee will:

- Arrange overnight loan and repayment with participant (pledgor).
- Receive facsimile copy 1 of pledge/release form from DTC.
- Sign copy 1 and facsimile-transmit back to DTC.

DTC will then:

- Receive signed facsimile copy 1 of pledge/release form from pledgee.
- Follow normal pledge processing routines, making the necessary bookkeeping entries to effect the movement of securities to pledged accounts, subject to participant's (pledgor's) having sufficient positions in general or interim free accounts.
- Sign copies 1, 2, 4, and 5 of original pledge/release form received from participant (pledgor).
- Sign facsimile copy 1 received from pledgee.
- Facsimile-transmit copy 2 of pledge/release form to pledgee (with DTC signature verifying pledge).
- Forward copies 2 and 4 to pledgee.
- Send copy 5 of pledge/release form to participant (pledgor).
- Retain copy 1 of original pledge/release form.
- Retain facsimile copy 1.

The pledgee will:

- Receive facsimile copy 2 of pledge/release form from DTC (with DTC signature verifying pledge).
- Disburse loan proceeds to participant (pledgor).

Procedures, Day 2

The participant (pledgor) will: Pay pledgee directly or effect a day loan, new pledge of securities, or other repayment arrangements previously agreed to with pledgee.

DTC will:

- Release securities from pledge at 9:30 A.M. on the business day (i.e., the day on which DTC is open for business) following the day of pledge (the time of the preauthorized release), unless directed otherwise by pledgee before that time.
  —*Participant's (pledgor's) note:* The released securities will be used to fill any recycling CNS, DBO, or MDO deliveries in accordance with the participant's (pledgor's) instructions.
  —*Pledgee's note:* To prevent automatic release of securities from pledge: Facsimile-transmit notification to DTC to cancel the auto-

matic release. Identify the release to be cancelled by the serial number, name of pledgee, and name of participant (pledgor) appearing on the pledge/release form. Be sure the notification carries an authorized signature of the pledgee.
- Be sure notification is received by DTC before 9:30 A.M. New York time on the business day (i.e., the day on which DTC is open for business) following the day of pledge.

Notification to cancel the automatic release may be given to DTC by telephone or by such other means as DTC may permit at the time. DTC will use its best efforts to cancel the release but takes no responsibility for the cancellation of the release except where written notification is given in accordance with the procedures described above.

Telephone notification may be given by calling the manager, Collateral Loan Section, before 9:30 A.M. New York time on the business day (i.e., the day on which DTC is open for business) following the day of pledge. The caller must identify him- or herself and the release to be cancelled by the serial number, name of pledgee, and name of participant (pledgor) appearing on the pledge/release form. Subsequently, written notification is to be facsimile-transmitted promptly to DTC.

The pledgee will: Receive payment from participant (pledgor) or put into effect other repayment arrangements as previously agreed to with the participant (pledgor).

CONVERSIONS

Certain debt securities and preferred stocks are convertible by their terms at the option of holders. Typically, these convertible securities can be exchanged without additional payment for "underlying securities" (another class of securities, usually common stock, of the issuing company). Conversion options are generally exercisable at any time throughout the life of the convertible securities at a fixed rate of conversion. Exercises of conversion options are irrevocable.

The DTC conversions program enables participants to exercise conversion options within the book-entry environment. DTC determines which convertible securities qualify for processing under the program. Qualifying convertible securities are announced by DTC in a notice sent to participants and pledgees.

Participants wishing to exercise a conversion option authorize DTC to surrender qualifying convertible securities on deposit to the conversion agent on their behalf. Upon receipt of the authorizations, DTC deducts the convertible securities from participants' accounts and adds the underlying securities to their accounts. The underlying securities are then available for the full range of DTC services, including book-entry delivery to other participants and book-entry pledge for collateral loans.

Thus, under the DTC conversion program, participants do not have to withdraw securities from the depository for the purpose of converting them;

do not have to deliver them to the conversion agent or pledge window tickets for collateral loans; do not have to borrow securities or delay delivery until the underlying securities are received; do not have to handle or store the underlying securities; and, where the underlying securities are to be delivered by book-entry, do not have to deposit them with DTC. In summary, the DTC program provides participants with an economical and orderly method for exercising conversion rights.

Notice of Qualifying Convertible Securities

From time to time, DTC notifies participants and pledgees of the convertible securities whose conversion options may be exercised under these procedures.

Where DTC is notified that a convertible security qualifying for conversion under these procedures is to be partially or fully called for redemption, DTC in its notice announcing the impending call specifies the cutoff date and time by which participants must submit to DTC exercises of the conversion option in called securities.

Exercise of the Option

A participant having on deposit with DTC qualifying uncalled or called convertible securities may exercise the conversion option in the following manner.

1. Check carefully DTC's notices to make certain that the convertible security qualifies for conversion under these procedures.
2. Type a Conversion Instructions form as follows:
   a. At the top of the form, enter the firm name and participant number.
   b. At the top of the form, enter under "Transaction Date" the current date if the instructions are to be delivered to DTC between 8:30 A.M. and 11:00 A.M. (Eastern time) on that date, or enter the next business date if the instructions are to be delivered to DTC between 4:00 P.M. and 6:00 P.M. (Eastern time) on the current date.

   Also, if the date entered under "Transaction Date" is the dividend record date for the underlying security and an earlier standard industry dividend cut-off date, if any, established for the underlying security by a dividend announcement service (such as Standard & Poor's) is not applicable to DTC or other firms located in New York City, check the box labeled "Dividend Record Date." If the date entered under "Transaction Date" is a standard industry dividend cut-off date established for the underlying security by a dividend announcement service (such as Standard & Poor's) and is applicable to DTC and other firms located in New York City, check the box labeled "Dividend Cut-Off Date."

Securities Transfer

DTC takes no responsibility for arranging the conversion of convertible securities subject of conversion instructions processed by DTC on the dividend record date or the standard industry dividend cut-off date, as the case may be, in time to obtain dividend protection on the underlying securities if the box required to be checked is not checked by the participant.

DTC may reject the conversion instructions if the participant checks a box not required to be checked.

    c. Under "Convertible Security Identification," enter the quantity, CUSIP number, and description of the qualifying securities to be surrendered in exercise of the conversion option.

       Where the convertible securities are bonds, enter the number of bonds as the quantity (that is, enter "1" for $1,000 bond, "2" for $2,000, etc.).

       Where the convertible securities to be surrendered are called securities resulting from a call for redemption, enter the CUSIP number and security description exactly as assigned by DTC to the called securities, referring to DTC's notice announcing the call to participants.

    d. In the "Conversion Rate" section of the form, enter the number of shares of the underlying security into which each $1,000 principal amount of convertible bonds is convertible or into which each share of convertible preferred stock is convertible, as appropriate.

       Always give numbers to four places past the decimal, even where the low-order positions are zeros (such as .0000 or .5000).

       Where in doubt as to the exact conversion rate, contact the conversion agent.

    e. Under "Underlying Security Identification," enter the quantity, CUSIP number, and description of the underlying securities into which the convertible securities are convertible.

       Quantity of underlying securities is obtained by multiplying the quantity of convertible securities by the conversion rate. Always give numbers to four places past the decimal, even where the low-order positions are zero.

    f. Under "Participant Coordinators," enter the name and telephone number of the person(s) that DTC should attempt to telephone if the conversion instructions are rejected by DTC or the agent.

3. Forward copies 1, 2, 3, 4, and 5 of the Conversion Instructions form to the DTC Reorganization Section between 8:30 A.M. and 11:00 A.M. (Eastern time) for same day processing and between 4:00 P.M. and 6:00 P.M. (Eastern time) for next day processing, but not later than the final time specified by DTC's notice where the conversion option being exercised is in called securities. Retain copy 6.

4. DTC will time-stamp incoming Conversion Instructions forms and return copy 5 to your messenger.

5. DTC will deduct the convertible securities from your general free account and add the underlying securities to your general free account, as specified by the conversion instructions.

    The underlying securities are added to your account normally in time for book-entry delivery to other participants on the same day.
6. DTC has no obligation to examine conversion instructions that have been submitted to it or, if it does examine them, to conduct a thorough or accurate examination. Nevertheless, if DTC makes such an examination and the instructions do not pass such examination, or if your general free position is at any time after submission of the instructions insufficient to permit deduction of the convertible securities, DTC may reject the instructions by making copy 4 of the instructions available for pick-up by your messenger at DTC's Central Delivery Department. DTC will attempt to notify participants by telephone of rejections, calling first the coordinator(s) at the telephone number(s) entered in the Instruction form, if any, but takes no responsibility therefore.
7. DTC will prepare an Agent Receipt and Confirmation form and forward it, together with the Conversion Instructions form and the convertible securities, to the conversion agent.

Pledge and Transfer by Book-Entry of Underlying Securities

When a participant instructs DTC to convert a quantity of convertible securities into a quantity of the underlying securities, DTC will deduct such quantity of convertible securities from the participant's free account and add the appropriate quantity of underlying securities to the participant's free account. Since the conversion process will not have been completed at the time of the addition of the underlying securities to the participant's free account, a credit to any participant's account or pledgee's account, whether or not they have participated in a conversion, of a quantity of the underlying securities will represent rights in (a) the quantity of underlying securities in the custody of DTC or of a custodian bank or of a nominee of either, including securities resulting from participants' conversion instructions that are held by the conversion agent; (b) the quantity of convertible securities subject of participant's conversion instructions that are in the custody of DTC or of a custodian bank or of a nominee of either, including such convertible securities that are held by the conversion agent; (c) the rights, if any, in the underlying securities prior to their issuance pursuant to the terms governing the convertible securities; and (d) the rights against the conversion agent and the issuer arising from the submission of convertible securities to the conversion agent.

Any instruction given by a participant or a pledgee to transfer, pledge, or release from pledge underlying securities by book-entry will be deemed for all purposes of DTC's Rules and Procedures to be an instruction to transfer, pledge or release from pledge the rights described in clauses (a), (b), (c), and (d) of the preceding sentence rather than the underlying securities identified in the instruction. Any instruction given by a participant or a pledgee to withdraw physical certificates representing underlying securities from DTC shall nevertheless be deemed to be an instruction to DTC to deliver only the quantity of underlying securities identified in the instruction. Should, for any reason, the underlying securities subject of such a withdrawal instruction exceed the amount of underlying securities available for withdrawal, that instruction may be rejected by DTC.

Payment of Fractional Interest

When DTC receives from the conversion agent payment of cash in lieu of fractional interest in the underlying securities, DTC distributes the payment to participants through the DTC net settlement system.

DTC Activity Reports

Book-entry security activity related to conversions (deductions of convertible securities and additions of underlying securities) appears in the daily participant activity statements for verification by participants in the usual manner against the conversion instructions submitted to DTC.

REORGANIZATION

DTC's Reorganization Department deals with such events as mergers, tenders, and exchanges when they affect eligibility of securities for DTC. Participants are immediately notified of the events by an Important Notice. Sample notices and the procedures that both DTC and the participants must follow are described in this section.

MANDATORY EXCHANGE

DTC will: In the case of a mandatory exchange of a DTC-eligible security (say, in a merger, reverse, split, redemption, etc.), forward an Important Notice to all participants stating the particulars as well as advising the participant of dissenters' rights and specifying when deposits and deliveries will not be accepted.

When and if the mandatory exchange is effective, DTC's Reorganization Department will surrender the participant's unpledged (free) position in the security and obtain the new security for the participant. At that time DTC will debit (reduce) the participant's position for the security being exchanged and either credit (increase) the position in the new security or disburse cash proceeds or cash-in-lieu-of-fractional-shares.

The exchange may, in certain instances, involve receipt of another security.

The participant must: Release any collateral loan. When the security involved is being used as collateral for a loan, it is the responsibility of the participant to release or substitute the security.

Name Change

DTC will:

- When a DTC-eligible security undergoes a name change, forward an Important Notice to all participants stating the date when all DTC transactions must be in the new name.
- Upon effectiveness of the name change, DTC will debit (reduce) the participant's general free account in the old security name and credit (increase) the participant's general free account in the new security name.

The participant must: Deliver securities subject to DTC balance orders outstanding at the date when all DTC transactions must be in the new name by using miscellaneous deliver orders filled out in the new name.

Spin-Off

DTC will:

- When there is a distribution of a DTC security, DTC will forward an Important Notice to all participants, advising them that the securities have been allocated to the participant's account. If securities are DTC ineligible, the notice will specify the date when the securities are to be exited.
- On exit date, DTC's Reorganization Department will prepare Withdrawal of Nominee Stock forms, reducing to zero the participant's account in the DTC-ineligible security and furnishing the participant with certificates withdrawn.

The participant must: Pick-up. Participants are responsible for picking up the securities on the date and at the time stated in the Important Notice, if the securities are DTC ineligible.

Voluntary Exchanges: Tender and Exchange Offers

DTC will: When a tender or exchange offer relates to a DTC-eligible security, forward an Important Notice to all participants giving the exit date.

- *Prior to exit date:* Participant receives an Important Notice from DTC specifying the date when the security becomes DTC ineligible. Effective on that date, the only DTC activity in this security will be withdrawal of nominee certificates.
- *Exit date:* DTC's Reorganization Department will prepare Withdrawal of Nominee Stock forms, reducing to zero the participant's entire unpledged (free) position in the security being exited.

Securities Transfer 247

The participant must:

- Release any collateral loan. When the security involved is being used as collateral for a loan, it is the responsibility of the participant to release or substitute the security.
- If the participant does not release the pledged securities prior to exit date, the participant may not receive the securities in time for tender or exchange.
- Pick-up. Participants are responsible for picking up the securities on the date and at the time stated in the Important Notice, if the securities are DTC ineligible.

DEPOSITORY FACILITIES

Procedures for participant and nonparticipant depositors are basically the same. The only differences involve the forms to be used and the requirement for the nonparticipant to notify the participant of the deposit being credited to the participant's DTC account.

To obtain credit with DTC for deposits through a depository facility, the participant (and the nonparticipant depositing to the account of a participant) must comply with the rules and general operating procedures of DTC.

The participant and/or nonparticipant must:

- Check DTC's Eligible Securities booklet to determine if the security to be deposited is eligible for deposit in DTC. Copies of this booklet are available for a fee upon application to DTC.
- Be sure DTC's nominee name (Cede & Co.) has been entered in the assignment area on the back of the certificate and, where applicable, the appropriate New York State tax waiver stamp has been affixed to the back of the certificate.
- A participant may use an assignment separate from certificate for deposits of more than one certificate of the same security and the same registration.
- Be sure the back of the certificate has been properly endorsed, i.e., contains all necessary signature and/or erasure guarantees as well as power of attorney releases, whenever applicable.
- Prepare DTC deposit ticket limiting one form to one security issue, making sure the security description, quantity (odd and round lots of the same security issue may be combined), CUSIP number, and DTC participant number are correct.

    Bonds: Quantity of bonds is entered in multiples of 1,000, "1" for $1,000, etc.

    Baby bonds (less than $1,000) will not be accepted.

- Attach by a paper clip or a staple all five copies of the deposit ticket to the left side of the securities, making sure the clip or staple is also at the left side of the deposit ticket forms.
- When the accumulated deposits are ready for delivery to the depository facility, the participant or nonparticipant must prepare a Depository Facility Transmittal form, making sure to complete the top part of the form and starting with line item 1, making sure to limit each deposit to one line.
  Depository Facility Deposit Transmittal Form must be used even if it covers deposit of only one security.
- Attach by a paper clip or a staple all four copies of the transmittal form to the left side of the deposit ticket(s), making sure the securities are attached to the deposit ticket(s) and that the paper clip or staple is also at the left side of the transmittal form.
- Receive without thoroughly examining each deposit; the depository facility will verify that all items listed on the transmittal form are attached and receipt copy 4 of the transmittal form, returning the receipted copy to the participant.
- After examination of all certificates and forms, the depository facility will receipt copy 5 of the deposit ticket, returning the duly receipted form to the participant.
- Retain. Participant should retain and compare all receipted forms to verify the participant's statements (daily and end-of-month). If a customer of a participant is making a deposit to the participant's account (a "piggy-back" deposit), the customer should retain all receipted forms for the participant's subsequent reconciliation.

ADR Deposits

A participant or a nonparticipant depositing American Depositary Receipts (ADRs) must include the acronym ADR in the security description portion of the deposit ticket and must write the name of the depositary that issued the ADR in the upper right-hand corner of the deposit ticket.

In certain instances there is more than one depositary for the same security. In this event, the participant is required to prepare a separate deposit ticket for each depositary, even though the security being deposited is identical in all other respects.

CNS Deposits

Depository Facility DTC/CNS Deposit Ticket as well as a Depository Facility CNS Deposit Transmittal. In other words, except for the forms to be used, and the requirement for separate submission, the procedures and requirements for a CNS deposit are exactly the same as for a non-CNS deposit.

After CNS processing has been completed, any remaining position is credited to the participant's general or interim free accounts in accordance with the procedures described in this section.

Legal Deposits

Certain registrations requiring legal documentation for sale or transfer will be accepted provided that, among other things, each submission is limited to a separate deposit ticket and accompanied by appropriate documentation authorizing the sale or transfer of the security.

A Depository Facility Legal Deposit Ticket, as well as a Depository Facility Deposit Transmittal Legal is necessary, and follow the preceding deposit procedures. In other words, except for the forms to be used, and the requirements of accompanying documentation and separate submission, the procedures and requirements for a legal deposit are exactly the same as for a nonlegal deposit.

Special Considerations. In the case of *record stock:* Stock deposited for same day credit that is record for dividends on the day deposited or stock deposited for next day credit that is record for dividends on the credit date will *not* be accepted. In addition, if the deposited securities cannot reach DTC, New York, prior to 11:30 A.M. (New York time) on the next business day after credit date, where the next business day is the dividend record date, the depository facility will *not* accept the deposit.

Hold: In the case of a *reorganization item:* Securities that become DTC ineligible (based on merger, corporate reorganization, change in state of incorporation, etc.) will *not* be accepted for deposit on the day prior to the effective date of DTC ineligibility. Reorganization items for next day credit will *not* be accepted two days prior to the effective date of DTC ineligibility.

Exception: If a participant is making a deposit in a DTC-ineligible security to cover a short position, the deposit ticket must be marked "Reorg-Short." If those words do not clearly appear, the deposit will be rejected.

How Deposits Are Credited. Deposited securities are credited to the participant's general free account with the following exception: When there is a stock distribution or an applicable stock dividend, deposits are credited to the participant's interim free account from the close of business on record date until settlement date of the distribution.

Securities in either the participant's general free account or interim free account are eligible for all DTC services. Deposits are reflected on the participant's statement at the opening of business the following business day.

Participant should check this statement carefully, noting any discrepancy on a DTC Notification of Participant Activity Difference List.

Rejected Deposits

The depository facility and DTC will attempt to correct deposits that cannot be accepted in the form submitted. However, since a rejected deposit deprives the participant of use of the securities and in some cases may result in a short position while the cause for rejection is being resolved, the participant should take every precaution to avoid deposit rejects.

The following are the most frequent causes of deposit rejects.

- Certificates are not properly prepared.
- Security being deposited is not DTC eligible or is in the process of reorganization.
- Deposit tickets are not properly completed.
- CUSIP number does not agree with the security being deposited.
- Quantity or security description listed on the deposit ticket differs from the securities being deposited.

A fee will be assessed for excessive deposit rejects.
The Depository Facility will:

- *Correctable:* If it determines a deposit is unacceptable and the depository facility is able to make the correction (e.g., incorrect CUSIP number), the facility may correct copies 1 through 3 of the transmittal form and copies 1 through 5 of the deposit ticket, notifying the participant of the correction and forwarding the corrected deposit to DTC in the usual manner. The corrected item will also be listed on the Depository Facility Deposit Rejection Ledger at the completion of the deposit examination cycle and transmitted to DTC.
- *Not Correctable:* If it determines a deposit is unacceptable and the correction cannot be made, the depository facility will sign and stamp "Reject" next to the unacceptable line item on the transmittal form copies 1 through 3, returning the physical securities together with copies 1 through 5 of the deposit ticket to the participant. The unacceptable item will also be listed on the Depository Facility Deposit Rejection Ledger at the completion of the deposit examination cycle and transmitted to DTC.
- *Correctable transmittal form transmissions:* If any errors are found on the transmission of the transmittal form (e.g., ineligible security), DTC will notify the facility by phone and then transmit the corrected transmittal form to the facility. The facility will make the corrections on the applicable transmittal form and deposit ticket as outlined in the correctable and unacceptable deposits section.

DTC may:

- *Correctable:* If, on physical receipt of the securities and forms DTC determines a deposit is unacceptable and DTC is able to make the correction, DTC will make the correction, completing a Deposit Reject Notice and forwarding the completed notice to the participant. The corrected item will also be listed on the Depository Facility Rejection

Ledger and then transmitted to the depository facility by the Interface Department.
- *Not Correctable:* If, on physical receipt of the securities and forms, DTC determines a deposit is unacceptable and DTC is unable to make the correction, DTC will automatically debit the participant's account to the extent it was credited by the deposit.

After debiting the participant's account, DTC will complete a Deposit Reject Notice, forwarding the notice together with the securities to the participant's New York office. If the participant does not have a New York office, the Deposit Reject Notice together with the securities will be forwarded to the participant or nonparticipant via the facility by DTC's Interface Department. The unacceptable item will also be listed on the Depository Facility Deposit Rejection Ledger and then transmitted to the depository facility by the Interface Department.

The transfer agent will: Should the transfer agent determine a deposit is unacceptable, the transfer agent will return the securities to DTC together with a transfer agent's Reject Notice. DTC will then follow the procedures outlined herein.

When a depository facility accepts a deposit, the information is electronically transmitted to DTC in New York. DTC credits the participant's account to the full extent of the deposit. At this point, the participant may use this position in whole or in part.

Upon physical receipt of the securities and forms from the depository facility, usually the next business day, DTC examines the deposit. Should DTC then determine that the deposit is unacceptable and the reason for reject cannot be immediately corrected, DTC will debit the participant's account to the full extent of the deposit. If this debit drives the participant's account into a short (or negative) position, DTC will automatically debit the participant's money account 130 percent of the current market value of the securities used. The debit will remain in effect until the matter has been resolved.

CALLABLE SECURITIES

When a call occurs, DTC allocates called amounts of securities among participants by an impartial lottery method. Using their lottery techniques, participants in turn allocate to customers their portion, if any, of the call on DTC's holdings. The DTC lottery results are recorded in participants' accounts and, subsequently, the called securities are redeemed on redemption date on behalf of participants.

Definitions

The terms defined below have the meanings specified for the purposes of these procedures:

- *Transfer agent:* The organization chosen by the issuer of registered bonds or preferred stock to maintain records of holders and to select securities for redemption when a call is declared.
- *Record date:* The date on which the transfer agent closes its registration books for the purpose of selecting securities for redemption.
- *Publication date:* The date on which serial numbers of certificates selected for redemption are made available by the transfer agent. On and after this date, called securities are not a good delivery except when an entire issue is called or when the transaction is specifically in called securities.
- *Redemption agent:* Organization chosen to exchange redemption cash values for called securities.
- *Redemption date:* The date on which the redemption agent redeems called securities.

Before the Call

The full range of DTC's regular bookkeeping and custodial services is available for callable securities before the first call and between calls. During these periods . . .

The participant must: Determine that certificates have not been called and are transferable prior to depositing callable securities with DTC. Deposit rejects and short positions are subject to regular DTC charges.

The Call Announced

DTC will: As promptly as possible, upon learning of the impending call from the transfer agent, notify participants and pledgees. The notice will include all pertinent information made available by the transfer agent, plus the following:

- Security description and CUSIP number reserved by DTC for called securities.

    The CUSIP number reserved by DTC for the called securities contains the same issuer number (first six digits) as assigned to the callable securities. The issue number (next two digits) for the called securities is the highest user code: 99 for preferreds and 9Y for bonds. For example:

	CUSIP Number		
	Issuer	Issue	CK
Benef Corp 5% Cum Pfd	081721	50	8
Benef Corp 5% Cum Pfd Cld	081721	99	5
Alabama Pwr Co 9% 2000	010392	AY	4
Alabama Pwr 9% 2000 Cld	010392	9Y	6

- Cut-off date for deposits of securities is the record date.
- Cut-off date for withdrawals by transfer of securities is the business day prior to record date.

Deliveries, collateral loans, withdrawals of nominee securities all continue without interruption. Deposits and W/Ts are reactivated after publication date, when the transfer agent's books are reopened.

The participant must:

- Cover any short positions in the callable securities with deposits by record date. Otherwise, DTC short position charges continue at least to publication date, unless covered by a pledge release or receipt of a bookkeeping delivery. The charge may continue to publication date because the transfer agent's books are closed from record date to publication date and deposits will not be accepted during this period. Securities represented by short positions are subject to call by the Transfer Agent outside DTC. This potential call can be avoided by covering short positions by record date.
- Consider substituting securities on any outstanding loans collateralized by the securities subject to the impending call.
- Reserve for internal processing and input to DTC the same CUSIP number reserved by DTC for called securities.

The Call Lottery

Once the record date is established, the transfer agent makes final changes in registrations, closes the books, selects securities for redemption pro rata or by lot, and publishes the serial numbers of certificates fully or partially called. These procedures can take two weeks or more to complete.

DTC will:

- Receive notification of called certificates in the late afternoon of the day prior to publication date.
- Determine the total called amount of bonds or preferred shares to be allocated by the number of fully or partially called Cede & Co. certificates in the possession of DTC.
- Conduct its lottery based on participants' positions as of the close of business the day prior to publication date.
- Allocate the total called amount by impartial lottery to participants' net long positions.

The portion of the total called amount allocated to a participant reduces the participant's position under the callable security description and increases the participant's position under the called security description and CUSIP number reserved when the call was announced. The participant's free, pledged, and/or investment identification callable accounts are reduced, in that sequence, to the extent that each is sufficient to cover the called amount. The participant's corresponding called accounts are increased. Where pledged accounts are affected, pledgees are randomly selected.

Certificates held outside DTC in Cede & Co. name, in street name, or in any other name, including any certificates represented by short positions in DTC participants' accounts, may be called by the transfer agent. The called amounts of such certificates are not, of course, includable in DTC's lottery. Control and redemption of such certificates is the responsibility of participants.

On the morning following the lottery, DTC distributes reports of its lottery results to participants and pledgees. A Called Securities System Impartial Lottery Results report is sent to each participant who had a position in the callable security at the close of business the prior day, whether or not a portion of the total called amount was allocated by the lottery to the participant. A Called Securities System Pledgee Bank Report is sent to each pledgee affected by the lottery.

All changes in positions from callable accounts to called accounts are effective on publication date and appear on regular participants' activity statements and pledgee reports sent that day.

In some circumstances DTC will be notified after publication date. In such cases DTC's notice will contain special instructions for the participant to follow concerning the call.

The participant can combine the result of the DTC lottery with any called amount of the same issue held by the participant in a fungible mass outside DTC. The participant conducts an impartial lottery to allocate called amounts to accounts for which the securities are being held.

The participant should:

- *Note:* On and after publication date, called certificates and DTC bookkeeping transfers of called security positions are not a delivery except when an entire issue is called, or when the transaction is specifically in called securities.
- Contact: Where a called amount has been allocated to pledged securities by DTC's lottery, it is recommended that the participant contact the pledgee to arrange release or substitution prior to redemption date. The redemption proceeds for securities still pledged on redemption date are paid to the pledgee.
- Consider: Where a called amount has been allocated by DTC's lottery to securities in investment identification status, the participant should consider releasing the securities from that status. Called securities still in investment identification status on redemption date will be redeemed together with all other called securities.
- Review: Regulations applicable to participant in regard to participant's lottery system, disclosure to customers, and favorable calls should be reviewed.

In the event that called securities remain pledged on redemption date, the redemption proceeds are paid to the pledgee.

After the Call

After the publication date when the transfer agent's books are reopened, the full range of DTC's services, including deposits and withdrawals by transfer, is once again available on the uncalled securities.

During the period from publication date until two days before redemption date, normally about thirty days, certain DTC services are available on the called securities. They may be withdrawn in Cede & Co. nominee name. They may be delivered to other participants by book-entry to complete a transaction in called securities. Pledged positions may be released.

All such activities in called securities appear under the assigned security description and CUSIP number in participants' activity statements and pledgee reports apart from activities in uncalled securities. Deposits and withdrawals by transfer of called securities cannot be accepted by DTC because the transfer agent's books are closed.

Transactions in called securities must be completed by normal closing schedules on the third business day prior to redemption date. During the final two days, DTC prepares to redeem the securities on behalf of participants.

The participant must: Observe: In documents prepared for input to DTC during the period from publication date through the third business day prior to redemption date, be sure to use the appropriate security description and CUSIP number for uncalled securities or called securities, as the case may be. It is only during this period that DTC activities are available in both uncalled and called securities of the same issue.

Redemption

All called securities remaining in DTC's inventory as of the close of business on the third day prior to redemption date are automatically submitted to the redemption agent. This action is treated as a withdrawal by transfer and appear as such on participants' activity statements.

When the cash proceeds of the redeemed securities are received from the redemption agent, they are allocated to the proper participant accounts by DTC's cash dividend accounting system. The allocated redemption proceeds then appear on participants' regular cash dividend settlement listings and are payable through normal daily net settlement procedures. Where a participant and pledgee have failed to release called securities from pledge, the proceeds are paid to the pledgee.

By timely submission of the called securities to the redemption agent, DTC expects to receive their cash proceeds in time to distribute the proceeds to participants on redemption. On participants' activity statements the redeemed securities appear as released from the transfer account.

Dividends/Interest Distributions on Called Securities

In the event there is an interest payment or dividend distribution payable as of the redemption date, these funds will be disbursed in accordance with the procedures described in the DTC manual.

VOLUNTARY OFFERINGS

Roll-Over Option on U.S. Treasury Bills

The Secretary of the Treasury invites tenders for new U.S. Treasury bills by public notice. Such a notice regularly provides an option whereby settlement for accepted tenders may be made in maturing bills accepted in exchange—in other words, an option whereby maturing bills can be "rolled over" for new bills.

New twelve-month, six-month, and three-month bills are issued every four weeks, usually on Thursdays, with the official closing tender date falling on the prior Friday for new twelve-month bills and on the prior Monday for the new six-month and three-month bills. The six-month bills are issued as an additional amount of that outstanding twelve-month bill that has six months of life remaining and, thereafter, the old and new amount are identified by that twelve-month bill's description and CUSIP number. The three-month bills are issued as an additional amount of that outstanding twelve-month bill that has three months of life remaining and, thereafter, the old and new amount are identified by that twelve-month bill's description and CUSIP number. The outstanding twelve-month bills maturing on the issuance date of the new twelve-month, six-month, and three-month bills can be rolled over for any of the new bills.

New six-month and three-month bills are also issued in those weeks when twelve-month bills are not issued. They are usually issued on Thursdays, with the official tender closing date falling on the prior Monday. The three-month bills are issued as an additional amount of that outstanding six-month bill that has three months of life remaining and thereafter the old and new amount are identified by the six-month bill's description and CUSIP number. The outstanding six-month bills maturing on the issuance date of the new three-month and six-month bills can be rolled over for either of the new bills.

Notice of Roll-Over Option. On or about the fifteenth day of each month, DTC publishes for participants and pledgees a Treasury bill roll-over notice with respect to Treasury bills that are eligible securities. The notice includes the complete schedule for exercises of noncompetitive roll-over options that may be processed in accordance with these procedures during the following calendar month. It also contains information relevant to processing exercises of the roll-over options by book-entry, as follows:

Securities Transfer

- Security descriptions and CUSIP numbers reserved by DTC (called "contra security identification") for recording the cumulative quantity of maturing bills subject to exercises of roll-over options submitted to DTC by participants and pending with the Federal Reserve Bank of New York (FRBNY), fiscal agent of the United States.
- "DTC input days" on which participants can submit to DTC exercises of roll-over options on Voluntary Offering Instructions forms.

Provisions of the roll-over notice may also modify or supplement these procedures with respect to a particular roll-over option. In such a case, such provisions will supersede or supplement these procedures for the purposes of the roll-over option as if they were a part of these procedures.

For each bill maturing during the following calendar month, the CUSIP number reserved by DTC for the contra securities contains the same issuer number (first six digits) as assigned to the bills maturing and to be surrendered. The issue number (next two digits) for the contra securities is a user code selected by DTC from range specified in the CUSIP directory. For maturing twelve-month bills, where three roll-over options are available (roll-over into new twelve-month, six-month, or three-month bills), three security descriptions and CUSIP numbers are reserved for corresponding contra securities. For example:

	Description	CUSIP NO.
Surrendered security	Bill 11/06/80	912793 4R 4
Contra security	Roll to 12 Mo Bill &	912793 9Y 4
Contra security	Roll to 6 Mo Bill &	912793 9S 7
Contra security	Roll to 3 Mo Bill &	912793 9G 3

In the security description, "roll" stands for roll-over option and "&" for contra security.

For maturing six-month bills, where two roll-over options are available (roll over into new three-month bills or roll over into new six-month bills), two security descriptions and CUSIP numbers are reserved for corresponding contra securities. For example:

	Description	CUSIP NO.
Surrendered security	Bill 11/13/80	912793 ZE 9
Contra security	Roll to 6 Mo Bill &	912793 9Q 1
Contra security	Roll to 3 Mo Bill &	912793 9E 8

The last time for participants to submit voluntary offering instructions to DTC is normally 11:00 A.M. (Eastern time) on Thursday, the last DTC input day each week.

Exercise of the Option. A participant having on deposit with DTC maturing U.S. Treasury bills may exercise a noncompetitive roll-over option in accordance with these procedures after receiving DTC's roll-over notice and only on the DTC input days specified for the particular option by the notice.

Exercises of roll-over options under these procedures are irrevocable.

1. Type a Voluntary Offering Instructions form as follows:
    a. At the top of the form, enter firm name and participant number. Also enter the current date if the instructions are to be delivered to DTC between 8:30 A.M. and 11:00 A.M. (Eastern time) on such date or enter the next DTC business date if the instructions are to be delivered to DTC between 4:00 P.M. and 6:00 P.M. (Eastern time) on the current date.
    b. Under "Surrendered Security Description," enter the quantity, CUSIP number, and the description of the maturing bills eligible for the roll-over option and to be surrendered.
    Enter the number of bills as the quantity (that is, enter "10" for a $10,000 bill, "15" for $15,000, etc.). The CUSIP number and security description may be taken directly from DTC's roll-over notice.
    c. Check off the Roll-Over box in the "Purpose" section of the Instructions form.
    d. Under "Contra Security Identification," enter the CUSIP number and security description exactly as assigned to the roll-over option, referring to DTC's roll-over notice.
    Exercise extreme caution when entering the contra security CUSIP number because by that entry you specify which rollover option will be exercised.
    e. Under "Participant Coordinators," enter the name and telephone number of the persons that DTC should attempt to telephone if the voluntary offering instructions are rejected by DTC or the FRBNY.
2. Type a Roll-Over Customer List for attachment to the voluntary offering instructions, as follows:
    a. At the top of the form, enter your name, participant number, and the date and preprinted serial number from the Voluntary Offering Instructions form just completed as described above.
    b. In the body of the form, enter your customers' names and the amounts bid and included in the quantity entered on the Voluntary Offering Instructions form.
    Note: Enter the number of bills as the amount bid (that is, enter "10" for $10,000 bill, etc.).
    The amount bid must be at least 10 bills ($10,000) and an even multiple of 5 bills ($5,000) per customer.
    The amount bid for each customer or for the participant's own account is not to exceed 500 bills ($500,000) through all sources.

Customers' bids for 25 bills and less ($25,000 and less) may be combined and the total entered on one line identified only by the number of such customers.

All bids are noncompetitive.
   c. At the bottom of the form, enter the columnar totals and the grand total, which must equal the quantity entered on the Voluntary Offering Instructions form.
3. Attach copy 1 of the Roll-Over Customer List behind copies 1, 2, 3, and 4, and 5 of the Voluntary Offering Instructions form by stapling through their stubs. Retain copy 6 of the instructions form and copy 2 of the Customer List for your records.
4. Forward the stapled forms to the DTC Reorganization Section between 8:30 A.M. and 11:00 A.M. (Eastern time) for same day processing on only those DTC input days specified in the roll-over schedule in DTC's roll-over notice, or between 4:00 P.M. and 6:00 P.M. (Eastern time) for next day processing on only those same DTC input days.

   Normally, the DTC input days each week are Monday, Tuesday, and Wednesday; the official tender closing date at the FRBNY is the following Friday for new twelve-month bills and the following Monday for new six-month and three-month bills; and the maturity/issuance day is the Thursday following the tender closing date.
5. DTC will time-stamp all copies of incoming voluntary offering instructions.
6. DTC will deduct the maturing bills being surrendered from your general free account and add the contra securities to your general free account, as specified by the voluntary offering instructions. The surrendered securities deducted from your account are held in DTC's FRBNY account, subject to their roll-over into the new Treasury bills pursuant to the irrevocable instructions of the participant or their payment on maturity (see "Rejection of Tender" below). For a description of the rights evidenced by the contra securities, see "Pledge of Contra Securities" below. You may not deliver, transfer, or withdraw contra securities from your account.
7. If voluntary offering instructions do not pass any review conducted by DTC or if your general free position is, at any time after submission of the instructions, insufficient to permit deduction of the quantity of bills to be surrendered, DTC may reject the instructions by making copy 4 available for pick-up by your messenger at DTC's Central Delivery Department. DTC will attempt to notify participants by telephone of rejections, calling first the coordinator(s) at the telephone(s) entered in the instructions form, if any, but takes no responsibility therefor. Participants are responsible for accurately completing the Voluntary Offering Instructions form, and DTC is not responsible for reviewing accurately any Voluntary Offering Instructions form.

8. DTC will prepare an official noncompetitive tender for the new bills and forward it, together with all voluntary offering instructions and Roll-Over Customer Lists, to the FRBNY by the official tender closing date.

Pledge of Contra Securities. A participant having exercised a noncompetitive roll-over option pursuant to these Procedures may pledge by book-entry the contra securities that have been added to its account. For the purposes of their pledge, the contra securities represent (i) the participant's rights in the maturing Treasury bills until their maturity, subject to their roll-over into new Treasury bills pursuant to the irrevocable instructions of the participant; and (ii) upon the maturity of such bills and the issuance of new Treasury bills and the accompanying roll-over proceeds on the maturity/issuance date, the participant's rights in the new Treasury bills and the roll-over cash proceeds and upon the rejection or proration of their tender, if any, the payment of the Treasury bills not rolled over on their maturity date.

1. Contact the pledgee to determine acceptability of the contra securities as collateral.
2. Complete the loan in the usual manner in accordance with DTC rules.

Obtain the release of the contra securities from pledge prior to the maturity/issuance date. Otherwise, the roll-over cash proceeds or any payment of Treasury bills not rolled over due to a rejection or proration of the tender will be paid to the pledgee, and the new Treasury bills become subject to the pledge.

Rejection of Tender. The Secretary of the Treasury expressly reserves the right on any occasion to reject any or all tenders or parts of tenders and to award less than the amount applied for, and any action he may take in any such respect or respects shall be final.

1. Upon notification of such action by the Secretary of the Treasury, DTC in turn notifies affected participants. DTC will attempt to notify participants by telephone of rejections, calling first the coordinator(s) at the telephone number(s) entered in the instructions form, if any, but takes no responsibility therefor.
2. If an entire tender submitted by DTC pursuant to these procedures is rejected, DTC reduces participants' positions in the contra security and increases participants' positions in the surrendered security to reflect the rejection.
3. If part of a tender submitted by DTC pursuant to these procedures is rejected or if an amount less than the amount applied for is awarded, DTC reduces participants' position in the contra security and correspondingly increases participants' positions in the surrendered security in such proportion as the amount of the tender rejected or not awarded bears to the total amount of the tender unless DTC is able and authorized to, and in

its sole discretion elects to, allocate the amount rejected to particular participants.

Payment. DTC receives payment (that is, the new Treasury bills and the roll-over cash proceeds) from the FRBNY on the maturity/issuance date, usually Thursday of each week.

1. DTC distributes Dividend Record Date Notices to participants, showing their final position in the contra security on DTC's books and the rate of payment.
2. DTC allocates payment when received to participants based on their positions in the contra security.
3. DTC sends to participants on payment date stock dividend distribution reports showing the new bills due to them. Dividend Settlement Listings sent to participants on the same day show the next cash roll-over proceeds paid through the DTC settlement system that day. The net cash roll-over proceeds equals the par value of the maturing bills less the issue price of the new bills.

DTC Activity Reports. Book-entry activity related to a roll-over option—exercises, pledges, releases, rejections, new bill payments—appears in daily participants' activity statements and pledgee reports, as appropriate, which reported activity must be verified by participants and pledgees in the usual manner against instructions submitted to DTC and notices of adjustments made by DTC in respect of rejections of tenders.

GOVERNMENT SECURITIES

U.S. Treasury bonds, notes and Federal Agency securities are eligible for DTC through a system developed with the Federal Reserve Bank of New York and the American Stock Exchange.

The system links the Federal Reserve's and DTC's book-entry systems so that all participants may deliver and store Government securities. Definitive Government securities (certificates in bearer or registered form) are thus rapidly eliminated, minimizing risk of their loss, theft, or destruction.

DTC does not handle or hold in its vault definitive Government securities.

Deposits

Participants may deposit securities in the DTC accounts by:

- moving securities by book-entry from their custodian accounts with banks that are members of the Federal Reserve,
- delivering definitive securities in registered or bearer form to a Federal Reserve Bank.

Withdrawals

Participants may withdraw securities from their DTC accounts by:

- moving them by book-entry to their custodian bank accounts,
- receiving definitive securities in registered or bearer form at the Federal Reserve Bank of New York (FRBNY).

Delivery and Settlement

Miscellaneous deliver orders (MDOs) are used to make deliveries by DTC book-entry. Those participants whose transactions in Government securities are cleared by the American Stock Exchange Clearing Corporation or acknowledged through DTC's Institutional Delivery (ID) system make deliveries via PDQ or deliver balance orders (DBOs). Participants may also pledge Government securities by book-entry through DTC's collateral loan program.

Interest Payments

Regular DTC services for collecting and distributing interest payments and redemption proceeds and for allocating calls by impartial lottery apply to Government securities. Transactions appear on the participant's statement (daily activity).

Deposits. It is important that participants note:

- DTC credits participants' accounts for deposits only upon notification from the FRBNY that the securities are in DTC's account at the FRBNY.
- DTC does not accept deposits of definitive Government securities on its premises.
- Participants may not deposit securities into another participant's DTC account.
- Nonparticipants may not piggy-back deposit/deliver Government securities into a participant's DTC accounts.
- Deposits must not be against payment.

Deposits of Book-Entry Securities. Eligible Government securities held by a bank in custody for a participant can be moved to the participant's DTC account through the Federal Reserve's book-entry system.

The participant must:

- Check DTC's Eligible Securities booklet to determine if the security to be deposited is eligible for deposit in DTC. DTC's Eligible Securities booklet is available at a fee from DTC.

Securities Transfer

- Instruct the custodian bank to deliver the appropriate securities to DTC's account at the FRBNY for the participant's account at DTC. In its Fed wire message, the participant's custodian bank must identify DTC's account at the FRBNY by number (026002066), name (DTC NYC) and type (CUST) and must identify the participant's account at DTC by Participant number and name; thus:

    . . . . Depository Trust . . . . Firm . . . .
    026002066 DTC NYC/CUST/999   Any Participant

    Securities will be added to the participant's account at DTC after receipt of the bank's wire message on DTC's Fed wire terminal. If the wire message is received by DTC before 11:00 A.M. New York time, the deposit will be credited in time to be used the same day for DTC book-entry deliveries.

- Obtain copy 3 of the deposit advice, which will be held for pick-up by the participant's messenger at DTC's Central Delivery Department.

    The participant must follow up with its custodian bank if the deposit advice is not received in a reasonable time. DTC is not aware of the deposit upon receipt of the advice via the Fed wire.

Deposits of Definitive Securities (Certificates) at FRBNY. Eligible definitive Government securities in registered or bearer form may be deposited in the participant's DTC account by delivering them (with appropriate instructions) to the FRBNY. Check DTC's Eligible Securities Booklet to determine if the security to be deposited is eligible for deposit in DTC. DTC's Eligible Securities booklet is available for a fee from DTC.

The participant must:

- Prepare securities and endorse them as specified in Section 306.121 of Sub-part "O" of the Department of Treasury Circular Number 300, as follows:

    To the Federal Reserve Bank of New York, as Fiscal Agent of the United States, for conversion to book-entry Treasury securities.

    The assignment must be executed and supported by evidence as set forth in Circular 300. Copies are available from the FRBNY, and a quick reference guide to Circular 300 for the most common types of transactions, prepared by the FRBNY, is available from DTC.

    Manual signatures are required for all assignments and supporting documents. The signatures must be witnessed and guaranteed by an authorized officer or employee of a member bank of the Federal Reserve or by another qualified person (See Section 306.45 of Subpart "F" of Circular 300), and the certifying bank's corporate seal or savings bond validating stamp must be affixed.

- Prepare the FRBNY's application form GB 622, which may be obtained from the FRBNY. Identify DTC account, number, name, type, and participant number and name thus:

Appendix F

```
. . . . Depository Trust . . . .          . . . . Firm . . . .
026002066 DTC NYC/CUST/999      ANY PARTICIPANT
```

- Deliver the registered securities and form GB622 to:
    Federal Reserve Bank of New York
    Government Bond Division, Registration Section
    33 Liberty Street
    2nd Floor, Window No. 15
- Take the bearer securities and form GB622 to the:
    Federal Reserve Bank of New York
    Safekeeping Division, Receiving Section
    33 Liberty Street
    Temporary location on 6th Floor
  DTC will add the securities to the participant's DTC account after the FRBNY's wire message is printed on DTC's terminal. Wired deposit advices received by DTC before 11:00 A.M. New York time create positions available for DTC book-entry deliveries on that day.
- Obtain copy 3 of the deposit advice, which will be held for pickup by the participant's messenger at DTC's Central Delivery Department.

  The participant must follow-up with the FRBNY if the deposit advice is not received in a reasonable time. DTC is not aware of the deposit until receipt of the advice via its Fed wire.

Note:

1. Bearer securities presented to the FRBNY are usually credited to DTC's account on the day they are presented by participants, particularly when they are presented early in the day.
2. Registered securities take at least one week for the FRBNY and the Department of the Treasury to process and credit to DTC's account. Complicated deposits might take longer.

   Treasury Department regulations mandate the closing of transfer books "for one full month preceding interest payment dates and call or maturity dates." The FRBNY adds two days to the closing period for its own processing requirements.

Deposits of Definitive Securities (Certificates) at Other Federal Reserve Banks. A participant may deposit DTC-eligible definitive Government securities in registered or bearer form in its DTC account by delivering them with appropriate instructions to the local Federal Reserve Bank (FRB). DTC's Eligible Securities booklet is available for a fee from DTC.

The participant must:

- Confirm that the local FRB offers the service and its exact requirements.

- Deposits of registered securities take considerably longer to complete than deposits of bearer securities, due to additional steps required to process and forward registered securities to DTC's account at the FRBNY.
- Instruct the FRB to move the securities by book-entry to DTC's account at the FRBNY for the participant's account at DTC.
- The participant must follow up with its custodian bank if the deposit advice is not received in a reasonable time. DTC is not aware of the deposit until receipt of the advice via the Fed wire.

Deposits of Definitive Securities (Certificates) at DTC Depository Facilities. A participant may deposit DTC-eligible definitive Government securities in registered or bearer form in its DTC account by delivering them with appropriate instructions to a DTC depository facility. DTC's Eligible Securities booklet is available monthly at a nominal fee from DTC.

The participant must:

- Confirm that the depository facility offers the service and its exact requirements.

    Deposits of registered securities take considerably longer to complete than deposits of bearer securities, due to additional steps required to process and forward registered securities to DTC's accounts at the FRBNY.
- Instruct the depository facility to deliver the securities to a Federal Reserve Bank, with instructions to move the securities by book-entry to DTC's account at FRBNY, for the participant's account at DTC. In performing this function, the depository facility bank is acting as the participant's servicing agent. The participant must follow up with its depository facility if the deposit advice is not received in a reasonable time. DTC is not aware of the deposit until receipt of the advice via the Fed wire.

Delivery and Settlement

Once eligible securities have been credited to a participant's DTC account, they are available for delivery by DTC bookkeeping entries to other participants. Deliveries can be made by deliver balance orders (DBOs) or via PDQ by those participants whose trades are cleared by the American Stock Exchange Clearing Corporation or are acknowledged through the Institutional Delivery (ID) system. Deliveries can also be made by miscellaneous deliver orders (MDOs).

Institutional Delivery (ID) System

Eligible Government securities are eligible for processing through the ID system.

Collateral Loans

Government securities on deposit in a participant's DTC account may be pledged by book entries in the usual manner as collateral for a bank loan or to secure the participant's obligation to the DTC Participants Fund.

In Pledge and Release forms as in other transactions, the quantity for Government securities must be entered in multiples of 1,000, e.g., "10" for $10,000, "50" for $50,000, etc.

Withdrawals. It is important to note:

- DTC accepts requests from participants for any type withdrawal of Government securities between 4:00 P.M. and 6:00 P.M. (New York time) for deduction from participants' DTC accounts on the next transaction day. DTC also accepts requests for book-entry withdrawals only between 8:30 A.M. and 11:00 A.M. (New York time) for processing the same day. All withdrawal requests must be submitted to the Government security window in DTC's Central Delivery Department.
- DTC does not hold definitive Government securities in its vault and does not issue securities on its premises against withdrawal requests.
- Withdrawals cannot be made against payment.
- Participants must sign a letter of indemnity with DTC in order to make registered or bearer withdrawals. Participants who have not signed such a letter should contact their participant services representative for further information.

Withdrawals of Book-Entry Securities. Government securities in a participant's DTC account can be moved to the participant's custodian bank account by book entry.

The participant must:

- Instruct its custodian bank to notify the Federal Reserve Bank or branch in its district to accept the book-entry delivery of securities from DTC for the participant's account at its custodian bank.
- Check its custodian bank's ABA number and its Fed wire name and the participant's Fed wire account type, number, and name.
- Prepare a WGS form as follows:
- Enter the participant's firm name at top of the WGS form.
    Line 2 Enter the participant's custodian bank's ABA number and type code 20.
    Line 4 Enter the participant's DTC number.
    Line 5 Enter bank's ABA name (e.g. WELLS SF), the participant's account type at the bank (e.g., CUST for custody, INV for investment), and the participant's account number and name at the bank (e.g., 234567 ANYPARTICIPANT). For example: WELLS SF/CUST/234567 ANYPARTICIPANT

Securities Transfer

> Line 8 Enter the standard name of the Government security, the CUSIP number, and (in the space just to the left of the pre-printed zeros) the number of bonds or notes to be withdrawn. DTC publishes the standard name and CUSIP number for each government security when it becomes DTC eligible.

- Check off box 2 at the bottom of the WGS form.
- Forward copies 1, 2, 3, and 4 of the WGS form to DTC. For same day processing they must reach DTC between 8:30 A.M. and 11:00 A.M. New York time. For next day processing, they must reach DTC between 4:00 P.M. and 6:00 P.M. New York time.
- Retain copy 5 as the participant's permanent record.

DTC will: Deduct the securities from the participant's DTC account and wire a withdrawal advice to FRBNY. The FRBNY computer will immediately acknowledge that the securities have been deducted from DTC's account at the FRBNY.

There is a charge for book-entry movement of securities out of the Federal Reserve Bank of New York's district (District 2).

The participant must: Obtain withdrawal advice and copy 3 of the WGS form from DTC's Central Delivery Department.

Once securities have been delivered by book entry to the participant's bank account, the participant may withdraw them in registered form or in bearer form, as required, by instructions given directly to the participant's bank.

Withdrawal of Bearer Securities at FRBNY. A participant may withdraw bearer securities from its DTC account by giving appropriate instructions to DTC. The bearer securities are made available for pick-up by participants at the FRBNY.

The participant must:

- Prepare a WGS form as follows:
- Enter the participant's firm name at the top of the WGS form.
    > Line 2 Enter the FRBNY's ABA number (021001208) and type code 82.
    > Line 4 Enter the participant's DTC number.
    > Line 5 Enter the FRBNY's ABA name (FRB NYC) followed by CUST/DEL TO and the participant's firm name. For example: FRB NYC/CUST DEL TO ANYPARTICIPANT
    > Line 6 Enter the desired number of pieces and denominations (e.g., 2 X 25,000) to be issued in bearer form.
    > Line 8 Enter the standard name of the Government security, its CUSIP number, and (in the space just to the left of the pre-printed zeros) the total number of bonds or notes to be withdrawn from the participant's account and issued in bearer form.

- Check off box 3 at the bottom of the WGS form.
- Forward copies 1, 2, 3, and 4 of the WGS form to DTC. For next day processing, they must reach DTC between 4:00 P.M. and 6:00 P.M. New York time.
- Retain copy 5 as the participant's permanent record.

DTC will: Deduct the securities from the participant's account and wire a withdrawal advice to the FRBNY in the morning of the next day. The FRBNY computer will immediately acknowledge that the securities have been deducted from DTC's account at the FRBNY.

The participant must: Obtain withdrawal advice and copy 3 of the WGS form from DTC's Central Delivery Department.

The FRBNY notifies the participant when the bearer securities are ready for pick-up (usually on the same day DTC wires the withdrawal advice to the FRBNY). For a messenger to pick up the bearer securities, the messenger must have a letter from the participant containing the messenger's signature and authorizing him or her to take delivery of the securities. The letter must be signed by an official of the participant whose signature is on file at the FRBNY. To file official signatures at the FRBNY, contact the chief of the FRBNY Safekeeping Division.

Withdrawals of Registered Securities at FRBNY. A participant may withdraw registered securities from its DTC account by giving appropriate instructions to DTC. The securities are made available for pick-up by participants at the FRBNY.

The participant must:

- Prepare a WGS form for each registration as follows:
- Enter the participant's firm name at the top of the WGS form.
    Line 2   Enter the FRBNY's ABA number (021001208) and type code 20.
    Line 4   Enter the participant's DTC number.
    Line 5   Enter the FRBNY's ABA name (FRB NYC) followed by CUST/DEL TO REGIS SECTION; that is enter
             FRB NYC/CUST/DEL TO REGIS SECTION
    Line 6   Enter the desired number of certificates and denominations (e.g., 3 X 10,000) to be registered in the same name.
    Line 8   Enter the standard name of the Government security, its CUSIP number, and (in the space just to the left of the pre-printed zeros) the total number of bonds or notes to be withdrawn and registered in the same name. Check off box 1 at the bottom of the WGS form.
- Prepare a FRBNY application form GB622. The form must be signed by a partner, officer, or other authorized employee of the participant firm.

Note: the application form must contain the social security number, or employer/tax identification number of the party in whose name the securities are to be registered.
- Attach, by a staple through their stubs, copies 1, 2, 3, and 4 of the WGS form and all copies of the GB622 form.
- Forward the forms to DTC. For next day processing they must reach DTC between 4:00 P.M. and 6:00 P.M. New York time.
- Retain copy 5 of the WGS form as the participant's permanent record.

DTC will: In the morning of the next day, deduct the securities from the participant's DTC account and forward copies 3 and 4 of the WGS form, with the GB622 form, to the FRBNY for validation. When the FRBNY returns the validated copy 3 of the WGS form and a receipted copy of the GB622 form to DTC (usually later the same day), DTC will wire a withdrawal advice (similar to Exhibit 4) to the FRBNY. The FRBNY computer will immediately acknowledge that the securities have been deducted from DTC's account at the FRBNY.

The participant must:

- Obtain withdrawal advice, copy 3 of the WGS form and the copy of the GB622 receipted by the FRBNY from DTC's Central Delivery Department.

  The FRBNY notifies the participant when the registered securities are ready for pick-up. The participant's messenger must then take to the FRBNY the receipted copy of the GB622 form previously picked up at DTC. This copy must first be signed by an authorized official of the participant and also by the messenger who is to pick up the securities. The messenger will be asked to sign again at the FRBNY for the release of the securities.
- Inquire of the FRBNY if registered securities are not received within a reasonable time.

  Ordinarily, it takes at least one week for the FRBNY to issue registered securities.

Special Considerations

Redemption proceeds of Government securities may be paid in federal funds upon request of participants.

Interest Payments

Interest is paid by DTC on Government securities based on participant's closing DTC positions on the day preceding the interest payment date.

The Federal Reserve's books are closed (normally one month and two days) to transfers of registrations prior to interest record dates. Therefore, there are no deposits and withdrawals of Government securities in registered form into and out of participants' DTC accounts that would affect DTC interest distributions.

Deposits of book-entry securities and definitive securities (certificates) in bearer form into participants' DTC accounts, which are credited to DTC's account at the FRBNY up through the business day prior to interest payment date, are included in participants' closing DTC positions and, therefore, are in turn properly included in the DTC interest distribution.

Withdrawal requests for bearer securities submitted by participants to DTC up through the afternoon of the second business day prior to an interest payment date are reflected in participants' closing DTC positions and excluded from the DTC interest distribution.

Withdrawal requests for book-entry securities submitted by participants to DTC before 11:00 A.M. New York time on the day prior to interest payment date are also properly reflected in participants' closing DTC positions and excluded from the DTC interest distribution.

Requests for withdrawals of Government securities submitted to DTC after the above-mentioned times are deducted from participants' positions on the next business day and, therefore, do not affect closing DTC positions or DTC interest distribution.

Interest payments appear on the participants' regular cash dividend settlement listings and are paid through DTC's normal daily net settlement system.

PROXIES

DTC does not directly exercise any voting rights of shares registered in the name of Cede & Co. Instead, DTC facilitates the voting of Cede & Co. shares by extending the voting rights to the appropriate DTC participants.

DTC will prepare:

- Notice of Stockholder Meeting listing impending record dates and meeting dates for DTC-eligible securities.
- Dividend/Proxy Take-Off Listing naming the security, identifying the participant maintaining a position in the security, and listing the number of shares held by each participant as of record date.
- Participant Name Listing giving full names of all DTC participants, along with abbreviations for the names used in the Dividend/Proxy Take-off Listing.
- Bank Contact List listing of all DTC bank participants, along with mailing addresses, names of contact(s), and telephone number(s).
- Omnibus proxy assigning voting rights to the full extent of each participant's position as listed on the Dividend/Proxy Take-Off Listing and authorizing the participant to vote the shares in the participant's firm or corporate name.
- Proxy Record Date Notice advising the participant of the delivery of omnibus proxy and Dividend/Proxy Take-Off Listing to the issuer and listing the number of shares the participant is entitled to vote.

DTC will forward to the issuer:

- Dividend/Proxy Take-Off Listing identifying the participants entitled to vote and number of shares.
- Participant Name Listing explaining the abbreviations used for participants' names.
- Bank Contact List listing DTC's bank participants together with names, addresses, and telephone numbers.
- Omnibus proxy assigning voting rights and authorizing the participants to exercise those rights in its own name.

DTC will forward to the participant:

- Notice of Stockholder Meeting advising the participant of impending record and meeting dates.
- Proxy Record Date Notice advising the participant of delivery to the issuer of omnibus proxy material and giving record date, meeting date, and number of shares of record.

Upon receipt of the Proxy Record Date Notice, it becomes the responsibility of the participant to contact the issuer direct for the appropriate sets of proxy material. It is also the responsibility of the participant to complete and execute proxy cards, returning them direct to the issuer.

Special Considerations

In the event that a participant's record date position must be adjusted due to, among other things, a rejected deposit or a proxy claim, a corrected Proxy Record Date Notice will be distributed to the participant.

In accordance with existing procedures, participants may withdraw from their DTC accounts certificates registered in the name Cede & Co. Although those securities are deleted from DTC's records and are thus not reflected in the name of Cede & Co. on record date. Participants holding such certificates may claim proxies in respect thereof by submitting to DTC a formal claim and proof that the certificates were outstanding in the name of Cede & Co. on record date and an indemnity agreement. After examining and approving the claim, DTC will adjust the number of shares shown opposite the participant's name on a Dividend/Proxy Record Date Listing and forward an adjusted omnibus proxy and the listing to the issuer.

On rare occasions, persons who are not participants claim voting rights attendant to certificates registered in the name of Cede & Co. that they held on record date. DTC will give such persons proxy cards executed by Cede & Co. and limited to the appropriate number of shares. Such persons will remain responsible for completing these cards and sending them direct to the issuer.

In the case of a shareholder consent in lieu of a meeting where a fixed record date is involved, DTC will follow the omnibus proxy procedures previously described.

APPENDIX G

New York Stock Exchange: Rules Pertaining to Securities Transfer and Processing

RULE 195: ASSIGNMENTS

(a) A certificate of stock, a registered bond, or other registered security shall be accompanied by a proper assignment, executed either on the certificate itself or on a separate paper, in which latter case there shall be a separate assignment for each certificate or bond.

Separate Assignments
(b) A separate assignment shall contain provision for the irrevocable appointment of an attorney, with power of substitution and a full description of the security, and shall be in the form approved by the Exchange. The number of shares of stock or the principal amount of a bond shall be expressed in both words and numerals.

RULE 196: POWER OF SUBSTITUTION

When the name of an individual or member organization has been inserted in an assignment, as attorney, a power of substitution shall be executed in blank by such attorney.

When the name of an individual or member organization has been inserted in a power of substitution, as substitute attorney, a new power of substitution shall be executed in blank by such substitute attorney.

When the name of Stock Clearing Corporation has been inserted in an assignment, as attorney, or in a power of substitution, as substitute attorney, a power of substitution shall be executed in blank by Stock Clearing Corporation as provided in Rule 200(e).

When the name of any nominee of Stock Clearing Corporation, in whose name is registered any security included within the Central Certificate Service established and maintained by Stock Clearing Corporation, has been inserted in an assignment, as attorney, or in a power of substitution, as substitute attorney, a power of substitution shall be executed in blank by such nominee as provided in Rule 200(f).

RULE 197: ALTERATIONS OR CORRECTIONS

Any alteration or correction in an assignment, power of substitution, or other instrument shall be accompanied by an explanation on the original instrument, signed by the person, firm, or corporation executing the same.

RULE 198: SIGNATURES

The signature to an assignment or power of substitution shall be technically correct; that is, it shall correspond with the name as written upon the certificate in every particular with alteration or enlargement, or any change whatever, except that in the case of a firm "and" or "&," "Company," or "Co." may be written either way.

RULE 199: CORPORATE ASSIGNMENTS

(a) A certificate in the name of a corporation (except as provided in paragraph (b) hereof) or an institution or in a name with official designation shall be a delivery only if the statement "Proper papers for transfer filed by assignor" is placed on the assignment and signed by the transfer agent.

Member corporations

(b) A certificate in the name of a member corporation shall be a delivery provided the assignment is executed either (1) by the manual signature of an officer of that member corporation or other person authorized pursuant to Rule 200(a) or (2) by the mechanically reproduced facsimile signature of an officer of that member corporation adopted in accordance with Rule 200(b), and the following statement appears on the assignment: "Authorizing resolutions filed with New York Stock Exchange."

RULE 200: ASSIGNMENT BY MEMBER ORGANIZATIONS

Member Corporations: By Authorized Persons

(a) A member corporation may authorize one or more of its officers or one or more other persons who are either its employees or who are officers or employees of Stock Clearing Corporation to assign registered securities in the name of the member corporation and on its behalf and to guarantee assignments, by filing with the Exchange in the form prescribed to it a certified copy of resolutions of its Board of Directors, authorizing such person or persons so to act.

Member Corporations: By Facsimile Signature of Officer

(b) A member corporation may assign securities registered in the name of such member corporation, and may execute powers of substitution by means of a mechanically reproduced facsimile signature of an officer of such member corporation, provided the member corporation shall have (1) executed and filed with the Exchange, in the form prescribed by it, an agreement with respect to the use of such facsimile signature; (2) filed with the Exchange, in the form prescribed by it a certified copy of resolutions of the Board of Directors of such member corporation authorizing the execution and filing with the Exchange of such agreement; and (3) complied with such other requirements as may be prescribed by the Exchange in connection with the use of facsimile signatures.

Members and Member Firms: By Authorized Persons

(c) A member or member firm may authorize one or more persons who are either his or its employees or who are officers or employees of Stock Clearing Corporation, to assign registered securities in the name of such member or member firm and to guarantee assignments, with the same effect as if the name of such member or firm had been signed under like circumstances by such member or by one of the partners of the firm, by executing and filing with the Exchange in the form prescribed by it a separate Power of Attorney for each person so authorized.

Members and Member Firms: By Facsimile Signature

(d) A member or member firm may assign securities registered in the name of such member or member firm and may execute powers of substitution, provided the member or member firms shall have executed and filed with the Exchange in the form prescribed by it an agreement with respect to the use of such facsimile signature and shall have complied with such other requirements as may be prescribed by the Exchange in connection with the use of facsimile signatures.

Stock Clearing Corporation: Powers of Substitution by Facsimile Signature

(a) Stock Clearing Corporation may execute powers of substitution by means of a mechanically reproduced facsimile signature of an officer of such corporation, provided such corporation shall have (1) executed and filed with the Exchange in the form prescribed by it an agreement with respect to the use of such facsimile signature; (2) filed with the Exchange in the form prescribed by it a certified copy of resolutions of the Board of Directors of such corporation authorizing the execution and filing with the Exchange of such agreement; and (3) complied with such other requirements as may be prescribed by the Exchange in connection with the use of facsimile signatures.

Detailed Procedure To Be Followed in Effecting Appointments Pursuant to Rule 200

.10 Assignments by member corporations. A member corporation desiring to authorize officers or other persons for the purposes set forth in Rules 199 (b) and 200(a) above, shall have adopted at a meeting of its Board of Directors resolutions in the forms prescribed by the Exchange authorizing such persons to act and file certified copies of such resolutions with the Department of Stock List.

The resolutions authorize the officers or other persons named therein, in the name and on behalf of the corporation, to assign registered securities, to guarantee signatures, and to make other necessary certifications or guarantees in connection with the transfer of securities.

The resolutions provide that any issuer of securities (whether or not listed on the Exchange), its transfer agents, and any bank, banker, or trust company, in whatever capacity it may act, having received at any time from the Exchange or from the member corporation (1) notice of the filing with the Exchange of certified copies of the resolutions, supporting certificates and specimen signatures, and (2) facsimiles of the specimen signatures of the persons authorized by the resolutions, may at any time rely on any instrument or paper that has been signed in accordance with the resolutions prior to the receipt by them from the Exchange or from the member corporation of written notice of the revocation of the authorization.

Two forms of corporate resolutions are provided, as follows:

(1) *Resolutions authorizing officers of the member corporation (designated by titles) to act.* These grant continuing authority to the persons from time to time holding the offices designated and become effective for those persons duly elected and certified by an Incumbency Certificate.

(2) *Resolutions authorizing specific persons (other than officers) to act.* These grant authority to the persons specifically named therein. Any subsequent authorization must be covered by a new set of resolutions.

A person authorized pursuant to this procedure will sign his name, over the designation "Authorized Signature," in conjunction with an imprint of the name of the Member corporation, which may be in the form of a rubber stamp, and reads as follows:

JOHN JONES & CO., INC.
By [signed] Richard Roe
Authorized Signature
(Authorizing resolutions filed
with New York Stock Exchange)

Resolutions authorizing officers to act must be accompanied by an Incumbency Certificate, executed by the Secretary or an Assistant Secretary, as to the names of the persons duly elected to the offices of the member corporation designated by the resolutions and the genuine signatures of such persons.

Resolutions authorizing persons other than officers must be accompanied by a certificate of the Secretary or an Assistant Secretary as to the genuine signatures of the persons authorized by the resolutions to act.

In either event, a legal opinion of the attorney for the member corporation that the member corporation has the power under its charter, by-laws, and the laws of the state under which it is organized to confer the authority and power given by the resolutions must be filed with the resolutions.

In filing resolutions (other than officers) the Exchange requires a covering letter stating that the person being authorized is an employee of the member corporation (or an officer or employee of Stock Clearing Corporation).

Cards in the form provided by the Exchange and containing specimens of the signatures to be used by the persons authorized also must accompany the resolutions, in order that the Exchange may have cards prepared bearing facsimiles of the signatures. These cards are sent by the Exchange to all transfer agents for listed securities, together with the notice of the filing of the certified resolutions, supporting certificates, and specimen signatures with the Exchange. This procedure makes it unnecessary for member corporations to file resolutions or signature cards with transfer agents for listed securities. A supply of the signature cards issued by the Exchange will be sent the member corporation for its use in connection with transfers of unlisted securities.

Notification in the following manner should be given the Exchange of the revocation of any authorization:

(1) *Officers.* Whenever it is desired to revoke the authority previously given by resolutions to an officer designated by title, a certificate to this effect, executed by the Secretary or an Assistant Secretary of the member corporation, shall be filed with the Exchange.

Whenever there is a change in the identity of a person holding an office that has been designated by title in a resolution filed with the Exchange and it is desired to revoke the authority of the person leaving that office and to establish the authority of the person succeeding to that office, a certificate, executed by the Secretary or an assistant secretary of the member corporation, evidencing the change in the identity of the person holding such office should be filed with the Exchange. In addition, a new Incumbency Certificate covering all officers of the member corporation who have authority to sign, executed by the Secretary or an assistant secretary of the member corporation, must be filed with the

Exchange, together with a signature card containing a specimen of the signature of any newly authorized officer.

(2) *Persons other than officers.* Whenever it is desired to revoke the authority previously given to any named person (other than an officer), a copy of the resolution of the Board of Directors of the member corporation revoking the authority previously given that person and stating that the authority previously given that person and stating that the authority previously granted the remaining named persons is being continued must be filed. This must be certified by the Secretary or an assistant secretary of the member corporation.

Whenever it is desired to authorize a new person (other than an officer) to sign, whether or not that new person is being substituted for a person whose authority is being revoked, the Exchange must be furnished with a new Certificate as to Authorized Persons covering the new person who is being authorized to sign and all other persons (other than officers) who will continue to sign, together with the necessary certified copy of resolution granting authority to the new person.

In order to defray in part the expenses of the Exchange in preparing signature cards and notifying transfer agents, a charge will be made by the Exchange on the filing of the resolutions, at the rate of $100 for one person being authorized, and $60 for each additional person being authorized at the same time.

.20 *Powers of attorney to employees.* A member or member firm desiring to appoint one or more employees for the purposes set forth in Rule 200(c), above, must execute and file with the Department of Stock List, in form prescribed by the Exchange, a separate power of attorney for each employee appointed, signed by either (1) all general and limited partners; or (2) above, an appropriate provision, in form approved by the Exchange, must be included in the partnership articles, or an amendment thereto, signed by all partners of the firm, both general and limited. A suggested form of such provision may be obtained from the Exchange. These powers of attorney will be kept on file by the Exchange.

Two forms of power of attorney are provided, authorizing an employee to sign for the firm as follows:

Type A power authorizes the employee to sign the firm name, i.e., "John Jones & Co."

Type B power authorizes the employee to sign his or her name in conjunction with an imprint of the firm name, i.e., "John Jones & Co. By [signed] Richard Roe, Attorney."

Only one type of power may be used at any one time by a firm in appointing attorneys for the firm.

A power of attorney filed with the Exchange must be accompanied by a specimen of the signature that will be used by the person appointed, together with a covering letter stating that the person being authorized is an employee of the member firm (or an officer or employee of Stock Clearing Corporation). On receipt of a power of attorney in proper form and a specimen signature, the Exchange will undertake to have cards prepared bearing facsimile signatures, which will be furnished to transfer agents of all listed securities, together with notice of the appointment.

A power of attorney is revocable by notice in writing to the Exchange and according to the provisions of the power. Transfer agents may rely on instruments executed by such attorneys until they receive written notice of revocation from the member or firm appointing the attorney or from the New York Stock Exchange.

The expenses of the Exchange in connection with the preparation of signature cards and notifying transfer agents are to be borne by the members and member firms availing themselves of the privilege. For this purpose, a charge is made on filing of the powers with the Exchange at the rate of $100 for one power and $60 for each additional power filed at the same time.

If powers of attorney are executed under (1) above, arrangements should also be made for the addition of the signatures of any new partners (general or limited) to any powers on file with the Exchange promptly after their admission to the firm.

.30 Machine-imprinted facsimile signatures. A member organization desiring to make use of a machine-imprinted facsimile signature for the purposes set forth in Rule 200, above, must file with the Department of Stock List an agreement in the form prescribed by the Exchange. In the case of a member firm, the agreement must be signed by either (1) all general and limited partners or (2) designated partners constituting a Special Committee appointed for that specific purpose under the partnership articles of the firm. If it is desired to execute the document under (2) above, an appropriate provision in form approved by the Exchange must be included in the partnership articles, or an amendment thereto, signed by all partners of the firm, both general and limited. A suggested form of such provision may be obtained from the Exchange. In the case of a member corporation, the agreement must be signed by an officer pursuant to resolutions, in form prescribed by the Exchange, of the Board of Directors of the corporation duly adopting the facsimile signature of a specified officer as the signature of the corporation and directing the filing of the agreement.

In the agreement the member organization agrees to indemnify the Exchange, any issuer of securities (whether or not listed on the Exchange), its transfer agents, and any bank, banker, or trust company, in whatever capacity it may act, that has received from the Exchange or from the member organization a specimen of the facsimile signature, from any loss or liability arising out of any act done in reliance upon the authenticity of the facsimile signature or one resembling or purporting to be the facsimile signature, when used as provided in the agreement.

In connection with the use by a member corporation of a mechanically reproduced facsimile signature, the member corporation must file with the Exchange a legal opinion of the attorney for the member corporation that the facsimile signature has been duly adopted by the member corporation, the agreement properly authorized, and the signature, the agreement, and the resolutions are effective and binding upon the corporation under its charter, bylaws, and the laws of the state under which it is organized.

The member organization must also file with the agreement an acknowledgment by their surety company of the issuance of a rider to their blanket bond to protect the member organization against loss resulting from their agreement, which may be in the form of a photostat of such rider.

Prior to the execution of such an agreement, full details of the procedure to be followed by the member organization and of the machine and signature plate to be used should be furnished the Department of Stock List so that the requirements for the use of machine signatures may be followed.

Upon approving the use of a particular facsimile signature by a member organization, the Exchange will send a notice to transfer agents for listing securities, together with a card containing a specimen of the facsimile signature imprinted from the actual signature plate to be used by the member organization. The imprinting of the signature on the cards for the Exchange will be done by the member organization using its own machine on cards furnished by the Exchange. A supply of the imprinted cards will be sent the member organization for its use in connection with transfers of unlisted securities.

The expenses of the Exchange in connection with the preparation of signature cards and notifying transfer agents are to be borne by member organizations availing themselves of this procedure. For this purpose, a charge of $100 is made on the filing of the agreement with the Exchange.

If the agreement is executed under (1) above, arrangements should also be made for the addition of the signatures of any new partners (general or limited) to the agreement on file with the Exchange promptly after their admission to the firm.

RULE 201: ASSIGNMENTS BY PERSONS SINCE DECEASED, TRUSTEES, GUARDIANS, ETC.

A certificate shall not be a delivery except as noted under (a), (b), or (c) below with an assignment of power of substitution executed by (1) a person since deceased; (2) a trustee or trustees, except trustees acting in the capacity of a board of directors of a corporation or association, in which case Rule 199 (a) shall apply; (3) a guardian; (4) an infant; (5) an executor; (6) an administrator; (7) a receiver in bankruptcy; (8) an agent; or (9) an attorney, except as provided in Rule 200(c).

Exceptions: (a) Domestic individual executor(s) or administrator(s). (b) Domestic individual trustee(s) under inter vivos or testamentary trusts. (c) Domestic guardian(s), including committees, conservators and curators.

Supplementary Material

.10 Exceptions, Domestic. The above exceptions to Rule 201 are to cover transfers that will be effected by transfer agents without additional documenta-

tion. Such exceptions apply only to securities of a domestic issuer (one organized under the laws of any state of the United States, and the District of Columbia) that bear the above domestic registrations set forth in (a), (b), and (c). Certificates bearing such registrations must be properly assigned, and the signature(s) to the assignment must be guaranteed pursuant to Rule 209.

RULE 202: ASSIGNMENT BY INSOLVENTS

A certificate with an assignment or power of substitution executed by an insolvent shall be a delivery only during the closing of the transfer books, during which time such a certificate shall be a delivery only if held by others than the insolvent and if accompanied by an affidavit that the said certificate was so held on a date prior to the insolvency and the signature to the assignment or power of substitution is guaranteed as provided in Rule 209.

RULE 203: ASSIGNMENTS BY DISSOLVED MEMBER ORGANIZATIONS

A certificate with an assignment or power of substitution executed by a member organization that has since ceased to exist shall be a delivery only during the closing of the transfer books, provided the execution of the assignment or power of substitution is properly acknowledged and the signature thereto is guaranteed as provided in Rule 209.

RULE 204: ASSIGNMENTS BY CONTINUING MEMBER ORGANIZATIONS

A certificate with an assignment or a power of substitution executed by a member organization that has since dissolved or ceased to be a member organization and is succeeded by either—

(1) A member firm or firms having as general partners one or more of the members or allied members in the dissolved or former member organization; or

(2) a member organization or corporations having as members or allied members one or more of the members or allied members in the dissolved or former member organization

shall be a delivery only if the new member organization or one of the new member organizations shall have signed the statement "Execution guaranteed" as of the date of, or a date subsequent to, the formation of the new member organization so signing.

RULE 205: ASSIGNMENTS—CHANGE IN MEMBER ORGANIZATION NAME

A certificate with an assignment or power of substitution executed by a member organization the name of which has since been changed shall be a delivery only if such member organization shall have signed the statement "Execution guaranteed" as of the date of, or a date subsequent to, the change in name.

RULE 206: JOINT TENANCY; SPECIAL DESIGNATION, etc.; TENANCY IN COMMON

A certificate with an inscription to indicate joint tenancy or with a qualification, restriction, or special designation shall not be a delivery.

A certificate with an inscription to indicate tenancy in common shall be a delivery only if signed by all co-tenants.

RULE 207: CERTIFICATES ISSUED IN TWO OR MORE NAMES

A certificate issued in the names of two or more individuals or firms shall be a delivery only if signed by all the registered owners.

RULE 208: MARRIED WOMEN

A certificate in the name of a married woman shall be a delivery except that, where applicable law limits the right of a married woman to transfer the certificate, such certificate shall be a delivery only when the assignment is executed jointly by husband and wife and acknowledged before a notary public or other qualified officer.

Note: The laws of Texas, Arizona, and New Mexico, and some foreign countries restrict the rights of married women to transfer certificates.

RULE 209: SIGNATURE GUARANTEE

Except with respect to registered securities of the United States Government, the signature to an assignment of a certificate not in the name of a member, a member organization, or a nominee of Stock Clearing Corporation in whose name is registered any security included within the Central Certificate Service established and maintained by Stock Clearing Corporation shall be guaranteed by a member or member organization or by a commercial bank or trust company, which bank or trust company either (a) is organized under the laws of the United States or of the State of New York and has its principal office in the vicinity of the Exchange or (b) does not have its principal of-

Securities Transfer

fice in the vicinity of the Exchange but is a national bank or other member of the Federal Reserve System and whose signatures are on file with and acceptable to the transfer agent for the security.

Each signature to a power of substitution executed by other than a member, member organization, Stock Clearing Corporation, or a nominee referred to in this rule shall be guaranteed in like manner.

.10 *"Vicinity of the Exchange."* The Exchange has determined that the words "vicinity of the Exchange" shall mean that part of the Borough of Manhattan, City of New York, located south of Chambers Street.

RULE 210: MEMBER SIGNATURE IS GUARANTEE

An endorsement or guarantee of an assignment or power of substitution shall be a guarantee of the signature to such assignment or power of substitution and shall also be a guarantee of the legal capacity and authority of the signer.

RULE 211: OUT-OF-TOWN MEMBER EXECUTIONS

(a) A certificate with an assignment or power of substitution executed or guaranteed by a member or member organization not having in the vicinity of the Exchange an office at which settlement of Exchange contracts is regularly effected shall be a delivery only if such assignment or power of substitution shall be (1) guaranteed by a member or member organization having such an office in the vicinity of the Exchange or (2) stamped as follows by such member or member organization first delivering it:

Delivered by _____
[Name of resident member
or member organization]

Guarantee by Commercial Bank or Trust Company

(b) A certificate with an assignment or power of substitution guaranteed by a commercial bank or trust company, as provided in Rule 209, shall be a delivery only if such assignment or power of substitution is (1) guaranteed by a member or member organization first delivering it:

Delivered by _____
[Name of member or
member organization]

RULE 212: GUARANTEE BY INSOLVENT

A certificate with an assignment or power of substitution guaranteed by an insolvent shall be a delivery only if reguaranteed as provided in Rule 209.

RULE 213: TRANSFER BOOKS CLOSED INDEFINITELY

The Exchange may in particular cases direct that assignments and powers of substitution on certificates of a company whose transfer books are closed indefinitely be properly acknowledged.

RULE 214: TRANSFEREES IN ERROR

A certificate of stock on which the name of a transferee has been filled in in error shall be a delivery during the closing of the transfer books, provided that:

(1) Statements as follows have been placed on the back of the certificate, signed, and properly acknowledged:

 (a) *By transferee:* "I (we) have no interest in the within certificate of stock."

 (b) *and by assignor:* "Above power of attorney cancelled by me (us) and a new detached assignment and power issued in lieu of it."

 (c) *and by attorneys (if any),* a separate statement, as follows, with proper acknowledgment by each attorney: "I (we) have no interest in the within certificate of stock, and within power of substitution dated _____ is hereby cancelled" (Acknowledgment Forms 13, 14, and 15) and

(2) the registered owner shall have executed a separate detached assignment (Form 2), and

(3) the papers shall have been presented to the Exchange and determined to be in order.

RULE 215: ACKNOWLEDGMENTS; AFFIDAVITS

Acknowledgments, affidavits, or depositions shall be executed before an officer having authority to take acknowledgments under the laws of the state in which such instruments are executed and shall bear the seal of the signing officer.

Any alteration or correction in an acknowledgment shall be properly noted by the signing officer.

RULE 216: ASSIGNMENTS OF "RIGHTS"

Rules 195 to 215, inclusive, shall apply to assignments of registered warrants for rights to subscribe, provided that warrants assigned by a trustee, guardian, executor, administrator, conservator, assignee, receiver in bankruptcy, or a corporation shall be a delivery if permitted by the Exchange.

RULE 217: CALLED STOCK OR REGISTERED BONDS

Certificates of stock or registered bonds that are called for redemption shall not be a delivery after the record date fixed by the corporation for the purpose of the drawing for redemption, or the date of the closing of transfer books thereof, except when an entire issue is called for redemption and except in respect of transactions in called securities dealt in specifically as such.

RULE 218: CALLED COUPON BONDS

Coupon bonds that are called for redemption shall not be a delivery on and after the date of availability, by publication or otherwise, of the serial numbers of the bonds drawn, except when an entire issue is called for redemption and except in respect to transactions in called bonds dealt in specifically as such.

RULE 219: PROPER COUPONS; WARRANTS

Coupon bonds shall have securely attached proper coupons, warrants, etc., of the same serial numbers as the bonds, the money value of a coupon missing from a bond may be substituted by mutual consent of the parties to the contract.

RULE 220: BONDS, REGISTERED AS TO PRINCIPAL OR FOR VOTING PURPOSES ONLY

Coupon bonds that have been registered as to principal shall be a delivery only if registered to bearer, or, while the transfer books are closed, only if accompanied by a proper assignment for each bond.

Coupon bonds that have been "registered for voting purposes only" shall be delivery only if such registration has been cancelled.

RULE 221: ENDORSED BONDS

A coupon bond bearing an endorsement of a definite name of a person, firm, corporation, association, etc., in conjunction with words of condition, qualification, direction, or restriction not properly pertaining thereto as a security shall not be a delivery unless sold specifically as an "endorsed bond."

This rule shall also apply to bonds with coupons bearing such endorsements.

RULE 222: RELEASED ENDORSED BONDS

A coupon bond bearing an endorsement indicating that the bond was deposited in accordance with a governmental requirement pertaining to banking institutions or insurance companies shall not be a delivery. If released, with such release acknowledged before an officer authorized to take acknowledgments, it may be delivered if sold specifically as a "released endorsed bond."

RULE 223: MUTILATED BONDS

A coupon bond that has become mutilated shall not be a delivery unless permitted by the Exchange.

RULE 224: MUTILATED COUPONS

A bond bearing a coupon that has been mutilated as to the bond number or signature or that has been cancelled in error shall not be a delivery unless appropriate endorsement in the form required by the Exchange shall have been placed upon the reverse of the coupon.

The endorsement shall be signed on behalf of the obligor by an officer thereof or, under authorization from the obligor, on behalf of the corporate trustee or paying agent by a duly authorized officer thereof or other person authorized to sign on behalf thereof.

.10 Mutilated Coupons. It is required that the following endorsement be placed upon the reverse of a coupon that has been mutilated as to bond number or signature.

> This coupon belongs to Bond No. _____ and is a valid obligation of the obligor.

In case a coupon has been cancelled in error, it is required that the following endorsement be placed upon the reverse of the coupon:

> This coupon, belonging to Bond No. _____, cancelled in error; it is a valid obligation of the obligor.

The endorsement shall be signed on behalf of the obligor by an officer thereof, or, under authorization from the obligor, on behalf of the corporate trustee or paying agent by a duly authorized officer thereof or other person authorized to sign on behalf thereof.

The Department of Stock List shall be notified in writing of the making of the endorsement, by the obligor, corporate trustee, or paying agent signing the endorsement, identifying the endorsed coupon and reciting the language of the endorsement. If the endorsement is by other than the obligor, such notification to the Exchange must include a certification that proper authorization to make the endorsement has been received from the obligor.

If the coupon has become detached from the bond, it shall be properly attached thereto.

RULE 225: DELIVERY OF EQUIVALENT SECURITIES

All contracts made in securities listed on the Exchange shall be subject to the condition that, unless otherwise specifically agreed between the parties, in the event that such securities become or are exchangeable for new or other securities under a plan or proposal relating to such securities, the Exchange may at its discretion direct that, upon admission to dealings of the new securities, settlement of such contracts, unless previously effected, may be made by delivery either of the securities contracted for or the equivalent in securities and cash or other property receivable under such plan or proposal.

RULE 496: REQUIREMENTS FOR INDEPENDENT AGENTS ACTING AS OR IN LIEU OF NEW YORK CITY TRANSFER AGENTS OF SECURITIES LISTED ON NEW YORK STOCK EXCHANGE, INC.

1. Office (hereinafter referred to as the office) satisfactory to the Exchange and the issuer to receive and redeliver securities must be located south of Chambers Street in the Borough of Manhattan, City of New York.
2. Routine transfers are to be processed and available for pick-up at the office under normal conditions within forty-eight hours, i.e., if received before noon on Monday must be available for pick-up not later than immediately after 1:00 P.M. on Wednesday.
3. The transfer agent must assume total responsibility and liability for securities from the time of deposit at the office until redelivered at the window, and the transfer agent must have capital, surplus (both capital and earned) undivided profits, and capital reserves aggregating at least $10 million.
4. Out-of-town agents having a drop in New York must make appropriate arrangements to pick up from and deliver to the Central Certificate Service normally within the forty-eight-hour period and framework mentioned above.
5. Personnel at the office must have sufficient experience to respond promptly to inquiries regarding transfers, including legal items.
6. Securities received before the close of business at the office on a record date or any other date involving the rights of a security holder must be recorded as of that date so as to establish the transferee's rights.
7. Facilities should be available for expediting transfer service when needed. No objection will be made if a reasonable charge is made for such special service.
8. Transfer agents maintaining a New York office or drop must maintain insurance coverage of at least $25 million to protect securities while in transit or in process.
9. The Exchange reserves the right to request termination of the office in the event of the failure of a transfer agent to conform to all the foregoing requirements.

For Listed Stock

>*Agencies to be Maintained in New York City.* A company having stock listed on the Exchange shall maintain, in the Borough of Manhattan, City of New York:
>
>1. An office or agency where:
>   (a) All stock of the company listed on the Exchange shall be transferable;
>   (b) Checks for dividends and other payments with respect to stock listed on the Exchange may be presented for immediate payment:
>   (c) Scrip issued to holders of a security listed on the Exchange and representing a fractional interest in a security listed on the Exchange will, during the period provided for consolidation thereof, be accepted for such purpose;
>   (d) A security listed on the Exchange that is convertible will be accepted for conversion:
>   (e) Subscription rights issued to holders of listed stock of the company shall be transferable, subscriptions shall be payable, and securities subscribed for shall be deliverable; and where all other rights or benefits pertaining to ownership of listed stock of the company, which may be issued, granted, or allotted by the company, shall be transferable, exercisable, payable, and deliverable.
>2. A registry office (hereinafter sometimes called the registrar) other than the transfer office or agency where all listed stock of the company shall be registerable. Such registrar shall be a bank or trust company located in the Borough of Manhattan, City of New York.

Number of Agencies in New York City: A registrar for a particular issue of stock listed on the Exchange (or, if a serial issue, for a particular series thereof), shall not be identical with a transfer agency for the same issue (or same series). With this exception, the facilities described above may be combined in one office or agency or distributed among several offices or agencies.

Location of Agencies in New York City: The transfer office or agency shall be located in the Borough of Manhattan and, if such transfer office or agency is at any time located north of Chambers Street, the company shall arrange for the registrar, or some other office satisfactory to the Exchange, located south of said street, in said borough, to receive and deliver, at the company's cost and expense, all listed stock there tendered for transfer.

Due to the concentration of brokerage firms, financial institutions, and other members of the securities industry of New York City in the area of Manhattan lying south of Chambers Street, it is essential to the orderly, convenient conduct of transactions in listed securities occurring in New York City that all agencies for the service of such securities be located south of Chambers Street in said borough.

Payment of Dividends in New York City: If checks for dividends or other payments with respect to stock listed on the Exchange are drawn on a bank located outside the City of New York, the company shall also make arrangements for payment of such checks at a bank, trust company, or other agency located in the Borough of Manhattan, City of New York, the name and address of which shall be imprinted on such checks.

Exchanges in New York City: The Exchange considers it essential to the orderly, convenient conduct of transactions occurring in New York City in a listed stock that is exchangeable for other securities of the issuing company that an office or agency for the exchange of said stock also be maintained south of Chambers Street in the Borough of Manhattan, City of New York.

The Exchange considers it equally essential that a similarly located agency be provided where an unlisted security is involved unless a concentration of holders of that security in another geographical area makes such an arrangement inappropriate.

Redemptions in New York City: Arrangements shall be made for an agency in the Borough of Manhattan, City of New York, where stock called for redemption may be presented for payment.

If funds for redemption are deposited in a bank located in a city other than New York, appropriate arrangements may be made for the payment of the redemption price through an agency in New York City, which may be the New York correspondent of such bank.

Transfer Agents and Registrars to be Acceptable to Exchange. Transfer agents and registrars for stock listed on the Exchange shall be (or shall have been) formally accepted by the Exchange as transfer agents and/or registrars for listed stocks before commencing to act in either of such capacities.

Most of the larger banks and trust companies in the United States already have been so accepted by the Exchange. The Department of Stock List of the Exchange will be pleased to advise whether a particular organization has been so accepted; and if it has not been so accepted, will upon request inform such organization as to the procedure by which Exchange acceptance may be obtained.

The general qualifications required by the Exchange of transfer agents and registrars for listed stocks and the procedure for obtaining acceptance by the Exchange are described below.

Required Qualifications of Transfer Agents and Registrars: Transfer agents and registrars for stock listed on the Exchange must be acceptable to the Exchange, and, before commencing to act in either of those capacities, shall be (or shall have been) formally accepted by the Exchange as transfer agents and/or registrars for listed stocks and shall have executed and filed with the Exchange for form of agreement regularly required by the Exchange in the circumstances. The procedure for obtaining formal acceptance of the Exchange is described below (see Procedure for Acceptance by Exchange). The various forms of agreement regularly required of transfer agents and registrars for listed stock by the Exchange are stated in full below, with indication as to the circumstances in which each such form is appropriate (see Agreements of Transfer Agents and Registrars with Exchange).

A registrar for a particular issue of stock listed on the Exchange (or, in a serial issue, for a particular series thereof) shall not be identical with a transfer agent for such issue (or such series.)

A registrar for stock listed on the Exchange shall be a bank or trust company.

If listed stock is transferred at an office of the company, the person acting as transfer agent shall be authorized specifically by the Board of Directors to countersign stock certificates in that capacity. Such person shall not also execute on behalf of the company certificates signed by him as transfer agents. It is not required in such case that such person be formally accepted by the Exchange as transfer agent or that the agreement above referred to be filed with the Exchange by such person.

Procedure for Acceptance by Exchange: A bank or trust company desiring to be accepted by the Exchange as a transfer agent and/or registrar for stock listed on the Exchange shall request such acceptance by letter addressed to the Department of Stock List of the Exchange. Such letter shall indicate the extent of the facilities of such bank or trust company for performance of the functions of transfer agent and/or registrar and shall enclose a list of its officers and directors and a copy of its latest available financial statement.

Such bank or trust company should also arrange to have two of its correspondent banks located in New York City advise the Department of Stock List in writing as to whether such bank or trust company, in their opinion, has facilities adequate for the performance of the functions of transfer agent and/or registrar for stocks listed on the Exchange.

After review of these data by the Exchange, such bank or trust company, if acceptable to the Exchange, will be furnished with copies of the appropriate form of agreement for execution and filing with the Exchange.

If stock listed on the Exchange is transferred at the company's office by a person acting as transfer agent, it is not required that prior acceptance of the Exchange in respect to such person be obtained or that any agreement be filed with the Exchange by such person.

Change of Transfer Agent or Registrar

Transfer Agent: Prior notice shall be given the Exchange of the appointment of a new transfer agent for listed stock, whether such new agent is appointed in addition to or in lieu of an existing agent.

If the stock is transferred at the office of the company and the change to be made is merely in the identity of the employee acting as transfer agent, the aforesaid notice is not required.

Registrar: Prior notice shall also be given the Exchange of the appointment of a new registrar for listed stock, whether such new registrar is appointed in addition to or in lieu of an existing registrar. If the new registrar is not qualified with the Exchange as a registrar for securities listed on the Exchange at the time of its appointment, such appointment shall not become effective until the new registrar has so qualified.

Time of Notice to Exchange: If the new appointee has not previously been formally accepted by the Exchange as transfer agent and/or registrar for listed stock, the required prior notice shall be given sufficiently early to permit the

Securities Transfer

Exchange, prior to the time the appointment became effective, to communicate with that appointee and receive the data and agreement requisite to acceptance of the appointee as described above (see Procedure for Acceptance by Exchange).

A period of not less than two weeks should be allowed for this purpose.

For Listed Bonds and Other Listed Securities Evidencing Indebtedness

The term "bond," as used below, shall be understood to include any security evidencing indebtedness.

Agencies to be Maintained in New York City. A company having bonds listed on the Exchange shall maintain an office or agency in the Borough of Manhattan, City of New York, where:

1. principal of and interest on all listed bonds of the company shall be payable;
2. all listed bonds of the company that are registerable as to principal and interest or as to principal only shall be so registerable;
3. scrip issued to holders of a security listed on the Exchange and representing a fractional interest in a security listed on the Exchange will, during the period provided for consolidation thereof, be accepted for such purpose:
4. a security listed on the Exchange that is convertible will be accepted for conversion; and
5. all rights or benefits pertaining to ownership of listed bonds of the company and issued, granted, or allotted by the company shall be transferable, deliverable, payable, or exercisable.

APPENDIX H

National Association of Securities Dealers: Rules Pertaining to Securities Transfer and Processing

DEFINITIONS

Section 3 (amended effective March 1, 1970)

Delivery Date
(a) The term "delivery date" as used in this Code shall be used interchangeably with "settlement date" and shall mean the date designated for the delivery of securities.

Written Notices
(b) The term "written notice" as used in this Code shall include a notice delivered by hand, by letter, teletype, telegraph, TWX, or other comparable media.
(c) The term "Committee" whenever used in this Code, unless the context otherwise requires, shall mean the National Uniform Practice Committee.

DELIVERY DATES

Section 4 (amended effective February 9, 1968; amended effective March 1, 1970)

For "Cash"
(a) In connection with a transaction for cash delivery shall be made at the office of the purchaser on the day of the transaction.

Regular Way

(b) In connection with a transaction regular way, delivery shall be made at the office of the purchaser on but not before the fifth business day following the date of the transaction; except that if the seller tenders delivery before the fifth business day, acceptance shall be at the option of the purchaser, and rejection of such delivery by the purchaser shall be without prejudice to his or her rights.

Seller's Option

(c) In connection with a transaction seller's option, delivery shall be made at the office of the purchaser on the date on which the option expires; except that delivery may be made by the seller on any business day after the fifth business day following the date of transaction and prior to the expiration of the option, provided the seller delivers at the office of the purchaser on a business day preceding the day of delivery written notice of intention to deliver. Contracts maturing on a Saturday, half-holiday, or holiday shall carry over to the next business day.

Buyer's Option

(d) In connection with a transaction buyer's option, delivery shall be made at the office of the purchaser on the date on which the option expires; except that if the seller tenders delivery before that time, acceptance shall be at the election of the purchaser, and rejection of such delivery by the purchaser shall be without prejudice to his or her rights. Contracts maturing on a Saturday, half-holiday, or holiday shall carry over to the next business day.

When, As, and If Issued

(e) In connection with a transaction in a security when, as, and if issued, delivery shall be made at the office of the purchaser on the date declared by the Committee; except that if no delivery date is so declared, (a) delivery may be made by the seller on the business day following the day upon which the seller has delivered at the office of the purchaser written notice of intention to deliver, and (b) open market when, as, and if issued contracts in securities currently being publicly offered through a syndicate or selling group shall be settled on the date such syndicate or selling group contracts are settled, provided, however, delivery of securities in accordance with this subsection shall be made during the normal delivery hours in the community where the buyer is located.

When, As, and If Distributed

(f) In connection with a transaction in a security when, as, and if distributed, delivery shall be made at the office of the purchaser on the date declared by the Committee; except that if no delivery date is declared, delivery may be made by the seller on the business day following the day upon which the seller has delivered at the office of the purchaser written notice of intention to deliver.

TRANSACTIONS IN SECURITIES EX-DIVIDEND, EX-RIGHTS, OR EX-WARRANTS

Section 5 (amended effective March 1, 1979)

Designation of Ex-Date

(a) All transactions in securities, except cash transactions shall be ex-dividend, ex-rights, or ex-warrants: (i) on the day specifically designated by the Committee after definitive information concerning the declaration and payment of a dividend or the issuance of rights or warrants has been received at the office of the Committee; or (ii) on the day specified as such by the appropriate national securities exchange that has received definitive information in accordance with the provisions of SC Rule 10b-17 concerning the declaration and payment of a dividend or the issuance of rights or warrants.

Normal Ex-Dividend Dates

(b) (1) In respect to cash or stock dividends, except as noted below, if definitive information is received sufficiently in advance of the record date, the date designated as the ex-dividend date shall be the fourth business day preceding the record date if the record date falls on a business day, or the fifth business day preceding the record date if the record date falls on a day designated by the Committee as a non-delivery date. In respect to stock dividends and/or splits that are twenty-five percent or greater, the ex-dividend date shall be the first business day following the payable date. In respect to stock dividends and/or splits relating to American Depository Receipts (ADRs) and foreign securities, the ex-dividend date shall be designated by the Committee.

Late Information Re Ex-Dividend Dates

(2) If definitive information is not received sufficiently in advance of the record date to permit designation of an ex-dividend date in accordance with paragraph (b) (1) hereof, the date designated shall be the first business day that, in the opinion of the Committee, will be practical having regard to the circumstances pertaining.

Ex-Dividend Dates for Investment Company Shares

(3) Notwithstanding the above, the ex-dividend date on stock of an open-end investment company shall be the date designated by the issuer or its principal underwriter.

Normal Ex-Rights Dates

(c) (1) In respect to rights subscription offerings, if definitive information is received sufficiently in advance of the effective date of the registration statement, the date designated as the ex-rights date shall be the first business day after the effective date of the registration statement.

Late Information Re Ex-Rights Dates

(2) If definitive information is not received sufficiently in advance of the effective date of the registration statement to permit designation of an ex-rights date in accordance with the paragraph (c) (1) hereof, the date designated shall be the first business day that, in the opinion of the Committee, is practical in respect to the circumstances pertaining.

Normal Ex-Warrants Dates

(d) (1) In respect to the issuance or distribution of warrants, if definitive information is received sufficiently in advance of the record date, the date designated as the ex-warrants date shall be the fourth business day preceding the record date if the record date falls on a business day, or the fifth business day preceding the record date if the record date falls on a day designated by the Committee as a non-delivery date.

Late Information Re Ex-Warrants Dates

(2) If definitive information is not received sufficiently in advance of the record date to permit designation of an ex-warrants date in accordance with paragraph (d) (1) hereof, the date designated shall be the first business day that, in the opinion of the Committee, is practical in respect to the circumstances pertaining.

EX-INTEREST TRANSACTIONS IN BONDS THAT ARE DEALT IN FLAT

Section 6 (amended effective February 9, 1968)

Transactions Except for Cash

(a) All transactions except cash transactions in bonds or similar evidences of indebtedness that are traded flat shall be ex-interest as prescribed by the following provisions:

(1) On the fourth business day preceding the record date if the record date falls on a business day.

(2) On the fifth business day preceding the record date if the record date falls on a day other than a business day.

(3) On the fifth business day preceding the date on which an interest payment is to be made if no record date has been fixed.

(4) If notice of payment of interest is not made public sufficiently in advance of the record date or the payment date, as the case may be, to permit the security to be dealt in ex-interest in accordance with the foregoing provisions, that security shall be dealt in ex-interest on the first business day following public notice of the record date or the payment date, as the case may be.

Record Date

(b) As used in this Section, the term "record date" means the date fixed by the trustee, registrar, paying agent, or issuer for the purpose of determining the holders of bonds or similar evidences of indebtedness entitled to receive interest payments.

EX LIQUIDATING PAYMENTS

Section 7

All transactions except cash transactions in stock, bonds or similar evidences of indebtedness shall be ex liquidating payments or payments on account of principal in accordance with the formula set forth in Section 5 of this Code.

TRANSACTIONS IN PART-REDEEMED BONDS

Section 8

In transactions in bonds that have been redeemed or paid in part, such bonds shall be designated as part-redeemed bonds. The settlement price of contracts in part-redeemed bonds shall be determined by multiplying the contract price by the original principal amount thereof, and contracts shall be made on the same basis.

DELIVERY OF SECURITIES

Section 12

Time and Place of Delivery

Delivery shall be made at the office of the purchaser between the hours established by rule or practice in the community where such office is located. If the purchaser maintains more than one office, delivery shall be made at the office with which the transaction was effected.

PAYMENT

Section 13

The party making delivery shall have the right to require the purchase money to be paid upon delivery by certified check, cashier's check, bank draft, or cash.

STAMP TAXES

Section 14 (amended effective January 1, 1973 and November 13, 1975)

Members shall, as required by the rules and regulations of jurisdictions imposing taxes on sales purchases or other transfers of securities, furnish tax stamps or pay the tax through securities clearing organizations.

In the event that taxes are due pursuant to state stock transfer taxes:

(a) The seller shall furnish to the buyer at the time of delivery a sale memorandum ticket to which shall be affixed and cancelled sufficient state transfer stamps as are required by the state in which the sale occurs, or the tax may be paid by the seller through securities clearing organizations.

Additional Stamps

(b) If any stamps in addition to those required by paragraph (a) hereof are desired by the buyer, the furnishing of such additional stamps by the seller may be made a part of the transaction.

Seller's Failure to Furnish Stamps

(c) If the buyer has requested the additional state stamps, provided by paragraph (b) and at the time of delivery of the security the seller does not furnish or has not made adequate provision for such stamps, the buyer may furnish and cancel such additional state transfer stamps and deduct the cost thereof from the purchase price.

PART DELIVERY

Section 15 (amended effective January 1, 1973)

The purchaser shall be required to accept a part delivery on any contract due, provided the portion remaining undelivered is not an amount that includes an odd lot that was not a part of the original transaction.

UNITS OF DELIVERY—STOCKS

Section 16 (amended effective July 8, 1969, and December 1, 1972)

(a) Stock certificates delivered in settlement of contracts:

(1) in which the transaction is for 100 shares may be in one certificate for the exact number of shares or certificates totaling 100 shares.

(2) in which the transaction is greater than 100 shares and a multiple of 100 shall be in the exact amount of the contract or in multiples of 100 shares or in amounts from which units of 100 shares can be made or a combination thereof equaling the amount of the contract.

(3) in which the transaction is for more than 100 shares but not in a multiple of 100 shall be in multiples of 100 shares or in amounts from which units of 100 shares can be made or a combination thereof, plus either the exact amount for the odd lot or smaller amounts equaling the odd lot.

(4) in which the transaction is for less than 100 shares shall be in the exact amount of the contract or for smaller units aggregating the amount of the contract.

Uniform delivery ticket

(b) A properly executed uniform delivery ticket must accompany the delivery of securities.

UNITS OF DELIVERY—BONDS

Section 17 (amended effective January 1, 1973)

Coupon Bonds

(a) Each delivery of bonds or similar evidences of indebtedness in coupon bearer form shall be made in denominations of $1,000 or in denominations of $100 or multiples thereof aggregating $1,000.

Registered Bonds

(b) Each delivery of bonds or similar evidences of indebtedness in fully registered bond issues shall be made in denominations of $1,000 or multiples thereof or in amounts of $100 or multiples aggregating $1,000, but in no event in denominations larger than $100,000.

(Section 17(b) amended effective July 8, 1968 and November 1, 1971.)

Bonds Issued in Both Coupon and Registered Form

(c) Unless otherwise specified at the time of execution, contracts in bonds that are issuable in either coupon or registered form shall be settled by delivery of bonds in either form pursuant to the denominations in subsections (a) and (b) above, notwithstanding that there may be a charge for interchanging one form with the other.

Units of Delivery by Agreement

(d) When a contract relating to (a), (b) and (c) above is for a principal amount that is not a multiple of $100, the parties shall agree at the time of entering into the contract as to the proper units of delivery.

UNITS OF DELIVERY— CERTIFICATES OF DEPOSIT FOR BONDS

Section 18

The units of delivery for certificates of deposit for bonds, shall be the same as prescribed for bonds in Section 17 of this Code.

DELIVERY OF SECURITIES WITH DRAFT ATTACHED

Section 19 (Section 19 and Note amended effective February 9, 1968)

Acceptance of Draft: Time of Presentation. Drafts accompanying the shipment of securities need be accepted only on a business day between the hours established by rule or practice in the community where the draft is presented. Acceptance of a draft at other times shall be at the option of the drawee, and the drawee shall not be liable for any expense arising out of his or her refusal of the draft when presented on a Saturday or half-holiday.

Note: For his or her own protection, the seller should instruct his or her bank or collecting agent that if the draft is received on a Saturday or half-holiday, it need not be presented to the drawee until the following business day.

Section 20

Prior to Settlement Date. The acceptance of a draft prior to the settlement date shall be at the option of the drawee.

Section 21

With Irregularities. The acceptance of a draft that contains irregularities shall be at the option of the drawee.

Section 22

Expense Due to Shipment. Expenses of shipment, including insurance, postage, draft, and collection charges, shall be paid by the seller.

Section 23 (amended effective February 9, 1968)

Expenses Due to Delay. Failure to accept a draft in which no irregularities exist when duly presented on a business day shall make the drawee liable for the payment of interest to the date the draft is paid and for other incidental expenses incurred because of the delay, including protest fees, if any, and wire charges.

Section 24

Claims for Irregularities. Claims with respect to such items as price, interest, protest fees or wire charges, and items of similar nature arising from the acceptance of draft shipments in which irregularities exist shall be presented not later than ten days after payment. This limitation shall not apply to matters covered hereinafter under "Reclamations" (Sections 51 to 57, inclusive, of this Code).

DELIVERY OF SECURITIES WITH RESTRICTIONS

Section 25

Delivery of Temporary Certificates. A temporary certificate shall not be a good delivery when permanent certificates are available.

Section 26 (amended effective September 1, 1970)

Delivery of Mutilated Securities

(a) A mutilated security shall not be a good delivery until appropriately authenticated by the trustee, registrar, transfer agent, or issuer.

(b) The delivery of a bond that bears a coupon that has been mutilated as to the bond number or signature or that bears a coupon that has been cancelled in error shall not be good delivery unless an appropriate endorsement by an official authorized by subparagraph (c) hereof, in the form required by the Committee, shall have been placed on the reverse of the coupon.

(c) The endorsement shall be signed on behalf of the obligor by an officer thereof or, under authorization from the obligor, on behalf of the corporate trustee or paying agent by a duly authorized officer thereof or other person authorized to sign on behalf thereof.

Section 27

Delivery of Securities Called for Redemption. A certificate of stock or a bond shall cease to be a good delivery upon publication of notice of call for redemption except when an entire issue is called for redemption and except against transactions in called stock or called bonds dealt in specifically as such.

Section 28

Delivery Under Government Regulations
Documents Required:

(a) When the laws, regulations, rulings, instructions, or orders of any government, government instrumentality, or agency or official thereof having jurisdiction, require a license, clearing certificate, affidavit of ownership, or any similar document in connection with the acquisition, disposition, transfer, or redemption of, or other dealing in or with respect to, any security, such security shall not be a good delivery unless accompanied by the document or documents so required.

Certificate Subject to Stoppage

(b) If a specific certificate tendered in settlement of a contract in foreign securities is on a black list, blocked list, or subject to similar stoppage from which an innocent holder in due course cannot have it removed by simple request, such certificate is not a good delivery, and reclamation may be made without limit of time.

ASSIGNMENTS AND POWERS OF SUBSTITUTION: DELIVERY OF REGISTERED SECURITIES

Section 29 (amended effective March 1, 1970, and December 1, 1972)

General Requirements

(a) Any registered security to be a good delivery must be accompanied by an assignment and a power of substitution (when such power of substitution is required under subsection (f) of this Section) conforming to the requirements set forth in Sections 29 through 38 of this Code. Any expense incurred through failure of a seller to meet these requirements shall be paid by the seller.

Assignment

(b) An assignment shall be executed on the certificate itself or on a separate paper, in which latter case there shall be a separate assignment for each certificate.

Signature Requirements

(c) The signature to an assignment or power of substitution shall be technically correct; that is, it shall correspond with the name as written upon the certificate in every particular without alteration or enlargement, or any change whatever, except that "and" or "&" and "Company" or "Co." may be written either way.

Detached Assignment Requirements

(d) A separate (detached) assignment shall contain provision for the irrevocable appointment of an attorney, with power of substitution, and a full description of the security, including name of issuer, issue, certificate number, and amount (expressed in words and numerals).

Alteration or Correction

(e) Any alteration or correction in an assignment or power of substitution shall be accompanied by an explanation on the original instrument signed by the person or firm executing the same.

Power of Substitution

(f) When the name of an individual or firm has been inserted in an assignment as attorney, a power of substitution shall be executed in blank by that individual or firm. When the name of an individual or firm has been inserted in a power of substitution as substitute attorney, a new power of substitution shall be executed in blank by that substitute attorney.

Guarantee

(g) Each assignment, endorsement, alteration, and erasure shall bear a guarantee acceptable to the transfer agent or registrar. It is not the intent of this subsection that a "New York," national securities exchange member, or other specific guarantee is required: rather, it is the intent only that the guarantee be acceptable to the transfer agent.

Foreign Internal Securities
(h) Except for Canadian Securities, American Depository Receipts, American Shares, New York Shares, and similar securities, the provisions of Section 29 (b) through (g) and Sections 33 and 35 shall not apply to foreign internal securities in registered form. In default of specific rules in the Code, the usual conditions of delivery and transfer of foreign internal securities in registered form in the foreign market where principally traded shall apply.

Uniform Transfer Instruction Form
(i) A properly executed Uniform Transfer Instruction Form must accompany securities presented for transfer.

Section 30

Witnesses to Assignments. Each signature to an assignment or power of substitution shall be witnessed by an individual and dated. Where there are two or more signatures to an assignment, the witness shall state definitely, in his or her own handwriting, to which signature he or she was witness. A certificate with either the assignment or power of substitution witnessed by a person since deceased is not a good delivery.

ACKNOWLEDGMENTS AND SAMPLE FORMS

Section 31

Certificate of Company Whose Transfer Books Are Closed
General Requirements:
(a) The assignment and each power of substitution pertaining to a certificate of a company whose transfer books are closed indefinitely for any reason shall be properly acknowledged before an officer having authority to take acknowledgments under the laws of the state in which such instruments are executed and shall bear the seal of the signing office, if required by statute. Any alteration or correction in an acknowledgment shall be properly noted by the signing officer.

Executed by Individual
(b) In an acknowledgment of an assignment or power of substitution executed by an individual, the officer before whom the acknowledgment is executed shall certify that he or she knows the person signing to be the person named in the certificate or in the power of substitution and that the signer acknowledged his or her signature.

Executed in Name of Firm
(c) In an acknowledgment of an assignment or a power of substitution executed in the name of a firm, the officer before whom the acknowledgment is

executed shall certify that he or she knows the person executing the acknowledgment and knows that person to be, or to have been on the date of execution of the assignment or power of substitution, a member of the firm or authorized to sign for the firm under a power of attorney and that that person acknowledged that he or she executed the assignment or power of substitution as the act or deed of the firm.

Section 32

Certificate in Name of Corporation, etc.
Transfer Books Open:
(a) A certificate in the name of a corporation or an institution or in a name with official designation shall be a good delivery only if the statement "Proper papers for transfer filed by assignor" is placed on the assignment and signed by the transfer agent.

Transfer Books Closed:
(b) Where a certificate, an assignment, or a power of attorney is in the name of a corporation and the transfer books of the issuing company are closed indefinitely for any reason, the certificate shall not be a good delivery unless the assignment or other instrument effecting transfer on the corporation's behalf is executed by an officer of such corporation, other than the secretary, and is accompanied by (1) a guarantee of such officer's signature by a bank that is a member of the Federal Deposit Insurance Corporation; (2) an acknowledgment in proper form of such execution by such officer; (3) a copy of a corporate resolution in proper form authorizing such execution by such officer, certified by the secretary or other appropriate corporate officer to be in effect on the date of such execution; (4) a certificate of incumbency executed by the secretary or other appropriate corporate officer, certifying as to the office and signature of the executing office as of the date of such execution; and (5) an acknowledgment in proper form of the certification of the resolution and the certificate of incumbency.

Foreign Internal Securities:
(c) The foregoing requirements shall not apply to foreign internal securities when the requirements do not correspond to the laws or customs of the country concerned; but instead such laws and customs shall govern such securities.

Section 33

Certificate in Name of Firm. Unless the endorsement specifies otherwise, there shall be a presumption that stock registered in a firm or business name is registered in the name of a partnership and not a corporation.

Section 34

Certificate in Name of Dissolved Firm Succeeded by New Firm. A certificate with an assignment or a power of substitution executed in the name of a firm that has since dissolved and is succeeded by a firm or firms having as general partners one or more of the general partners of the dissolved firm shall be a good delivery only if the new firm or one of the new firms shall have signed the statement "Execution Guaranteed" under a date subsequent to the formation of the new firm so signing.

Section 35

Certificate in Name of Married Woman
(a) Married Women. A certificate in the name of a married woman shall be a good delivery, except that, where applicable law limits the right of a married woman to transfer the certificate, such certificate shall be a good delivery only when the assignment shall be executed jointly by husband and wife and acknowledged before a notary public or other qualified officer.

Certificate in Name of Unmarried Woman
(b) Unmarried Women. A certificate in the name of an unmarried woman with the prefix "Miss" shall be a good delivery without acknowledgment if signed "Miss," unless an acknowledgment is required by any pertinent state law. A certificate in the name of an unmarried woman without the prefix "Miss" shall be a good delivery only if the assignment is accompanied by an acknowledgment in proper form executed before a notary public or other qualified officer.

Section 36 (amended effective July 1, 1974)

Certificate in Name of Deceased Person, Trustee, etc.
(a) A certificate shall not be a good delivery with an assignment or power of substitution executed by (1) (a) person since deceased; (2) a trustee or trustees, except as provided in paragraph (b) below, or except for trustees acting in the capacity of a board of directors of a corporation or association, in which case Section 32(a) shall apply; (3) a guardian, except as provided in paragraph (b) below; (4) an infant; (5) an executor, except as provided in paragraph (b) below; (6) an administrator, except as provided in paragraph (b) below; (7) a receiver in bankruptcy; (8) an agent; (9) an attorney; (10) or with a qualification, restriction, or special designation.

(b) A certificate shall be a good delivery with an assignment or a power of substitution executed by (1) domestic individual executor(s) or administrator(s); (2) domestic individual trustee(s) under an inter vivos or testamentary trust; or (3) domestic guardian(s), including committees, conservators, and curators. These exceptions to paragraph (a) above are to cover transfers that will be effected by transfer agents without additional documentation. This paragraph (b) shall apply only to securities of a domestic issuer (organized under the laws of any state in the United States or District of Columbia) that are registered in the name(s) of (1), (2), or (3) of this paragraph (b). Certificates delivered pursuant to this paragraph (b) must be properly assigned, and the signature(s) to the assignment must be guaranteed pursuant to Section 29(g).

(c) Section 36 does not apply to certificates registered under a statutory Gifts to Minors Act.

Section 37

Joint Tenants, etc. A certificate with an inscription to indicate joint tenancy or tenancy in common shall be a good delivery only if signed by all co-tenants.

Section 38

Two or More Names. A certificate registered in the names of two or more individuals or firms shall be a good delivery only if signed by all the registered owners.

DELIVERY OF BONDS AND OTHER EVIDENCES OF INDEBTEDNESS

Section 39

Liability for Expenses. Failure of the seller to meet the requirements of good delivery relating to bonds and similar evidences of indebtedness as set forth in Sections 40 through 45 of this Code shall make the seller liable for any expense incurred as a result of such failure.

Section 40

Coupon Bonds
(a) A coupon bond shall have securely attached in the correct place proper coupons, warrants, etc., of the same serial number as the bond. Acceptance of cash or check in lieu of missing coupons shall be at the option of the purchaser.

Endorsed Bonds
(b) A coupon bond bearing an endorsement of a definite name of a person, firm, corporation, association, etc., in conjunction with words of condition, qualification, direction, or restriction not properly pertaining thereto as a security shall not be a good delivery unless sold specifically as an endorsed bond. This rule shall also apply to bonds with coupons bearing such endorsements.

Interest in Default
(c) A bond upon which interest is in default shall carry all unpaid coupons.

Section 41

Registerable as to Principal. A coupon bond registerable as to principal shall be a good delivery only if registered to bearer.

Section 42

Endorsements for Banking or Insurance Requirements. A coupon bond bearing an endorsement indicating that the bond was deposited in accordance

Section 43

Coupon Detached Prior to Delivery

(a) A bond dealt in "and interest" for delivery on or after the date on which interest is due and payable shall be delivered without the coupon payable on such date.

Late Delivery

(b) In the settlement of contracts in bonds dealt in "and interest" where delivery is due prior to the interest payment date but is made on or after the interest payment date, bonds may be delivered without coupons payable on such date, and the seller may present such detached, unpaid coupons to the buyer for payment, the buyer bearing the risk of non-payment.

Section 44

Stamped Bonds

(a) If a plan of reorganization that has been declared operative or an amendment or supplement to an indenture provides that the bonds covered thereby shall be stamped to reflect the adoption of such plan or the amendment or supplement to the indenture, bonds so stamped shall be a good delivery and bonds not so stamped shall not be a good delivery.

Stamped "Tax Paid"

(b) The fact that a bond has been stamped "tax paid" by any authority vested with the power to tax, if the stamp does not indicate ownership, shall not prevent such bonds from being a good delivery.

Section 45

Certificates of Deposits. Certificates of deposit issued by committees or depositaries other than those specified at time of trade shall not be a good delivery.

COMPUTATION OF INTEREST

Section 46

Interest To Be Added to the Dollar Price

(a) In the settlement of contracts in interest-paying securities other than for cash, there shall be added to the dollar price interest at the rate specified in the bond, which shall be computed up to but not including the fifth business day following the date of transaction. In transactions for cash, interest shall be added to the dollar price at the rate specified in the bond up to but not including the date of transaction.

(Section 46(a) amended effective February 9, 1968.)

Basis of Interest

(b) Interest shall be computed on the basis of a 360-day year; that is, every calendar month shall be considered to be one-twelfth of 360 days; every period from a date in one month to the same date in the following month shall be considered to be thirty days.

Note: the number of elapsed days should be computed in accordance with the examples given in the following list:

From 1st to 30th of the same month to be figured as 29 days.

From 1st to 31st of the same month to be figured as 30 days.

From 1st to 1st of the following month to be figured as 30 days.

From 1st to 28th of February to be figured as 27 days.

From the 23rd of February to the 3rd of March is to be figured as 10 days.

From the 15th of May to the 6th of June is to be figured as 21 days.

Where interest is payable on the thirtieth or thirty-first of the month:

From 30th or 31st to 1st of the following month to be figured as 1 day.

From 30th or 31st to 30th of the following month to be figured as 30 days.

From 30th or 31st to 31st of the following month to be figured as 30 days.

From 30th or 31st to 1st of second following month to be figured as 1 month, 1 day.

(Note to Section 46(b) amended effective January 2, 1968.)

Registered Bonds Traded "and Interest"

(c) When a delivery of a registered bond traded "and interest" is made between the record date fixed for the purpose of determining the holder entitled to receive interest and the interest payment date, a deduction equivalent to the full amount of the interest to be paid by the obligor shall be made on settlement.

Registered Bonds Traded Flat

(d) When delivery of a registered bond traded flat is made after the record date fixed for the purpose of determining the holder entitled to receive interest in the settlement of a contract made prior to the date on which the issue of bonds was traded ex-interest, a due-bill check for the full amount of the interest to be paid by the obligor shall accompany the delivery.

(Section 46(d) amended effective February 21, 1969.)

Income Bonds

(e) Income bonds shall be dealt in flat even though such bonds are paying interest, except that where a certain fixed rate is guaranteed in the indenture and provision is made for additional contingent payment, they shall be dealt in and-interest at the fixed rate guaranteed in the indenture (so long as interest payments at such fixed rate are not in default and no announcement of intention to default has been made).

Fractions of a Cent
(f) In all transactions involving the payment of interest, fractions of cent equaling or exceeding five mills shall be regarded as one cent; fractions of a cent less than five mills shall be disregarded.

DUE-BILLS AND DUE-BILL CHECKS

Section 48

Definition of Due Bills
(a) The term "due-bill" as used in this section means an instrument employed for the purpose of evidencing the transfer of title to any security or rights pertaining to any security contracted for or evidencing the obligation of a seller to deliver such to a subsequent purchaser. A due-bill shall not be transferable or assignable by the purchaser.

Definition of Due-Bill Checks
(b) The term "due-bill checks" as used in this section means a due-bill in the form of a check payable on the date of payment of a cash dividend or interest on registered bonds, which prior to such date shall be considered as a due-bill as defined in paragraph (a) above for the amount of such dividend or interest on registered bonds.

Due-Bills for Stock Dividends and Rights
(c) A security sold before it trades ex-dividend (for stock and scrip dividends) or ex-rights and delivered too late for transfer on or before the record date shall be accompanied by a due-bill for the distribution to be made. When a due-bill accompanying a delivery evidences the obligation of the seller to deliver stock, the purchaser shall prorate the value of the contract, and shall make payment of the balance upon redemption of the due-bill.

The requirement to prorate the value of the contract as described above shall not apply to stock dividends less than ten percent or to spin-offs or rights.

Due-Bill Checks for Cash Distributions and Interest
(d) Due-bill checks for a cash distribution or interest on registered bonds shall accompany securities delivered too late for transfer on or before the record date.

Redemption of Due-Bills
(e) Due-bills for any security or rights pertaining to any security shall be redeemable on the date on which the security or rights are issued by the corporation or as soon thereafter as the signor or guarantor of the due-bill can obtain transfer of the security or rights into denominations necessary to effect the redemption of the due-bills.

Default Upon Redemption of Due-Bills

(f) A due-bill for any security or rights pertaining to any security issued pursuant to paragraph (c) of this section and presented for redemption pursuant to the terms of paragraph (e) of this section and not honored by the seller may, at the option of the buyer, be treated as a "fail to receive" from the seller, and the distribution evidenced by such due-bill may be bought-in for the account and risk of the seller pursuant to the terms of Section 59 of this Code. However, buy-ins executed in accordance with this paragraph must be executed after the payable date of such securities as determined by the issuing corporation.

(Section 48 amended effective February 21, 1969; amended effective March 1, 1970; amended effective November 1, 1971 and November 1, 1972.)

CLAIMS FOR DIVIDENDS, RIGHTS, INTEREST, etc.

Section 49

Dividends or Rights

(a) A buyer of stock who has the certificate in his or her possession in time to enable him or her to effect transfer prior to the closing of the books or to the record date shall have no claim upon the seller (unless the seller is the registered holder) for the dividend or rights pertaining to such certificate; but the seller, upon request of the buyer, shall use his best efforts to collect the same for the buyer.

Substantiating Claims

(b) When a buyer of stock who has failed to have said stock transferred in time requests the seller to collect the dividends or rights pertaining thereto, the seller may require from the buyer the presentation of the certificate or a letter from the transfer agent substantiating the claim or the buyer's written statement that he or his customer was the holder on the record date and a guarantee of indemnity for liability arising out of any further demand for said dividend or rights.

Interest on Rights on Registered Bonds

(c) The provisions of subsections (a) and (b) of this section shall be equally applicable to interest or rights pertaining to registered bonds.

TRANSFER FEES

Section 50

The party at whose instance a transfer of securities is made shall pay all service charges of the transfer agent.

RECLAMATIONS AND REJECTIONS

Section 51 *(amended effective September 1, 1969)*

Definitions. The term "reclamation" as used in this Code shall mean a claim for the right to return or the right to demand the return of a security that has been previously accepted. Securities that have been presented for delivery on a transaction and have been refused for a valid reason shall, within the meaning of Sections 52 through 57, be deemed a rejection for the purpose of these sections.

Section 52

Uniform Reclamation Form. Form Must Accompany Securities:

(a) A properly executed Uniform Reclamation Form must accompany securities on reclamation or return.

Absence of Form Permits Sell-Out:

(b) Any security reclaimed or returned on a transaction without a properly executed Uniform Reclamation Form as prescribed within this section may, at the option of the receiving broker, be sold-out pursuant to Section 60 of the Code, but in no event later than three business days after receipt of the receiving broker or his or her agent.

Section 53

Time for Delivery on Reclamation and Manner of Settlement. A security with an irregularity having been delivered may be returned or reclaimed between the hours established by rule or practice in the community where the delivery or reclamation is to be made.

(b) When a security is returned or reclaimed, the party who originally delivered it shall immediately give the party returning it either the security in proper form for delivery in exchange for the security originally delivered or the money amount of the contract. In the latter case, unless otherwise agreed, the party to whom the security is returned shall be deemed to be failing to deliver the security until such time as a proper delivery is made.

Section 54

Minor Irregularities. Reclamation for an irregularity that affects only the currency of the security in the market shall be made within fifteen days from the day of original delivery, except that, if the security is issued under the jurisdiction of a foreign country, the period for reclamation under this section shall be forty-five days from the day of original delivery.

Section 55

Wrong Form of Certificate. Reclamation by reason of the fact that a form of certificate was delivered that was not a good delivery, but that is exchangeable without charge for a certificate that is a good delivery shall be made within fifteen days from the day of original delivery.

Section 56

Irregular Delivery—Transfer Refused; Lost or Stolen Securities
Irregular Delivery:
(a) Reclamation by reason of the fact of an irregularity in the delivery of a security shall be within thirty months after the settlement date of the contract. For purposes of this section, the term "irregular delivery" shall include, among other things, wrong, duplicate, misdirected, and overdelivery.
Transfer Refused:
(b) Reclamation by reason of the fact that a specific certificate tendered in settlement of a contract has been presented for transfer and transfer thereof has been refused by the transfer agent shall be within thirty months after the settlement date of the contract.
Lost or stolen securities:
(c) Reclamation by reason of the fact that a security is lost or stolen shall be within thirty months after the settlement date of the contract.
(d) The running of the thirty-month period described in Section 56 shall not be deemed to foreclose a member's rights to pursue its claim via other open avenues, including but not limited to the Association's arbitration procedure.
(Section 56 amended effective January 2, 1968. September 1, 1971, and April 1, 1974.)

Section 57 (amended effective January 2, 1968)

Called Securities. Reclamation by reason of the fact that a security was delivered after publication of notice of call for its redemption may be made without limit of time, and such security may be returned to the party who held it at the time of such publication, except that this rule shall not apply when an entire issue is called for redemption or when the security involved was dealt in specifically as a called security.

Section 58 (amended effective February 21, 1969 and March 1, 1970)

Marking to the Market
Demand for Deposit:
(a) The party who is partially unsecured by reason of a change in the market value of the subject of a contract in securities may demand from the other party a deposit equal to the difference between the contract price and the market price without being required to make a mutual deposit. Such deposit shall be made either with the member demanding same or with a mutually agreed-on depositary or, on failure to agree on a depositary, with any member of the Federal Reserve System with an office in the financial district of the city where the unsecured party maintains its office.

Assignment of Contract:

(b) Either party to a contract in securities may assign the contract, either at the time the transaction is effected or at the time a request is made for funds to mark to the market, provided the other party to the contract assents to the assignment.

Refund of Deposit:

(c) If the market value of the subject of the contract changes so as to permit a total or partial refund of any deposits that have been made in accordance with subsection (a) of this section, such refunds shall be made on demand.

Delivery of Demand for Deposit or Refund:

(d) All demands for deposits or refunds shall be in writing and shall be delivered at the office of the party upon whom the demand is made during the business hours of member banks of the Federal Reserve System located in the community where such party maintains his or her office, and such demands shall be complied with immediately.

Failure to Comply with Demand:

(e) Failure of a party to comply with a demand for a deposit or refund made in accordance with subsections (a), (c), and (d) of this section shall entitle the party making the demand to close the contract without notice by making offsetting purchase or sale contracts in the best available market for the account and liability of the party failing to comply with said demand.

Contract Closure:

(f) No contract shall be closed pursuant to subsection (e) of this section prior to the expiration of regular delivery time in the community where the party making the demand maintains his or her office on the next business day following the day when notice of such demand was received by the other party.

Notice of Offsetting Purchase or Sale:

(g) The party making such offsetting purchase or sale contracts shall as promptly as possible on the day on which they are made (1) notify the other party via telegram, TWX, or other comparable written media, and (2) mail or deliver formal confirmation of same to the other party and a copy of said confirmation to the Committee.

Section 59

Close-Out Procedure

Buying In. A contract that has not been completed by the seller according to its terms may be closed by the buyer not sooner than the third business day following the date delivery was due, in accordance with the following procedure:

Notice of Buy-In:

(a) Written notice of buy-in shall be delivered to the seller at his or her office not later than noon, seller's time, two business days preceding the execution of the proposed buy-in. Attached to or accompanying each notice of buy-in shall be a copy of the original comparison or other written statement of the broker/dealer to be "bought-in," evidencing the contract to be closed out.

Information Contained in Buy-In Notice:

(b) 1. Every notice of buy-in shall state the date of the contract to be closed and the quantity and contract price of the securities covered by said contract and shall state further that unless delivery is effected at or before a certain specified time, which may not be prior to 11:30 A.M. local time in the community where the buyer maintains his or her office; the securities may be bought-in on the date specified for the account of the seller. Every notice of buy-in transmitted pursuant to a buy-in issued by a registered clearing agency must contain the buy-in reference number, if any, assigned by such registered clearing agency. This number, if preceded by the letters "EXT," will also indicate that the buy-in has already been extended seven calendar days past its original proposed execution date pursuant to Section 59(g) of the UPC. Each buy-in notice shall also state the name of the individual with whom further discussions concerning the buy-in may be carried on or the telephone extension where an individual authorized to pursue further discussions can be reached.

2. Notice may be redelivered immediately to another broker/dealer from whom the securities involved are due in the form of a retransmitted notice (retransmit). Retransmitted notice of buy-in must be delivered to subsequent broker/dealers not later than one business day preceding the time and date of execution of the proposed buy-in.

3. A broker/dealer retransmitting to another broker/dealer a buy-in issued by a registered clearing agency must, in order to do so, retransmit the buy-in pursuant to the time period set forth in subsection (a) hereof, using the same time and execution date as appears on such buy-in notice. Subsequent retransmittals of such buy-ins will be treated in the manner prescribed in subsection (b)2. Also, any subsequent retransmittals of such buy-in must contain the buy-in reference number as provided in subsection (b) 1 hereof.

Section 61 (amended effective September 1, 1969, and March 1, 1970)

Rights and Warrants

Definition—Rights:

(a) The term "rights" or "rights to subscribe" as used in this section is the privilege offered to holders of record of issued securities to subscribe (usually on a pro rata basis) for additional securities of the same class, of a different class, or of a different issuer, as the case may be.

Definition—Warrants:

(b) The term "warrants" or "stock purchase warrants" as used in this section is an instrument issued separately or accompanying other securities, but not necessarily issued to stockholders of record as of a specific date, that is, warrants issued with or attached to bonds, common stock, preferred stocks, etc.

The instrument represents the privilege to purchase securities at a stipulated price or prices and is usually valid for several years.

Basis and Unit of Trading—Rights:

(c) Except as otherwise designated by the Committee, transactions in rights to subscribe shall be on the basis of one right accruing to each share of issued stock, and the unit of trading in rights shall be 100 rights unless otherwise specified.

Securities Transfer 315

Basis and Unit of Trading—Warrants:

(d) Except as otherwise agreed or designated by the Committee, transactions in stock purchase warrants shall be on the basis of one warrant representing the right of the purchaser to receive one warrant in settlement of such transaction, and the unit of trading shall be 100 warrants.

Members must ascertain how many warrants they have to sell, what each warrant entitles the holder to purchase, the purchase price, and the current price of the warrant relative to the price of the underlying security that may be purchased. Trades in warrants should be properly described on comparisons and confirmations.

Section 62

CUSIP Number. The CUSIP number must be used on the Uniform Transfer Instruction Form, Uniform Delivery Ticket, and the Uniform Comparison or Confirmation.

APPENDIX I

Uniform Disposition of Unclaimed Property

The following states and district have adopted escheat laws pertaining to unclaimed securities, dividends, and interests in the possession of transfer agents, banks, brokers, and financial institutions. Annual reports must be filed in these states if the financial institution is unable to locate the true owner of the security, dividends, and interests. After a period of time, these properties are turned over to the state.

Alabama	Kentucky	Ohio
Alaska	Louisiana	Oklahoma
Arizona	Maine	Oregon
Arkansas	Maryland	Pennsylvania
California	Massachusetts	Puerto Rico
Colorado	Michigan	Rhode Island
Connecticut	Minnesota	South Carolina
Delaware	Missouri	South Dakota
District of Columbia	Montana	Texas
Florida	Nebraska	Utah
Georgia	Nevada	Vermont
Hawaii	New Hampshire	Virginia
Idaho	New Jersey	Washington
Illinois	New Mexico	West Virginia
Indiana	New York	Wisconsin
Iowa	North Carolina	Wyoming
	North Dakota	

DIVIDEND REPORTING

The following states require an annual report of dividend payments from dividend disbursing agents in addition to the reporting requirement of forms 1096 and 1099 for the Internal Revenue Service.

Alabama	Iowa	North Carolina
Alaska	Kansas	North Dakota
Arizona	Louisiana	Oklahoma
Arkansas	Maine	Oregon
California	Massachusetts	Pennsylvania
Delaware	Michigan	Puerto Rico
District of Columbia	Minnesota	Rhode Island
Georgia	Mississippi	South Carolina
Hawaii	Montana	Tennessee
Idaho	New Hampshire	Virginia
Indiana	New Jersey	Wisconsin

LIST OF STOCKHOLDERS

Reporting Requirements

The following states require that transfer agents and/or corporate secretaries file an annual report of lists of stockholders.

Alabama	Michigan
Delaware	Minnesota
Florida	North Carolina
Georgia	North Dakota
Indiana	Ohio
Iowa	Texas
Kansas	Virginia
Kentucky	West Virginia
Maryland	Wisconsin

Index

Administrators of estate, 93
   multiple, 95–96
ADRs (American Depository Receipts)
   deposits, 206, 248
Affidavit of domicile
   for California inheritance tax waiver, 113
   for joint tenancy with right of survivorship, 84
   for partnerships, 63
   for will/estate, 94
Agent-originated envelopes, 152
American Depository Receipts (ADRs), depositing, 206, 248
American Stock Exchange, Rule 891 of, 146
American Stock Exchange Clearing Corporation,
   distribution service of, 149–154
AMEX (American Stock Exchange), 146, 149–154
Appropriate person, definition, 15, 17
Assignment, 15–26
   blank, 20
   form of, 5
   legal aspects of, 15, 16
   rules for, 15, 17; *see also* Assignment rules, NYSE
Assignment rules, NYSE, 273–284
   acknowledgments; affidavits, 284
   alterations or corrections, 274
   with certificates issued in two or more names, 282
   with change in member organization name, 282
   corporate, 274
   guarantee by insolvent, 283
   by insolvents, 281
   joint tenancy; special designation, etc.; tenancy in common, 282
   by member organizations, 274–280
      continuing organizations, 281
      detailed procedure, 276–280
      dissolved organizations, 281
      member corporations, 274–275
      members and member firms, 275
      stock clearing corporation, 275–276

Assignment rules, NYSE (cont.)
   member signature as guarantee, 283
   out-of-town member executions, 283
   by persons since deceased, trustees, guardians, etc., 280–281
   power of substitution and, 273–274
   for "rights," 284
   signature guarantee, 282–283
   signatures, technically correct, 274
   transfer books closed indefinitely, 284
   transferees in error, 284
Attorney designated in error, 20
Attorney-in-fact, 72
   and authority of committee, 79
   statement, 20

Bankruptcy and receivership, 72–73
Bearer bonds, municipal, 210–228
Bearer form, security in, 190
Beneficial ownership, 127–130
   disclosure of, 129–130
   factors in definition of, 128
Beneficial purpose of street name registration, 128–129
Beneficiary of estate, death of, 95
Birth and death certificates, offices issuing, 117–122
Bond certificate, 6–12
   coupons, 9, 11–12
   face of, 6–7
   reverse side of, 8–9
Bond for missing securities
   indemnity, 159–160
   open penalty, 160
Bond power, 10; *see also* Stock/bond power
Bonds
   "baby," 205
   bearer, 10, 13
   municipal, 210–228

Bonds (cont.)
  dealt in flat, ex-interest transactions in, 296–297
  delivery of
    acceptable denominations for, 124–125
    other evidences of indebtedness and, 306–307
    part-redeemed, transactions in, 297
    registered, 10
    NYSE rules for, 285
    transfer of other instruments and, 10
    units of delivery for, 299
BOWT ("broker originated window ticket"), 149–152
British stocks, 22, 23–24
Broker originated window ticket (BOWT), 149–152
"Brokers' transactions" in SEC, Rule 155, 139–140

Callable securities, 251–256
Called securities, 312
  distributions on, 256
  stock or registered bonds, rules for, 285
Canadian securities, transfers of, 99–104
  Alberta, 100
  British Columbia, 100–101
  Manitoba, 102
  New Brunswick, 102
  Newfoundland, 102
  Nova Scotia, 102–103
  Ontario, 103
  Prince Edward Island, 103
  Quebec, 103
  Saskatchewan, 104
  Yukon Territory, 104
Cash contracts, 123
Cash distributions and interest, due-bill checks for, 309
Certificates
  bond, 6–12
  federal transfer, for inheritance tax waiver, 112, 113
  inscriptions on, 30–31
  issued in two or more names, assignment and, 282
  of internal foreign securities, 304
  lost in delivery, 156, 186
  nominee, for municipal bearer bond, 224–227
  registration of, 27–31
    abbreviations in, 29–30
    in corporate name of brokerage firm, 17, 19
    in married name and maiden name of woman, 20
    methods and practices in, 27–29
  stock, 1–6
  wrong form of, 311–312
Certificates of deposit for bonds, units of delivery for, 299
Certifications, 171–173

Churches and religious orders, 70
Clifford trust, 34
CNS, *see* Continuous-net-settlement *entries*
Collateral loans
  at Depository Trust Company, 234–236
  facsimile transmission and, 239–241
  on U.S. Government securities, 266–269
Committee and conservatorship, 78–79
Community property, 87–88
Conservatorship, 78–79
Continuous-net-settlement deposit (CNS), 206, 248–249
  and institutional delivery system, 215
  of municipal bearer bonds, 211
Continuous-net-settlement (CNS) release of collateral loan, 235–236
Convertible securities provisions, 241–245
  exercise of option, 242
  notice of qualifying security, 242–244
  payment of fractional interest, 245
  pledge and transfer by book-entry of underlying securities, 244–245
Corporate name
  change of, 69
  sale of stock in, 67
  transfer of stock from, into name of officer, 67–68
Corporate resolutions, 67, 68
Corporations, 67–69
  dissolution of, 69
Counterfeit securities, 156
  reporting, and inquiry with respect to, 185–188
Coupon bonds
  delivery of, 306
  deposit of, 208–210
  NYSE rules for, 285
Coupons, bond, 9, 11–12
  detached prior to delivery, 307
  mutilated, 286
  proper, 225
  and warrants, etc., NYSE rules for, 285, 286
Crummey trust, 34
Custodian(s) to minor, 33–59
  accounting by, 49
  change of residence of, from one state to another, 37, 39
  death of, 21, 47, 57–58
  delivery of registered securities in the account of, 37
  duties and powers of, 37, 45–46
  eligibility of, 37
  expenses, compensation, bond and liabilities of, 46–47
  nomination of, in UTMA, 51
  number of, 41
  resignation of, 40
  or death or removal, 47–49
  transfer of securities from decedent to, 41

Index

Death
  of beneficiary of will, 95
  of brokerage client, 93–96
  of custodian of minor, 21, 47, 57–58
  of executor, 92
  of joint tenant(s), 84–85
  of life tenant, 86
  of minor, 40–41
  of partner, 62, 63
  of sole proprietor, 61
  of tenant(s) in common, 85
  of trustee, 75–76
Death and birth certificates, offices issuing, 117–122
Decedent/deceased person, 93–96
  assignment by, 280–281
  Canada, 100
  certificate in name of, 305–306
  dividends issued after death of, 95
  nonresident, federal transfer certificate for, 112, 113
  transfer of securities from, to custodian of minor, 41
  with will, 89–92
  without will, 92–93
Declaration of transmission, Canada, 100, 101
Delivery of securities, 196–200, 297
  acceptable denominations for
    bonds, 124–125
    stocks, 124–125
  assignments and powers of substitution, 302–303
  bonds and other evidences of indebtedness, 306–307
    municipal bearer bonds, 219–224
  dates of, 293–294
  with draft attached, 300
  equivalent securities, 286–287
  items "good for transfer or," 125
  NASDAQ rules for, 297
  part, 298
  registered securities
    in account of custodian to minor, 37
    assignments and powers of substitution, 302–303
    with restrictions, 301
  rules of, 123–125
  securities lost during, 156, 186
  and settlement of U.S. Government securities, 265
  types of, 123–124
    cash contracts, 123
    regular way contracts, 123
    seller's option, 124
  units of
    bonds, 299
    certificates of deposit for bonds, 299
    stocks, 298–299
Depository Trust Company, participant operating procedures at, 205–271

Depository Trust Company, participant operating procedures at (cont.)
  for callable securities, 251–256
  for collateral loan, 234–241
    overnight, 236–241
    pledge/release of collateral with banks using facsimile transmission, 239–241
  for conversions, 241–245
  depository facilities, 247–251
    ADR deposits, 248
    CNS deposits, 248–249
    legal deposits, 249
    rejected deposits, 249–251
  for deposits, 205–210
  for dividends and interest payments, 222, 229–234
    dividend reinvestment service, 231–234
  for government securities, 261–270
  for municipal bearer bonds, 210–228
  for proxies, 270–271
  for reorganization, 245
    mandatory exchange, 245–247
    name change, 246
    spin-off, 246
    voluntary exchanges: tender and exchange offers, 246–247
  roll-over option on U.S. Treasury bills, 256–261
  for voluntary offerings, 256–261
Deposits
  ADR, 206, 248
  CNS, 206
  of coupon bonds, 208–210
  demand for, 313
  facilities for, 247–251
  how to make, 205–206
  legal, 206–207
  of municipal bearer bonds, 210–213
  rejected, 249–251
  special considerations, 207–208
Destroyed, lost and stolen securities, 204
Disclosure of beneficial ownership, 129–130
Distribution; see also Dividends/interest
  person not engaged in, definition, 133–134
  and sale of stock in estate, under court order, 94
  service of AMEX Clearing Corporation, 149–154
Dividends/interest
  claims for, 310
  distributions on called securities, 256
  issued after death of decedent, 95
  payments of, at Depository Trust Company, 222, 229–234
    dividend reinvestment service, 231–234
  reporting of, on unclaimed property, 318
  and rights, etc., claims for, 310
Due-bills and due-bill checks, 309–310

Economic Recovery Act of 1981, estate and gift tax provisions under, 96–97
Endorsed bonds, delivery of, 306
Endorsements (indorsements), 15, 17–20, 306–307
  for banking or insurance requirements, 306–307
  forms of, 17–20
  unauthorized, 17
  Uniform Commercial Code provisions for, 196–198
    effective, 201–202
Estates(s) 89–98; *see also* Wills
  administrators of, 93
    multiple, 95–96
  affidavit of domicile and, 94
  death of brokerage client and, 93–96
  of decedents with last will and testament, 89–92
  of decedents without will, 92–93
  executor(s) of, 91–93
    death of, 92
    multiple, 95–96
  SEC Rule 144 for, 137
  settlement of small, without administration, 94–95
  taxes and
    Economic Recovery Act of 1981, 96–97
    inheritance tax waiver, 94, 95
    Tax Reform Act of 1986, 97–98
Estate and gift tax provisions under Economic Recovery Act of 1981, 96–97; *see also* Inheritance tax *entries*
Ex-dividend dates, 295
Ex-interest transactions in bonds dealt in flat, 296–297
Ex-liquidating payments, 297
Ex-rights dates, 295–296
Ex-warrants dates, 296
Executor(s) of estate, 91–93
  administrators
    Canada, 99, 100–104
    England, 104
  multiple, 95–96
Exoneration statutes for legal entities, 65–67

Facsimile transmission, pledge/release of collateral with banks using, 239–241
Fast and transfer agent custodian (TAC), 152–153
Federal transfer certificate for inheritance tax waiver, 112, 113
Fiduciary relationships using nominee registrations, 127–128
Fiduciary transferee, 28
Fiduciary transfers, 71–79
  bankruptcy and receivership and, 72–73
  committee and conservatorship and, 78–79
  guardianship and, 77–78
  power of attorney and, 71–72
  trusts and, 73–77

Foreign securities
  internal, certificates of, 304
  transfers of, 99–104
    Canada, 99–104
    England, 104
Forged endorsement, 22
  signature guarantor and, 17
Frauds, statute of, 100

Gift tax provisions under Economic Recovery Act of 1981, 96–97
Gifts of securities under SEC Rule 144, 137
"Good for transfer" versus "good for delivery," 125
Guardian, assignment by, 280–281
Guardianship, 77–78
  to minor, *see also* Custodian(s) to minor; Minor
    Canada, 100–104
    England, 104
  to person declared incompetent
    Canada, 100–104
    England, 104

Income trust, 34
Incompetent, guardianship to person declared
  Canada, 100–104
  England, 104
Indemnity, letter of, 20, 21
Indemnity bond for lost securities, 159–160
Indorsements, *see* Endorsements
Inheritance tax, Canada, 100, 113
Inheritance tax waivers, 94, 95, 111–122
  Canada, 100
  factors determining necessity of, 111
  offices issuing, 112, 114–116
  states and Canadian provinces requiring, 112–113
  states requiring special affidavits in lieu of, 112
Insolvents
  assignment by, 281
  guarantee by, 283
Institutional Delivery System (IDS)
  for municipal bearer bonds, 213–219
  for U.S. Government securities, 265
Institutions, ownership of securities by, 28
Inter vivos trust, Canada, 99
Interest; *see also* Dividends/interest
  bond, in default, 306
  claims for, 310
  computation of, 307–309
  payment of
    Depository Trust Company procedures for, 222, 229–234
    fractional, 245
  on U.S. Government securities, 269–270
Investment clubs, 62–65

Index

323

Joint ownership
  in Canada, 100–104
  death of tenant(s) and, 84, 85
  in England, 104
  registrations describing, 29
  types of, 81–88
    community property, 87–88
    in 50 states and District of Columbia 82–84
    joint life tenancy, 86
    joint tenancy in common, 85–86
    joint tenancy with right of survivorship, 81–85
    tenants by entirety, 86
Joint tenancy, 81–86
  assignment and, 282
  Economic Recovery Act of 1981 and, 97

Laws, rules, and codes
  Economic Recovery Act of 1981, 96–97
  exoneration statutes, 65–67
  SEC rules
    13D, 130
    17f-1 (missing, lost, counterfeit or stolen securities), 155–160
    144, 131–141; see also SEC rule 144
    for registration of transfer agents, 153–154
    for turnaround, 143
    Securities Act of 1933, 131
    Securities Exchange Act of 1934, 129–130
    Securities Investor Protection Act of 1970, 129
  Tax Equity and Fiscal Responsibility Act of 1982, 10, 13
  Tax Reform Act, 1986, 97–98
  UCC, see Uniform Commercial Code provisions
  UGMA, see Uniform Gifts to Minors Act
  Uniform Act for Simplification of Fiduciary Transfers, 66–67
  UTMA, see Uniform Transfers to Minors Act, provisions of
Legal deposits, 206–207, 249
Legal entities, 61–70
  exoneration statutes and, 65–67
  types of
    churches and religious orders, 70
    corporations, 67–69
    investment clubs, 62–65
    partnerships, 61–62
    sole proprietorships, 61
    unincorporated associations, 69
Letter of indemnity, 20, 21
Life tenancy, 86
Living trusts, 74–76
Loan, overnight, 236–241
Lost or missing securities, see Missing or lost securities

Marking to market, 313
Married woman, 282
  certificate in name of, 305
  married name and maiden name, 20
  right of, to transfer securities, 19
Medallion signature guarantee, 26
Minor
  custodian to, see Custodian(s) to minor
  death of, 40–41
  definition of, 35, 36
  gifts to, see Uniform Gifts to Minors Act
  guardianship to
    Canada, 100–104
    England, 104
  reaching majority, 40
  registration of securities for, 35, 38–39
  transfer requirements for, 34
  transfers to, see Uniform Transfers to Minors Act, provisions of
Missing or lost securities, 155–160
  bonds for
    indemnity, 159–160
    open penalty, 160
  destroyed and stolen and, 204
  exceptions to rule, 158
  liability for certificates with NTS, 149–150
  method of inquiry, 157–158
  open penalty bonds for, 160
  recordkeeping, 158
  replacement of lost certificates, 158–159
    procedure for, 159–160
  requirement for inquiry, 157, 185–188
  reporting institutions, 155–156
  reporting method, 157
  reporting requirements, 156–157, 185–188
Model Law and Uniform Gifts to Minors Act, 34–35
Municipal bearer bonds
  activity verification for, 212
  deliveries of, 219–224
  institutional delivery (ID) system for, 213–219
  procedures for deposit of, 210–212
  rejected deposits of, 212–213
  withdrawal of nominee certificates for, 224–227
  withdrawals of, 227–228

National Association of Securities Dealers rules, 293–315
  acknowledgments and sample forms, 303–306
  bond interest in default, 306
  called securities, 313
  certificate in name of deceased person, trustee, etc., 305–306
  certificate in name of married or unmarried woman, 305

National Association of Securities Dealers rules (cont.)
   claims for dividends, rights, interest, etc., 310
   computation of interest, 307–309
   definitions, 293
   delivery
      dates of, 293–294
      irregular, 312
      of bonds and other forms of indebtedness, 306–307
      of securities, 297
      of securities with draft attached, 300
      of securities with restrictions, 301
      part, 298
   demand for deposit, 313
   due-bills and due-bill checks, 309–310
   ex-dividend, ex-rights, or ex-warrants transactions, 295–296
   ex-interest transactions in bonds dealt in flat, 296–297
   ex-liquidating payments, 297
   foreign internal securities certificates, 304
   marking to market, 313
   part-redeemed bonds, 297
   payment of purchase money, 297
   rights, 314
   stamp taxes, 297–298
   transfer fees, 310
   units of delivery, 298–299
      bonds, 299
      certificates of deposit for bonds, 299
      stocks, 298–299
   warrants, 314–315
   wrong form of certificate, 311–312
National Transfer Service (NTS), 149–152
   procedure for record date transfers in New York through, 151–152
New York Stock Exchange rules pertaining to securities transfer and processing, 273–291
   for assignments, 273–284; *see also* Assignments, NYSE rules for
   for bonds
      called coupon, 285
      endorsed, 285
      mutilated, 286
      registered, 285
      registered as to principal or for voting purposes only, 285
      released endorsed, 285
      for called stock, 285
   for coupons
      mutilated, 286
      proper, 285
   delivery of equivalent securities, 286–287
   requirements for independent agents, 287–291
   turnaround Rule 496, 146–148
      transfer agents in and outside New York City, 146–148
   for warrants, 285

New York State Tax Commission
   rebate procedure devised by, 105–109
   transfer tax rates, 106
      maximum tax, 106
Nominee partnership, 127
Nominee registrations, 127
   for municipal bearer bonds, 224–227
Notary public, 22
NTS (National Transfer Service), 149–152

"Open penalty bonds" for missing certificates and, 160
"Overissue," 190
Overnight loan at Depository Trust Company, 236–241

Partnerships, 61–62
   investments clubs as, 64
   nominee, 127
Power of attorney, 20, 71–72
   discretionary, 72
   revocation of, 72
Power of substitution, 125
   NYSE rules for, 302–303
Proxies, operating procedures for, 270–271

Receivership, bankruptcy and, 72–73
Reclamations and rejections, 311–315
Record date transfers, procedure for, in New York through NTS, 151–152
Record stock, 249
Registered form, security in, 189
Registration of certificates, 27–31
   describing joint ownership, 29
   nominee, 127
   fiduciary relationships using, 127–128
   of securities of minor, 35, 38–39
   street, 127–129
Regular way contracts, 123
Reorganization item, 249
Restricted securities, 134–135
   delivery of, 301
   holding period for, 135–137
Rights
   assignments of, 284
   claims for, 310
   due-bills for dividends and, 309
   NASD rules for, 314
   voting, and beneficial ownership, 128
Rollover option on U.S. Treasury bills, 256–261

Index

"Search letter," 128
SEC, *see* Securities and Exchange Commission
Securities Act of 1933, 131
Securities and Exchange Commission
  lost and stolen securities program of, 185–188
  rules and regulations of
    13D, 130
    17f-1, 155–160
    144, *see* Securities and Exchange Commission Rule 144
      for registration of transfer agents, 153–154
      for turnaround, 143; *see also* Securities and Exchange Commission rules of transfer agents turnaround
Securities and Exchange Commission Rule 144, 131–141
  provisions of, 132–141
    bona fide intention to sell, 141
    brokers' transactions, 139–140
    conditions to be met, 134–135
    current public information, 135
    definitions, 134
    filing of reports, 135
    holding period for restricted securities, 135–137
    limitation on amount of securities sold, 137–139
    manner of sale, 139
    non-exclusive rule, 141
    notice of proposed sale, 140–141
    person not engaged in distribution, 133–134
    "restricted securities," 134–135
    termination of certain restrictions, 141
    underwriter, definition, 132–133
  purpose of, 32
Securities and Exchange Commission rules of transfer agents turnaround (§§ 240.17Ad-1 through 17Ad-7), 175–184
  applicability, 179
  definitions, 175–176
  limitations on expansion, 178–179
  record retention, 183–184
  recordkeeping, 181–182
  turnaround, processing, and forwarding of items, 177–178
  written inquiries and requests, 180–181
Securities Exchange Act of 1934, 129–130
Securities Information Center, Inc. (SIC), 155
Securities Investor Protection Act of 1970, 129
Seller's option, 124
Signature guarantee, 22, 25–26, 197–198
  forged endorsement and, 17
  guidelines for, 25–26
  medallion, 26
  NYSE rules for, 282–283
  under Uniform Commercial Code, 25–26

Signatures
  facsimile, 275–276, 279–280
  technically correct, 274
Sole proprietorships, 61
Stamp taxes, 297–298
Stamped bonds, delivery of, 307
Stock/bond power, 15, 16, 19, 20
Stock certificates, 1–6
  design and workmanship of, 5–6
  face of, 1–3, 5
  reverse side of, 4, 5, 18
Stockholder's identifying number, 5
Stockholders, list of, 318
Stolen securities, 155–160, 204; *see also* Missing or lost securities
  requirements for reporting and inquiry with respect to, 185–188
Street registration, 127
  purpose of, 128–129

TAC (transfer agent custodian), 152–153
Tax
  estate and gift, under Economic Recovery Act of 1981, 96–97
  inheritance, *see* Inheritance tax *entries*
  on securities transactions and transfer, 105–109
    exempt transactions, 108–109
    maximum tax, 106
    New York State transfer tax rates, 106
    nontaxable transactions, 108
    plan of operation, 105–106
    rebate procedure, 105–109
    taxable transactions, 106–107
  stamp, 297–298
Tax Equity and Fiscal Responsibility Act of 1982, bearer bonds and, 10, 13
"Tax paid," bond stamped, 307
Tax Reform Act of 1986, highlights of, 97–98
Tenancy, joint, 81–86
  in common, 85–86
    assignment and, 282
    death of tenant(s) in, 85
  life, 86
  with right of survivorship, 81–85
Tenants by entirety, 86
Testamentary trusts, 76–77
  Canada, 99
Theft of securities, 155; *see also* Stolen securities
Transfer(s)
  of bonds and other instruments, 10
  within central depository systems, pledge or, 200–201
  definition, 175–176
  fiduciary, 71–79
  of foreign securities, 99–104
  items "good for" delivery or, 125

Transfer(s) (cont.)
  to minors, 34; *see also* Uniform Transfers to Minors Act, provisions of preventing wrongful, 17
Transfer agent custodian (TAC), 152–153
Transfer agent drop facility in New York, 147–148
Transfer agents
  located outside New York City, 146
  SEC rules for registration of, 153–154
Transfer fees, 310
Transfer services, stock, 149–154
  agent-originated envelopes, 152
  AMEX Clearing Corporation, 149–154
  broker-originated window ticket (BOWT), 149–152
  National Transfer Service, 149–152
  procedure for record date transfers in New York through, 151–152
  transfer agent custodian (TAC), 152–153
  registration of, 153–154
Transfer turnaround rules, 143–148
  American Stock Exchange, 146
  New York Stock Exchange, 146–148
  provisions of
    applicability of rules and exceptions, 144
    limitations on expansion, 144
    processing of transfer, 143–144
    record retention, 146
    recordkeeping, 145–146
    written inquiries and requests, 145
  SEC, 143–146
Transfer taxation, 105–109
Transferee
  in error, 20, 284
  fiduciary, 28
Trustees
  assignment by, 280–281
  authenticating
    duty of, 204
    effect of signature of, 194
  certificate in name of, 305–306
Trusts
  Clifford, 34
  Crummey, 34
  income, 34
  inter vivos, Canada, 99
  living, 74–76
  under SEC Rule 144, 137
  short-term revocable, 34
  testamentary, 76–77
    Canada, 99
"Turnaround", definition, 176; *see also* Transfer turnaround rules

UGMA, *see* Uniform Gifts to Minors Act
Unclaimed property, uniform disposition of, 317–318
Underwriter, definition, 132–133
Uniform Act for Simplification of Fiduciary Security Transfers, 66–67
Uniform Commercial Code provisions, 66, 189–204
  "adverse claim," 194–195
  applicability, 191
  attachment of levy upon security, 199–200
  completion or alteration of instrument, 193
  definitions and index of definitions, 189–190
  delivery, 196–200
  duty of authenticating trustee, transfer agent or registrar, 204
  effect of issuer's restrictions on transfer, 193
  effect of overissue, 190
  effect of signature of authenticating trustee, registrar or transfer agent, 194
  effect of unauthorized signature on issue, 193
  indorsement(s), 196–198
    effective, 201–202
  issue-issuer, 191–194
  issuer's lien, 190
  issuer's responsibility and defenses, 192–193
  limited duty of inquiry, 202–203
  lost, destroyed and stolen securities, 158, 204
  purchase, 194–201
  purchaser's right to requisites for registration of transfer on books, 199
  registration, 201–204
    liability and non-liability for, 203–204
  rights of issuer with respect to registered owners, 193–194
  securities deliverable; action for price, 191
  securities negotiable; presumptions, 191
  signature guarantee under, 25–26
  statute of frauds, 200
  transfer or pledge with central depository system, 200–201
  warranties on presentment and transfer, 195–196
  wrongful transfer, 199
Uniform disposition of unclaimed property, 317–318
Uniform Gifts to Minors Act (UGMA), 33–34
  application of, 35
  complete text of, 41–49
  Model Law and, 34–35
Uniform Transfers to Minors Act (UTMA), provisions of, 33, 49–59
  accounting by, and determination of liability of, custodian, 58
  custodian's expenses, compensation and bond, 56

Index

Uniform Transfers to Minors Act (UTMA) (cont.)
   manner of creating custodial property and effecting transfer; designation of initial custodian, control, 52–54
   means of transfer, 51–52
   nomination of custodian, 51
   renunciation, resignation, death, or removal of custodian, 57–58
   termination of custodianship, 58
   third person and liability, 56–57
   validity and effect of transfer, 54–55
Unincorporated associations, 69
Unmarried woman, certificate in name of, 305
U.S. Government securities, 261–270
   collateral loans on, 266–269
   delivery and settlement, 262, 265
      institutional delivery system, 265
   deposits of, 261
   interests payments on, 262–265
   withdrawals of, 262
U.S. Treasury bills, rollover option on, 256–261

UTMA, see Uniform Transfers to Minors Act, provisions of

Warrants
   NASD rules for, 314–315
   NYSE rules for, 285, 286
Wills, 89–92; see also Estates
   death of beneficiary of, 95
   decedents with, 89–92
   decedents without, 92–93
   formal witnessed, 89–90
   holographic, or handwritten, 89
   noncupative, 89
   probating of, 90–91
Withdrawals
   of municipal bearer bonds, 227–228
      nominee certificates for, 224–227
   of U.S. Government securities, 262
Witness, 22
Woman, see Married woman